The Application of the Theory of Efficient Breach in Contract Law

A Comparative Law and Economics Perspective

Wenqing Liao

The Application of the Theory of Efficient Breach in Contract Law

A Comparative Law and Economics Perspective

intersentia

METRO

Ius Commune Europaeum

Wenqing Liao

The Application of the Theory of Efficient Breach in Contract Law
A Comparative Law and Economics Perspective

Intersentia Publishing Ltd.
Sheraton House | Castle Park
Cambridge | CB3 0AX | United Kingdom
Tel.: +44 1223 370 170 | Email: mail@intersentia.co.uk

ISBN 978-1-78068-356-0
D/2015/7849/133
NUR 822

British Library Cataloguing in Publication Data. A catalogue record for this book is available from the British Library.

ACKNOWLEDGEMENTS

Four and half years ago when I was sitting in the library of Peking University, I only had an initially unshaped idea that I was going to write a thesis about the theory of efficient breach. Then I came to Maastricht, one of the oldest cities in the Netherlands and started a fantastic journey to become a PhD researcher. After four years, the results of my research have finally turned into a book: "The Application of the Theory of Efficient Breach in Contract Law, A Comparative Law and Economics Perspective". I realise that the completion of this book would never been possible if I did not have supports and help from many individuals and organizations.

First, I would like to send my acknowledgement to my supervisors– Prof. Michael Faure and Dr. Niels Philipsen– and their families– Hui (Michael's wife) and Tony (Michael and Hui's son) as well as Lili (Niels' wife), Timo and Mika (Niels and Lili's sons). When I just started my PhD, I actually did not have a clear picture in my mind about what exactly I should do in the coming four years. Michael and Niels guided me step by step to build the structure of a doctorate thesis and to write every paragraph of each chapter. They read every word of my writings, gave feedbacks frequently and even corrected linguistic errors and punctuation mistakes. In addition to being the supervisors of my PhD research, Michael and Niels gave me a lot of emotional supports and social supports. I was one of the frequent visitors to their houses during all kinds of events (weekends, festivals and birthdays), where I received not only tasty food but also greetings, accompanies and encouragement.

I also feel very grateful to the professors and other researchers who have provided various useful information and suggestions to me when I was writing my thesis. I have many thanks to Dr. George Zhou who helped me to better understand my topic and to search correct information about English law. He was also sitting at the reading committee of my thesis and showed his patience when reading and commenting my thesis. My gratitude also goes to other members of my assessment committee, including Prof. Jan Smits, Prof. Jacques Herbots and Dr. Caroline Cauffman. They gave me plenty of pertinent comments and suggestions, which have touched the fundamental problems in both contract law and economic analysis of law. Those comments helped me to improve my research. In addition, I want to express my gratefulness to Prof. Chang Peng'ao from the Law School of Peking University. He did not only supervise my master thesis, but also became a friend of me, providing me advises regarding my work and my life.

In the last four years, as a PhD researcher, I shared a lot of pleasures with my colleagues in the law faculty of Maastricht University. Specially, my acknowledgement goes to Dr. Jing Liu, who is my colleague, officemate and a close friend. Our friendship started from 2011 when I just arrived at Maastricht without finding any accommodation and since then she has been treating me as her younger sister by offering me with tasty food, nice gifts, valuable suggestions and countless times of accompanies. In the law faculty, I have a long list of names, which I will never forget in my whole life. They are Kevine Kindij, Ancui Liu, Bo Chen, Catalina Goanta, Grace Gan, Huizhen Chen, Jiangqiu Ge, Junping Liu, Jie Wang, Julia Pedraza Laynez, Mengxing Lv, Mengmeng Shi, Mark Kawakami, Mehdi Piri Damagh, Kelly Shang, Laura Tilindyte, Liuhu Luo, Rosa Ristawati, Sarah Schoenmaekers, Sascha Hardt, Taotao Yue, Tianxiang He, Tian Lv, Jaqueline Albino, Tobias Heldt, Viorelia Gasca, William Bull, Xiahong Chen, Xiaowei Yu, Xi Chen, Xuesong Li, Yaojing Peng, Yuan Gao, Yang Gao, Yu Zhao, Yu Yan, Guang Shen and Zamira Xhaferri. We attended seminars and conferences together, had drinks and dinners now and then, and also celebrated some festivals together. Being in the same faculty for four years, we are not only colleagues with each other, but also friends in the end. Another group of people in the law faculty, to whom I should always remember is our secretary, including Yleen Simonis, Elke Hundhausen, Chantal Kuijpers, Marina Jodogne, Marijo Mullers and Marlies Lijten. They are the people who deal with all kinds of detailed things for me and for every member in METRO, from scheduling every meeting to arranging the publication of PhD thesis. Whenever there is an issue on my hand, their office door is always open, with warm smile on their faces and timely help for me.

After I came to Europe, I was lucky to know a large group of new friends, owing to whom I did not feel lonely and homesick any more. Those friends include Zhenglong Sun, Ao Rong, Ai Li, Chan Huang, Haiyan Li, Haokun Liu, Hua Zhang, Hong Wei, Lotte Chin Kon Sung, Jinjin Zhao, Jun Hou, Qian Qu, Sheng Zhong, Shuang Zhou, Shilpi Bhattacharya, Li You, Min Lin, Mary Ma, Maik Peeters, Wei Zhao, Wenzhao Qiao, Xun Xiao, Yuzhe Li, Yu Rao, Jie Zhou and so on. Because of them, I have the possibility to taste Sichuan hot pot, Cantonese Dim Sum, Indonesia food and Chinese Barbeque even in the Netherlands. Among the above Chinese friends, I have my special thanks to Zhenglong Sun. His accompany has added a lot of pleasure to my life in Europe and his encouragement has lighted my hopes when I was in my hardest time. On the other side of the world right in China, I have my closest friends who are always standing beside me, such as Jianxing Luo, Sisi Wu, Li Jiang, Fan Zhang, Xuewen Fu, Yang Zhao, Yan Fang, Yan Liu, Yiyun Zhang and so on. The physical distance between them and me has not affected our friendship. Whenever I need help from anyone of them, a simple message or a call is enough for me to reach a hand immediately.

In addition to the above-mentioned people, there are some institutes and entities that have supported both of my research and my life in Europe. I have my gratefulness to the

Chinese Scholarship Commission and the Chinese Embassy in the Netherlands. Without the funding provided by the Chinese Scholarship Commission, I could neither have the opportunity to conduct my PhD research nor have a proper life. Owing to the support of the Chinese embassy, the life in the Netherlands became much easier because I always felt that my country is standing behind me. In addition, I want to express my gratitude to the law faculty of Maastricht University, which has provided me with opportunities to work in my own office, to enjoy nice coffees every day, to attend the Ius Commune research school, to present in different workshops and most importantly to defend my thesis.

In the end, I owe my gratefulness to my mother Daolan Huang and my father Chengliang Liao. Their support always gives me sufficient motivation to move on and never to give up.

Wenqing Liao
Maastricht

CONTENTS

LIST OF ABBREVIATIONS

CCL	Contract Law of the People's Republic of China
CESL	Directive on Common European Sales Law Directive COM (2011) 635 final
CISG	Convention on Contracts for the International Sales of Goods
CPC	Communist Party of People's Republic of China
CPL	Civil Procedure Law of the People's Republic of China
DCFR	Draft Common Frame of Reference of European Private Law
ECL	The Economic Contract Law of the People's Republic of China
FECL	Law of the People's Republic of China on Economic Contracts Involving Foreign Interest
GPCL	The General Principles of Civil Law of the People's Republic of China
NPC	National People's Congress
PCR	People's Republic of China
PECL	Principles of European Contract Law
Prop. CESL	a Proposal for a Regulation for Common European Sales Law
SGA	The Sales of Goods Act 1893
SGA 1979	The Sales of Goods Act 1979
SPC	Supreme People's Court of the People's Republic of China
TCL	The Law of the People's Republic of China on Technology Contracts
TEC	European Union Treaty Establishing the European Community
TFEU	Treaty on Functioning of the European Union;
UPICC	UNIDROIT Principles of International Commercial Contracts 1994.

LIST OF TABLES

Chapter 1

INTRODUCTION

1. Background

Against a background where commercial trading is growing and becoming more complex in modern society, private parties are appealing for more flexibility and freedom in taking commercial decisions, rather than strictly abiding by the documents they have signed. Correspondingly, the traditional study of contract law, which offers a fundamental legal structure for trade, has received more theoretical debate. The traditional legal idea that breach of contract is wrong and should be avoided has been challenged.[1] Law and Economics, with its efficient breach theory, obviously provides one of the strongest voices and provides a utilitarian approach to explain contract and promissory obligations, which have been influenced greatly by the traditional notion of *pacta sunt servanda*[2] and the moralistic nature of obligations.[3] In 1897, Judge Oliver Wendell Holmes wrote in his well-known book 'The Path of the Law' that: "The duty to keep a contract at common law means a prediction that you must pay damages if you do not keep it, and nothing else."[4] Afterwards, this illustration of contract became a strong support for the theory of

1 Statistics show that, generally, people have a moral aversion to breach of contract, and think that a contractual obligation implies performing the promise as specified, even when this would lead to a greater loss to the promisor than the profit to him. According to the traditional contract law theory, the promisee in a contract is entitled to the right of strict performance and profits derived from breach must be restored. *See* Stolle & Slain 1997, p. 83–94; Waddams 2000, p. 1–29; Wilkinson-Ryan & Baron 2009.

2 *See* Wehberg 1959, p. 775–786. Pacta sunt servanda is Latin for "agreement must be kept". According to traditional perception, the principle of sanctity of contracts is an essential condition for any social community, from the private relationship, to the vertical relationship between public organizations and private individuals, and even to international society. *See also* Havighurst 1961, p. 64. It was assumed that "the social interest is served when promises are performed".

3 Moralism is based on the general rule of good faith and reliance, which describes the promissory obligation in a way that it should be abided by according to moral standards of keeping one's word and respecting the promisee's reliance. It has been pointed out that the freedom of the promisor is restricted by his own decision and an individual normally has an intuitive moral thinking which is fostered automatically. Hence, moralism has been deeply rooted in the contract law rules. Dawson wrote that "prevention of profit through mere breach of contract is yet not an approved aim of our legal order..." See Menetrez 2000, p. 859–885.

4 See Holmes 1897, p. 462.

efficient breach, which is assumed to have been clarified first in Birmingham in 1970[5] and received its name by Goetz & Scott 1977.[6]

Structured on the contract's functions of optimally allocating goods and factors of production as well as enhancing social welfare, the theory of efficient breach is stipulated to count all gains and losses in monetary value in the period between the birth and death of a contract. In the early stage, after the theory was born, it was used mainly to describe a desirable kind of breach,[7] where the promisor's gain from breach, after paying expectation damages, exceeds his profit from performance.[8] This sort of breach was assumed to be a movement toward economic efficiency and consistent with the contract parties' economic preference. Scholarly efforts were made to justify this theory from an economic perspective. Before that, there was Coase's statement that "once the costs of carrying out market transactions are taken into account it is clear that such a rearrangement of rights will only be undertaken when the increase in the value of production consequent upon the rearrangement is greater than the costs which would be involved in bringing it about."[9] Birmingham reached a similar conclusion when illustrating the case where an employee gets a better job.[10] Moreover, grounded on the theory of efficient breach, more and more studies were done in order to provide economic implications for shaping an efficient contract remedy system and motivating people to behave efficiently. As is pointed out by Birmingham, "an efficient damage standard may do nothing more than lower negotiating expense, since presumably the bound party confronted with a more attractive opportunity can buy his freedom by offering to share the gain with his promise." In this sense, the common law remedy of expectation damages is considered to be efficient for giving a promisor the options of adhering to the agreement or buying his way out of a contract at an optimal court-determined price.[11] A similar idea was presented by Posner 1973 as well as by Cooter & Eisenberg 1985.[12] Goetz & Scott concluded that damages for breaches of contract should be set at a reasonable level which would lead to just compensation as well as efficient breaches.[13] In this sense, any remedy that aims to prevent and punish breaches is considered to be inefficient. Literature supporting the efficient breach theory at this period, before the 1990s, concentrated either on building some concise models of efficient breach by using basic economic instruments or providing economic justifications for compensatory damages and rejecting any rules that punish breaches.[14]

5 As is described, "Repudiation of obligations should be encouraged where the promisor is able to profit from his default after placing his promisee in as good a position as he would have occupied had performance been rendered". *See* Birmingham 1970, p. 273–284.

6 *See* Goetz & Scott 1977, p. 554–594.

7 Some scholars may call the theory a simple efficient breach model which just makes a comparison between the cost of performance and the expected benefit.

8 For more discussion of the concept of efficient breach, see chapter 3, section 1.2.

9 Coase 1960, p. 15–16.

10 Birmingham 1970, p. 286–289.

11 Id, p. 292.

12 Posner 1973 as well as Cooter & Eisenberg 1985.

13 Goetz & Scott 1977, p. 558–559.

14 *See id*, p. 554–594; Macneil, 1982, p. 947–969.

The theory of efficient breach gained both theoretical and empirical development as well as challenges after its birth. The development of this theory is indicated in the scholars' efforts to integrate the concept of efficiency into contract law rules on a broader basis beyond the remedy of compensatory damages. For instance, some scholars re-examined the efficiency of the remedy of specific performance[15] by taking into account litigation costs, re-negotiations, court error, etc. Another question raised by law and economics scholarship is how to resolve the conflicts between economic theories and the existing legal rules or legal doctrines,[16] such as the theories of tortuous inference[17]and incomplete contracts.[18] Recently, the concept of efficient breach has gained access to more comprehensive legal areas, such as international law[19] and intellectual property law.[20] In addition, the development of modern law and economics and the efficient breach theory has been promoted by an impetus that is based on new methodologies and perspectives. More and more recent studies grounded on empirical statistics and experiments have added to the development of the theory of efficient breach and efficient contract rules by assessing the factual relationship between contract law and business activities. For example, there are examples of experiments, which investigated how a certain type of remedy would affect people's decisions, such as the decisions of breach or negotiation.[21]

The flourishing of methodologies and new theories, however, also brought out a trend criticizing and attacking the so-called efficient breach theory. For example, some recent research based on empirical data shows that the legal realities are incompatible with the theory of efficient breach. Businessmen in practice place a higher value on trust and long-term relationships than on economic surplus from breaches in the short-term.[22] Even in the US where this theory was first raised, judges reject the use of the term efficient breach in their judgments.[23] In addition, we may find literature arguing that the consequence-based efficient breach theory only works for financial values but it violates ethical values, which are deeply rooted in political and moral culture.[24] Such an argument, from a

15 See e.g. Ulen 1984, p. 364–395; Brooks 1989–1990, p. 687–771.
16 Perillo 2000, p. 1093–1098.
17 See Mc Chesney 1999, p. 131–186; Perillo 2000, P. 1090.
18 According to a traditional division between complete and incomplete contract, a contract has gaps in its terms, which will leave the content undefined unless the law supplements it with some gap-filling rules. A complete contract stands on the opposite side. However, this understanding is superficial according to some law and economics scholars, in whose eyes, most of the contracts are incomplete because it is impossible and not necessary to specify the contract terms without any flaw when the contract was signed. *See e.g.* Craswell 2005, p. 151–168. For more discussions concerning incomplete contract, *see* chapter 2, section 1.3.2.
19 *See* e.g. Morrison 1994–1995; Pelc 2010; Pelc & Urpelainen 2010; Posner & Sykes 2011–2012.
20 Cahoy 2003.
21 For example, Depoorter & Tontrup 2012 examine the influence of specific performance on contract parties' incentive to cooperate and negotiate; and another experiment conducted in Wilkinson-Ryan 2010 deals with the relationship between liquidated damages and people's decisions of breach.
22 *See* Bernstein 1994; Bernstein 1996.
23 Warkol 1998–1999, p. 321–354.
24 The efficient breach theory is always labelled as consequentialist and immoral, which provides a single principle, namely, that one must always act so as to produce the best consequences by which every

moralistic perspective, stands for one of the strongest voices against the efficient breach theory. Besides, there is another argument, suggesting that the efficient breach theory illustrated in the previous literature should be modified and revised. Markovits & Schwartz 2011 proposes a theory called "dual-performance" in replacement of the efficient breach doctrine. According to this theory, a typical contract obligation contains dual alternatives, namely, to deliver goods or services in return for a price or to make a monetary transfer to the promisee in place of delivery.[25] Thus, the payment of expectation damages should be treated as a substitutive method of enforcing the contract and be justified. Against various doubts and critiques, more and more contract theorists accept that the theory of efficient breach described in the early work is too simple, since it neglects other elements affecting the efficiency of breaches. Since 2000, more literature has raised radical attacks against this doctrine and suggested to put an end to it.[26] After almost 40 years since this theory was first proposed, it seems that the traditional theory of efficient breach has been losing its attraction to scholars gradually and almost nobody is still defending the so called "simple" efficient breach theory.[27]

2. Research Question

The development of efficient breach theory reflects scholarly efforts to solve specific design problems in contract law. More specifically, the questions to be answered by contract theorists are: what goals do we want contract law to reach? Can contract law reach this goal and how should contract law be designed in order to achieve the expected goals? Moralists may point to ethical reasons for recognizing and enforcing contracts, such as the morality of keeping promises or the value of corrective justice.[28] Economists, however, provide their answers to such questions by assuming that the goal of contract law is to maximize social welfare. What some contract theorists called a simple efficient breach theory focuses on a specific question: what remedy should be selected for breaches

action can and should be appraised. However, it is argued that this theory has neglected either the social effect or moral effect of an individual's activities. For more discussion, *see* chapter 4, section 4. *See* also Menetrez 2000; Perillo 2000; Sidhu 2006; Russell 2007; Bayern 2011 & Thel & Siegelman 2009.

25 *Actually, a similar assumption could be derived from Holms' previous exposition of a contractual duty as performance or payment of an equivalent amount of money. And after that, Richard Craswell raised a similar statement that "the equivalent of the promised performance itself depends on the full and exact scope of what was promised including the exact scope of what was promised in the event of a breach."* See *Craswell 1989, p. 513; Craswell 2006, p. 12; 20–21. In 2011, Daniel Markovits and Alan Schwartz raise the concept of dual performance in a sum. They divided contract terms into action terms, which require the parties to take actual movement of performance, and transfer term, accorded by expectation damages paid by the breach party. On this view, the promisor "breaches" only when he fails to comply with either aspect of his promise, that is, he fails to deliver and he refuses to pay.* See *Markovits & Schwartz 2011.*

26 Sidhu 2011, p. 360.

27 Klass 2013, p, 2.

28 Fried 1981 explained the moral foundation for contracts. According to him, a contract essentially is based on a promise, which provides a way for the promisor to bind himself to the promisee so that the promisee may expect a future performance and such a binding capacity of the promise is what the promisor expects. The obligation to keep a promise is grounded in respect for individual autonomy and in trust. A similar idea has been expressed by Atiyah 1981 and Macneil 1980.

of contracts in order to encourage efficient breaches and in the end to produce welfare maximization? In response to this question, some researchers use economic variables and formulas for building perfect efficient breach models and designing efficient remedy rules. Many early law and economics studies on efficient breach theory have chosen such a solution. However, many of them have not produced theoretical predictions that are determinate, nor normative suggestions that are plausible and justifiable.[29] One important explanation for such a result, according to Posner 2003, is that the so-called economic analysis of contract law failed to "explain the current system of contract law". Besides, when scholars tried to find out the optimal remedy for promoting efficient breach, they failed to consider the factors such as transaction costs, the possibility of renegotiations, the specific form of a contract as well as the effect of expectation damages on contract parties' other behaviour besides breach, etc.[30] As a result, the theory of efficient breach failed to provide a solid basis for criticizing and reforming contract law."[31] Facing all kinds of questions from both economic and non-economic arguments, we might ask whether or not the efficient breach doctrine is still useful in the modern study of contract law.

The goal of this thesis is to re-assess the problems to be solved by efficient breach theory and to fit the findings deriving from this theory into the context of different legal systems. In order to avoid exercising a general theory on all types of contracts, this thesis will merely focus on one type of contracts, namely, a commercial sales contract, in which both the buyer and the seller are commercial parties and the seller's obligation is generalized as to deliver or produce goods as required by the contract.[32] As for commercial parties, they usually include companies, partnerships and other forms of business entities, which work for economic interests and can be expected to base their activities on the calculation of benefits and costs. It is hypothesized that both parties to such a contract will choose to maximize their economic profits through efficient ex-post trade and efficient ex-ante investment and, at the same time, a state's policy choices and the possibility of cognitive errors play a less important role in influencing the contractual relationship.[33] Following this logic, we assume that the role of contract law in commercial

29 Posner 2002, p. 830.

30 *Id*, p. 834–836.

31 *See Id*, p. 830. Although many law and economic studies before the 20th century failed to provide a solid economic basis for explaining and reforming contract law, "this is not to say that the economic approach has not produced any wisdom, but that the nature of its accomplishment turns out to be subtle and will become clear only after an extended discussion".

32 *See* Schwartz & Scott 2003, p. 544. Besides a transaction between two business parties, there are three other transactional categories, including: 1) an individual sells to another individual; (2) a business seller sells to an individual; and (3) an individual sells to a business buyer. These three types of transactions are primarily regulated by other laws instead of by contract law. For instance, transactions between a business seller and an individual are usually regulated by consumer protection law or property law or security law.

33 See id, p. 545–546. The idea that commercial parties make contracts for maximizing profits might be criticized for several reasons. Some people may argue that the possibility of cognitive errors might deter a party from making profit-maximizing acts. Besides, it is also argued that the values to be pursued by traders are not restricted to economic profits, but also include fairness and environmental friendliness, etc. In order to carry out those values, a state will carry out certain policies and this has a great impact

sales, in brief, is merely to "facilitate the efforts of contracting parties to maximize the joint gains (the 'contractual surplus') from transactions", but nothing else.[34] This is the starting point for re-examining the theory of efficient breach and the problems to be solved by this theory.

Traditionally, the theory of efficient breach focuses on one single question, namely, which remedy will promote efficient breach? It has been suggested that the contract remedy rules should be structured in a way that breaches will be encouraged if, and only if, they are efficient. Instead of simply studying the relationship between the remedy of expectation damages and contract parties' breach-or-performance decisions, this thesis develops the analysis of efficient breach theory against a legal context in a way that contract law rules are treated as an integrated one. It starts from the hypothesis that there is a possibility that a seller's performance of a contract may turn out to be inefficient even if it seemed to be efficient at the time when the contract was concluded. If this takes place, non-performance of a contract will be economically more desirable than performance. We assume that such a contract falls into a zone where performance of the contract should be avoided. In order to avoid the performance of such a contract, the seller might choose to breach the contract or to renegotiate with the buyer in search of better contract terms. The question of how the law can encourage efficient breaches is then switched into how the law can promote efficiency, if performance of a contract turns out to be less efficient than non-performance. We assume that not only contract remedy rules but also other rules of contract law may influence a seller's acts in the aforementioned case.[35] A number of more detailed questions will be addressed, including: 1) Why do people make contracts and why do they need contract laws? 2) What is the doctrine of efficient breach in the existing law and economic literature and what are the limits of this doctrine? 3) How will different remedy rules impact people's ex-post acts after the conclusion of a contract (particularly the acts of performance, breach or re-negotiations)? 3) In which circumstances is breach efficient and what kind of problem does the theory of efficient breach try to solve; and 4) What implications can we infer from the doctrine of efficient breach for shaping an efficient set of contract law rules?

on trade as well. However, according to Schwartz & Scott, the aforementioned elements play an insignificant role in shaping pure commercial contracts. Cognitive errors are more likely to take place in contracts between individuals or between a business and an individual and this would be solved through, for example, consumer law. Further, a state's policies of protecting the environment or promoting competition deal with the externality problems in contracts, but will not affect the relationship between contract parties.

34 Id, p. 544.

35 In existing literature, it has been generally agreed that contract remedy rules tend to affect a promisor's incentives to breach a contract. The topic about the interactive relationship between contract remedies and a promisor's incentive to breach has been discussed broadly. For instance, Birmingham 1969 is one of the earliest articles, which has discussed the economic effects of motivations created by contract damages. However, what has been largely ignored is the potential impact of remedy rules on contract parties' other decisions, such as the contract price as well as whether or not to enter into a contract. Moreover, not only remedy rules, but also other contract law rules will influence contract parties' acts after the conclusion of a contract if the rules of contract are considered as a whole. See Barnes 1998, p. 398; Klass 2013, p. 19–26.

The findings deriving from the doctrine of efficient breach will be tested in different sales law systems as well. In fact, there already exists some research, assessing the extent to which the efficient breach theory can be tested in the setting of judicial or commercial practices.[36] Nevertheless, it has been widely accepted in that research that the efficient breach doctrine is rarely adopted in practice. Scalise (2007) concludes that any idea of efficient breach is denied by civil law scholars and judges and is unlikely to be accepted by them at any time in the near future.[37] According to him, the doctrine of efficient breach is incompatible with the civil law principle of good faith, the default specific performance rule as well as many other structural and cultural elements existing in civil law. Even in the US, where this concept was first debated, judges would hardly express this terminology explicitly.[38] This might be true for the simple efficient breach theory, according to which contract remedies should only serve to create incentives for a promisor to breach a contract in seeking economic surplus.[39] Does this mean that there is no space for extending the law and economic theory of efficient breach into legal systems? The answer is "no" if the focus is placed on the problem that the efficient theory is dealing with as well as different legal systems' reactions to such a problem. Are the reactions of different legal systems consistent with the theory of efficient breach? This will be answered in the final part of this thesis. Furthermore, a fundamental goal that economists want contract law to achieve is to facilitate contracting parties' capacities for welfare maximization in transactions. Starting from this assumption, it may be useful to know to what extent different legal systems are pointing in such a direction and whether one system is more efficient than the others. The doctrine of efficient breach in this thesis provides one perspective to answer such a question. It enables us to study how well different legal systems work in shaping a promisor's (a seller's) incentives to perform-or-breach a contract as well as in addressing the problems to be solved by such a doctrine.

3. Methodology

This thesis adopts both economic analysis and comparative law and economics studies in addressing the theory of efficient breach as well the application of this doctrine in specific legal systems.

36 *See* e.g. Warkol 1998–1999; Lando & Rose 2003; Zhu 2005; Scalise 2007; Zhou 2008.

37 *See* Scalise 2007, p. 763.

38 Warkol 1998–1999, p. 334.

"Efficient breach is rarely adopted by judges. With a few notable exceptions, most judges do not explicitly adhere to the precepts of the theory of efficient breach in their decisions. In cases where judges could apply the theory of efficient breach to strengthen their conclusions, they often fail to do so. Also, when judges seem to embrace the theory, they often write in terms of equity and avoid the language of "efficiency" in their opinions."

39 Klass 2013, p. 17.

3.1. *Law and Economics*

3.1.1. Application of the Economic Analysis of Law

As one of the most influential approaches to analyzing contract law, law and economics study has extended into a wide range of legal fields, covering property law, tort law, antitrust law, corporation law, public regulation, etc.[40] This methodology, which has been contributed to greatly by the Chicago school, derives from a conviction that economics is a powerful tool for analyzing various legal questions.[41] Traditionally, the application of such an approach is grounded on the important presumption that: "individuals have preferences over outcomes, that these preferences obey basic consistency conditions, and that individuals satisfy these preferences subject to an exogenous budget constraint."[42] It is assumed that individuals are forward-looking and prefer acts that maximize their welfare.

Provided that individuals on average act rationally, it is possible to predict the influence of a certain legal rule on individual behavior. This is one type of question that law and economics scholars try to answer in their research. There are many examples of this kind of question. Will higher fines for speeding on the highway cause drivers to slow down? Will harsher punishments deter violent crime? Do businesses take too many or too few precautions when the law holds them strictly liable for injuries to consumers?[43] To answer those questions, economists introduced a behavioral theory by making assumptions concerning an individual's desire, knowledge, and capacities. Answers to those questions are usually neutral. Another type of question that is involved in law and economics studies concerns the social desirability of a legal rule.[44] Economists refer to the concept of social welfare and they use the criterion of efficiency to evaluate legal rules.[45] Cooter & Ulen 2011 gave an example showing how to assess the effect of a legal

40 Posner 2004, p. 66.

41 As to the definition and purpose of law and economics, there are various expressions in current textbooks, in which, Posner 2004 and Cooter & Ulen 2011 have a great influence.
According to Posner 2004,

> *"[e]conomic analysis of law has heuristic, descriptive, and normative aspects, As a heuristic, it seeks to display underlying unities in legal doctrines and institutions; in its descriptive mode, it seeks to identify the economic logic and effects of doctrines and institutions and the economic causes of legal change; and in its normative aspect it advises judges and other policymakers on the most efficient methods of regulating conduct through law."*

Cooter & Ulen 2011 summarizes that:

> *"Economics provided a scientific theory to predict the effects of legal sanctions on behavior, a behavioral theory to predict how people respond to laws, a method of prediction for social values of efficiency and the distribution of income, help for law makers to design a good legal system, which keeps the profitability of business and the welfare of people aligned."*

See Posner 2004, p. 67; Cooter & Ulen 2011, p. 3.

42 Posner 2003, p. 832.

43 Cooter & Ulen 2011, p. 2.

44 Shavell 2004, p. 1.

45 *Id*, p. 3.

rule according to a social welfare standard.[46] If a study shows that a higher punishment will decrease the number of drivers speeding on the highway, this result is neutral and we cannot judge whether a harsh punishment is socially desirable or not. However, if the study also shows that the additional cost of imposing higher fines exceeds the benefit from having fewer accidents, higher fines are considered to be inefficient and would decrease social welfare.

Economic analysis in this thesis is used for building a theoretical framework for analyzing the efficient breach doctrine in specific contract law systems as well as creating economic criteria for assessing those systems. This thesis begins from a hypothesis that people make contracts in order to maximize their mutual welfare. A transaction is deemed as a reciprocal process by which goods and services are transferred to the user who values them highest, provided it has no third-party effect and both parties are rational. Thus, rather than being a zero-sum game[47], transactions are productive because they bring out mutual benefits to both of the participants and create an economic surplus for the whole society. Under this premise, the thesis adopts some basic economic doctrines concerning efficiency (especially Kaldor-Hicks efficiency) and welfare maximization. The traditional cost-benefit analysis accompanied by some basic graphics and functions will be applied to explain the efficient breach theory. Beyond the cost-benefit analysis, this research will also consider other factors, such as uncertainties, risk-allocation and the existing behavioral evidence. Furthermore, this thesis is developed from both a positive and a normative perspective. On the one hand, it will explain how contract law rules can influence a seller's acts, such as his acts of performance. On the other hand, this research will try to provide some normative suggestions for shaping an efficient contract law. Before any further analysis, section 3.1.2 and section 3.1.3 will explain two basic economic terms, which are crucial for defining an efficient contract law system, namely, efficiency and transaction costs.

3.1.2. Efficiency

The term efficiency in economics usually refers to productive efficiency or allocative efficiency.[48]

Productive efficiency is evaluated by comparing the respective profit and cost of a process.[49] It's possible to improve productive efficiency either through increasing profits or lowering costs. An optimal extent of productive efficiency could be gained, where the

46 Cooter & Ulen 2011, p. 4.

47 A zero-sum game refers to a case, in which the gain of one party is always the loss of the other one.

48 Cooter & Ulen 2011, p. 13–14.

49 Productive efficiency is used to describe a factory's activity of production in the simple economic category. According to Cooter & Ulen 2011:

> "A production process is considered to be productively efficient if either of two conditions holds: 1. it is not possible to produce the same amount of output using a lower-cost combination of inputs, or; 2. it is not possible to produce more output using the same combination of inputs."

See id.

cost is minimal and the profit is greatest. Accordingly, we could say that a process is efficient if the benefit it produces exceeds the cost.

The other notion, *allocative efficiency*, concerns the satisfaction of individual preferences. After Coase raised the theorem of transaction costs, Posner's definition of efficiency in his early work has been cited frequently by scholars.[50] According to him, efficiency refers to "allocation of resources in which value (human satisfaction as measured by aggregate willingness to pay for goods and services) is maximized" from the perspective of utilitarianism.[51] However, such a definition has been questioned for its opaqueness and indeterminacy. For instance, Margolis (1987) argued that the elements of the court's role as well as the cost of allocation have been excluded from Posner's definition.[52] The problems in the utilitarian approach have encouraged economists to search for new definitions of efficiency. One of the most famous definitions of efficiency refers to the definition of Pareto efficiency, which is to confine the term efficiency to "outcomes of voluntary transactions".[53] A Pareto superior movement is one that makes at least one person better off without making anyone worse off.[54] It is considered that such a status will be achieved through voluntary transactions, which convey goods and services to the users who value them most. In comparison to Pareto superiority, what is more frequently applied to real world transactions is the criterion of Kaldor-Hicks efficiency.[55] Coleman (1984) defines Kaldor-Hicks efficiency as that: "*S1 is Kaldor-Hicks efficient to S if and only if in going from S to S1 the winners could compensate the losers so that no individuals would be worse off than they were in S and at least one person would be better off than he or she was in S.*" Any move is considered to be Kaldor-Hicks efficient if and only if the winners from such a move could compensate the losers. Once

50 See e.g. Baker 1980. P. 964; Kronman 1980, p. 240–241.

51 See Posner 2007, p. 11; see also Margolis 1987, p. 471. The concept utilitarianism is closely related to the definitions of "value" and "utility". In economics, value refers to "how much someone is willing to pay for something or, if he has it already, how much he demands for giving it away". In contrast, "utility is used by philosophers of utilitarianism, meaning happiness". Utility will be influenced by an individual's risk preference as well as his budget. Posner gave an example showing the difference between these two concepts. Suppose a poor person is willing to spend 10 euros on something (*S*) that he urgently needs and; a rich man wants to spend 100 euros on it but such a thing produces less happiness to the rich man than to the poor man. In this case, the value of (*S*) is higher to the rich man than to the poor man, because value is measured by willingness to pay. However, (*S*) confers greater happiness in the hands of the poor man than in the rich man.

52 Margolis 1987, p. 472–474.

53 Posner 2007, p. 12.

54 The concepts of "Pareto superiority" and "Pareto optimality" are used by economists to indicate what Pareto efficiency stands for. Suppose there are two groups: S1 and S2. The number of the members in S1 is exactly the same as that in S2. In economics, S1 is Pareto superior to S2 if and only if there is at least one person in S1, who gets better off than in S2 and no one gets worse off in S1, than in S2. Pareto optimality is based on Pareto superiority. A group is Pareto optimal if and only if no other group is Pareto superior to it. It is difficult to achieve the status of Pareto optimality. *See* Coleman 1984, p. 649–650; Menetrez 2000, p.870.

55 According to Posner 2007, the criterion of Pareto superiority has few applications in the real world because most transactions will have effects on third parties. Besides, each party to a transaction has to lose something in order to exchange for his expected value from the transaction, *See* Posner 2007, p. 12–13.

compensation had been paid to the losers, "a Kaldor-Hicks efficient move would become a Pareto superior one" because the result is that no one becomes worse off from this move.[56] In this sense, the term of Kaldor-Hicks efficiency is also called potential Pareto Superiority.[57]

3.1.3. Transaction Cost

Besides the term efficiency, transaction cost is another crucial concept for making economic evaluation of legal rules. Economists use the concept of transaction costs to describe the costs resulting from trading.[58] Within the market, suppose that people are able to transfer properties or services freely so that the contracting parties can both maximize their utility.[59] In the end, resources will be re-allocated in society and the social welfare is thus maximized. However, an ideal model of transactions only exists in an experimental world. In the real world, transactions are costly, in which various types of costs are involved. Those costs refer to what people give up in order to get some benefits within the transactions.[60] It is stated that transaction costs create obstacles and impediments to bargaining in the market.[61]

Transaction costs can arise from any parts of the market. Before a contract is signed, people need to find each other, approach each other, exchange information, communicate and negotiate with each other.[62] After the contract is signed, costs still emerge in the

56 Coleman 1984, p. 651–652.

57 Any Pareto improvement is a Kaldor-Hicks improvement, but not every Kaldor-Hicks improvement is a Pareto improvement.

58 As to the definition of transaction costs, there are two major different approaches. One refers to the property right approach which is derived from the Coase theorem (Coase 1937) and was promoted by scholars such as Cheung (1969), McManus (1975), Jensen and Meckling (1976), Cooter (1982) and Eggertsson (1990), etc. The transaction cost was defined as the costs of establishing and maintaining property rights. In this sense, the concept of transaction cost includes all kinds of costs involved in establishing, transferring, maintaining or protecting property rights. The other approach limits the transaction costs to the costs of transferring property. This approach, which is also referred to as the neo-classical approach, was mainly proposed by Hick (1935) and Demsetz (1964). Accordingly, the transaction costs only include the costs of exchanging ownership titles within the market and the enforcement-type costs within firms are not transaction costs. But no matter which type of definition is used, the underlying theme for transaction costs is similar. An important point is that transaction costs work as impediments to market coordination. In this chapter, we use the broader definition of transaction cost. See Allen 2000, p. 895–905; Demsetz 1968, p. 35. Cooter & Ulen 2011, p. 84, p. 85.

59 Schäfer & Ott 2004, p. 273.

60 In economics, the cost of something is what you give up to get it. For instance, if you go to school, then what you can obtain is enhancement of your knowledge and improvement of some skills. However, you also need to sacrifice something to achieve it. For example, you spend several years in the school, you pay the tuition fee and you need to make an effort to grasp knowledge. Mankiw 2008, p. 5.

61 Hicks 1935, p. 6.

62 For some scholars, the transaction costs arising from the formation of contracts are mainly information costs. For example, Barzel (1982, 1985) stresses that "information costs are at the heart of transaction costs because they lead to measurement". Niehans (1987) also recognizes that since the information is not common and sufficient, then negotiation, fraud, communication and contract stipulation will come about. However, it is argued that although information costs constitute the majority of transaction

whole process of executing and enforcing the contract. Goods need to be described, inspected, weighed, measured and transported. Title has to be transferred and lawyers may be involved. Sometimes, conflicts might occur between the contracting parties and the parties might turn to courts or arbitration agencies.[63] In all of those occasions, resources, money, time as well as subjective elements (emotion, opportunity, etc) will be invested and all those elements constitute the costs of transacting.[64] In general, transaction costs can have effects both on the transactions themselves and on the institutions governing how to allocate resources.

Firstly, the existence of transaction costs has an impact on both the quantity and the form of transaction. Given the existence of transaction costs, negotiations and transactions are restricted and deterred directly to some extent. For instance, the volume of trade will be influenced because people may compare the benefits and the costs when making decisions in the market. If the costs of transacting are much higher than the total benefits, then individuals will rationally hold their money and be reluctant to make investments in the market.[65] Moreover, people may also react to the problem by changing their way of trading. They prefer those arrangements under which the costs of transacting are much lower. A typical example is that a person would prefer investing money for long periods rather than short periods and this is to some extent because he can save the brokerage charges and the stamp duties.[66] Secondly, what is affected by transaction costs is the way resources are allocated, in other words, the institutions governing the establishment and maintenance of resources. According to the Coase Theorem, a transaction (or contract) is just one method that will allocate the resources.[67] In an ideal world where there is no transaction cost and people are rational, an efficient allocation and use of resources results from private bargaining, regardless of the legal assignment of property rights.[68] Since private bargaining is costless, people can always negotiate

costs, it is still necessary to distinguish transaction costs from information costs. Transaction costs also include the costs of monitoring and implementing contracts. Allen 2000, p. 906; Stavins 1995, p. 134.

63 Allen 2000, p. 906.

64 Id, p. 901.

65 Id.

66 Hicks 1935, p. 6.

67 Coase defined the transaction cost as the cost of using the price mechanism. Within the market, the price is the major tool that helps allocate resources when people choose to transact. When this method has its costs, it will compete with other institutions. See Allen 2000, p. 895.

68 The classical example that Coase uses to describe a zero transaction cost situation comes from his paper "The Problem of Social Cost", which has been frequently cited in literature. Cooter & Ulen in their book suppose a case that is similar to Coase's: the farmer grows corn on some of his land and his neighbor a rancher runs cattle over all her land. The cattle often wander onto the farm and damage the corn. The damage can be reduced if the famer builds a fence or grows less corn; or if the rancher invests in supervising his cattle or decreases the number of the cattle. All of the approaches are costly and the core issue here is to whom this cost should be allocated. Coase indicates that in the situation when transaction is costless, every approach can lead to an efficient result and the original arrangement is irrelevant. The rancher could always negotiate with the farmer. He may agree to pay the farmer to leave the land uncultivated or he rents the land by paying the farmer an amount slightly greater than the farmer would pay. The final result would be the same and would maximize the value of production. Coase 1960, p. 2–5; Cooter & Ulen 2011, p. 82–85.

with each other and come to agreements or settlements. Subsequently, all misallocations of resources will be fully cured in the market and all the conflicts around resources will also be solved within the market.[69] Therefore, the contents of law or regulation are irrelevant. In contrast, in the situation where transaction costs are positive, it is sometimes too costly and difficult for people to coordinate resources through market arrangements.[70] Then the market mechanism competes with other allocating institutions like firms, property law, tax or judicial decisions which are normally established by the states.[71] If those state-established institutions can be enforced at a comparatively lower cost, then they will become the alternatives in resource distribution. For example, when the transaction cost is high and bargaining is prevented, a well-defined system of property rights is important for providing a preliminary framework of how the property rights are established.[72] Similarly, a well-defined property rights system will increase people's gains from trade because it can lower the transaction costs and facilitate market coordination.[73] Hence, given the costs of transacting, it is required that an efficient contract law system should be constructed in a way that "property rights are assigned and liability rules are formulated so that the value of the things present in society, as measured by people's willingness to pay, is maximized over all alternative legal environments".[74]

3.2. *Comparative Law and Economics*

The failure of theoretical economic analysis to produce determinate and justifiable theories has received great attention among scholars. As mentioned by both Posner (2002)[75] and by Mattei & Monti (2001), many law and economic studies mostly work on producing ideal predictions based on abstract concepts while they neglect to discuss specific legal institutions as well as legal rules.[76] In view of this concern, this research also adopts a comparative law and economic analysis in order to extend the findings derived from the economic theory of efficient breach into specific legal systems. In this research, economic analysis is adopted for analyzing efficient breach models and

69 Calabresi 1968, p. 68.

70 Demsetz also indicates the transaction costs as "the costs of coordinating resources through market arrangements". Allen 2000, p. 903.

71 Also note that establishing and executing institutions will incur administrative costs. Then it is important to compare the costs of the market and the costs of other institutions and decide when it is cheaper for the market to allocate resources. "At times, firms and direct management supersede the market, while at other times market prices are used in directing goods and service." For instance, those public goods such as military goods or environmental goods and services are usually established and managed by states, rather than by private persons. Id, p. 895.

72 Cooter & Ulen 2011, p. 85.

73 Allen 2000, p. 898.

74 Margolis 1987, p. 473–474.

75 Posner 2002, p. 830.

76 Mattei 2003, p. 9. It is mentioned:

> *"Most of the founding contributions to the field of law and economics, in fact, tend to deal with general, abstract and sometimes misleading legal concepts – such as the naturalistic notion of "property right" – and to presume a static institutional framework clearly modelled on the American legal process (comprising an effective court system, strong incentives to litigation, etc.)."*

producing criteria of comparison for the different solutions adopted by different sales law systems. In contrast, a comparative perspective enables this thesis to establish to what extent the legal rules and legal institutions of different sales law systems are identical and different in motivating efficient breach and producing efficiency. The comparison is grounded on an observation of the factual laws as well as the operational rules applied by the courts in the given sales law systems.[77] Such a comparison is helpful for assessing the conditions upon which the efficient breach doctrine can be best applied and measuring the distance that separates each sales law system from the efficient breach models at the theoretical level. As a result, the applicability of the economic theories concerning efficient breach will be tested on the basis of practical evidence. The comparative inquiry in this research will be accomplished in two steps:

3.2.1. Choosing Legal Systems

The legal systems that will be analyzed in this research include English law, Chinese Law and European Union contract law. Among these three legal systems, English law belongs to the category of the common law systems, in which judicial cases have offered an important resource for their development. In some previous literature, it has been argued that a common law system is largely consistent with the criterion of economic efficiency while a statute law system is more concerned with the goal of distribution and the protection of special interests.[78] Following this logic, it might be assumed that the doctrine of efficient breach is well applied in UK sales law. However, at the moment, there is very little research analysing this doctrine on the basis of English contract law, while most studies of the efficient breach theory have been conducted under the premise of the American law system in which this theory was first raised. Hereby, this thesis chooses English sales law instead of American law as one jurisdiction for comparison. In contrast with English law, European Union contract law mainly refers to laws derived from the recent achievements of the Europeanization of contract law. Those achievements are presented as several different types of European contract law instruments including, directives and regulations promulgated by the European Commission or by the European Parliament, soft laws grounded on scholarly efforts and so on.[79] Many rules of European Union sales contract law have been affected by the contract laws and principles of the member states. For instance, the Latin maxim *pacta sunt servanda* has a great impact on the design of remedy rules in for instance Germany, France, Spain, Greece and Italy,[80]

[77] Traditionally, when people talk about comparative studies, they always think about the following four steps, including:

> *"First, a comparative analysis starts with preliminary considerations, deciding on the research question and the choice of legal systems. Second, the comparatist has to describe the laws of these countries. Third, she has to compare them, in particular exploring the reasons for unexpected similarities and differences. Fourth, she should critically evaluate her findings, possibly also making policy recommendations."*

See Siems, 2014, p. 13.

[78] For instance, see Rubin 1977, p. 61; Rubin 1982, p. 205.

[79] For more discussion about the development of European Union contract law, see chapter 6, section 1.

[80] Scalise Jr. 2007, p. 726–734.

and this also influences the choice of default remedy in European Union law. At the first sight, some people might take it for granted that European Union contract law has a general preference for the remedy of specific performance and the idea that contracts should be performed. Hence, it might be true that this legal system is incompatible with any idea of efficient breach. The third system chosen for comparison is Chinese law, which is basically modern Chinese sales contract law. Chinese contract law stands for a developing contract law system in China and the establishment of it has been influenced by Chinese culture and traditions, the political and economic elements in China and even the contract law rules in other legal systems. As China now is becoming one of the largest markets in the world, the growth of Chinese law in relation to trades has gained more and more attention from scholars in other countries. But scholars might worry that political orders and business customs in China pre-date laws and take a prevailing role in determining the formation and the performance of a contract. It seems that the new-born Chinese contract law has little to do with the criterion of efficiency.

3.2.2. Choosing the Topics to be Compared

Facing the aforementioned questions and hypotheses, this thesis takes a comparative approach in order to re-test those hypotheses and furthermore tries to answer whether one legal system produces a higher level of efficiency than others. Under each legal system, two major questions are raised. First of all, the comparative study starts from an observation about how each legal system encourages a seller to perform a contract that has been concluded. This is closely related to each system's design of contract remedy rules, which indicates the consequences of the breach and hence influences a seller's incentive to perform the contract. The emphasis will be placed on three major types of remedy, including specific performance and compensation, as well as remedies stipulated by contract parties. Another issue to be studied concerns the specific mechanisms offered by each legal system for dealing with the situations where the performance of a contract is considered to be inefficient. With regard to this aspect, each system has provided some particular rules indicating solutions that are available to contract parties, such as *force majeure*,[81] the hardship rule, the impracticability rule, etc.

4. Structure of the Thesis

This thesis contains two major parts. After an Introduction (chapter 1), Part I offers the theoretical framework for the efficient breach theory. This part aims to provide a general idea about what the efficient breach theory is, what limits this theory has and what implications can be derived from the theory. The findings from the theoretical analysis will be applied to specific sales law systems and this will be dealt with in Part II. The

81 *Force majeure* is the term that has been used by French law. In European Union contract law instruments, what has been used is the term "excuse" which has the same meaning as *force majeure* does; while in China the term "*force majeure*" is quite often adopted by judges and Chinese contract law scholars. This thesis will choose the term of *force majeure* in order keep a consistence.

question to be answered in part II is: How EU law, English law and Chinese law react to the problems that are to be solved by the efficient breach doctrine and to what extent does each legal system follow this doctrine? At the end of the thesis, some policy recommendations will be provided.

Four chapters will be included in Part I. Chapter 2 will introduce some basic economic theories of contract, contract law and contract remedies. Afterwards, Chapter 3 will summarize the doctrine of efficient breach in existing literature, regarding its definition, economic justifications, economic model and conditions. This theory, since the first time it was proposed, has been receiving all kinds of doubts and critiques both from an economic perspective and from a moralistic aspect. A re-assessment of the theory and its limits will then be conducted in chapter 4. Chapter 5 will analyze the relationship between the efficient breach doctrine and different kinds of remedies, consisting of expectation damages, specific performance, reliance damages, and disgorgement as well as remedies created upon agreement. Moreover, some implications deriving from the efficient breach theory will be given at the end of chapter 5.

Part II mainly deals with the application of the efficient breach doctrine to EU law, English law and Chinese law and each legal system will be analyzed within one chapter. Chapter 6 concerns the application of the efficient breach theory to EU sales contract law. At the beginning of this chapter, an introduction to European Union contract law will be provided in order to give an idea about what belongs to European Union contract law as well as how it developed. Afterwards, section 2 will indicate the general remedy rules of EU contract law, regarding the application of specific performance, damage rules as well as party-agreed damages. Section 3 will particularly deal with the reactions of EU law to contracts that have fallen into a zone where strict performance is inefficient. The difficulties for applying the efficient breach theory to EU law will be explained in section 4. Afterwards, section 5 is going to make a law and economic analysis and section 6 will conclude. Chapter 7 (English sales law) and Chapter 8 (Chinese sales law) will be structured in a similar way that is used in chapter 6. Both of these chapters contain five sections, indicating the development of one legal system, the remedy rules in this system, the rules concerning the efficient breach zone, economic analysis as well as the concluding remarks. Based on the studies of the above three legal systems, chapter 9 will make a comparative law and economic analysis. The purpose of this chapter is to discover the similarities and the differences among those legal systems in shaping contract parties' incentives to perform as well as to avoid inefficient performance.

In the end, some concluding remarks will also be given through which it is hoped that this thesis could contribute some suggestions and implications to the future economic analysis of contract law (Chapter 10).

Chapter 2

ECONOMIC ANALYSIS OF CONTRACT AND CONTRACT LAW

In voluntary transactions, efficiency is enhanced because goods and services will be allocated to the best user and surpluses will be created. But the time lapse between the formation of a contract and its performance creates risks and uncertainties. This problem will be increased by the problems of opportunism, distrust and incomplete contracts. Thus the efficiency of transactions can be endangered. Since the market cannot always work efficiently, it is required that contract law is introduced as a supplementary mechanism for transactions. Economists assume that there is a close relationship between the structure of contract damage rules, people's behaviour and social efficiency. An efficient law is able to facilitate people's capacity for welfare maximization in the transactions, and to promote social efficiency. This chapter will first indicate the economic reasons why people make contracts and what would happen if there were no contract law. Afterwards, the economic functions of contract law will be provided in section 2. Section 3 will further provide the economic theory of the binding effect of a contract. One important result of the binding effect is that if one party to a contract breaches, the non-breaching party will be entitled to contract remedies. A basic economic theory of contract remedies will be included in section 4. Section 5 will conclude.

1. Economic Analysis of Contracts

1.1. Voluntary Transactions and Efficiency

Voluntary transactions are justified both in the traditional legal theory and from an economic perspective. Lawyers relate them to the principle of freedom of contract.[82] But economists pay more attention to the welfare that can be created through transactions. Suppose there are two parties *Y* and *X*. *Y* has a machine that is worth 50 euros to him but is worth 150 euros to *X*. According to economists, a rational person is assumed to be interested in welfare maximization and he will take actions which make him better off.

82 The principle of freedom of contract has been supported by a number of traditional textbooks and articles. For instance, Kessler and Sharp wrote: "[P]art of contract law is the counterpart, if not the product, of free enterprise capitalism. Contract, in this point of view, is the legal machinery appropriate to an economic system which relies on free exchange rather than tradition and custom or command for the distribution of resources". *See* Birmingham 1970, p. 274.

In this case, *X* might obtain this machine either through producing a similar one for himself or buying it from *Y* at a price lower than 150 euros. But *Y* would be willing to give up the machine only if he could acquire more than 50 euros. If the cost of transaction between *X* and *Y* is extremely low or even negligible, then the transaction creates a joint profit of 100. If X and Y agree on a price of 100 euro, then the transaction makes each party obtain a net profit of 50 euro. Under this ideal model, the transaction is deemed as a reciprocal process by which goods and services are converted into their most valuable uses. Thus, rather than being a zero-sum game[83], voluntary transactions are productive because they bring out mutual benefits to both of the participants and create an economic surplus for each party and for society. Thus our preliminary conclusion on transaction and contract is that: ***economic surplus motivates people to transact.*** The way in which each trader can increase his welfare is shown in the table as follows:

Table 1. Economic Surplus from a Voluntary Transaction

Transaction cost	Value of the machine		Price (50 < P < 150)	Surplus		
	For *X*	For Y		X	Y	Joint
Low	150	50	100	50	50	100

The value of a transaction is easy to be realized when the exchange between two parties occurs instantly and simultaneously. A simple case is where a buyer hands over the money and at the same time a seller delivers the goods. This is because the exchange creates surpluses immediately at the time when it is concluded. Thus the space for the role of promises or agreements is small in those simultaneous and instantaneous exchanges. However, there are many occasions where the simultaneity condition does not hold. Transactions often involve a passage of time for their completion and the products or services will be exchanged in the future. For instance, a transport company may have to deliver a particular cargo by a specified delivery date or a seller agrees to provide 300 bottles of red wine at the wedding day of a customer. In those circumstances, if a well-organized market does not exist,[84] the private parties need to arrange their own commitments of taking future performances through promises. Hence, agreements (or contracts) become an important method of confirming commitments.

1.2. Contract Formation: Negotiating Over the Uncertainty

What makes the exchanges that involve future performance (*deferred exchanges*) different from the instantaneous exchanges is the factor of time. Imagine there are three models of promise: "*one party pays now for the other party's promise to deliver goods later*

83 A zero-sum game refers to a case, in which the gain of one party is always the loss of the other one.

84 In a well-organized market, in which products and services are abundant and information is transparent, there is no reason for promise of future supply because the required products or services could be obtained on the spot. For instance, if we need a bottle of cola in next week, we don't need to sign a contract right now since we are able to find it at that moment. Shavell 2004, p. 296.

('payment for a promise'); one party delivers goods now for the other's promise to pay later ('goods for a promise'); one party promises to deliver goods later and the other party promises to pay when the goods are delivered ('promise for a promise')".[85] Within the basic structure of those models, the one who offers a promise is referred to as promisor and the other one who receives a promise is regarded as promisee. Our basic question is: as time passes by, will the parties still have incentives to implement their original promises and perform the agreed transaction?

1.2.1. The Problem of Uncertainty

No matter in which situation, when the promise is made initially, both parties want it to be enforceable so as to realize their purpose from the transaction. The buyer wants to obtain the ownership of the goods and the seller wishes to earn a surplus after selling the goods. Nevertheless, the passage of time between the moment when a promise was made and the moment when this promise should be carried out creates various uncertainties and possibilities. After the promise is made, a lot of things might happen. Thus the value or the cost of the performance may not be the same as what is expected by the parties at the time when they made promises. For instance, if an unexpectedly high temperature makes it hard to preserve the goods until the date of delivery, the seller has to take costly measures before all the goods get spoilt. Or a buyer may receive a new offer, from a seller who can deliver the desired product of a higher quality and at a lower price. Or there may have been a live concert by a famous singer, but she develops a throat infection before the date of the concert. In those events, the promisor has to bear an extra burden or lose an excellent opportunity if he wants to carry out what he has promised. So the cost of performing agreements will be increased or the value of the transaction will be decreased. We call those "bad events" *adverse risks*.[86] Similarly, some intervening events may be favourable, provided that they can lead to a decrease in the cost of the transaction or an increase in the surplus that is created by the transaction. One can imagine that an umbrella retailer will be very happy if rainy weather lasts for two months and his deal with a producer becomes more desirable, since people are more willing to buy umbrellas.

Given the possibility that various favourable or adverse events might happen in the future, the value and cost of a transaction is unstable and uncertain. Thus at the time when the promises are exchanged, the trading parties' anticipations of earning profits cannot be ascertained. Consequently, this type of uncertainty will also influence people's behaviour. As has been indicated, people will participate in the transaction when it can create an economic surplus for each party. However, when the time comes, completion of the original agreement might not be desirable anymore for the promisor, for instance, if he cannot earn any surplus. In this case, a promisor may just change his mind and break his promise.

85 Cooter & Ulen 2011, p. 283.

86 Since adverse risk refers to those contingencies that threaten to increase the cost of performance of a contractual obligation or decrease the value of performance, it is always correlated to the doctrine of contract frustration. Triantis 1992, p. 454.

1.2.2. Contract Formation

Our major explanation of contract formation comes from the problem of uncertainty. Since the purpose of most transactions is to enhance the economic value, each party has the motivation to control the uncertainty in their transaction through a careful ex-ante design of contract clauses. In the beginning when people approach each other for trade, they may negotiate over the contingencies which might arise in the transaction and make a desirable contract. On the one hand, either a promisor or a promisee is assumed to be the best judge of his own interest. Each of them has the incentive to estimate how much surplus can be brought out by a transaction when deciding whether or not to make it. In order to make the estimation, they need to consider various intervening events, which may increase or decrease the value (or the cost) of the performance. On the other hand, contractual parties are also the best persons[87] to deal with the risks related to the contract. They may make an arrangement dealing with all the prospective uncertainties and risks that may arise after the promise is made. On the one hand, the parties may evaluate the probability of a particular adverse risk, the cost of precautions against it, the severity of its consequences and so on in order to decide whether to control such a risk or to bear the consequences of it. This is called risk management in economic theory.[88] On the other hand, the parties may also discuss how to share a risk. After analysing their comparative advantages in risk management, the parties may allocate the risk to the one who can manage it at the lowest cost.[89]

By the consensus of the two parties, those risk arrangements will be fixed by some contract terms. In other words, the contract will specify some possible contingencies and the actions that the parties are going to take if a contingency happens. For instance, suppose the contract is for goods which are sensitive to temperature. If the parties know that there is going to be a sharp increase in the temperature, they may agree on the seller's duty to properly store the goods. Because the goods are still under the control of the seller before the delivery date, the seller is able to control the risk with a lower cost. Nevertheless, the stipulated price for the product will be increased as well so as to compensate for the cost of storage.

87 Compared to any other third person, the parties to a contract are the best who can make the best arrangement of their benefits and risks.

88 The parties may decide to take cost-effective measures against the undesirable risk in order to minimize the cost, if the cost of doing so is lower than the loss brought out by the risk. This is what we call "risk control". Normally, contract parties can control a risk by reducing its probability and severity of its consequence. However there are still some risks which cannot be eliminated completely. As to those residual risks, the contractual parties have to agree on bearing the consequences of them or only take some secondary strategies, such as insurance, to diminish the loss. *See* Triantis 1992, p. 454.

89 According to Posner & Rosenfield 1977, the optimal allocation means that, "a given risk should be borne by the party who can implement measures to control it at the lower cost," provided that all the other things are equal. Thus the risk might be allocated to the superior risk bearer whose performance is affected by the risk or the party that demands the lower price. "For instance, a risk may be allocated entirely to the promisor under a fixed price contract or to the promisee by a clause that discharges the promisor's obligations upon materialization of the risk or that passes all the resulting cost increase to the promisee under a price escalation clause." *See* Polinsky 1987, p.27; Posner & Rosenfield 1977, p. 111; Triantis 1992, p. 454–455.

1.3. *Problems in Contracts without Legal Interference*

Until now, transactions have been structured under a model without legal intervention. After the contract is made, the arrangement of future benefits and risks has been fixed to some extent and both of the parties are required to comply with what they have agreed upon. It seems that the problem of uncertainty can be resolved through private negotiations and contractual arrangements. But the contract is still extended into the future and the transaction still has a time dimension. Besides, there are at least two problems that will hamper the function of contracts in enhancing mutual welfare. First, it is uncertain that each party will make and perform a contract in good faith. Second, it is difficult to be sure that the contract has been drafted perfectly.

1.3.1. Problems of Opportunism and Distrust

1.3.1.1. Opportunism

Basically, commercial exchanges are ruled by the market. It is common for traders to act in their own rational self-interests within the framework of the market. As described in a recent work, economic agents are considered as utility maximizers who will take any measure to increase their return when there is no risk in doing so.[90] The seller might hide some important information about the product and charge the same price for an inferior product (information is hidden). Or the debtor might invest in an extremely risky project, which might cause his insolvency and thus impair the benefit of the creditor (action is hidden).[91] Or the debtor might appropriate the money he had borrowed from the creditor and would not be forced to pay the money back if there is no punishment at all. Those cases are relevant to what we call *opportunism*. The trading parties' behaviour such as hiding information or appropriating money is regarded as *opportunistic behaviour*. A classical definition of opportunistic behaviour by Williamson was given as: "self-interest

90 Oliver Williamson was the one who criticized neo-classical microeconomics for its assumptions that economic agents act in fair and law-abiding ways and the market will mediate transactions between technologically separable entities in a natural, hence efficient way. According to Williamson, on the one hand, the economic agents are motivated by economic profits. On the other hand, the human agents that populate the firms and markets differ from complete economic man in that they are less competent in calculation and less trustworthy and reliable in action. *See* Williamson 1981, p. 1545; Schäfer & Ott 2004, p. 277.

91 These are two examples associated with opportunism, where either information is hidden (adverse selection) or action is hidden (moral hazard). Suppose there are two parties, A and B. "the former describes the situation in which A doesn't know ex ante the true characteristics of B; while the latter describes the situation that B's incentive to act optimally from A's point of view is reduced because A can observe only the outcome of B's action and not the action itself. " The concept of moral hazard is a technical term from insurance literature. It is referred to an ex post insurance condition in which one party's behaviour would be changed because of the existence of the insurance. The other concept, adverse selection refers to an ex ante insurance screening problem. See Williamson 1981, p. 1545; Lyons & Mehta 1997, p. 241.

seeking with guile".[92] It indicates that the party who engages in opportunistic behaviour usually has a "weak moral"[93] or bad intention when he is trying to make more profit from the transaction.

As to contracts, ex-ante opportunism, which happens before the formation of a contract, can be distinguished from ex-post opportunism, which happens after a contract has been signed. During the negotiation, opportunism typically presents itself as particular behaviour such as deliberate misrepresentation or duress. The purpose of this behaviour is to mislead or force the other party to sign a contract that is disadvantageous to him. After the contract is signed, opportunism may also manifest itself "in the form of evasion of obligations in the on-going relationship".[94] It always occurs in such a way that the promisor takes advantage of the existing contract with little regard for the adverse effect on the promisee.[95] For instance, ex-post opportunistic behaviour may take the form that a promisor appropriates the payment made by the promisee and escapes from providing reciprocal performance.

Opportunism is described as exploiting the trust of the other party and earning an extra profit.[96] At the beginning, trust has been aroused in the injured party when the two parties approach each other for a transaction, but will be systematically exploited in the end. This situation is quite typical in a *specific investment* relationship where the subjects of a contract are specific items. Since one party's investment is more profitable in this relationship than elsewhere, he has little choice but to comply with the contract.[97]

1.3.1.2. Distrust

Given the existence of potential opportunistic behaviour, a new problem of uncertainty has arisen that both of the contractual parties face a degree of uncertainty about the other party's behaviour.[98] The potential opportunism leaves each party uncertain about whether the information disclosed by his partner is adequate and real or not, or whether the contract will be performed properly by his partner or not. Since the purpose of the

92 In the subsequent work of Williamson, he described guile as "lying, stealing, cheating, and calculated efforts to mislead, distort, disguise, obfuscate, or otherwise confuse". *See* Lyons & Mehta 1997, p. 242; Williamson 1981, p. 1545; Williamson 1985, p. 47.

93 Douglas 1990.

94 Wathne & Heide 2000, p. 38.

95 *Id*, p. 39.

96 As illustrated by Schäfer and Ott, a relationship of trust is built so that information can be exchanged between the contractual parties. "The person who behaves in accord with this trust will also receive a goodwill premium and a person who is a member of an organized group or association can draw on a collective goodwill premium when all members of the group also behave in a trustworthy manner. In contrast, opportunism is that kind of behaviour that awakes trust in another and then systematically exploits it. The profit from such behaviour is the opportunism premium." Schäfer & Ott 2004, p. 368–369.

97 Schäfer and Ott gave an example of selling one kind of specific component. As they indicate, if the buyer pushes the price to a very low level that only covers the supplier's variable costs, the supplier is forced to accept it because he will bear a larger loss if this contract were ruptured completely. Schäfer and Ott 2004, p. 369–370.

98 Here the concept of behaviour has a broad meaning, which includes not only the positive actions, but also the passive ones, such as failure to perform or passive acquiescence.

transaction is to enhance the joint profits of the parties, there is a reciprocal relationship between the contractual parties that each one will orient his behaviour to his expectation of the other.[99] Without some form of assurance that the other will be honest and trustful, each party might also just act in his own interest even if this might be against the joint interest of both parties. As a result, businessmen who dislike risks cannot be motivated to fully participate in anonymous transactions or they may just reduce their investments in transactions. Shavell gives some examples to indicate the harm of opportunism. Supposing a debtor is able to refuse to return the money that he has borrowed from the creditor, then loans will become impossible.[100]

1.3.1.3. Insufficiency of Market Mechanisms

To some extent, the market itself offers a kind of assurance because it works as a filter. In the long run, honest players are favoured while opportunist and dishonest players will be punished and dispelled. So in order to retain trust and reputation in the mutual playing field, each actor may consciously adhere to certain behavioural rules established in this field. To some extent, those rules may motivate people to execute contracts that have been concluded. However, the effect of market mechanisms is unstable and flexible, particularly with regard to the size of a market. Some empirical studies show that it is normally easier for people to achieve cooperation and compromise in small trading communities or between the parties who want a long-term cooperation. In those situations, reputation plays a significant role since the players are more familiar with each other or they want to preserve their business relationships. Moreover, when there is a breach of contract, the parties might easily enter into settlements through various ways, for example, the victim might ignore the breach, or the violator would apologize or promise a price reduction in the future.[101] On the contrary, in a highly mobile place where anonymous transactions prevail, reputation plays a weaker role in deterring opportunistic behaviour and the frustrated player can only choose to tolerate his loss. Besides, a problem of information asymmetry often takes place in such a mobile and complex market, which offers the party who has better access to information a good opportunity to cheat. This is why we can observe that cheating occurs more frequently in tourist sites.[102] If the market itself cannot always regulate transactions perfectly, there is a danger that, opportunism might be aggregated and hence the social welfare might be decreased.

In this sense, beside the uncertainty rising from market conditions (or conditions beyond either party's control, such as weather, market price, war, etc.), potential

99 *See* Lyons & Mehta 1997, p. 240.

100 Shavell 2004, p. 297.

101 For instance, in a report by Beal and Dugdale on the handling of complaints about defects in products supplied within a business relation, it was showed that the solution is normally an offer of repair without charge or a promise to reduce the price in the future transaction by the sellers. *See* Beale & Dugdale 1984, p. 45, 59; there are also some other discussions on this point, *See* Bernstein 2001, p. 1734; Schwartz & Scott 2003, P 557.

102 *Id.*

opportunism is another factor that hampers the success of collaboration between the trading parties. As the market cannot offer sufficient guarantees that every trading party is trustworthy and trusting,[103] an additional system is needed on which to establish more trust and good cooperation.

1.3.2. The Problem of Incomplete Contracts

As is proposed in the previous part, a contract is supposed to allocate the risks and benefits in the process of transactions, so that the uncertainty in the future could be diminished to some extent. However, to what extent the uncertainty of transactions can be decreased depends on many factors. One important factor is the extent to which the risk arrangements are complete.

1.3.2.1. Hypothesis of a Complete Contract

In a situation where the parties could anticipate all the contingencies concerning contract execution with perfect certainty, then they would negotiate over those contingencies and try to correctly specify an explicit provision for every contingency. This is related to what is called a *complete contract* or a *fully specified contract*.[104] Based on the assumption of a complete contract, the trading parties have to consider every risk, all consequences, and possible opportunistic behaviour of the other party, etc ("contingent completeness"). Correspondingly, the contract should specify the exact actions that one party should perform when every risk happens, for example, it should include the time, place, manner and quality of performance ("obligational completeness").[105] Meanwhile, the obligations and benefits of each party should be perfectly balanced in the contract as well. A significant requirement is that the price set in the contract can properly reflect the expected value of the risks. To put it simply, the parties will agree that the one who bears more risks could charge an extra price as much as the expected value of these risks (*the expected value can be calculated by multiplying the value of damage and the probability that the damage will happen*).[106] If the two conditions of completeness and perfectness can be satisfied in a contract, then there is very little ground for error or breach.

[103] *See* Lyons & Mehta 1997, p. 241. When we say a trading party is trustworthy, it means that he would choose to refrain from opportunism. While a trusting person is the one who would believe that the other is trustworthy.

[104] Schäfer & Ott 2004, p. 278; Caswell 2005–2006, p. 154.

[105] *See* Ayres & Gertner 1992, p. 730. Ayres and Gertner make a distinction between "obligationally incomplete contract" and "contingently incomplete contract". As observed by the two authors, the term of "obligationally incomplete contract" refers to contracts in which the obligations are not fully specified and this concept is more used by legal scholars. But the concept of "contingently incomplete contract" (or "insufficiently state contingent contract") is used mostly by economics scholars, which refers to contracts that fail to fully realize the potential gains from trade in all states of the world.

[106] *See* Schäfer & Ott 2004, p. 279. For instance, within the market, it is easy to find that the more risks that fall on the supplier, the higher the price of the product or service will be; or the more risk that the consumer is willing to absorb, the lower the price he would pay.

1.3.2.2. Reality: Incomplete and Imperfect Contracts

A complete and perfect contract, nevertheless, only belongs to the hypothetical world. In the real world, contracts are incomplete. Scholars have given several reasons for the existence of incompleteness and imperfection of contracts.

Firstly, it is considered that the incompleteness of contracts is caused by people's limited foresight. If the performance is extended into the future, the number of potential events that would happen is infinite. Then it may be generally more difficult to predict future contingencies and design perfect clauses for those contracts which need to be completed over a longer time.[107] Secondly, the existence of transaction cost increases the difficulty of drafting complete contracts. The cost of negotiation (including the costs of searching for information, engaging in communications and drafting contract terms, etc.) decreases the possibility of predicting every contingency and specifying each of them in the contract.[108] In this sense, economically rational parties will ignore some contingencies either unintentionally or intentionally. In particular they may exclude some insignificant contingencies, such as low possibility events which happen rarely, or irrelevant events which cause negligible damages to the trading parties. Over these two types of contingencies, the effort and cost of negotiation is much higher than the expected loss (equal to the expected value of a risk)[109] from this type of exclusion. Or at the time of bargaining, the parties may expect to rely on other mechanisms[110] for reallocating the risks if the expected unimportant risks turn out to change the utility of the contract afterwards. So insignificant contingencies are excluded deliberately by the bargainers at the time when they are making the contract. Shavell uses the case of a wedding photography contract as an example. According to his analysis, it is not necessary for the contracting parties to specify a car accident that might happen on the photographer's way to the wedding, because the possibility of such a contingency is very low. In addition, if the wedding is to be held in London, then whether it rains or not in New York should not be included in the contract as well, since such an event is irrelevant to the performance of contract. The last point to be mentioned concerns the necessity of ex-post interpretation. Even if there is a complete contract which has included every contingency in a perfect manner, the terms and expressions used in the contract may still cause ambiguities. In such a case, it is necessary to interpret the contract ex-post in order to understand and clarify the contract terms.

A contract cannot be complete and perfect, as potential gaps, errors and vagueness exist in every transaction. Thus, besides opportunism, incompleteness becomes another

107 Posner 2007, p. 95.

108 Hart & Moore 1988, p. 755–785.

109 The expected loss of exclusion of a certain contingency can be calculated by multiplying the damage caused by the contingency and the likelihood that the damage will occur. For example, suppose the cost of negotiating over a certain risk is *C*, the possibility of it is *P* and the damage caused by the risk is *D*. Then the party will specify this risk in their contract if $C<P*D$ but exclude it if $C>P*D$. *See* Shavell 2004, p. 299–301.

110 For instance, the parties may enter re-negotiations or resort to a third party's mediation. *See id,* p. 301; *see also* Hart & Moore 1988, p. 756.

factor that will increase the uncertainty problem in transactions. The parties are faced with a new question about what they should do if some un-anticipated or unspecified events[111] really happen. Of course, one solution the parties can choose is merely to fill in the contract gaps by themselves through renegotiation.[112] Take the previous photography contract as an example. The parties can just agree that the photographer be exempted from performance after a car accident really happens. In addition, in the real world, price alternation is another typical solution fostered in commercial traditions. It occurs quite often when there is a huge price fluctuation in a market.[113] However, as has been indicated, negotiation is costly because it involves time, money, information and effort. Therefore, the conflicting parties may not be able to solve the problem by re-negotiation every time. In an occasion when renegotiation is not available, the parties have to resort to other approaches to fill in the contract gaps.

2. Economic Function of Contract Law

Owing to the existence of opportunism and the unexpected risks arising after the conclusion of a contract, the contract will not always be as efficient as what had been expected at the time of contract formation and the uncertainty problem arising in transactions is hence still there. In addition, in the absence of a perfect market mechanism or a complete contract or a successful re-negotiation over those uncertainties, the parties cannot always have sufficient incentives to fully enforce the contract according to their original intentions. Starting from this consideration, another implication concerning contracts is given as: the introduction of contract law is aimed at optimizing the contracting parties' incentives to take efficient actions, or in other words, facilitating their abilities to maximize welfare from transactions.[114] This is assumed as the primary goal of contract law in this thesis. Basic on this, the next question is: "How can the contract law motivate the parties to take efficient actions?" To be brief: "what can the law offer to a contract (the economic function of contract law)?" Before answering this question, this section will first analyse the following cases.

111 Unspecified events refer to previously discussed low possibility events which can be predicted but are ignored by the parties on purpose.

112 Posner specifies four approaches to minimize the error costs arising from imperfect foresight: 1) the parties can shorten the duration of their contract, since the near future is more predictable than the distant future; or 2) they can just agree on a few things and leave the rest for re-negotiation; 3) or they may take the substitution of vertical integration for contracting (it means the market agent can choose to produce the goods by himself rather than buy the input); 4) or they leave the contract open so that a third party can fill in any gap when the gap emerges and precipitates a dispute. See Posner 2007, p. 96–97.

113 Suppose there is a deal that a buyer B wants to obtain a kind of machine from a seller *A* with 10,000 euro. After 3 months when A finds the cost of producing this kind of machine has been increased. Then, A can just re-negotiate with B and make an agreement on raising the price. Or if the market price of the same machine decreases, B can propose a price reduction.

114 Schwartz & Scott 2003, p. 544.

- **Case 2.1:** *Y1 promised to sell a farm to X1 for 10,000 euros. After X1 transferred the money, he got the farm but found there was no public water supply. Y1 knew that X1 was about to grow wheat on the farm. So X1 wants to get his money back.*[115]

- **Case 2.2:** *Y2 promised to supply X2 with 20 tons of potatoes in 1 month, but the potato crop failed totally because of an unforeseeable increase in temperature. This type of potatoes can only produced by Y2 with a special technique. Now X2 wants Y2 to perform the contract.*[116]

- **Case 2.3:** *Y3 promised to supply X3 with 20 tons of potatoes in 1 month. When the time comes, Y3 refuses to offer anything unless X3 raises the price. At that moment, X3 has prepared all the other equipment for storing the potatoes and he cannot find any substitute.*

- **Case 2.4:** *Y4 and X4, two important electricity providers in their local city, contracted to create a cartel and to increase the price of the product that they provide in the local city. Now Y4 does not want to keep the agreement anymore and X4 sues.*

2.1. How Does a Court apply Contract Law in a Contract Case?

Suppose there is a contract case, if one of the parties goes to court, then the state authorized law will be involved.[117] Let's generalize how contract law is employed by the court in this process. In case 2.1, Y1 failed to disclose the information that there is no connection between the farm and the public water supply. But this information is crucial for X1 to decide whether or not to take over the farm. According to the rules concerning the formation of contracts, the court may support X1's claim.[118] In case 2.2, the abrupt warm weather is beyond the foresight of both X2 and Y2. The contract has a gap concerning this contingency. Under these circumstances, the court may fill in the gap with the relevant rules (concerning impossibility or impracticability)[119] and allow Y2 to

115 The original version of this case is from Schäfer & Ott 2004, p. 276.

116 This case is modified from one in Posner 2007, p. 100–101.

117 Except the courts, other entities or organizations can also make a firm decision under the instruction of contract law, such as an arbitration organization, a trade association or a religious group. All of those institutes or organizations solve the contract conflicts and enforce contract law as an impartial third party. See Shavell 2004, p. 293.

118 The case concerns the issue of information disclosure. To some extent, all the contract systems impose an obligation of disclosing relevant information (especially defects in the goods) to at least professional sellers. If this obligation is violated, the seller will be liable to pay damages. *See* Beale, Fauvarque-Cosson, Rutgers, Tallon & Vogenauer 2010, p. 511–512.

119 Impossibility refers to the situation when a party's performance has become physically impossible, while impracticability may be applied in circumstances in which a party's performance is physically possible but will cause severe hardship, such as extremely high cost. Those two concepts are closely relevant to the doctrine of contract frustration and they will be analyzed in Chapters 6, 7, 8, and 9. Nowadays, a lot of countries have established the rule that a party could be excused from performance if his performance has become impossible or impracticable. *See* id, p. 1093–1094, 1127–1129; Smythe 2009, p. 3.

relinquish the duty of providing 20 tons of potatoes. The situation in case 2.3 is different since Y3 does not have any justifiable reason for his non-performance and for demanding the price increase. Thus remedy rules (specific performance or damages) in contract law will be employed. Case 2.4 involves a contract that has violated public policy (to foster competition) and the court will normally refuse to enforce this type of contract because it endangers market policy or social security policy.[120] Moreover, rules from other areas might also be applied to contracts concerning public policy, for instance, crimes, torts, property or regulations.

In summary, the contract law approach is an ex-post way which is activated by litigation. Under this mechanism, a court, which is mainly understood as a state-authorized court,[121] makes a significant connection between contract law and private transactions. Based on contract law, courts may undertake several tasks. They will judge whether or not the contract has been formed validly (case 2.1 and 2.4); or they ought to fill in the contract gaps with correct contract rules (case 2.2); or they have to clarify some specific terms in the contract when ambiguity has occurred; or they should decide whether or not there is a breach and impose sanctions on the offender (that is to say, entail remedies to the injured (case 2.3).[122] To carry out those assignments, the court needs to find the most relevant legal rules which are embodied in legislation, precedents or customs and then take those legal rules as the grounds for its judicial decision.[123] For instance, in case 2.1, since there is a fact that the seller Y1 failed to disclose the information that could have affected the transaction, the court will probably associate the case with the rules concerning the disclosure of information and the formation of contracts. In the end, the court is authorized to make a formal judicial decision, which defines the rights, obligations and liabilities of both parties. In this sense, the contract law, supported by the state power, plays an important role on the interests of the private parties who have decided to submit their case to a court. The next part will show how the law is related to contracting parties' behaviours.

2.2. *Contract Law and Rational Behaviour*

2.2.1. Standard Behaviour Models

According to the economists, each business man is assumed to be rational. In order to maximize economic welfare, contracting parties will attempt to consider every potential factor that might influence their benefits. Starting from this assumption, contract law is supposed to affect businessmen's behaviour both ex-ante and ex-post.

The first way is to influence people's decision-making before a certain event happens. Generally, contract law rules underlie a causal relationship between various behaviour

120 For example, hiring a person to murder another person is a kind of transaction, which violates social security policy. Courts will also refuse to enforce this kind of contracts.

121 Shavell 2004, p. 293, p. 294.

122 Id.

123 Pound 1923, p. 810.

models and different legal consequences.[124] Due to this kind of relationship, every business man can predict the legal consequence of his own behaviour. Thus, it is assumed that each contract party would act properly or refrain from a particular act under the consideration of the legal rules. For instance, Article 1643 of the French *Code Civil* states: "*He (the seller) is liable for latent defects, even though he did not know of them, unless he has stipulated that he would not be bound to any warranty in that case.*" The logic inside this article is abstracted as: the seller can avoid any liability if there is no latent defect or he has stipulated that he would not be bound to any warranty in that case.

The second way of influencing people's behaviour is to offer substitutes when the contractual parties are unwilling or unable to enter into an agreement over some specific issues. In this sense, the process of negotiation and contract formation is also affected. Since the parties should know that the law would determine what they fail to agree on, they can decide whether or not to negotiate a particular issue.[125] They may not make any effort to specify a certain problem if they prefer the way in which contract law deals with it.

In a summary, contract law may influence trading people's behaviour by indicating the legal consequence of different kinds of behaviour. Contract parties can choose to behave opportunistically and bear the liability incurred by law or to refrain from opportunism and lose the profit from it. Or they can choose whether or not to allocate a specific risk expressly. If they decide not to do so, the only result is that they will have to accept what has already been defined in law. Conversely, they will have to bear the cost of negotiating over that specific risk if they refuse the rules offered by contract law.

2.2.2. Illustration of the Cases

Let us take the cases 2.2 and 2.3 which concern an issue of non-performance as the example. As a major premise, contract law will give answers to two major questions, namely, whether to treat a failure to carry out an undertaking as a breach and what extent liability is to be imposed on the breaching party. Then, a simple picture of how the law can change the trading parties' behaviour will be indicated as follows:

- **Case 2.3**: *This is an instance of specific investment where the seller has an advantageous position and the buyer is vulnerable to the behaviour of his contracting partner. Since the buyer cannot find a substitute outside this particular contractual relationship, he*

124 Within the structure of most legal rules, a physical transaction is simplified into an abstract model, including abstract entities (promisor and promisee), standard behaviours and legal consequences (normally indicated as liabilities, or in other words, remedies for the injured). This is what we call abstractionism of the legal rule. Abstractionism is described as making the process of judicial reasoning atomistic because it helps the judge confine the problem to the two parties of the contract. This opinion gained support in traditional contract law studies, while it is challenged in modern practices and theories, where some qualities of the people are also involved in general terms, such as consumers or employees. This tendency towards differentiation is mostly aimed at protecting the weak party of the contractual relationship. However, differentiation still might linger to a certain extent; otherwise the stability and universality of legal solutions would be diminished with more arbitrariness. *See* Wilhelmsson 1993, P. 22.

125 Kornhauser 1986, p. 690.

has little choice but to count on the seller's performance.[126] *In case 2.3, Y3 refuses to perform unless X3 agrees to pay more for the potatoes, but nothing has happened to support Y3's request of extra charge. Y3 will be treated as an opportunist. As for X3, he probably just accepts the request of Y3 out of concern that the contract would break down totally and he would lose what he has already invested in the deal. At the same time, there is no ex-ante or ex-post negotiation over Y3's non-performance; hence, this contract can also be considered as incomplete. But contract law is hypothesized to change this situation through a careful design. When the parties have not stipulated specific measures to deal with non-performance of a contract, remedies provided by contract law naturally become a substitute for the missing contract terms. Based on remedy rules, the court may take a negative attitude toward opportunism by treating Y3's behaviour as breach and depriving him of all the gains from the breach. Then Y3 should understand the consequences of his decision under a comparison between the extent of liability and the profit from opportunism. He will refrain from opportunism if the profit from it is comparatively small and decide to comply with the contract consciously.*

- **Case 2.2**: *If we change some facts of this case by providing the seller with a plausible excuse for his non-performance, the situation will be different. As is shown in case 2.2, unforeseeable warm weather destroyed Y2's crop totally and Y2 is the only one who can produce the exact type of potatoes that X2 is looking for. Therefore, it is impossible for Y2 to complete his obligation as agreed. Suppose the high temperature is unseasonal, it is normal for X2 and Y2 to omit any extra precautions against this warm weather or any statement about whether or not Y2 is to perform if the potato crop is destroyed totally. Compared to case 2.3, case 2.2 indicates more about the problem of ex-post allocation of unforeseeable risk. Then the parties are faced with two options. They can either solve the problem by re-negotiation or just keep silent and accept what has been arranged in contract law. Before making decisions, the parties can make a comparison between these two ways. If the cost of re-negotiation is affordable, the parties are more likely to reject the application of state-designed rules by replacing their original contract with a more efficient one.*

2.3. Economic functions of contract law

At the outset, we noted that people contract to solve the uncertainty problem in those exchanges which are extended into the future, so as to maximize the surplus from the exchanges. Within the frame of the market mechanism, transacting parties will decide the content of the contract and the whole process of transaction (contract formation,

126 At the same time, "the party who makes specific investments as part of a contract has very little room to behave opportunistically because the consequences are costly." If the contractual relationship collapses, the specific investment becomes worthless. Schäfer and Ott used an example of marriage to indicate this doctrine. Investment in marriage for women is specific. "A woman often loses her human capital completely with child rearing and any special knowledge she obtains from being a mother is very difficult to capitalize on outside the marriage." Schäfer and Ott 2004, p. 370.

contract enforcement and resolution of contract disputes).[127] In this sense, contract law is basically assumed to work only as a supplement for the market. Furthermore, another assumption about legal interference with contracts is: it is possible to motivate people to act efficiently through the design of contract law To make this statement less abstract, four major economic functions of contract law are summarized as follows:

2.3.1. To Deter Inefficient Opportunism[128] and Increase Guarantee to Trust

Contract law contains a bundle of legally enforceable rules and instructions which indicate the legal consequences of different behaviour models. A significant issue is that the sanctions imposed on opportunism by law may render this type of behaviour unprofitable. On this basis, opportunism can be deterred and reduced both at the stage of contract formation and contract enforcement. For example in the previous case 2.1, Y1 noticed at the pre-contractual stage that a failure to disclose the irrigation information accurately and properly will cause an additional cost imposed by law. This cost comes from the legal consequences that their contract might be avoided later or Y1's liability for compensation might be enforced. Suppose that for Y1 the cost of non-disclosure exceeds the profit from it, non-disclosure is inefficient. Then, it is possible to assume that the parties would properly cooperate and refrain from misstatement or fraud because they want to save the legal costs incurred by the failure to disclose. Besides, at the stage after a contract has been signed, contract law can reduce opportunistic behaviour as well. For instance, the law may impose a standard of good-faith performance on the parties. According to this standard, people are motivated to refrain from taking advantage of the vulnerabilities created by the contractual relationship when performing the contract.[129] In the same way, each party is able to expect that his partner would take the same standard of behaviour as well. Therefore, a sense of security and trust can be enhanced to some extent even among anonymous transactions.[130]

127 It is also called "the Freedom of contract", which is one of the most important doctrines in legal study. Markesinis, Unberath & Johnston 2006, p. 45.

128 By offering legally enforceable rules, opportunism can be reduced both at the pre-contractual stage and at the stage when the contract is performed. Some literature uses other expressions to describe this economic function of contract law. For example, Shavell explained the reasons for why enforcement is desired for contracts. He states that an enforceable contract can reduce the number of appropriating funds that had been paid before contract performance. Besides, enforceability can reduce the inefficient non-performance. Other indications about contract law's function in reducing opportunism can be found in relevant literature. See Shavell 2004, p. 297–298; Posner 2007, p. 94–95; Schäfer & Ott 2004, p. 277.

129 Id.

130 But opportunism can not be eliminated absolutely by contract law. The extent to which opportunism is reduced depends on many factors, such as the level of how perfect a judicial system is. If the judicial system is well organized, the court can have more access to precise and reliable information about the relationship of the parties and the sanction imposed by the court has a more powerful impact on transactions. In this case, inefficient opportunism can be reduced to a higher level. See Schäfer & Ott 2004, p. 278.

2.3.2. To Fill the Gaps in Contracts

As is stated in the previous part, when a contingency not specified in the contract occurs and it precipitates a dispute, the parties can either renegotiate or resort to a particular authority (a court or an arbitrator) to resolve the matter. In the later case, the contract gap will be filled with some standard rules, which are called *default rules*. Gap-filling by a good law has an obvious advantage over renegotiation, in that it may help the parties to save transaction costs. Within the standard gap-filling rules, different solutions are given in response to some typical contingencies that may influence the value of the transaction. Therefore, bargainers do not need to negotiate over these typical contingencies in every trade unless they expressly reject to use those default rules in their agreement.[131] In this sense, the quality of gap-filling rules is significant because the bargainers only want those terms that maximize their welfare but the inefficient default rules will just be contracted out. Then the question is what kind of default rule is the one that bargainers consider as efficient?

It is assumed that an efficient default rule should be an imitation of the parties' mutual intentions,[132] rather than a rule that is based on the state's paternal concern for fairness and equality. Or in another way, the law maker ought to stand at the position of the trading parties. For example, the law maker may consider which party is better at managing a risk and then allocating the increased cost to that party. In the previous case 2.2, there is a presumed contract term that would have released Y2 from performing in the situation of impossibility, had the parties included this term. Courts will just adopt this presumed contract term and discharge Y2 from performance. Moreover, unification and legal certainty is set as another criterion for a good default rule. Since the rules will apply to every contracting pair within a certain commercial community, a good gap-filling rule should be most close to what the majority of trading agents would choose for themselves had they negotiated over that contingency.[133]

2.3.3. To Disambiguate Contract Terms

One significant role that a court is playing in a contract case is to ascertain what has been agreed on between the contractual parties.[134] This is called contract interpretation, which is also referred to as disambiguating contract terms and determining the legal effect created by those contract terms.[135] Just like the undertaking of filling contract

131 Most gap-filling rules are default rules, which can be contracted out of by the parties. Since the contractual parties are the best judges of their own benefits, the state cannot use its rules to replace the real intentions of contractual parties. Besides, in a large economy, there are heterogeneous agents and people don't like the same things. They should be allowed to modify or replace the state-supplied terms they dislike. An exception is the mandatory rules in contract law, which have sufficient justification. See Schwartz & Scott 2003, p. 595–597.

132 Id.

133 Kornhauser 1986, p. 692.

134 Schwartz & Scott 2003, p. 569.

135 Herbots 2012, p. 421.

gaps, disambiguating contract terms is also aimed at explaining the content of the contract before the contract is enforced by the court. In this way, both gap-filling and disambiguating have an "interpretative" sense.[136] Nevertheless, courts only interpret a specific term which has already been included in the contract when the words used in this term leave a doubt between the parties. So it is suggested that judges should merely focus on the written contract and treat it as if it was complete by adopting a textualist interpretative approach.[137] A judge must not impute his own values into the contract, but simply disambiguate the contract in clear and simple terms. While in an incomplete contract case, the contract lacks words to be interpreted, so that the court will plug a ready-made clause into the contract gap.[138]

2.3.4. To "Regulate Contracts" through Mandatory Rules

People contract to maximize the utility of their trade. So, contract law, in most occasions, is to facilitate people's capacity in transactions and it should respect people's freedom to make contracts.[139] But sometimes, the trade has some imperfections, related to harmful externalities,[140] asymmetric information or individual rationality. For example, contract parties might sign a contract in order to create a cartel (case 2.4) or to forbid one party to bring out lawsuits. In those situations, contract law will regulate contracts by setting up some mandatory rules to replace the explicit terms in the contract and bargainers cannot negate or remove mandatory terms by consensus.[141] For example, rules concerning individual competency may prevail in a contract of which the signing parties are juveniles. If a promise is made by a juvenile and this kind of promise is deemed as beyond his legal capacity, the court probably will not enforce the promise.

136 Some literature treats the courts' activity of interpreting contracts the same as their job of filling contract gaps. Shavell 2004, p. 301–304; Cooter & Ulen 2011, p. 291–299.

137 Schwartz & Scott 2003, p. 583.

138 Id, p. 594–595.

139 This is what we call "freedom of contract", which includes at least three implications: 1) freedom to conclude a contract 2) freedom to choose the contractual partner 3) freedom to determine the content of the contract that people signed. Some legal systems justify the freedom of contract as "unfolding of the personality" (see Article.2 of the German Constitution). Its constitutional idea is that a person in possession of legal capacity, not influenced by mistake or undue pressure, is fully capable of determining his fate as far as legal relationships of private law are concerned. Markesinis, Unberath & Johnston 2006, p. 45.

140 An externality refers to the spill-over effect of a contract. Since a contract is only binding between the parties who have agreed on it, a third party will not be able to obtain contract remedies when he has been affected by a contract. Therefore, a contract in some situations might create an externality problem. For example, sales of cocaine and other addictive drugs have a problem of endangering public health; purchasing a ton of inferior coal for manufacture will cause severe air pollution in the neighbourhood; and a cartel contract may create entry barriers and obstacles to competitors and a high price for consumers. In these situations, it is costly for a specific victim to negotiate with the drug dealer, the manufacturer or the parties to a cartel contract separately. In order to avoid costly negotiations over every externality problem, legislators may draft mandatory rules to regulate contracts. For a discussion about the information asymmetry and individual rationality, see section 3.2 in this chapter. Shavell 2004, p. 320–322.

141 Cooter & Ulen 2011, p. 292.

3. Economic Analysis of Contract Enforcement

From an economic perspective, contract law should facilitate business men's ability to maximize economic efficiency by providing external mechanisms. In addition, those external mechanisms are presented as a bundle of enforceable rules, most of which will become implied terms of each contract if there is no express negation.[142] In this way, contract law supplements (default rules) and regulates (mandatory rules) contracts in the legal perspective. But before any further discussion, it is necessary to answer a prerequisite question of whether or a contract should be enforced by the law. The question involves the doctrine of legally binding contracts.

3.1. A Binding Contract and the Justification for its Enforceability

By definition, a binding contract means that both of the contractual parties are "bound" to it and contract law offers remedies when the contract is not performed.[143] Or in other words, a binding contract is an enforceable contract.

The binding nature of the contract has been justified both in legal and economic doctrines. In traditional legal doctrine, enforceability derives from the value of freedom of contract. Thus, a contract based on the mutual consensus of the parties should be valid and enforceable.[144] While in the economic approach, the binding nature of a contract can be justified for at least two reasons:

First, the enforceability of a contract is desirable for motivating the attachment of mutually compatible plans (or contracts). In any exchange economy where many agents are closely inter-dependent, the benefit of one trader is vulnerable to the deviant behaviours of other traders without any assurance.[145] In order to modify the market's deviant behaviours and sustain some common rules of their activities, the parties wanted to have their contracts enforceable at the time when the contracts were made.[146] Thus the enforceability of contracts comes from this inner logic of the market and contract law is there just to approve this logic. In this way, mutual commitment is achieved between the contracting parties and the parties are able to make credible promises to each other.[147]

142 But as to the mandatory rules set up by contract law, they will naturally become the implied terms in every contract no matter whether the parties agree on them or not.

143 Beale, Fauvarque-Cosson, Rutgers, Tallon & Vogenauer, 2010, P. 64.

144 The question concerning the foundation of the enforceability has been controversial for many years. An early doctrine called "will theory" stressed that contract rules derived from the basic tenet of liberalism that an individual has the right to determine his future conduct by his own decision and his will must be respected by the court. A latter promise principle is held that "an indicial is morally bound to keep his promises because he has intentionally invoked a convention whose function is to give moral ground for another party to expect the promised performance". While for many common law scholars, there is a bargain theory that a contract is binding if it has a bargain, which is considered as the performance interest or the reliance interest. *See* Kötz, 1998, p. 7–9.

145 Landa 1976, p. 906.

146 Cooter & Ulen 2011, p. 283.

147 As what has been outlined previously, the market itself also offers a type of assurance and credit between the traders. So contracts, at their initial bases, should be enforced by the parties. But when the

Second, traders are induced to make rational decisions ex-ante in order to make their contracts legally binding. In this sense, a binding contract also promotes efficient contracting. Above all, a binding contract should be a valid contract.

3.2. *What is a Valid Contract?*

In legal doctrine, a contract is valid because both parties agreed with it. Although different legal systems impose some different requirements on making a contract, the fundamental substance in a valid contract is all the same, namely, a meeting of the minds.[148] Lawyers and economists think differently when they want to answer what is a valid contract and why a contract should be valid. Lawyers usually focus on whether or not the parties have reached an agreement and they consider a contract based on an agreement to be valid, while economists focus on the function of a contract and consider that a contract which can increase the utility of the parties is valid.[149] From an ex-ante perspective, enforceability is desirable in an efficient contract because the parties think the value of enforcing it will be higher than the cost. Since the parties themselves are normally the best judges of their own interest, it is plausible to believe that the contract based on their rational choices and free expressions is efficient. From this idea, two conditions for a valid contract can be inferred:

- **Rationality**: *The decision maker should be rational, which means he is able to define his own preferences and utility. On the contrary, a contract is irrationally made in the case where the preferences of one party are sufficiently unstable or disorderly or one party made a promise in a desperate position.*
- **Sufficient information**: *the decision to conclude a contract should be made based on sufficient information. A negative example is shown when a party has been deceived and made a contract based on wrong information.*

sanctions (normally present as reputation punishment) and incentives (such as price signals) offered by the market (reputation) have a weak effect and the parties decide to turn to the court, the contract will fall in the state-enforcing range. Schwartz & Scott 2003, p. 557–562.

148 On the one hand, different countries impose some minimum requirements as to the content of a declaration in order to qualify it as an offer that can ripen into a contract by acceptance. For instance, in English and German law, it is generally assumed that, in addition to the intention requirement, an offer must contain the essential elements of the contracts, in other words, it has sufficiency of agreement. Besides, some countries also ask whether or not there is a consideration or cause. For example, a valid contract in French law (Article 1108 of Code Civil) should contain four elements: 1) the consent of the party who binds himself; 2) his capacity to contract; 3) a definite object which forms the subject-matter of the undertaking; 4) a lawful cause in the obligation. Generally, common law countries require that consideration be a necessary element in a valid contract. For instance, in English law, a contract must have "a valuable consideration", which "in the sense of the law, may consist either of some right, interest, profit or benefit accruing to the one party, or some forbearance, detriment, loss or responsibility given, suffered or undertaken by the other". See Beale, Fauvarque-Cosson, Rutgers, Tallon & Vogenauer 2010, p. 169–170; p.189–190; p. 241–242; see also *Currie v. Misa* (1875) LR 10 Ex 153.

149 Schäfer & Ott 2004, p. 297.

When the conditions of rationality and sufficient information do not hold, a contract is deemed as irrational and enforcement of it is undesirable. Because this type of contract is supposed to lower the net social product by making one party worse off and by channelling resources into threats, fraud or misstatement.[150] In addition, the misled party would have not agreed with it had he been rational and obtained enough information at the time of signature. Accordingly, contract law fosters a series of legal doctrines to recognize a legally valid contract, such as the doctrines of legal capacity, necessity, duress or fraud.[151] Contracts that have been made by an insane person or extracted by fraud are contestable or invalid and courts may not accept or enforce them. In this way, contracts which are inefficient can be excluded ex ante. Table 2 shows different types of irrational contracts and the corresponding legal doctrines.

Table 2. Irrational Contract

Type	Legal doctrine
Irrational Trader	*Incompetency; Incapacity; Duress; Necessity.*
Bad Information	*Fraud; Failure to disclose; Mistake; Other abuse of circumstances.*

3.3. *Enforcement of a Contract*

After recognizing a valid contract, attention now returns to the previous issue concerning contract enforcement. A valid contract is enforceable and both parties are bound to it. Departing from the traditional legal notion that contracts are promises,[152] economists think that enforcement of contracts is more than simply requiring the parties to perform their promises.[153] But it involves the whole ongoing relationship between the parties. So all kinds of commitments that can prompt the parties to communicate and cooperate are related to the issue of enforcing a contract, such as one party's commitment to privacy protection. One of the most important issues is that parties are committed to be legally responsible for the non-performance of their promises.[154] It is indicated that the law defines legal consequence when non-performance of contract occurs. In particular the question of the applicable remedy will arise when a breach of contract is proved.

150 Posner 2007, p. 115.

151 A person whose preferences are sufficiently unstable and disorderly, he or she is legally incompetent and can not make enforceable contracts, such as children and insane people. Necessity refers to a situation when a promise is extracted from a desperate promisor, and in this case non-performance can be excused. Duress also refers to a situation where a promisor is in dire circumstances. But in a duress case, the cause of this desperation is usually the promisee. Fraud refers to a case where the beneficiary of the promise extracted it by lies. See Cooter &Ulen 2011, p. 295–297.

152 As Rechard Craswell observed, traditional conception requires that "promises must either (1) oblige the promisor to perform the promised actions or (2) have no moral force at all". Brooks 2006, p. 570.

153 There are a lot of discussions about the separation of contract and promise. Barnett 2011; Kraus 2009; Shiffrin 2007.

154 Barnett 2011, p. 10.

The typical contract remedy is manifested as monetary damages or specific performance. The former, monetary damages, is considered as the primary form of remedy in most common law countries. It is required that a breacher must pay a certain amount of damages to the aggrieved party. However, in civil law countries, imposition of specific performance is more common when a breach happens. In this situation, the aggrieved party can apply to the court to have the breacher perform the contract.[155]

4. An Introduction to Economic Analysis of contract remedies

After a contract is held valid, contract law will provide several mechanisms for keeping the binding effect of the contract. Within the mechanisms that are offered by contract law, a crucial one is that the law offers remedies when a contract suffers from disruption, which is mainly referred to as a breach of the contract. Then, the initial criterion that a good contract law should motivate efficient actions also works for the remedy rules. To see this, it is useful to start from the possible actions that the contracting parties will take after the signature of a contract. After a sales contract has been signed, the seller might start to prepare the goods, store the goods in a proper way, and take some necessary precautions against any deterioration of the product. Or he may wait for another higher bid and invest less in preparing the performance. While the buyer may decide to prepare the payment and be ready to accept the goods or do nothing after he signed the contract. In this part, some basic concepts and issues will be identified from a multitude of inter-related behaviours that may arise in the contract enforcement stage. Then we will establish our hypothesis on the economic relationship between remedy rules and contractual behaviours.

4.1. Basic hypothesis: Remedy as an Incentive

Since the parties have created a contract according to their own desires and preferences, the contract is assumed to be profit-enhancing ex-ante. Besides, the market also imposes a reputational sanction on behaviour that does not comply with the social norms and rules established in the market. Then the parties have reasons to enforce it by themselves. However, the previous observations on incomplete and imperfect contracts indicate that the actual value and cost in a transaction is uncertain and unstable. So parties will orient their decisions of performance, breach or reliance to the signals of value and cost in their trades. In this sense, the liability rules may also influence the contracting parties' behaviour, for example, by changing the cost of breach. In this sense, the remedy rules operate as a price mechanism. To make the hypothesis easier, let us categorize some typical behaviours that the promisor and promisee may show in a simple model.

- ***Case 2.5:*** *On January 1st, X5 and Y5 make a sales contract. X5 agrees to order a machine from Y5 and Y5 agrees to hand over the machine on June 1st. X5 estimates that he can gain 150 by using this machine to produce clothes, and Y5 will spend 50 on producing the machine. They agree on a price of 100.*

155 Schäfer & Ott 2004, p. 320.

4.1.1. Promisor's Behaviour

In our normal logic, when we talk about a promisor's post-contract behaviour, the concepts of breach, non-performance and liability (or remedy) are always correlated. However, a failure to perform can be caused by a number of reasons, either by some unexpected external events or by the intentional behaviour of the promisor. Non-performance of a contract is given a broader meaning and it may be either excusable or non-excusable. For example, Article 1:301(4) of the Principles of European Contract Law (hereinafter PECL)[156] defines non-performance as "any failure to perform an obligation under the contract, whether or not excused, and includes delayed performance, defective performance and failure to co-operate in order to give full effect to the contract".[157] In comparison, a breach is normally considered as a non-excused failure to perform the contract and contract liability will be imposed on the party who breaches the contract. However, if the promisor's non-performance is excused, no liability will be incurred. As is shown, when a promisor engages in different behaviour, it will cause different legal consequences. In this sense, it is assumed that the law can offer a party an incentive to avoid breach or choose to breach.[158]

If a breach is un-excusable, this implies that the law imposes liability on the breacher. That is, when a party to a contract breaches his promise, the victim may ask for a remedy. The contract remedy may be monetary damages or an order of specific performance.[159] But no matter in which form the remedy is made, it will reduce the breacher's benefit from breach or increase his cost of breach. In order to reduce the chance of breach, the promisor may take some ex-ante precautions against breach.[160] In case 2.5, a breach happens if Y5 fails to finish the production on time, or the machine has defects. To avert those situations, the seller Y5 may hire more workers to increase the probability of finishing the production on time, or he may buy new measuring equipment to ensure that the machine works precisely.

156 For more explanation of the PECL, see Chapter 6.

157 The concept of non-performance has also been used in statutes or other conventions. For example, in the Unidroit Principles for International Commercial Contracts, the words "breach of contract" has never been included. Rather, the Principles have chosen to talk of performance and non-performance. Non-performance may be excused, for example, by unexpected external events outside the control of the non-performing party (Article 7.1.6). Furmston 1992, p. 671, p. 672.

158 Distinguished from breach, the situation when it is impossible for the parties to fulfil a contract is called "impossibility". Normally, a failure to perform the contract in the circumstance of impossibility will be excused by the law. This will be discussed in a more detailed way. Schäfer & Ott 2004, p. 320.

159 Specific performance is mostly used in the civil law countries as the legal remedy for breach. Such as in German law, the aggrieved party can ask the court to have the breacher perform the contract. But in the common law countries, specific performance is used in the equity law. It will be issued by the courts only when there are some irreparable injuries which can not be compensated by damages. This will be discussed in the later chapters.

160 Cooter & Ulen 2011, p. 289, p. 290.

4.1.2. Promisee's Behaviour

Now consider the promisee's potential behaviours. After a promise has been made, the promisee may rely on it and take some action so as to increase his gain from the performance. In case 2.5, relying on the promise, Y5 will transfer the clothes machine in September, X5 may start to arrange the transportation or accept more clothing orders or rent a big retail store before he receives any performance. Because of the investment in this type of behaviour, the promisee's position is different from what it was before the promise was made. The concept of reliance is used to denote a change in the promisee's position which is induced by the promise.[161] Reliance is distinguished from pre-payment, which is also taken by the promisee. Pre-payment, in several cases, is required by the contract and it enriches the promisor before the contract is fully performed. But reliance may not necessarily transfer the value from the promisee to the promisor.

Reliance plays an important role in measuring the benefit enhanced in performance and the loss from a breach.[162] In the case when a contract has been fully performed, reliance would increase the promisee's gain from the transaction. Suppose Y5 has handed over the machine and it works well. Then for X5, accepting more orders and renting a big retail store will increase his profit since the sale of clothes is expanded accordingly. Conversely, reliance may also increase the promisee's loss from breach. When there is a breach, what the promisee has invested in reliance may become useless if he cannot receive any performance. In this sense, the actual value from the reliance investment is uncertain when it is made and the promisee may not invest before he gets any guarantee for his profit. The remedy rules can provide this kind of guarantee.

4.1.3. How Do Remedy Rules Shape the Parties' Incentives

Businessmen will seek a contract that maximizes their own profits. After contracting their expected payoffs (expected value-expected cost) from the contract has been fixed, but the actual values and costs in the transaction are still uncertain. Accordingly, the remedy rules can motivate the parties to perform or to invest in reliance by changing the cost of breach.[163] This incentive mechanism derives from the logic that the parties are bound to the contract so that in the event of a breach the victim can obtain legal remedies. Thus, the cost of breach increases.

4.1.3.1. Assumption

Certain assumptions can be made to see how the remedy rules can change the behaviours of a promisor and a promisee. To go further into this topic, we can start from the

[161] Fuller & Perdue 1936, p. 54.
[162] Cooter & Ulen 2011, p. 289, p. 290.
[163] A similar case is the imposition of criminal liabilities. For instance, a fine imposed on a crime has increased the cost of it, thus deterring this type of crime. See Ogus 2006, p. 11.

relationship between contract damages and a promisor's incentives to perform the contract or a promisee's incentives to invest in reliance.

- **No remedy**: Supposing that the law denies the promisee any remedies, in the case of 2.5, either X5 or Y5 is assumed to earn a payoff of 50 (expected profit). Since there is no remedy attached to Y5's breach, Y5 is unlikely to perform the contract if doing so will cost more than 50. By the same token, X5 may not expend any resources on reliance, since he was about to receive nothing in the event of non-performance. Therefore, if remedies are not available, breaches will become cost-free from an economic perspective. As a result, contract law cannot offer contract parties any incentive to perform the contract or to invest in reliance.[164]
- **Monetary damages**: The situation, however, will be different as the extent of the remedy is enhanced. Assume that the law requires a breacher to pay 200 to the aggrieved party and the cost of producing the machine is 10. Hence, the cost of breach is increased to 200. Y5 has a stronger motivation to perform because his gain from performance (50–10) is much higher than his gain from breach (-200). At the same time, Y5 probably will take a higher level of precaution so that he can decrease the chance of breach. In addition, X5 is guaranteed that he will receive either the machine or remedy from Y5. In order to gain more from the use of the machine, Y5 is more likely to increase his reliance by accepting more orders or renting a bigger retail store.

Thus, it is concluded that the higher the cost of the remedy, the more expensive the breach is and the stronger incentive the parties have to perform.[165] This is the third implication about contract law and contract remedy. In some extreme cases where a breacher would have to compensate the aggrieved party with treble damages or he would be put in prison, then the parties are assumed to always have strong incentives to obey the contract. In those extreme cases, the law cuts off any opportunity to breach.

4.1.3.2. The Complicated Reality

A lot of factors, however, will complicate this analysis. As pointed out in section 1, contracts are incomplete in nature. Many unexpected contingencies might happen after the conclusion of a contract and change the cost or the value of the performance. For example, in case 2.2, unseasonal warm weather destroyed the potato crop so that it is impossible for Y2 to perform the contract or performing the contract is uneconomic (Y2 might invest a lot in finding enough alternative ice). So it is not always good for contract law to provide the parties with strong motivations to perform. Therefore, a new question arises as: what degree of remedy is optimal for motivating efficient behaviour? This will

164 In this case, the parties may still obey the contract, which is motivated by the market. As we have noted previously, the parties have to follow some rules fostered by the market. In order to sustain the reputation in the mutual commercial society, a party to a contract will try to comply with the contract even if it is unprofitable for him to do so.

165 Shavell 2004, p. 305.

be analysed at the end of this thesis. What is more, people's behaviour in the real world will be influenced by a multitude of factors. Other complications, such as the effectiveness of a litigation system, people's accessibility to legal remedies will also affect this incentive question.[166] In a community where the litigation system works weakly, the mechanism of remedy incentive may not function as anticipated. A lot of contract cases would not enter the courts, but rather they will be resolved through private solutions created by the parties. For example, studies show that the traditional dispute solution based on judicial procedures plays a very limited role in solving disputes arising from on-line sales. According to Henry Jr, the Internet is geographically open to every person and most participants involved in the electronic market are small entities and individuals physically located in different places. This also means that the costs of litigation for those participants are often much higher than the benefits from it and hence the participants are more willing to resort to alternative dispute resolutions.[167] As a result, contract law remedies are less likely to provide sufficient incentives to the participants involved in an electronic market.

4.2. Basic Hypothesis: Remedy Rules as Default Rules

Recall that in the models of incomplete and imperfect contracts, those contracts which are not Pareto-superior at the time of formation can be supplemented and corrected later by the parties. By the same token, remedy rules can be recognized as gap-filling rules offered by the law since most contracts do not specify the remedies for a breach.[168] In this sense, a legally valid contract also contains an implied term that: if the parties decide to make a contract, there is a reasonably certain basis for giving a remedy in the case of breach.[169] Then when a breach of contract happens and the parties cannot achieve re-negotiation over it, contract remedy rules will apply.

The idea of treating remedy rules as contract gap-filling rules has been accepted by most commentators and it is recognized that parties may alter those remedy rules through ex-ante or ex-post negotiation.[170] In this sense, legal rights to remedies are marketable and contracting parties are allowed to design their own remedy rules which are different from the default remedy rules. However, controversies still arise over the question of to what extent this deviation is acceptable.[171] The fewer the restrictions which are imposed on contractually specified remedies, the more deviation from the default

166 Until now, the economic analysis has also done some empirical studies about those factors which make their results more precise, but the effects are still limited. Posner 2003, p. 831; Kornhauser 1986, p. 694.

167 Henry Jr, 1999–2000, p. 675.

168 Ayres & Gertner 1992, p. 731.

169 This idea has been incorporated into the Uniform Commercial Code (U.C.C.) of the USA. Clause 2–204(3) states that:" Even though one or more terms are left open a contract for sale does not fail because it is vague if the parties have intended to make a contract and there is a reasonably certain basis for giving an appropriate remedy."

170 Barmes 1998, P.403.

171 In some legal practices and theoretical discussions, it is recognized that significant departure from the default remedy rules are unenforceable. Id.

remedy rules can be reached. If the law doesn't restrict the parties' creation of remedy rules at all, then the parties can decide whatever they consider as desirable. In this case, parties may even choose penalty clauses so as to increase their incentives to obey the contract.

Another question involved in the assumption of default rules concerns the criterion for determining good default rules. As noted previously, those rules that are closest to the contracting parties' intentions are considered as efficient and desirable to the parties. The reason is that the probability for the parties to contract out of this type of default rules is relatively low. Thus, an important label attached to a good default remedy rule is the parties' reaction to breach. Or one might ask, what would the parties have agreed, had they specified the breach in their contract? Moreover, in the beginning of this chapter, also it was stated that people want to maximize welfare through contracting. At the pre-contract stage, people enter a contract because they think the profit from it is higher than the cost of it, otherwise, they would not sign the contract.[172] Identically, after the conclusion of a contract, the parties want efficient behaviour, which can help them take best advantage of the contract and maximize their profits. In general, we will assume that the parties may agree on a remedy rule, which is able to increase the cost of breaches and hence to promote efficient actions.

5. Conclusion

Each potential party to a trade hopes that the transaction will improve his welfare. But when the condition of simultaneous exchange does not hold, this expectation might be frustrated by various risks and uncertainty arising after the contract is made (uncertainty about various contingencies and uncertainty about the behaviour of the other party). In order to maximize economic efficiency, trading parties have incentives to arrange those contingencies that they consider significant, and stipulate an optimal contract. This is an important reason why people make contracts.

If a contract has been perfectly drafted and the parties make every effort to carry out their agreement consciously, a voluntary transaction will be advantageous for both of them. Then the contract can work well by itself and there is no need to create an external mechanism (or contract law) to enforce the contract. But a complete contract is just a hypothesis. There is still much space for error and uncertainty if people cannot design a complete and perfect contract. Therefore, the uncertainty problem cannot be managed at the stage of contract formation. Moreover, potential opportunism causes a distrust question and aggravates the problem of uncertainty. In absence of a perfect market mechanism, there is a demand for introducing contract laws in order to help contract parties to maximize their welfare in transactions. In this thesis, it is assumed that contract law plays four significant types of roles, including deterring opportunism, filling the contract gaps, clarifying contract terms as well as regulating contracts.

A precondition for the contract law to further exercise its role in contracts is to recognize the enforceability of contracts, which are created through voluntary

172 The pre-condition for this hypothesis is that both of the parties are business-men.

agreements. A valid contract is enforceable. This means that the contract parties on the one hand are required to perform the contract as required (such as deliver the goods as agreed) and on the other hand the party who fails to do so has to bear the consequences defined by the law. In this sense, contract remedies provide an important legal mechanism for shaping people's motivations, particularly when the parties have no contrary stipulations. It is assumed that remedy rules can put a price on breach and thus offer contract parties' a certain range of incentives to breach, perform or invest in reliance. The greater the extent of the remedy, the more expensive the breach is and the stronger incentive the parties have to perform. On this basis, the remedy rules that are set at a perfect level will optimally motivate people to breach or perform the contract to a desirable extent. Another question arises concerning the definition of a desirable extent of performance and breach, which will be discussed in Chapter 3.

Chapter 3

EFFICIENT BREACH IN LAW AND ECONOMICS THEORY

It has been noted that the commercial transaction involves a core undertaking of utility maximization. A contract that is extended into the future is faced with a major problem of uncertainty, which may be exacerbated by being incomplete and potentially opportunist. As a result, people may not always have an incentive to adhere to what they agreed. On this basis, the introduction of contract law is assumed to offer people good rules and to facilitate their capacities of welfare maximization. On the one hand, the law may ideally fill in the gaps in a contract; on the other hand, the law may offer people incentives to behave efficiently. One of the most important mechanisms provided by contract law is the remedy rules. Accordingly, it is assumed that people can make their decisions of breach or performance taking into consideration their loss incurred by the legal remedy. In this Chapter, we will focus on a promisor's decision of breach and recognize a situation where breach is desirable and preferable. Section 1 will first give an overview of the doctrine of efficient breach in existing literature. An ideal model of efficient breach will be given and the formula for it will be explained in section 2. Afterwards, section 3 will summarize two types of contingencies that probably alter the utility of a contract and hence make it efficient for the parties to breach the contract. The concluding remarks will be provided in section 4.

1. What is the Efficient Breach Theory?

1.1. Why Do People Breach?

As has been observed, people make contracts because they think that by so doing they can increase their utility. At the time when two parties sign a contract, each one expects a profit. But why do the parties later breach a contract which they previously considered as profitable? There are at least three economic reasons for the breach:

Uncertain risks: It is stated that transaction is costly so that it is impossible for the parties to specify all the contingencies and draft a complete contract. In this sense, provided that a simultaneity condition doesn't hold, the actual value and cost in a contract is uncertain at the time when it is made. A contract which was expected to be efficiency-enhancing may turn out to be disadvantageous to one or both of the parties later.[173] Therefore, the unpredictable risks increase one or both of the parties' incentives to breach. In the previous case 2.5, it is easy to understand that Y5 may not produce the machine as agreed if the cost of doing so becomes much higher than his expected gain (50) from the contract.

Opportunistic behaviour: It was noted that opportunism may also arise after the contract is signed and it is often presented in "a form of shirking or evasion of obligations".[174] In these circumstances, "the promisor breaches for no other reason except to make money".[175] Posner gives an example for this: "A pays B in advance for goods and instead of delivering them B uses the money to build a swimming pool for himself."[176]

Alternative to pay damages: The third economic explanation for breach derives from the availability of the damages mechanism. It is presumed that the damages mechanism prices the breach and allows people to perform or to pay damages. Owing to the existence of damage rules, the immorality of breach will be decreased[177] and people are more likely to breach by paying for it. Clearly, we can trace this cognition back to the famous remark of Justice Oliver Wendell Holmes that, "The duty to keep a contract at common law means a prediction that you must pay damages if you do not keep it and nothing else– ".[178]

1.2. *Definition of Efficient Breach*

1.2.1. The Concept of Efficient Breach

Economists observe that there are some occasions when a party to a contract should not be forced to perform[179], because his non-performance will increase the welfare of the society. This situation indicates what is called efficient breach, namely, it is efficient for a contract party to breach rather than to perform.

The first statement of efficient breach, which is included in Birmingham 1970, is presented as: "*Repudiation of obligations should be encouraged where the promisor is able to profit from his default after placing his promisee in as good a position as he would have occupied had performance been rendered.*"[180] At around the same time as when this statement was made, another paper by Scott and Goetz first used the concept of efficient

173 Schäfer & Ott 2004, p. 297, p. 298; Posner 2003, p. 831.
174 Wathne & Heide 2000, p. 38.
175 Roberts 2008, p. 139.
176 Posner 2007, p. 119.
177 "It is not the policy of the law to compel adherence to contracts but only to require each party to choose between performing in accordance with the contract and compensating the other party for any injury resulting from a failure to perform". Posner 2007, p.119.
178 Holmes 1897, p. 457, p. 462.
179 Barnes 1998, p. 399.
180 Birmingham 1970, p. 284.

breach.[181] So far, there are a number of authors giving definitions of this concept and Judge Posner's definition of efficient breach in his book "Economic Analysis of Law" is probably the best-known one. According to him, "*In some cases a party [to a contract] would be tempted to breach the contract simply because his profit from breach would exceed his expected profit from completion of the contract. If his profit from breach would also exceed the expected profit to the other party from completion of the contract, and if damages are limited to loss of expected profit, there will be an incentive to commit a breach.*"[182]

The doctrine of efficient breach has been largely cited as the basis for the common law remedy of expectation damages.[183] It is required that the breacher ought to pay damages in an amount that would make the victim of breach as well off as he would have been had the breach not occurred.[184] A party to a contract, therefore, is induced to breach as long as he compensates the expectation of the other party. By this way, if a contract turns out to be disadvantageous and wasteful after it is signed, the parties will abandon it without costly renegotiation; similarly, if a contract stays valuable after its formation, the parties will complete it as agreed.[185]

In addition to supporting expectation damages, scholars also raise critiques over punitive damages for the reason that punitive damages will deter efficient breaches. It is considered that punitive damages, which are sometimes created through a damage agreement between the parties, have a danger of causing over-compensation.[186] That is, the breacher is compelled to pay damages to an amount which is higher than the actual loss of the victim. As a result, the parties are forced to perform the contract for fear of the penalty, even if it would be more economically efficient to breach. Similarly, any other kind of remedy exceeding the degree of compensatory damages, such as specific performance or disgorgement, might also lead to an effect that promisors are forced to comply with contracts and hence efficient breaches are deterred.

181 Scott and Goetz 1977, p. 555.

182 Posner 2007, p. 120.

183 For instance, the Restatement (Second) of Contracts in the USA states: "The traditional goal of the law of contract remedies has not been compulsion of the promisor to perform his promise but compensation of the promisee for the loss resulting from breach. 'Wilful' breaches have not been distinguished from other breaches, punitive damages have not been awarded for breach of contract, and specific performance has not been granted where compensation in damages is an adequate substitute for the injured party. In general, therefore, a party may find it advantageous to refuse to perform a contract if he will still have a net gain after he has fully compensated the injured party for the resulting loss." See Linzer 1981, p. 111.

184 Adler, 2008, p. 1680–1681.

185 Id.

186 Moreno, 2010, p. 5.

1.2.2. Traditional Theories of Efficient Breach

Although we can find various definitions of efficient breach[187]exist, the basic content in this famous concept involves two questions: (1) when it is more efficient for a party to breach than to perform (economic basis)? (2) Which kind of contract rules will give promisors incentives to breach efficiently (optimal rules)? This section intends to provide answers to the first question. To analyse the concept of efficient breach, we will make at least three inferences from it as follows:

1.2.2.1. Kaldor-Hicks Efficiency

The efficient breach is justified for enhancing economic efficiency by creating a surplus. From the stand point of the breaching party, if his profits from the breach exceed his expected profit of performance, breach is efficient for him because he is "better off" than performing the contract after paying compensation. At the same time, the non-breacher can claim for expectation damages so that he will be in the same position as if there had been performance. This situation is in accord with the Potential Pareto Improvement (or Kaldor-Hicks improvement).[188] That is: if a movement creates a winner and a loser, but the winner gains more than the loser's loss and it is possible for the loser to claim for compensation of his loss, then this movement is efficient. Since the winner can still have a surplus after compensating the loser, the total gain is still larger than the total loss.

1.2.2.2. Just Compensation

The goal of the damage rule is just to make a breacher compensate the victim, rather than to punish the breacher.[189] Accordingly, the court should award a just compensation to the victim if the other party breaches the contract.[190] On the one hand, the amount of compensation should be equal to the promisee's expected profit on the transaction.[191] On the other hand, a breacher ought not to be liable for punitive damages which are much higher than the promisee's expected profit.[192] Furthermore, the application of liquidated damages should be limited to a very narrow scope. Scott and Goetz 1977

[187] For example, Posner states: "not all breaches are blameworthy. The promisor may simply have discovered that his performance is worth more to someone else. If so, efficiency is promoted by allowing him to break his promise, provided he makes good the promisee's actual losses. If he is forced to pay more than that, an efficient breach may be deterred, and the law does not want to bring about such a result."

[188] The potential Pareto efficiency is the modification of Pareto efficiency. The later one refers to a movement that makes at least one person better off and nobody worse off. It requires the gainer to explicitly compensate the loser in any change. If there is no payment, the loser can veto any change. So any change is by unanimous consent. For more discussions, *see* chapter 1. Section 3.1.2; *see also* Cooter &Ulen 2011, p. 42.

[189] Shiffrin 2007, p. 730.

[190] Scott and Goetz 1977, p. 555.

[191] Posner, *Supra* note 2, §4.9, p. 89–90.

[192] Birmingham 1970, p. 284, 285; Scott and Goetz 1977, p. 559–562.

summarized two conditions for enforcing a liquidated damages clause, including: "1) the stipulated amount must be a reasonable estimate of just compensation in the light of the harm anticipated by the parties; 2) the anticipated damages that may arise from the breach must be uncertain and difficult to calculate".[193]

1.2.2.3. Incentive to Breach Efficiently

By issuing the expectation damages, contract law is able to give the parties incentives to breach a contract when the result of breach is efficient, conversely, to fulfil their promise when that is inefficient. In order to induce a party not to perform an inefficient commitment, the law entitles him to the remaining part of the surplus created by his breach after compensating the victim's expected profit.[194] In contrast, a party is induced to perform when it is efficient to adhere to the contract. The motivation for this party to perform derives from the way in which his breach is rendered unprofitable after compensation. Moreover, since the promisee is able to claim for the expectation compensation, he is indifferent to whether or not the contract is performed.[195]

2. Hypothesis of Efficient Breach

- **Case 3.1**: X1 hires Y1 to construct a building and they agree on a price of 10,000. Suppose the value of construction is 14,000 for X1 and the cost of construction is 18,000 at the time set for performance.[196]

- **Case 3.2**: X2 hires Y2 to construct a building and they agree on a price of 10,000. Suppose the value of construction is 14,000 for X2 and the cost of construction is 12,000 at the time set for performance.

- **Case 3.3**: Y3 agrees to deliver 100 custom-made widgets at 10 each to X3 for use in his boiler factory. After Y3 has delivered 10, Z3 comes to Y3. Z3 explains that he desperately needs 25 widgets at once and he would offer 15 each for them. Suppose the unit value of the widget is 14 for X3.[197]

2.1. Analysis of Cases

Either case 3.1 or 3.2 refers to a situation where performance turns out to be more costly than the promisor presumed when he signed the contract. However, case 2.7 differs from case 3.1 in the amount of construction cost. Within the mechanism of expectation damages, if the constructor (Y2 or Y1) breaches, he is required to compensate the house

193 Scott and Goetz 1977, p. 559; Moreno 2009, p. 6.
194 Id.
195 Posner 2007, p. 120.
196 Shavell 1980, p. 466.
197 Posner 2007, p. 120.

owner (X2 or X1) for the difference between the value of performance (14,000) and the contract price (10,000), namely 4000. Under this background, Y2 is able to compare his loss from breach and his loss from performance.[198]

- **Case 3.1:** The construction cost is 18,000. Y1 is supposed to be better off if he tries to escape from the duty of performance by paying 14,000 rather than 18,000. This is one of what is called efficient breach cases.[199]

- **Case 3.2:** It refers to what is called an inefficient breach case where it is assumed that breach (14,000) is more costly than performance (12,000). Thus, Y2 is motivated to perform the contract because he could lose less by doing so.

On the other hand, case 3.2 refers to another situation, where the promisor is tempted to breach because he can gain more profit from breach. By transferring those 25 widgets to the second buyer Z3, Y3 will earn an extra profit of 125 (25 × 15 – 25 × 10). At the same time, the first buyer X3 is going to lose an expected profit of 100 (25 × (14 – 10). Y3 will still earn a gain of 25 (125 – 100) even after reimbursing X3 for his loss. In the end, this breach is Pareto superior for making both the seller (Y3) and the second buyer (Z3) better off without making the first buyer (X3) worse off. But if we suppose that the second buyer only offers a price of 12, then the seller is induced not to breach. In this case, breach is inefficient because the profit earned from breach (12 × 25 – 10 × 25) is less than the cost of breach (100).

2.2. *Formulate the Ideal Efficient Breach*

From the above analysis, some situations can be identified where non-performance becomes more efficient than performance. It was observed that the expectation damages rule allows the promisor be released from performance by paying damages to the other party. In this way, the breaching party can avert a larger loss or obtain a higher profit by getting rid of the agreed obligation. To make the illustration of efficient breach easier, Cooter and Ulen have translated this process into some basic formulas. Now suppose a seller *Y* and a buyer *X*, let *Npy* and *Nby* denote seller *Y*'s net profits[200] from performing and breaching separately and *Npx* and *Nbx* denote buyer *X*'s. Let *L* denote *Y*'s liability for breaching. *Y* might follow this rule to make the decision of breach or performance:[201]

- only if $Npy > Nby - L$, then Y will perform the contract;
- only if $Npy < Nby - L$, then Y will breach the contract.

198 Adler 2008, p. 1689.

199 Id.

200 Net profit, also called net revenue, is a measure of the profitability of a venture after accounting for all costs. In simplistic terms, net profit is the money left over after paying all the expenses of an endeavour, which could be denoted in the formula, *Np* =Value – Cost. Barnes 1998, p. 421.

201 Cooter & Ulen, p. 288–289.

In order to restore X to the position that he would have enjoyed had the performance happened, the law should award X perfect expectation damages, that is, $L = Npx - Nbx$.[202] If the value for L is incorporated into the rule regarding how Y makes his decision, it is derived that:[203]

- *when* $Npx + Npy > Nbx + Nby$, Y will perform the contract;
- *when* $Npx + Npy < Nbx + Nby$, Y will breach the contract.

In this sense, if perfect expectation damages are available, a promisor (Y) will breach a contract only when the net profits gained by both parties's from the breach are larger than those from the performance. In conclusion, it is shown that the perfect expectation damages lead to two ideal results: 1) rather than being obliged to perform a contract, the promisor would take an efficient level of commitment to keep it or break it; 2) a breach creates no victims since the promisee is able to get full compensation.[204] In this sense, what efficiency should solve is more than merely to recognize an efficient breach case and to release this breacher from performance. Efficiency also becomes a crucial criterion for evaluating the economic effect of a remedy rule, and this will be analyzed in the next chapter.

3. Models of Efficient Breach

In law and economics theory, an efficient breach case refers to a situation where non-performance of a contract is more advantageous than performance. At the time when two parties decided to enter a contract, obviously both of them assumed that performance of this contract was advantageous, because otherwise they would not sign it. However, due to the existance of transaction costs and contract parties' limited foresight, there are a number of unexpected contigencies that might arise in the ongoing contractual relationship. Those contigencies will possibly change an advantageous contract into a disadvantageous one by changing the cost of performance or the value of breach. From the previous illustration, we may summarize two types of contigencies that probably alter the utility of a contract, including. fortunate contigencies and unfortunate contigencies.[205]

202 Id.

203 Id.

204 There is a pre-condition for reaching this conclusion, that is, the contract does not have any external effect. So the result of solving any conflicts in a contract only affects the contract parties. Cooter &Ulen 2011, p. 289.

205 Id.

3.1. *Unfortunate Contingencies*

An unfortunate contingency refers to a case where the cost of performing a contract becomes much higher than anticipated.[206] Case 3.1 in this chapter probably involves an unfortunate contingency. After the contract is signed, the workers hired by Y1 may ask for an increased salary; or unseasonal cold weather may occur and make the construction more difficult. Thus the construction becomes more costly. In these circumstances, Y1 would do better not to perform in order to avert a larger loss. This refers to the first scenario of efficient breach, namely a breach for decreasing losses.

3.1.1. The Increased Performance Cost

Suppose Y agrees to sell a product to X at the price of P. This product is worth Vx for X and Vy for Y. Besides, the cost of performance is expected as C at the time when the parties sign the contract. Then the net profit (*the money left over after costs have been paid*) of performance is expected as $(P - Vy - C)$ for Y and $(Vx - P)$ for X.[207] The total expected surplus created by this contract is calculated as:

- $Npx + Npy = (Vx - P) + (P - Vy - C) = Vx - Vy - C$[208]

Besides, at the time when the contract is formed, the net profits of performing the contract for both parties should be larger than zero, otherwise they would not sign this contract.[209] Therefore, we assume that the contract is efficient if:

- $P - Vy - C > 0$ or $C < P - Vy$ and;
- $Vx - p > 0$ and;
- $Vx - Vy - C > 0$ or $C < Vx - Vy$

Suppose an unfortunate contigency incurs an extra cost to Y and the total cost of performance C is thus increased.[210] Three possibilities arise:

- $C < P - Vy$: *The total cost of performance is still lower than the promisor's expected profit from the contract. In this case, it is efficient for Y to perform the contract since he can still earn a surplus by doing so.*

206 Cooter & Ulen 2011, p. 325.
207 Schäfer & Ott 2004, p. 324.
208 Id.
209 Id; Kornhauser 1986, p. 697.
210 Notice that we ignore reliance cost in the whole process. If the reliance cost occurs before the unfortunate contingency, then it becomes sunk cost and cannot be taken into account in making future decisions. But if the reliance cost occurs after the unfortunate contingency, the contract case probably involves another issue of mitigation. That is, the promisee should take reasonable measures to mitigate the injury from the breach. Schäfer & Ott 2004, p. 324; Adler 2008, p. 1721–1723.

- ***P* – *Vy* < *C* < *Vx* – *Vy*:***The cost becomes higher than the promisor's expected profit but lower than the total expected profit from the contract. Then the performance of the contract would lead to a loss for Y but it still creates some joint surplus ($Vx - Vy - C > 0$).*[211] *In this case, Y might want to avoid the performance, but it is still efficient for him to perform the contract.*

- ***C>Vx-Vy:*** *When the cost of performance exceeds the total expected profit, performance becomes undesirable. In this situation, the cost of performance consumes the total profits that X and Y expected from performance of the contract at the time when the contract was concluded ($Vx - Vy - C < 0$).*[212] *Therefore, it is efficient for Y to terminate this contract.*

To conclude, a minor increase in the cost of performance would not necessarily create a case for efficient breach. If, and only if, the extent of the increase is unacceptable and well beyond the normal range, performance of the contract will become inefficient.[213] To be more precise, the promisor should only be prevented from performing in the case that the cost of performance is higher than the expected profit that both parties together anticipated when the contract was signed.[214]

3.1.2. Solutions to the Problem of Increased Cost

In a case where an unfortunate contingency occurs, the cost of performance will be increased. We note that performing the original contract will become inefficient only when its cost has increased dramatically. In this case, the cost of this contract is disproportionate to the value of it. The consequence is clear: to compel performance of the contract in this situation would just waste resources.[215] However, the promisor may want to avert performance whenever the cost of performance is increased above his expected surplus from the contract. He may try to avoid a contract even when performing it is efficient (recall the situation when $P - Vy < C < Vx - Vy$). Therefore, what matters in an unfortunate contingency case is: how can the law motivate the promisor to save the cost of performance when it is inefficient to perform and to invest in performance when it is efficient to do so? Obviously, the doctrine of efficient breach is not the only solution to this question. We can assume several possible approaches to deal with this situation.[216]

211 Id.
212 Id.
213 The standard here is similar to the standard that is imposed on the principle of impracticability. A comment to the Restatement (2ed) describes it as: "extreme or unreasonable difficulty, expense, injury, or loss to one of the parties involved" or "a risk of injury to person or to property, of one of the parties or of others, that is disproportionate to the ends to be attained by performance" De Geest 2012, p. 31.
214 Schäfer & Ott 2004, p. 320, p. 324.
215 Posner 2007, p. 120.
216 Adler 2008, p. 1690; Cooter & Ulen 2011, p. 326–328.

3.1.2.1. Breach and Full Compensation

The law may allow breach and design expectation damages rules to promote efficient breach and efficient performance. Accordingly, the promisor has the freedom to breach a contract which he considers as inefficient and he needs to fully compensate the expected profit of the other party. Let us translate this statement into a formula.

Suppose the liability incurred by breach is L. If the aggrieved promisee is able to obtain full compensation, then L is equal to the promisee's (X's) net profit from the performance, that is, $L = Npx = Vx - p$. Besides, in a case of unfortunate contingency, the promisor Y won't earn any additional surplus from breach, therefore Nby is zero:

- $Nby = 0;$
- $Npy = P - Vy - C;$
- $L = Vx - P$

If Y is a rational person, he will breach only if his net profit from breach is higher than that from performance after paying damages, that is, $Npy < Nby - L$. If the value of Nby, Npy and L is incorporated into the decision rule of the promisor, Y will breach when:

- $P - Vy - C < 0 - (Vx - P).$

It can be concluded that Y will breach only when $Vx - Vy < C$ *or* $Vx - Vy - C < 0,$ namely the cost of performance is larger than the total profit that X and Y expected from the contract when the contract was signed. It is expected that perfect expectation damages can achieve an ideal result in a non-contingency case. That is: the situtaion where the promisor will breach is identical to the situation where performance is inefficient[217] (Remember that only when C > Vx – Vy, is the performance of the contract inefficient).

3.1.2.2. Re-negotiations

Besides breach, the promisor may initiate a renegotiation with the promisee to resolve the problem of unacceptable cost. By re-negotiation, the parties will try to use a more efficient contract to replace the previous one.[218] The seller Y may prefer to give the buyer X any amount less than his cost of performance or may ask Y to increase the payment to the level that covers his cost. Since the parties are the best judges of their own benefits, the approach of re-negotiation may also achieve an efficient result. Based on this, some people have argued that the legal rules are irrelevant and the content of the remedy rules would not make any difference, because people can always contract the remedy rules out by consensus.[219]

217 Cooter & Ulen 2011, p. 289.

218 Id, p. 326.

219 This argument has been cited in attacking the efficient breach doctrine. As is said, whether or not the legal rules can motivate efficient breach is unimportant, "because a party contemplating breach can

Negotiations, however, are costly. According to the Coase Theorem, transaction costs interfere with efficient contracting and a successful re-negotiation only occurs when the transaction costs are low.[220] Besides, "the terms of the re-negotiated contract depend on the bargaining power of the parties, which is also influenced by the legal remedy in the event that bargaining fails".[221] In a case when the cost of performance exceeds the promisor's expected profit, either performance of the contract or compensation of the other party's loss will cause a loss to the promisor. In order to avoid both problems of performance and liability, a desperate promisor may just accept some disadvantageous terms. Therefore, it is necessary for the law to design the remedy rules so as to promote efficient breach and efficient performance. (In the previous part, the law's role in filling contract gaps was noted.)

3.1.2.3. Specific Performance

As an alternative, the law can also ignore the cost of performance and simply hold the parties to their contract. This will be discussed in chapter 5.

3.2. *Fortunate Contingencies*

The previous case 3.3 concerns a fortunate contingency. After the contract was signed, Z3 offers a higher price (15 each) than that in the first contract (10 each). Therefore, the alternative contract (with Z3) is more profitable for Y3 than the original contract (with X3). A fortunate contingency is always indicated in the model that one party to a contract gets some better opportunities after he has signed the contract.[222] As opposed to an unfortunate contingency, a fortunate contingency may not necessarily enhance the direct cost of performance,[223] but it seduces the promisor to break his promise in order to obtain more profit from the second offer. Again, this situation will be explained through some formulas.

3.2.1. Another Offer

Suppose *Y* agrees to sell a product to *X* at the price of *Px*. This product is worth *Vx* for *X* and *Vy* for *Y*. The net profit of performing this contract is expected as (*Px* - *Vy)* for *Y* and (*Vx* - *Px)* for *X* at the time when X and Y signed the contract. Therefore, the total expected surplus created by the first contract is calculated as:

always renegotiate the deal." More discussions concerning re-negotiations will be provided in Chapter 4 and chapter 5. *See* Barnes 1998, p. 401–403. Craswell 1988, p. 635–636; Adler 2008, p. 1698–1690.

220 Cooter & Ulen 2011, p, 326.

221 Id.

222 Id, p. 325, p. 328.

223 We can explain the case of fortunate contingency in a way that performance of the first contract may deprive the promisor of a better opportunity. We may also say that a fortunate contingency has increased the cost of performance. But this causal relation is indirect since performing the first contract doesn't cause a direct loss to the promisor.

- $Npx + Npy = (Vx - Px) + (Px - Vy) = Vx - Vy$[224]

After the contract is signed, *Z* comes to *Y* and wants to buy the product at the price of *Pz*.[225] Suppose that *Z* estimates the value of this product at *Vz*. In the second contract, the net profit that Y estimates is (*Npy'* or *Pz – Vy)* and the net profit that Z expects is (*Npz* or *Vz – Px)*. Hence, the total expected surplus created by the second contract is calculated as:

- $Npz + Npy' = (Vz - Pz) + (Pz - Vy) = Vz - Vy$

According to the standard of efficiency, it is required to compare the total surplus generated by the first contract and the total surplus generated by the alternative contract. If, and only if, performing the second contract generates more wealth than performing the first one, breach is efficient. Namely:

- $Npz + Npy' > Npx + Npy$.

Hence, breach will be efficient if:

- $Vz > Vx$

To conclude, the product should be allocated to the second buyer if, and only if, this product is valued higher by the second buyer than by the first buyer.[226]In these circumstances, it is assumed that the second buyer's use of the resource will generate a higher surplus than use by the first one. What is more, the surplus created by performing the second contract will cover the loss caused by failing to perform the first contract.

3.2.2. A Higher Price[227]

In the real situation, however, a party contemplating breach does not know exactly how much surplus an alternative user will earn from using the resource he has. In our example, when the second buyer Z approaches the seller Y, how can Y know that Z values the product more than the first buyer X does? Obviously, the information available for Y to decide whether or not it is more profitable to perform the alternative contract is manifested in the price that the second party offers. In order to answer this question, it

224 The direct cost of performance is neglected here. Since a fortunate contingency will not increase the direct cost of performance, then this part of the cost is irrelevant to the parties' decisions. Besides, we may assume that the parties should have considered the potential cost of performance and internalized this cost into the price when they enter a contract.

225 The same analysis applies if a buyer receives a more favorable offer from a second seller.

226 Craswell 1988, p. 634–636.

227 The doctrine also applies to the case when a buyer is contemplating breach. Then the situation is that, a lower price offer from another seller comes to a buyer after he has agreed to buy something from a seller.

is necessary to differentiate between the ***contract price*** that a party would actually have to pay and the ***reservation price***[228] that a party is willing to pay.

Economists use the terminology of reservation price to describe the maximum price that a buyer is willing to pay for a product (or certain service) or the minimum price that a seller is willing to accept in exchange for his performance.[229] The maximum price that one would bid is calculated as the left over from the total revenues that one person expects after he has paid the enhancing cost to produce that revenue.[230]But the minimum price that one would accept equals his cost of producing that product (or service).[231] In contrast to the reservation price, the contract price refers to the actual price that has been set in a contract.[232] To a large extent, that depends on people's ability to bargain.[233] A buyer who is good at bargaining is able to lower the price to the minimum level that the seller would accept and a seller who is good at bargaining may enhance the price to the maximum level that the buyer is willing to pay. Professor Barnes uses an example to show the difference between reservation price and contract price as well as how the reservation price may affect people's bargains.[234]

Suppose both X and Z want to buy an old car from Y. The buyer X can resell the car for 400 after he invests 375 in repairing it; and the buyer Z will resell the car for 200 just after he cleans it at a cost of 50. Suppose delivering the car will cost Y 10. In this case, although X can obtain a bigger enhancement (400) than Z does (200), it incurs a larger cost (375) for X to get the enhancement. Table 3 shows each party's reservation price,

Table 3. Each Party's Reservation Price

	Total revenue	Enhancing cost	Reservation price	Contract price
X	400	375	25	11
Z	200	50	150	20

As indicated in the above table, the maximum price that X is willing to pay is 25 and that Z would pay is 150, while the minimum price that Y would accept is 10.[235] Therefore, a larger surplus will be created if the product is transferred to the person with a higher reservation price. However, the real contract price may not truly reflect this. For example, if Z is a good bargainer, then he may make Y accept a price as low as that slightly higher than Y's reservation price (10), such as 11. In contrast, suppose X is a bad bargainer and he can only make Y agree on a price of 20.[236] In such a situation, the contract price set

228 The complete discussion about reservation price can be find in Cooter & Ulen 2011, p. 31.
229 Barnes 1998, p. 421–423.
230 Id.
231 Id.
232 Id.
233 Id.
234 Id.
235 Id.
236 Maybe Z has used some personal resource to persuade Y to accept a low price, for instance, he may bribe Y; or maybe Z has a good business relation with Y.

between Z and Y is lower than that set between X and Y, but it does not necessarily prove that Z values the car less than X.

In an economic sense, the preferable user is a buyer with a higher reservation price, or in other words, it is the buyer who is willing to pay a higher price that can use the resource best.[237] Thus, the resource should be allocated to this party. To return to the initial analysis of efficiency and assume a bidding war,[238] when an alternative user approaches one of the contractual parties, it is assumed that the alternative user will express a price that he is willing to pay (Reservation price: *Pz'*). At the same time, suppose that the first buyer may increase his bid after he learns what has happened. The first seller is willing to pay *Px'* instead of *Px*. There are three possibilities:

- ***Pz' < Px****: Z is only willing to pay a price that is lower than the price that has been set in the first contract. According to the price doctrine, Y will not choose the alternative bidder.*[239]

- ***Px < Pz' < Px'****: Z comes to Y and would offer a higher price than the price which has been set in the first contract. If X knows this and he thinks the product is more valuable than the new price, X will increase his bid to Px' and make Px' higher than the new price.*[240] *In this sense, allocating the product to X will be more efficient. It is efficient for Y to carry out the original contract.*

- ***Pz' > px'****: Z comes to Y and would offer a higher price than the price which has been set in the first contract. After that, X wants to increase his bid but the maximum amount that X wants to pay is still lower than Z's offer. In this case, Z values the product more than X does. It is efficient to avoid the first contract and perform the second one.*

In conclusion, if an alternative user comes with a price that is higher than the price set in the original contract, it does not sufficiently indicate that performing the second contract is more efficient. If, and only if, the price offered by the alternative buyer is higher than the highest price that the first buyer would pay, then performing the original contract is inefficient.

3.2.3. Reactions to a Fortunate Contingency

In the case when a seller receives another higher offer after he has signed a contract, it means he gets a fortunate opportunity; in the same way, a buyer meets a fortunate opportunity if he receives another lower price offer. For the promisor, however, he is willing to accept an offer whenever he notices that it comes with a better price than has

237 Similarly, the more preferable buyer is the one with a lower reservation price. In this sense, this buyer is able to produce the product at a lower cost. Barnes 1998, p. 421–423.

238 Craswell 1988, p. 635.

239 We exclude the possibility that Z will offer Y some additional profits, for instance, Z might bribe Y.

240 The first buyer will not bid an amount greater than the amount at which he values the resource.

already been set in the original contract. He might sign the new contract directly without letting the first buyer know it. Then it is possible for the promisor to quit the original contract even when it is inefficient to do so (recall the instance when $Px < Pz' < Px'$).

If, and only if, the price offered by the alternative bargainer is much better so that the alternative contract is able to create a higher surplus than the original contract, then performing the alternative contract will be efficient.[241] In these circumstances, resources will be moved to a better user. Besides, the loss from failing to perform the original contract is lower than the profits yielded by the alternative contract. Therefore, breach may lead to an additional surplus. On this basis, there are two questions to resolve in the case involving a fortunate contingency: (1) how can the law motivate people to transfer the resources to a better user?[242] (2) how can the law efficiently allocate the surplus created by a breach? There are several possible answers to these questions:

3.2.3.1. Breach and Compensation

The law may allow breach and ask a breacher to pay damages. In the case when breach is caused by a fortunate contingency, additional gains will be incurred. Thus the design of the damage measurement determines how much the promisor must share his gains from breaching with the promisee. There are several options:

A. Expectation damages:

It requires the promisor to pay damages equal to the promisee's expected loss of surplus. It is assumed that the approach of expectation damages has several advantages:

(1) It gives the promisor incentives to act efficiently. He will breach when he is able to earn a greater surplus from the alternative contract than the amount of damages he needs to pay to the promisee.[243] Then, after breaching and paying the damages, the promisor is still better off.
(2) It promotes efficient allocation of resources. An alternative buyer will be willing to offer a higher price because he values the promisor's performance more. Or an alternative seller wants to offer a lower price because he could produce the same goods at a lower cost. Then breach is efficient for making the alternative bargainer better off.
(3) The promisee is indifferent. Since the principle of expectation damages requires a breacher to fully compensate the expected loss of the victim,[244] the promisee won't be worse off. As a result of breach and compensation, two parties are better off without making anyone worse off.[245] Then, a Pareto superior reallocation is yielded.

241 Craswell 1988, p. 634.
242 Id.
243 Id.
244 Barnes 1998, p. 425; Craswell 1988, p. 634.
245 Id.

We may translate this statement into a formula as well. From the previous case, suppose the liability incurred by breach is L, then L equals the promisee's (X's) expected profit from the performance, that is, $L = Npx = Vx - Px$. Suppose the alternative bargainer Z offers a price of Pz. In a case of fortunate contigency, the promisor's net profit from breach is his net profit created by the alternative contract, namely, $Nby = Npy' = Pz - Vy$. We get:

- $Nby = Pz - Vy$;
- $Npy = Px - Vy$;
- $L = Vx - Px$

Y follows a decision rule that he will breach only if $Npy < Nby - L$. If we substitute the value of Nby, Npy and L into the decision rule of the promisor, we get:

- Only if $Px - Vy < (Pz - Vy) - (Vx - Px)$, will Y Breach the contract with X.

We further conclude that Y will choose to breach the contract with X when Pz > Vx. This is consistent with the creterion of efficiency established in section 3.2.2. Recall that Vx is also the maximum price that X is willing to pay, so Vx = Px'. Then the conclusion is reached that Y will breach when Pz > Px'.

Arising from this, the perfect expectation damages can achieve an ideal result in a fortunate contingency case as well. That is: the situation where the promisor will breach is identical to the situation where performing the alternative contract is efficient.

B. Other measurements

Beside the expectation damages, the law may also offer other measures of damage. For instance, the promisor may only be required to pay the damages covering the reliance loss of the victim (reliance damages). Or the law may issue the restitution damages and ask the promisor to return what he has received from the promisee, such as the payment that the promisor has received. Or the law may deprive a breacher of all the surpluses created by his behaviour.[246] Those alternative damage measurements will be compared with the expectation damages in chapter 5.

3.2.3.2. Re-negotiations

Provided that the transaction cost is low or zero, the parties will choose to solve the problem by negotiations.[247] Negotiation may happen in different ways, such as re-negotiation or re-sell.[248] For example, after a second bargainer comes to a party to a contract, all the parties involved in this transaction may gather together and re-discuss

246 Posner 2007, p. 118, 119.
247 Cooter & Ulen 2011, p. 289.
248 Craswell 1988, p. 635.

the price. Through this approach, a bidding war may occur and thus prevent the promisor from performing the less efficient contract. What's more, if a seller fails to sell a product to a higher-valuing buyer[249], this buyer can always do business with the buyer who has the product. In this way, resources will also be allocated to the best user in the end. However, the basic point here is quite similar to what was concluded in an unfortunate contingency case. That is, only when the transaction cost is relatively low, will re-negotiation or re-sell be a good way of allocating products and services.

4. Conclusion

Contracting, in the economic sense, is a way for people to maximize their utility and hence to maximize social welfare. In many circumstances, the time for performing a contract is different from the time when the contract is signed. Since contracts can never be perfect and complete, a contract which the parties considered as efficient may turn into an inefficient one later. One factor that may cause this change is a contingency rising after a contract has been signed.

If a contingency happens and increases the cost of performance, it is called an unfortunate contingency. In the case when an unfortunate contingency has increased the cost of performance dramatically, the contract usually becomes inefficient. Under these circumstances, the surplus that both of the parties anticipated from their contract will be consumed by the cost of performing it. In addition, if one party to a contract receives another price offer after he has signed a contract, it means a fortunate contingency occurs to this party. The original contract may also become inefficient when there is a fortunate contingency. This happens when the alternative bargainer is willing to offer a better price than the first bargainer does. Therefore, performing the second contract can yield a larger surplus. In both cases, some strict criteria should be applied for assessing inefficient contracts. Only if the performance cost increases dramatically or the price offered by an outsider is much higher than that offered by the original buyer[250], performance is considered inefficient. From an economic perspective, no-one wants the promisor to perform those types of contract. After recognizing the situations when performance becomes inefficient, it is necessary to find the solution to make people's behaviour accord with efficiency. There are different ways to achieve it. For instance, people may re-negotiate over the issues and enter a desirable consequence by themselves. Besides, the law may also offer people good incentives not to perform a contract when it is inefficient to do so. The logic under this derives from the interactive relationship

[249] Maybe the law imposes large damages on the breacher. In this case, a seller contemplating a breach is frightened to do so and he will just deliver the product as agreed, even when the buyer doesn't value this product as much as another buyer does. Or maybe the lower valuing buyer has already got the goods according to the property law. For instance, in many civil law countries, registration is an important requirement for obtaining the ownership over a real property. Suppose there are two people wanting to buy a house. If the first buyer has done the registration in the public authority, the second buyer cannot get the property even when he is willing to pay a higher price.

[250] In the case where a buyer is contemplating to breach, the price offered by an outsider should be much lower than that by the original seller.

between contract law and people's motivations. By making a breaching party remedy the other party's loss, a party who is contemplating breaching the contract will consider both the benefit and the cost generated by such a decision. But the question is at what level the remedy should be set in order to provide contract parties with incentives to make efficient decisions.

In the law and economics literature, a doctrine of efficient breach is raised. According to this doctrine, a contract that becomes inefficient (caused by a fortunate or unfortunate contingency) could be breached by the promisor. In addition, the promoters use the efficient breach doctrine to justify the common law systems of expectation damages. It is assumed that efficiency is promoted by allowing a party to a contract to break their promise, provided they compensate the promisee's actual losses. In this sense, the common law remedy of expectation damages is favoured by the doctrine of efficient breach. In the next chapter, this idea will be examined by taking into account several elements that may affect the efficiency in the scenario of efficient breach.

Chapter 4

A RE-EXAMINATION OF THE OPTIMAL RULE TO ENHANCE EFFICIENCY

Applying the standard of efficiency, law and economics scholars have defined the concept of efficient breach as a situation where breach is more efficient than performance. In this situation, breach of contract, compared to performance, will make the promisor better off without making the promisee worse off. Hence, performing the original contract is undesirable for the promisor. Conversely, it is more efficient for the promisor to seek a release from the original contract so as to save the cost of performance (unfortunate contingency) or to implement another more profitable contract (fortunate contingency). In order to achieve that, the promisor may breach the contract by breaking his promise, or he may start to re-negotiate with the other party and modify the original contract.[251]

Accordingly, it is assumed that the contract remedy rules should encourage breach when breach is efficient and discourage it otherwise.[252] Based on this standard, some law and economics scholars have reached a consensus about the form of remedy that is most likely to promote efficient breach. They observed that expectation damages[253] which put the non-breaching party in a position as if breach had not occurred will best motivate the promisor to take efficient breach. There is also literature clarifying the interactive relationship between the remedy of expectation damages and efficient breach.[254]

The efficient breach doctrine, in its simplest form, stops here. However, on this basis it is still difficult to draw a conclusion about the relationship between contract remedies, efficient breach and efficiency. On the one hand, we need more empirical evidence to show that people indeed take more efficient breach and avoid inefficient breach under a particular type of contract remedy. On the other hand, it is unclear whether or not the remedy system which can best promote efficient breach will in fact contribute to welfare-enhancement. Moreover, criticism also comes from subjectivists and moralists.[255] Whether

251 In the situation where an alternative bargainer comes to the promisor, the parties may also solve the problem without breaching the contract or re-negotiation. For example, if a second buyer also wants to get the product, he could buy it from the first buyer. We call this situation re-sell. But similar to re-negotiation, re-sell also involves negotiation between the parties and it will induce transaction costs. Craswell 1988, p. 635; Cooter & Ulen 2011, p. 325.

252 Ulen 1984, p. 343.

253 The definition of expectation damages was presented in the previous chapter.

254 Barton 1972, p. 278; Birmingham 1970, p. 284–286.

255 What is argued by the subjectivists is that the costs and benefits incurred by an economic actor should only be assessed by the actor himself and not by a third party. Therefore, compensation based on the

or not efficiency should be the sole criterion for contract remedies is still being debated in the literature. The goal of this chapter is to examine how the doctrine of efficient breach is incorporated into legal rules and what is the limit of the integration.

To carry out the goal of this chapter, a summary of various re-examinations of the traditional concept of efficient breach and contract remedies will be provided. Two questions are raised: firstly, will the expectation damages be the best way to promote efficient breach and; secondly, will breach be the most efficient way to deal with the situation when performance is inefficient? This chapter will be developed in four steps. First, Section 1 will establish the basic theoretical framework for the analysis by indicating the contract models and remedy models to be used. Section 2 will provide an outline of expectation damages in traditional law and economics doctrine. In more detail, it will discuss the interactive relationship between expectation damages and efficient breach by means of a simple example, including only a seller (or a producer) and a buyer, the duty to convey a product (or to produce a product) and a price. In section 3, the model of efficient breach will be extended by some correlative factors. For example, the surplus of breach (Section 3.1), the loss from breach (Section 3.2), transaction costs (Section 3.3) and people's preference of risk (Section 3.4) may influence the promisor's decisions of breach or performance and the efficiency of the results in real contract cases. These factors will be added to the analysis in order to try to find out their impacts on the relationship between the different remedy rules and efficiency. Afterwards, this chapter will summarize some critiques over the story of efficient breach both from an economic and moralistic perspective (section 4). Section 5 will conclude.

1. Theoretical Framework of Analysis

In the previous chapter, we concluded that there are two major situations where non-performance of a contract is economically superior to performance. The first situation exists where the cost of performance turns out to be much higher than initially expected so that it consumes the total profits generated by the contract. The second situation where breach is assumed to be efficient and desirable occurs if the profit from the contract with a third party is higher than that from the original contract. To deal with those situations, the parties could either negotiate over every possibility ex-ante or ex-post or just accept what has been established by contract default rules in contract law.

Law and economics scholars have tried to propose an optimal remedy to shape incentives for efficient breach. Undeniably, it is difficult to reach a conclusion only by theoretical inference. In the real-world, transactions are costly and flexible[256] and people engage in market activities through different types of contracts. It can be a sales contract concerning the transfer of ownership; or it can be a service contract involving one type

assessment of a court shouldn't become the substitute for performance. According to moralists, the efficient breach theory has violated moral principles and undermines the moral basis of society. The later sections of this chapter will integrate more of this discussion. See Schäfer & Ott 2005, p. 329; Friedmann 1989, p. 13–20.

256 In a real situation, the parties would also design their own mechanism and institutions to govern the on-going relationship between each other.

of specific behaviour. Moreover, people's preferences and bargaining capacities in transactions are different as well. Transactions may take place between two professional businessmen or between one company and an individual consumer. Can we still say that one individual remedy can best motivate efficient breach in all those occasions without sufficient empirical evidence? The answer will undoubtedly be no. However, theoretical models are still valuable for giving us some reflections of the economic analysis of contract remedies.

1.1. Shavell Model

In the previous chapter, two hypothetical types of efficient breach were presented. One type of breach is committed to avert a larger loss; and the other one is made because the profit from breach is greater than the profits from performing the contract.[257] Those two types of efficient breach, according to Shavell, normally fit in two different contractual contexts, namely, contracts to produce new goods or to provide services and contracts to convey existing properties.[258]

In Shavell's paper, a distinction is made between contracts to produce material goods and contracts to convey a property with a "production cost" explanation.[259] In both contractual contexts, Shavell considered that the promisor may want to commit breach because contingencies will arise after the contract is signed. Besides, he assumed that uncertainty may arise in different forms when the content of performance is changed. As to the contracts to produce things, uncertainty is often caused by the performance cost.[260] The promisor might want to breach if the cost of performance turns out to be high and the way of breach is indicated by a refusal to accomplish the stipulated production or service. This situation will fit into the model of unfortunate contingency. In contrast, Shavell considers that uncertainty exists in those contracts to convey goods, in most situations, because of an outsider's bid.[261] In the case that an outsider offers a high bid, the promisor will be tempted to commit a breach. He might be willing to transfer the existing property to the outsider rather than to the original promisee.

An efficient breach, accordingly, presents accomplishing different tasks in those two contractual contexts: 1) to save the performance cost; and 2) to transfer the goods to the most valuable user. Moreover, as shown in the previous chapter, if the contract remedy is set as expectation damages, people will breach either when the performance cost turns out to be high or an outsider bids a much higher price. Thus, our starting points are two earlier conclusions which were summarized in the previous chapter. The first conclusion

257 Posner 2007, p. 120.

258 The contracts to produce goods, to some extent, share a lot of similarities with contacts to provide services. Shavell 2006, p. 837–838.

259 Shavell 2004, p. 339.

260 In general, there are also other uncertainties that the two parties might face. For instance, the value of the goods (or service) might be disappointing or the demand of the product might be decreased.

261 In reality, uncertainty about bids from outsiders may also exist in the contracts to produce goods. But for the convenience of discussion, Shavell discussed the contracts to produce goods just with the consideration of production costs. Shavell 2006, p. 838.

is that the rule of expectation damages is able to motivate people to commit efficient breach. Secondly, the consequence caused by breach complies with the concerns of performance costs and most valuable use. Besides, in order to simplify the model, an isolated contract[262] to produce goods and a contract to convey a property will serve as examples. In both of the models, there is only a seller (or a producer), a buyer, a duty to convey a property (or to produce goods) and a price.[263] The question is whether the mechanism of achieving efficiency will be different or not when it comes to different types of contracts.

1.2. *The Remedy Model*

After establishing the contractual contexts, attention will turn to the remedy models and give a basic framework of remedy rules. As already known from the last chapter, to deal with a situation that a contract turns out to be inefficient after it has been signed, the parties have multiple solutions, either ex-ante or ex-post. Through ex-ante negotiation, the parties can specify each other's rights and obligations in reaction to the possible uncertainties, such as a sharp increase in performance cost or a higher outside bid. Or they can decide how to react to those contingencies by ex-post re-negotiation after disputes arise. The other way that the parties may choose is to resort to legal rules, especially, remedy rules (Table 4).

Table 4. Ex-ante and Ex-post Solutions

	Ex-ante	Ex-post
Contract parties	Negotiation	Renegotiation
Law	Mandatory law	Legal remedy

1.2.1. Party-designed Remedies, Default Remedies and Mandatory Rules

The first approach to deal with uncertainties and breach derives from contract parties' negotiation. Sometimes it is indicated as a liquidated clause specifying the amount of compensation that a breaching party should pay if the contract is broken. Or, the parties may also agree that the promisor should offer a certain asset as a deposit.[264] The promisee is entitled to enjoy the value of this asset in the case that the contract is broken.[265]

262 The concept of isolated contract, means that the transaction happens only once between the two parties. In this chapter, those long-term transactions which occur repeatedly between the parties are not mentioned.

263 In this chapter, the concepts of "seller" and "buyer" will also be used in the same meaning as the words of "promisor" and "promisee".

264 Sometimes, it is a third person that offers the guarantee. Normally the asset is a real property, such as a house or farm. Cooter & Ulen 2011, p. 321.

265 The non-breaching party may sell the property and enjoy the money from the sale; or he can get the asset by himself.

Another approach to deal with breach refers to legal remedy rules. Basically, legal remedy rules work as default rules. This is what was concluded in chapter 2. Saying that remedy rules are default rules has two implications. First, legal remedy rules work as gap-filling rules. Namely, in a case when the private arrangement of breach and remedy is unavailable, the legal remedy mechanism needs to function as a substitute. Second, if the remedy rules are default rules, this also means that parties can contract around them by ex-ante agreement or ex-post agreement. A typical case is that the parties may, at the time of contract formation, write liquidated clauses into their contracts.

What contract law can also provide, however, are mandatory rules that limit parties' freedom in choosing their own remedies. Mandatory rules on contract remedy are established for several concerns.[266] For example, as to the issue of stipulated remedy, the legislators or the courts may be sceptical of the unfairness of the negotiation, which is normally caused by asymmetric bargaining power between the contract parties. Hence, some courts are rigorous about the remedies clauses in a contract, especially the amount of compensation set by the contract parties. In many cases where a contract specified an amount of damages that is significantly larger than the actual loss caused by a breach, a court may apply the mandatory rule regarding party-agreed damages and refuse to enforce the stipulated damages clause.[267] Another example of mandatory rules can be found in consumer contract law, namely, the rule of punitive damages. According to some legislation, in a case where a consumer party experiences unfair and deceptive treatment from a business party, he is entitled to receive up to double or treble the amount of money that was lost at the hands of the business party.[268] In either of these examples, contract law imposes immutable rules on contracts parties so as to restrict the negotiation of contract remedies. The more mandatory rules there are, the less space parties have in choosing their own remedies or other alternatives to breach.

1.2.2. Choosing the Optimal Default Remedy

As to the form of default remedy, there are several choices that the law may make. For instance, a remedy rule may allow a party to a contact to break his primary obligation and bear the secondary obligation to pay damages *in lieu* of the primary one he has disclaimed. Then a damage remedy is the applicable default. Or, an aggrieved party can apply to the court to have the breacher perform the contractual obligation as agreed. In this case, the routine remedy presents as an order of specific performance.[269] Or, in some

266 In chapter 2, we summarized the major arguments around establishing mandatory rules. They are always related to market monopoly, externality, asymmetric information or individual rationality.

267 Goetz & Scott 1977, p. 555, p. 556.

268 For instance, Article 49 of the Chinese consumer protection law allows the consumer to ask for increasing the compensation of his losses in the case when a business party engages in fraudulent activities in supplying commodities or services. A similar rule can also be found in the consumer protection law in US. Under chapter 93A (9) in Massachusetts consumer protection law, recovery of a consumer's losses shall be in the amount of double or treble damages if a business's actions are unfair or deceptive.

269 The later part in this chapter will give more discussion on specific performance.

occasions, the law may allow the aggrieved party to apply for performance of the obligation as well as for compensation of damages.[270] Then which form of default rule is the most preferable? Controversy over this question has existed for a long time.

Some law and economics scholars have reached a consensus in that the optimal default rules should be close to what the parties would agree had they specified the remedies in their contract. So the parties' preference is a crucial factor that legislators have to consider. If we incorporate this issue into the topic of efficient breach theory, we assume that efficient breach is preferred by both of the parties. Because it is presumed that efficient breach would enhance the welfare of a contract-breaker without making the innocent party worse off. To be more specific, from the early law and economics literature, some standards can be deduced for assessing an efficient legal remedy from two perspectives.

> **From the ex-post perspective:** An efficient legal remedy should be able to solve the cases where non-performance of the original contract is efficient. There are two typical cases where non-performance of a contract is more desirable than performance. The standard of an efficient solution is that the result led by it is acceptable to the conflicting parties. This has two implications. Firstly, the rule allows non-performance of a contract so as to save the performance cost or to transfer goods (services) to the best user. This settlement which is achieved in a court, at the same time, is accepted by both of the parties in the contract dispute. Then, another one concerns the surpluses (or profits) yielded by breach. The surpluses include both the costs avoided by the breach and the profits yielded from the performance of another contract. So the court should decide how to distribute the surpluses from a breach between the contractual parties as well. This is normally achieved through the design of damages measurement.

> **From the ex-ante perspective:** Another task of an efficient remedy involves the issue of motivation. Contract law should complete contracts by providing remedy rules which can encourage efficient breach (or performance) and discourage inefficient behaviour. This is another preliminary statement from which we develop our analysis. The justification for this statement derives from an assumption of parties' preferences. Generally, we may agree that the parties are seeking for a maximization of utility. If we translate this to the pre-contractual stage, we may agree that people want each other to comply with their contract if it is efficient and to excuse it otherwise.[271] Suppose, for example, a contract to produce a product. The producer will only accept a price (P) higher than his production cost (C) and the buyer will only accept a price lower than the value (V) he places on the product. That is: $C<P<V$. If, at the stage of contract formation, a seller knows that C will exceed V, then these two parties will never enter a contract. Because "there would be no price that the buyer would pay for which the

270 For instance, in German law, when an obligor fails to accomplish the contract within the agreed time, then the obligee is allowed to apply for both specific performance and monetary damages. He may ask the court to have the obligor finish the remaining part of the obligation, besides, to compensate his losses caused by the delay. Schäfer &Ott 2004, p. 320.

271 Kornhauser 1986, P. 697–698.

seller would agree to produce".[272] Or suppose a contract to convey a product. If, at the stage of contract formation, another bidder is willing to offer a higher price, there would be a bidding war. The bidder who values the product most may bid a higher price than the other one does and the seller probably will transfer the product to him so as to earn a higher profit.[273] If the third party is the one who is willing to pay a higher price, then he will probably win the product. In this sense, a producer or seller's decision whether to enter a contract depends on the relative costs and benefits of performance and non-performance. A good remedy rule should complete the contract. The simplest possible way is to permit efficient breaches and to penalize inefficient breaches.[274] Through this way, the legal rule can induce a promisor to perform when the parties would agree, and in other case to provide appropriate alternative such as damages.[275]

2. Traditional Idea: Promote Efficient Breach through Expectation damages

In our simple model presented in the previous chapter, it was shown that the expectation damages will induce a seller (or producer) to break his promise only when the result of performance is an inefficient use of resources in both contracts to produce goods and contracts to convey properties. In that case, expectation damages are able to motivate efficient breaches and to deter inefficient performance. This idea has also been expressed in several early works of law and economics scholars.[276]

Expectation damages, furthermore, are justified for several reasons, which are in accordance with the main standards set for an efficient remedy: 1) It sets a price for breach as the amount of the expectation value of the other party, hence, encourages a promisor to make a cost-benefit judgement. A promisor is required to pay compensation if he breaks the contract and the amount of compensation is equal to the expected loss of the other party. Therefore, "if the promisor is willing to breach and pay damages equal to the promisee's lost surplus, he must be earning a surplus from breach that is greater than the surplus yielded from performing the contract."[277] Otherwise, the promisor will just fulfil his promise as agreed because performance is estimated as efficient. In this sense, expectation damages facilitate a promisor to make a reasonable judgement by calculating his benefits and losses from breach and performance. 2) The rule of expectation damages

272 Id.

273 A criticism, however, is proposed against this price doctrine. It is presented as: the price of a product depends on several factors. For example, the bargaining power of the seller or the relationship between the buyer and the seller will also influence the price set by the two parties. So a seller might sell the product to somebody who values it less because this buyer has a long-term busy relationship with him or because this buyer has a better bargaining power. This chapter will discuss the problem later. *See* Friedmann 1989, p. 4–8; see also Menetrez 2000, p. 871–872.

274 Geest 2012, p. 27.

275 Kornhauser 1986, P. 697–698.

276 "The bulk of the scholarship on efficient remedies has concerned the award of money damages, and a consensus has been reached on the form of damages that is most likely to promote economic efficiency." See Ulen 1984, p. 343; Edlin 1998, p. 15.

277 Barnes 1998, p. 425.

is assumed to be able to motivate efficient breach. By encouraging efficient breach, the expectation damages will prevent excessive performance and only promote those contracts which lead to efficient use of resources.[278] So performance will happen if, and only if, it is efficient.[279] 3) From an ex-post perspective, the dispute of breach will be resolved in a way that is acceptable to both of the parties. As long as the disappointed promisee obtains full-compensation, nobody is worse off in a breach case.

Allowing breach and awarding expectation damages, thus, is a possible approach to dealing with the situation where non-performance is efficient. However, then one may ask whether or not this approach is the optimal one to achieve a desirable result in all the situations. The answer to this question may lie in comparing the expectation damages with other possible solutions by considering elements that may affect the efficiency of "efficient breach" models. But before doing so, an outline of expectation damages will be provided:

- **Measure of expectation**: If a court needs to apply expectation damages in a contract-breach case, it has to determine how much that the defendant should compensate the plaintiff. This involves an issue of damage measure, which is defined as the rule or formula determining the amount of compensation that a breaching party should pay.[280] Ideally, the expectation damages should put the non-breaching party in as good a position as he would have been in had the contract been performed.[281] The measure for expectation equals the value of performance.
- **Define the scope of expectation**: There are some principles involved in defining the scope of expectation. One refers to the "*Rule of Hadley*". In the case of Hadley & Baxendale (1854), the court set a rule to limit the expectation to a foreseeable zone. That is: promisors are not liable for losses that are not "foreseeable" at the time when they sign the contracts.[282] Moreover, the "*reasonably certain*" doctrine requires a promisee to prove its loss is reasonably certain[283]; and the principle of "*emotional distress*" excludes the emotional distress that a promisee suffers from the scope of expectation damages.[284] By applying those limiting doctrines, courts always define a promisee's expectation within an ex-ante foreseeable frame rather than seek ex-post accuracy.[285]

3. What may Influence Efficiency?

This part will summarize several factors that probably influence the efficiency of the means of breach, which will directly influence the contract parties' decisions of breach,

278 Birmingham 1970, p. 284–286.
279 Barton 1972, p. 278; Shavell 2004, p. 308.
280 Shavell 2004, p. 304.
281 Cooter & Ulen 2011, p. 309; Shavell 2004, p. 307.
282 Posner (A) 2000, p. 163–169.
283 In practice, a promisee has to "prove his loss with a greater degree of certainty than that required by the preponderance of evidence test that governs the other elements of civil actions." Posner (A) 2000, p. 176.
284 Id.
285 Liu & Avraham 2012, p. 339.

performance, renegotiation, etc. It starts with a sales case (contract to convey a property).

- **Case 4.1:** *Y1 agrees to sell an old car to X1 at a price of 12,000. Suppose at the time when X1 and Y1 enter the contract, Y1 values the car at 5,000 but X1 estimates he can resell the car for 15,000.*[286]

3.1. *The Profits Based Efficiency*[287]

Ideally, case 4.1 is an ex-ante efficient contract, by which a surplus of 10,000 will be created. In this case, what creates the efficiency is not the transfer of money (12,000) from X1 to Y1,[288] because this is merely a redistribution of money. Rather, what matters is the allocation of the car. Profit is created by converting the car to the more valuable user. At the time when X1 and Y1 enter the contract, performance in the form of converting the car from Y1 to X1 is assumed to be efficient because it may create a surplus of 10,000. Similarly, we presume that non-performance of the contract will be efficient in some cases where non-performance can yield more surpluses.

3.1.1. The Profits in a Sales Contract

Case 4.1 can be complicated by several possibilities.

- **Possibility 1:** *Suppose Y1 also agreed to deliver the car. After he signed the contract, he found the cost of delivery had increased to 11,000.*

- **Possibility 2:** *Suppose after Y1 signed the contract and before he delivers the car Y1 found actually he could earn some money by using the car to transport goods for other people. At this time he estimates he can earn 16,000 if he uses the car by himself.*

- **Possibility 3:** *After Y1 has signed the contract Z1 explains that he desperately needs this car and the highest price he is willing to pay is 20,000.*

- **Possibility 4:** *Suppose Y1 also agreed to deliver the car to X1 and he estimates the cost of delivery is 2,000 at the time of the signature of the contract. After Y has signed the contract Z1 explains that he desperately needs this car and he is willing to pay the same price at 12,000. Suppose that Z1 is willing to pick up the car himself and Z1 also thinks the value of the car is 15,000.*

286 This case is modified from Brooks' example. See Brooks 2006, p. 579.
287 Some literature also uses the concept of surplus or gain.
288 Except from the hypothesis that maybe X or Y can make better use of this 12,000. For instance, maybe one of the parties is better at investment and he probably invests this 12,000 in a profitable activity.

In the previous chapter, there were two typical hypothetical cases where breach is more efficient than performance. They refer to the situations when an unspecified contingency increases the promisor's cost of performance or offers the promisor a better opportunity. Then we want the promisor to save the cost of performance or transfer the performance to the more valuable user. This goal can be realized by more than one approach, such as breaching the original contract, re-negotiation or re-selling. By the same token, one can also think of several approaches to solve those possibilities involved in the case 4.1 above. So the substantive issue here is not merely whether the promisor *Y1* should breach, but also to whom the car should be allocated. As to this question, our assumption is that the car should be allocated to the user who can generate a greater total net profit[289], instead of the presumption that the car should be converted to the more valuable uses.[290] This presumption can be examined in our previous cases.

Possibility 1: If *Y1* retains the car, no profit will be created. But if Y1 delivers the car to *X1*, the net profit is -1,000.[291]

Possibility 2: If *Y1* retains the car, the total net profit is 11,000. But if *Y1* transfers the car to X, the net profit is 10,000.[292]

Possibility 3: If *Y1* transfers the car to *Z1*, the total net profit is 15,000. But if *Y1* transfers the car to *X1*, the total net profit is 10,000.[293]

Possibility 4: If *Y1* transfers the car to *Z1*, the total net profit is 10,000. But if Y1 transfers the car to *X1*, the total net profit is 8,000.[294]

In all these cases, the promisor has two alternatives: either to allocate his performance to the original promisee and obtain the surplus from doing so, or to allocate the performance to the substitute user (himself or a third party) and obtain its surplus. We may agree that the performance should be allocated to the more valuable use. However, the concept of value reflects all the pleasure that a party expects to obtain, "some of which will be offset by the costs he has incurred and the balance going to profit".[295] Then a person who values

289 Barnes 1996, p. 20.

290 The traditional efficient breach doctrine assumes that breach is efficient when it can allocate the goods to a more highly valuable use. Craswell 1988, p. 634.

291 It is calculated by deducting the cost of performance from the surplus of performance, namely 10,000–11,000.

292 The surplus from Y's use of the car is calculated as 16,000–5,000; but the surplus from transferring the car to X is obtained as 15,000–5,000.

293 20,000 is Z's reservation price and the surplus from allocating the car to Z is calculated as 20,000–5,000. In contrast, the surplus from allocating the car to X is calculated as 15,000–5,000.

294 Although the price that either Z or X offers is 12,000 and the value that either Z or X places on the car is 15,000, the difference exists in the cost of performance. The surplus from allocating the car to Z is calculated as 15,000–5,000–2,000.

295 The Restatement (Second) of Contract (USA) intends to separate surplus from value. It contends that the value includes more than simply the net gain (whether consumer surplus or profit). Barnes 1996, p. 4–9.

a product more may also need to invest more money in using it. But only the concept of "surplus" or "profit" stands for the amount of pleasure left after subtracting the cost of inducing it.[296] Therefore, the most valuable user means the user that can create the largest profits and devoting the performance to him is efficient.[297] Take the first and the fourth cases as examples. In both cases, allocating the car to the buyer *X1* is inefficient. But the reason is not that the original buyer *X1* places a lower value on the car. Rather, it is because the seller has an additional obligation of delivery that diminishes the net profit of performance. The initial question, i.e. when breach is efficient, hence is changed into the question when allocating the performance to the original promisee is inefficient.[298] In a contract to convey properties, one can conclude that: if the possible profit from the alternative contract is high enough to exceed the entire profit from performing the first contract, then the performance of the original contract is inefficient.

When this story is applied to a contract to produce goods, it also works. As is noted in Shavell's model, the uncertainty in contracts to produce goods, in most situations, occurs in the production cost. If the cost of performance is so high that it consumes the entire utility yielded by performing the contract, then performing the original contract cannot generate any surplus. Therefore, a decision to stop producing is efficient.

To summarize, in all the cases above, non-performance of the original contract is efficient because non-performance is assumed to bring out a higher economic surplus in total. There are two implications:

> ***Efficient breach is distinguished from inefficient behaviour.*** Since economic efficiency is judged most directly on a profit or surplus basis, one can distinguish efficient behaviour from inefficient behaviour. Efficient breach is justified for creating social surplus or profit. Conversely, a category of breach which may put the non-breaching party in a worse position and decrease the total economic profit is regarded as inefficient breach. In most cases, inefficient breach is also recognized as opportunistic breach that ought to be deterred.[299]
>
> ***Surplus provides an incentive***: The promisor who is contemplating breaking the contract weighs the benefit against the cost and calculates his profit from breach, just

[296] Id.

[297] Id.

[298] The question can also be stated as: in which situation is non-performance of the original contract efficient?

[299] As to the definition of opportunistic breach, there are still a lot of debates. Posner recognizes a category of opportunistic breach where the promisor breaks the contract for no other reason but "to make money". William defines it as occurring "if the breaching party attempts to get more than he bargained for at the expense of the non-breaching party". What's more, the "Restatement (Third) of Restitution and Unjust Enrichment (Tentative Draft No. 4, 2005)" requires the opportunistic breach to be "deliberate" and "profitable", and the injured party has to prove that the ordinary damages would be inadequate. Although there is no uniform definition, it is well-accepted that "opportunistic breach" is exploitative, selfish, advantageous and it creates inefficiency. See Roberts 2008, p. 137–139; Craswell 2009, p. 1509.

as a consumer weighs the benefit of a product against the price.[300] Or we may say, what actually motivates the promisor's breach is the greater profit yielded from the breach.[301] Furthermore, the net profit of breach is yielded through the way that the promisor avoids the costs of performance or obtains an additional surplus. Accordingly, the surpluses are either the costs avoided by the promisor's breach or the profits subsequent to the breach.[302]

3.1.2. The Models of Profits

It is recognized that, what motivates and justifies a breach is neither whether or not there is an alternative bargainer coming to the promisor, nor whether or not there is an additional cost in performance, but it is whether or not the surplus from breach of the contract exceeds the surplus from performance. Besides, what matters in a specific case is not whether or not breaches should be encouraged. Rather, what does matter is to whom the entitlement to the performance should go, or whether the promisor should stop production.[303] Then, we can define economically efficient behaviour by comparing the surplus of non-performance and the surplus of performance (Table 5).

Table 5. The Model of Profits

	Efficient behaviour	
	Non-performance is Efficient	Performance is Efficient
High	*Net profits from the non-performance*	*Net profits from the performance*
Low	*Net profits from the performance*	*Net profits from the non-performance*

According to the standard of efficiency, it is required that non-performance should be encouraged when the profit from it exceeds the profit from the performance, and vice versa. There is still the ideal formula of efficient breach, namely: $Npx + Npy < Nbx + Nby$. In order to achieve this ideal result, a contract-breacher should be able to know both parties' net-profits from performing the contract or breaking it. The contract-breacher (*Y1*) may be capable of estimating his profits from performing a contract (*Npy*) or from breaking a contract (*Nby*). But he can hardly correctly assess the total surplus from performing the original contract or the surplus from non-performance.[304] Because he doesn't have enough incentives to estimate how much his performance is worth for the promise (*Npx*), or he has no incentive to appraise the damage that the breach will cause

300 Cooter 1984, p. 1545.
301 Barnes 1996, p. 20.
302 Siems 2003, p. 29.
303 Brooks 2006, p. 572.
304 Criticisms against the efficient breach doctrine proposed that the promisor (for instance, a seller) would rarely be sufficiently informed of the other party's loss (for instance, a buyer) from breach. This is a crucial argument against the efficient breach doctrine.

to the other party (*Nbx*).[305] In response to this problem, the mechanism of remedy rules are required to provide the parties with incentives and possibilities to choose a more profitable contract or to avoid a less profitable contract. The one important function of contract remedy is to put a price on the behaviour of breach and let a contractual party to decide whether or not he is going to buy this behaviour. Then it is possible to correlate the price of breach to the non-breaching party's net profits from performance or non-performance. In this way, a party who is contemplating a breach has to both consider his partner and his own surpluses from breach. Accordingly, it is assumed that those properly designed remedy rules are able to motivate contractual parties to take an efficient breach and avoid an inefficient one. Finally economic surplus in transactions will be promoted.

3.2. *Just Compensation*

Besides the criterion of surplus, another issue that may influence the efficiency of breach refers to whether or not the compensation of the non-breaching party's loss is just.[306] According to Kaldor-Hicks efficiency, if a movement creates a winner and a loser but the winner can compensate the loser and still have some gain left, then the movement is efficient.[307] Breach of a contract can be Kaldor-Hicks Efficient, but not Pareto Efficient. The breach may create a loser (promisee) although it can generate a higher surplus and enhance the net welfare. Therefore, only if the breacher can still be better off after he fully compensates the other party's loss, will the breach eventually create a Pareto efficient state. It is noted that the compensation by a contract-breacher should place the victim in the position that he would have been in had the contract been performed. Basically the loss that a non-breaching party suffers is the value of the difference between the position that he is in after the breach occurs and the position that he would have enjoyed had the contract been performed. But determining this discrepancy is complicated in the real world.

3.2.1. A Buyer's Loss from Breach

An intentional breach of contract may occur in different occasions and bring out different results. In the case 4.1 above, after *X1* and *Y1* concluded the sales contract, *Y1* may break his promise in several ways. For instance, various situations may occur at the time when Y refuses to transfer the car. At that moment, maybe *X1* has not made any actions as well; or maybe that *X1* has already done the payment of 12,000; or maybe *X1* has invested 200 in renting a parking space. Then how much should the promisee (*X1*) be compensated in those situations? Should he get back all the money that he has lost? What's more, the breach may also be present in a different form, such as in the form of defective performance. Suppose that Y has already handed over the car but the brake doesn't work, or even worse, Y gets personal injury because of the broken brake. Typically, we can categorize the promisee's loss from breach as follows:

305 Siems 2003, p. 52.
306 Zhou 2008, p. 3–4.
307 Id.

3.2.1.1. Expectation Loss

A breach of contract may not cause any actual loss when there is no performance begun by either party or no alternative transaction arranged by either party after the contract has been concluded. In this situation, a non-breaching party may suffer no actual loss. But the loss that a non-breaching party does incur is just his expectation loss,[308] which is calculated as the improvement or enhancement that the non-breaching party would have realized had the breach not occurred.

In sales contracts, a non-breaching party's expectation loss can be calculated on the basis of market price difference or the value difference. When a seller breaches, the expectation loss of the buyer is normally calculated as the difference between the contract price and the value that the buyer places on the goods to be sold. In theory, there are at least three elements determining the buyer's value of the product. The first and more important element to be considered is the market price of the goods at the time when the buyer learns the fact of breach. As a result, the buyer will be able to obtain a substitute product from the market with the money he obtains from the breaching seller and theoretically he suffers no loss in the end. Another element contributing to a buyer's loss from breach is the extra money that he has to pay for a substitute if the aggrieved buyer has arranged an alternative transaction. In such a circumstance, what the buyer has actually lost is the discrepancy between the price set in the substitute contract and the price set in the original contract.[309] However, it may also be argued that the difference between the alternative price and the original contract price is dependent on the buyer's bargaining capacity rather than directly caused by the breach. Beside these two elements, another element that may affect a buyer's loss from breach is the expected profit to be obtained by the buyer from using or reselling the product, particularly in relation to the case where there is no relevant market for measuring the price of the goods. For instance, suppose a seller and a buyer have agreed on a price of 10,000 at the time of contract formation and the buyer expected to resell the product to a third party at 15,000. The buyer's expected loss from breach in this case will be 5,000.

To summarize, the baseline for computing expectation loss is the expected value of performance. However, this baseline is not always that clear. In the following situations, it is controversial whether or not the scope of expectation loss should be extended.

1. **Breach-related Loss (Consequential Loss)**: *Sometimes, a breach may make the injured party bear some extra losses outside their transaction. We call those losses* "breach-related costs", *including any personal injury or property damages or additional expense (such as the expense on repairing the defective product) imposed on the injured party.*

[308] The way of measuring expectation loss is the same as how to measure the amount of expectation damages. Barnes 1996, p. 3.

[309] Cooter & Ulen 2011, p. 309, p. 310.

2. **Opportunity loss:** *in every case, a party to a contract loses an opportunity to enter another contract. We call this opportunity loss.*[310] *A promisee may forgo an opportunity to make an alternative contract if he relies on a promise.*

3. **Partial performance, delay of performance and the promisee's loss:** *Sometimes, a breach occurs because a party has partially or defectively performed. Accordingly, the injured party could realize a part of the value expected from the other's performance. His loss is calculated as the difference between the value anticipated from performance and the actual value received.*[311] *Or sometimes, the promisor is unable to finish the performance at the agreed time and this is a case of delay where the loss of value is similar to that in a case of partial performance.*

3.2.1.2. Reliance Loss[312]

As is noted in chapter 2, based on the anticipation of a promisor's performance, the promisee may invest in reliance so as to enhance the value of performance. Then if the contract is broken, the value of what has been invested in the contractual relationship will also be diminished or destroyed. This refers to the reliance loss of a non-breaching party. The logic is: the more that a promisee invests in reliance, the greater the loss he will suffer. Take the previous assumption (case 4.1 in this chapter) as an example; *X1* cannot use the parking place anymore if he does not have a car. In this case, *X1* loses the 200 that he has invested in renting the parking space. Taking the reliance loss into account, scholars also discuss the impacts of remedy rules on people's reliance investment. This will be considered in the next chapter.

3.2.1.3. Loss of Restitution Interest

Restitution interest refers to the interest conferred by a promisee to the promisor.[313] Loss of restitution interest is usually incurred in the situation where he has "begun performance by, for instance, making a prepayment or beginning to supply the product or service required by the contract".[314] In our example where *X1* has already made the payment of 12,000, the performance loss is presented as this 12,000 transferred by *X1*.

3.2.2. The Indifference Principle

- **Case 4.2:** *X2 has a restaurant and needs a car to offer door-to door service. Y2 has a car and would sell it to X2 for 12,000. They signed a contract on January. 1st and agreed*

310 Id, p. 311–312.
311 Barnes 1998, p. 444.
312 The concept of reliance which is used here is the same as the one defined in chapter 2. Reliance is the change in the promisee's position which is induced by a promise.
313 Eisenberg 2006, p. 560.
314 Barnes 1998, p. 406.

that X2 should pay the money on February. 1st and Y2 deliver the car on February. 15th. After signing the contract, X2 paid 200 as renting fee for a parking space. X2 transferred the money on Feb. 1st but until March.1st he still has not obtained the car because Y2 had sold the car to Z2. Suppose X2 estimates the car's value as 15,000. Besides, without the car, X2's restaurant lost at least 100 orders.

As is noted, whether or not a non-breaching party can obtain just compensation is an important criterion for assessing efficient breach. But then the question is which kind of compensation should be deemed as just compensation. Applying the standard of Kaldor-Hicks efficiency, it is required that the compensation obtained by a promisee should be able to make him indifferent between performance and breach. This is what we call indifference principle (Table 6).

Table 6. Indifference Principle

- **The Indifference Principle:** *If a contract is broken, the promisee will be worse off, compared to the position that he would have enjoyed had the contract been performed. In order to assure that none of the contract parties would be worse off, the legal rule should make sure that the non-breaching party is indifferent, between having the breacher breach and pay damages or having the breacher perform the contract.*[315]
- **Economic justification for the indifference Principle:** As was noted, the liability mechanism could change people's behaviour by providing them with incentives to behave. This story can be applied to the scope of contract compensation. If the compensation is below the value of the promisee's expectation, the promisor would not have the incentive to consider the full value of the contract to the promisee.[316] Therefore, the promisor would take too little precaution or breach too frequently, and the promisee may lower his investment in reliance and performance since he cannot get the guarantee that his expectation will be realized.[317] In another way, over-compensation increases the cost of breach and may create an excessive-performance problem.[318]

When applying the requirement of just compensation into legal practice, however, there are still some problems: 1) Firstly, an important question that a court has to decide on is the scope of compensation, namely, how much a contract breaker should compensate the victim. This question will be more complicated if the loss that a promisee has to bear is extended. Take the case 4.2 as an example. In case 4.2, because of *Y2*'s breach, *X2* has paid 200 as the parking fee (reliance loss), 12,000 as the car's price (loss of restitution interest), he has lost 100 orders (breach-related loss) and he couldn't get the car (3,000 as expectation loss). When the indifference principle is simply applied, then we may agree that the compensation should cover all the losses of *X2* so that the breach cannot make *X2* worse off. However, this simple conclusion may

315 Richard Craswell defined the indifference Principle as: "the stated goal of contract damages is to put the plaintiff in as good a position as he would have been in had the defendant kept his contract". Craswell 1988, p. 636.

316 Eisenberg 2005, p. 980.

317 Id; Mahoney 2000, p. 122–124.

318 Bishop 1985, p. 299–300.

not make us convinced and the question here still needs to be considered. The court may use the "Hardly Rule" and the "Reasonable Certainty Rule" to deny X's claim for recovery of his breach-related loss. Thus, the principle of indifference may not be realized. 2) Secondly, evaluation of a non-breaching party's loss is complicated. Especially, it is difficult for a third party (a court) to measure a loss, such as the loss of personal enjoyment of the goods or service.

3.3. *Transaction Costs under Different approaches to resolve disputes*

Under the circumstances that both the surplus and the loss from the breach are taken into account, it seems that *Y1* should better breach no matter which possibility occurs to the case 4.1. However, it is too arbitrary to make this conclusion since the transaction costs haven't been considered. Suppose that the reputation loss[319] of *Y1* will be 50,000 under the damages rule if he breaches. But if *Y1* chooses to renegotiate with *X1*, he will incur a cost of 10,000. When those costs are taken into account, *Y1* may bear a larger loss or obtain a smaller surplus after breaking the contract, in comparison to re-negotiating with the other party *X1*. Then we can neither assert that *Y1* will definitely decide to breach nor claim that the expectation damages will lead to efficiency, because the efficiency is measured by his final surplus from breach after all costs have been subtracted. This is just one simple example showing the influence of transaction costs on efficiency.[320]

In general, as to the conflicts concerning enforcement of a contact, the parties may solve the problem either by bargaining or resorting to courts. When taking the factor of transaction costs into account, we assume that contractual parties' decision of efficient breach and the efficiency of each approach may also be influenced by the relative transaction costs of operating under that approach.[321] Based on this, if either bargaining or a remedy rule imposed by courts may permit allocating resources to the user who values them more, then the difference in efficiency of the rules is related to the transaction costs under different rules.[322] Contractual parties are supposed to prefer the approach which is less costly so that their net profits from transactions will be maximized. Moreover, if a contract dispute has been brought to a court, then the problem that the court should also recognize is the level of transaction costs facing the plaintiff and the defendant under different remedy rules.[323] Then the question is switched to: what kind of transaction costs do the parties have to incur under different approaches and by which approach will the parties invest the least costs?

319 Reputation loss is the cost of breaching a contract. In this chapter, the concept of transaction cost is used in a broader sense, which includes any costs incurred in transactions. In this sense, the reputation costs are also taken into account as one part of the costs yielded by breach. Macneil 1982, p. 954–955.

320 Id.

321 Macneil 1982, p. 957.

322 Id.

323 Ulen 1984, p. 369.

3.3.1. Types of Transaction Cost

Before comparing the transaction costs to the parties under different approaches, one should first recognize what kind of transaction costs parties normally have to bear. Although this is predominantly an empirical question, from a theoretical perspective one can summarize some typical categories of transaction costs rather than use one general concept of transaction cost in the model. The transaction costs that may influence the efficiency of different institutions governing resource allocation contain:

- **Pre-breach transaction costs**: This refers to the costs of initial planning in the original contract.[324] For instance, this includes the costs of finding each other, exchanging information, negotiation, drafting the contracts, insuring against frustration of the contracts and non-performance[325] and so on. Besides, transaction costs will also rise if the parties to a contract negotiate over breach and damages ex-ante. In that case, the parties will agree on a certain amount of money that the breaching party has to pay to the innocent party and confirm it through a liquidated damage clause.[326] Nevertheless, the ex-ante assessment, negotiating remedies or tailoring remedies to the parties' preferences is costly and this causes extra transaction costs.

- **Post-breach transaction costs**: An important issue that has always been neglected by scholars when discussing the doctrine of efficient breach is the transaction costs incurred ex-post. In the previous case 4.1 in this chapter, disputes arising from allocating the car (either to the promisee *X1* or to the alternative user *Y1* or *Z1*) may be resolved either by the parties themselves or by a court. What is important is through which approach is the transaction cost to the parties of resolving their disputes, lower. If the parties decide to negotiate a mutually satisfactory conclusion to the breach, they have to bear the costs of negotiating with each other, re-evaluating the car, or offering other guarantees, etc. While if a court is involved in resolving the contract dispute, different types of costs will be incurred. The parties have to participate in litigation, hire legal counsel, gather information, or even take the risk of losing the lawsuit. The court is involved, obtaining information, evaluating the contractual parties' subject interests and making correct judicial decisions, and the decisions will be enforced, etc. Those actions are costly. Nevertheless, the emphasis should not be placed on the general amount of transaction costs incurred in using litigation. Rather, a comparison should be made between different remedy systems, namely, the costs of operating different remedy mechanisms.[327] For instance, when

324 Macneil 1982, p. 958.

325 When the parties sign a contract, they want to make sure that the contract will be well performed. For example, a lender may require the borrower to provide him with some guarantee that the borrower would return the money and pay the interest.

326 Cooter &Ulen, p. 321. As to the concept of liquidated damages, it will be discussed in chapter 5.

327 The most common comparison is made between the systems of money damages and specific performance. Ulen 1984, p. 383–384.

the mechanism of money damages prevails, it is indicated that the "informational demands on a court in reaching the efficient level of damages are extremely large". But at the same time, it is also argued that the supervisory costs and enforcement cost are low under this mechanism.[328]

3.3.2. Hypothesis of Transaction Costs

Whether the transaction costs in real-world trading are high or low depends on the specific circumstances of the cases, and hence involve an empirical study. Even so, the models and hypothesis can still give some indication of the relationship between efficiency, breach and legal rules:

- **Transaction costs are zero**: We have noted that in the absence of transaction costs, negotiations between parties will always lead to an efficient allocation of resource. As a result, the parties can always negotiate with each other to reach an efficient conclusion of resource allocation and breach probably becomes the last choice that is taken by bargainers. Take the previous case 4.1 as an example again and let us assume a zero transaction cost world. Suppose allocating the car to a third party *Z1* is the most efficient choice, then either re-negotiation (among *X1*, *Y1* and *Z1*), reselling (from *X1* to *Z1*) or breach (*Y1*) will realize this result. Besides, neither of these methods costs more than the other. Accordingly, no matter which type of remedy rule is applied, the car will be assigned to the most efficient user in the end. In this sense, as long as the remedy rule is not mandatory, the content of the rule is irrelevant in the absence of transaction costs, because the parties can always contract the rule out by bargaining if they dislike it.[329]

- **Transaction costs are positive**: In the real world, transaction costs are positive and impediments to transaction are common. When those costs are taken into account, the efficiency of different dispute solutions also depends on the relative transaction costs generated by each solution.[330] Applied to the hypothesis of efficient breach, the most efficient remedy should minimize the transaction costs of moving the goods (or services) to the highest valued use.[331]

328 In order to decide the amount of compensation, a court needs to get adequate and accurate information and determine the innocent party's expectation interest. But the extent of difficulty in evaluating the expectation interest also depends on a lot of factors, such as the type of goods involved in the contract. Normally, it is more difficult to estimate the value of unique goods which are irreplaceable in the market. As to the influence of transaction cost on legal remedy rules, a more detailed discussion follows later (See section 3 below). Id, p. 384–385.

329 Craswell 1988, p. 632.

330 Macneil 1982, p. 952.

331 Cooter &Ulen 2011, p. 330; Barnes 1998, p. 402.

3.4. *Risk Preference?*

Another possible factor related to efficiency is the risk preference of contracting parties. "The risk preference describes what one does when faced with a risky option and a safer alternative; it is an important predictor of one's behaviour under risk".[332] Within a complex commercial context, some people are in favour of gambling and therefore will take an option even when the probability of benefiting from this option is low. In contrast, some parties might be willing to prefer an option only with a high degree of certainty.[333] Economists use the concept of risk preference to describe people's attitude toward risks.

3.4.1. People's Attitude toward Risk

Suppose there are two options. D1 is a certain option which will generate a profit of 1,000. But D2 is an uncertain one with a 1% chance of generating 10,000 profits. Therefore Both D1 and D2 can create an expected profit of 1,000.[334]

One group of people will take the option D1 because it provides a guaranteed return. In economics, this type of person is said to be "risk-averse". Or in other words, a risk-averse person considers the utility of a certain prospect of money income to be higher than the utility of an uncertain prospect with an equal expected monetary value.[335] Conversely, another group of people are indifferent between the option D1 and D2 as long as the expected values of these two options are same. This group of people is referred to as being "risk-neutral".[336]

In the real-world, most people are assumed to be averse toward risk. They are willing to pay a certain premium to insure against the uncertain loss. This provides an explanation for the existence of insurance contract, which may exchange the possibility of a loss for a smaller, but certain, cost.[337] But some people are assumed to be either neutral toward risk or risk preferring. For instance, gamblers, rock climbers and car drivers are typical groups who are indifferent or favour risks.[338]

3.4.2. Risk and Contract Remedies

The theory of risk may also be applied to the study of contract law. For instance, there is a lot of contract law literature discussing the issues of risk allocation or risk shifting.[339] For example, as indicated by Posner, ordinary commercial contracts have a risk-shifting function so that contracts basically work as insurance. "A contract, by its nature, commits

332 Hsee& Weber 1999, p. 45.
333 Cooter & Ulen 2011, p. 44.
334 The expected profit from D2 is calculated as 1% × 10,000 = 1,000.
335 Cooter & Ulen 2011, p. 45.
336 Id; Kornhauser 1986, p. 688.
337 Posner 2007, p. 105.
338 Cooter & Ulen 2011, p. 45.
339 There are several studies concerning risk-allocation through the institutions of impossibility, foreseeability and contract remedies, such as Posner & Rosenfield 1977; Shavell 1980; Triantis 1992.

both of the parties to a future course of action; and the future is uncertain."[340] So if one party fails to perform a contract and the failure is induced by reasons out of his control, then he is exempted. This offers a basic explanation for the doctrine of impossibility.[341]

What is discussed here, however, is the impact of risk-preference on contract remedies. Kornhauser (1986) used a sale contract to show this. For the buyer, the possibility of non-performance is a risk, which may decrease his profits from contract; while for the seller the risk exists in the possibility of being liable for breach.[342] As was noted, a risk-averse person prefers a certain cost to an uncertain loss. Similarly, a risk-averse buyer may prefer a guarantee of premium from performance, such as a fixed amount of compensation. A risk-averse seller may also prefer a certain amount of profits. If an insurance market is available, then a risk-averse party may insure against a particular risk of non-performance. Otherwise, both the buyer's risk of non-performance and the seller's risk of liability cannot be eliminated.

Now the case 4.1 set in the beginning of this chapter can be reviewed. Both the buyer and seller should understand that there is a risk of a higher outsider bid before the car is delivered. It is also possible that the third party values the goods more than the original buyer.[343] However, the buyer doesn't know whether or not the seller will break his promise, so his expected profit from the sale is uncertain. For the seller, he doesn't know whether the third party comes with a high bid (suppose it is 20,000) or with a low bid (suppose it is 16,000), his expected profit is uncertain as well. By the same token, both of the parties in a contract to produce goods are also faced with a risk that the production cost will be high.

As to risky situations, it is desirable to lower the risks imposed on a risk-averse person. This will be achieved by guaranteeing that a risk-averse party can obtain a certain profit in the event of breach. But the problem is how to know that traders are risk-averse or risk neutral? We can assume four models:[344]

1) Both parties are risk neutral;
2) Both parties are risk averse;
3) A risk-neutral seller & a risk-averse buyer;
4) A risk-averse seller & a risk-neutral buyer.

If the first model is applied, then both the seller and the buyer are indifferent to risks. Then the choice of contract remedy will not affect the efficiency of the risk allocation.[345] So the models to which attention should be paid are those in which one party is risk averse or both the parties are risk averse.[346]

340 Posner 2007, p. 106–108.
341 Id.
342 Kornhauser 1986, p. 705–707.
343 Polinksy 1983, p. 429.
344 Id, p. 431, p. 432.
345 *"Obviously, if both parties are risk neutral, then every damage payment is equally desirable in terms of risk allocation."*Id, p. 431.
346 Discussion about a specific risk model will be shown in chapter 5.

To conclude, in this section, several factors have been discussed that will influence the efficiency of breach and contract remedies. The analysis is developed from a problem that performing a contract may lead to an inefficient result and there are several approaches to cope with this problem. Breach in this situation is assumed to be efficient and the efficient remedy is assumed to be expectation damages. However, such a statement seems to be questionable when the elements that may influence the efficiency of a decision are taken into account. For instance, there must be more arguments supporting that expectation damages will in fact make a non-breaching party indifferent between performance and breach of a contract. In chapter 5 there will be an estimation of whether or not the approach of expectation damages will ultimately promote welfare enhancement.

4. Critiques on the Efficient Breach Doctrine

The doctrine of efficient breach, since its first appearance in the 1970's, has been controversial. In the early work of law and economics, efficient breach theory offered a baseline for supporting the common-law system of expectation damages. The theory was developed within a simple model that expectation damages give people an incentive to perform when, and only when, performance will increase social welfare and to breach would do otherwise. Turning to the stage of contract formation; it is assumed that parties would contract for expectation damages because they are able to "maximize the contract gain for the parties to share".[347] However, as indicated in the previous sections, this simple version of efficient breach, which lacks consideration about the types of contract, the influence of transaction costs and the adequacy of remedy, has been found unsatisfactory. When more factors influencing efficiency and people's behaviour are taken into consideration, the possibility that efficient breach takes place under expectation damages is low. Moreover, observations from judicial activities and empirical evidence point out a divergence between the legal doctrine and actual practice.[348] Several explanations have been proposed to explain this discrepancy between theory and reality. In additional to various moral concerns, another important line of argument derives from the flaws and limits in the theory itself. All of those opposing opinions point to a trend of rejecting the efficient breach doctrine as the normative criterion in the contract system.[349]

4.1. *Economic Critique*

From a law and economics perspective, doubts and questions around the simple efficient breach theory mainly derive from two concerns. 1) More and more scholars are sceptical concerning the possibility that efficient breach takes place in the real world. 2) The simple

347 *"As long as the law requires the seller to pay the promisee's gain if she breaches, she will perform, nevertheless unless her gain from breach would exceed the promisee's gain from performance. Protecting the expectation with a liability rule thus is ex post (that is, at the performance/breach stage) efficient. A promisor breaches only if breach would produce a greater gain overall than performance would have done; otherwise, she performs"* Markovits & Schwartz 1911, p. 1944.

348 Wakol 1999, P. 334–343.

349 Perillo 2000, p. 1106.

combination of efficient breach and expectation damages has no longer been promoted. Rather, efforts are made to establish a more complete framework of contract remedies. "Economically oriented scholars" put their attentions to a broader area rather than focus on the "single perform-or-breach decision". For instance, they found that contract remedies have multiple functions "across the whole of a transaction";[350] they recognize opportunistic breaches which are not merely uneconomic and so on.[351]

4.1.1. Problems in the Economic Basis of Efficient Breach

Within the arguments in law and economic studies, the efficient breach theory is rejected mainly for being cultivated in a simple and short-term perspective. In the eyes of some scholars, the doctrine is established in an ex-post judgement that both of the contract parties will be made better off by ending the contract and by having the promisor pay expectation damages. However, this hypothesis is built upon a hypothesis of a single transaction without concerns of long-term consequences and effects on third parties or the social collective. It is also simply based on the idea that people are motivated to perform contracts because of the threat of legal liability. When it comes to real-life transactions, it is observed that individuals are more likely to prefer cooperation, compromise and negotiation rather than breach.[352] Moreover, some empirical studies also show that people in fact consider more factors than just economic profits and the potential liabilities when making decisions,[353] such as the benefit of retaining reputation and trustworthiness in the market. Then, breach will not become a good choice even when it turns out to be inefficient to perform a contract. Finally, the study of efficient breach only considered a single type of non-performance in the scenario of sales contracts, without taking other types of breach into account. In addition to a seller's non-performance, some breaches might be presented as a delay or a defective performance; some breaches might be committed by a buyer rather than by the seller; some breaches are not only inefficient but also opportunistic[354] and some breaches may occur in labour contracts or lease contracts, etc. Those situations are largely ignored in the simple model of efficient breach.

4.1.2. Weakness in the Compensatory Damages

The rule of compensatory damages (expectation damages), which is grounded upon the efficient breach doctrine has been attacked as well. Attention has been paid to the weaknesses in this compensatory rule. A fatal attack on the efficient breach doctrine is raised upon the inability of expectation damages to fully compensate the non-breaching

[350] For instance, the design of contract remedies will influence the contract price, risk-allocation, contract formation, contract re-negotiations and so on.

[351] Klass 2013, p. 9.

[352] Sidhu 2011, p. 397.

[353] Wakol 1999, p. 344. Klass 2013, p. 8.

[354] Klass 2013, p. 9.

party.[355] Thus, economists conclude that the rule of expectation damages offers insufficient deterrence to inefficient breach[356] and actual promisors will have inadequate incentives to perform and excessive incentives to breach.[357] In this sense, an "efficient breach" may not be efficient anymore, if the non-breaching party can hardly receive enough compensation for his losses.[358]

Conflicting opinions: Will Expectation Damages Induce Over-reliance or Under-reliance?
Expectation damages are criticised for inducing inefficient reliance in addition to being under-compensatory. However, there are some conflicts over the issue whether efficient breach will cause a problem of over-reliance or under-reliance.

- **Over-reliance:** *Theoretically, the rule of expectation damages is justified for being able to fully compensate the expected loss of the promisee and induce the promisor to breach efficiently. However, the mechanism of full compensation is not perfect since it is likely to have a negative impact on the promisee's behaviour.*[359] *If the expectation damages cover all the cost of reliance, it gives rise to a new problem of over-reliance. It is assumed that the expectation damages would remove the incentive for the promisee to consider the risks of breach. The promisee is indifferent to his partner's behaviour of breach or performance, because he can get fully compensated for his loss. Then he will just spend as much as he likes in reliance investment.*

- **Under-reliance:** *In contract, the under-reliance problem is based on the hypothesis that the expectation damages can not offer the promisee full compensation. It is argued that the guarantee from specific performance has a lock-in effect, which allows the promisee to confidently engage in making productive reliance and helps the contract parties sustain long-term cooperation.*[360] *In contrast, expectation damages can always be insufficient to provide this guarantee. A pre-condition is that what a promisee cares about in the transaction is not merely a promise or the right to win a lawsuit. So in our real word, if the promisee is told that his partner can either perform the contract or break his promise and just pay damages, he will also react in a negative way by lowering his investment in reliance.*[361]

355 Section 3.2.2.A gave several explanations to the problem of under-compensatory problem in expectation damages.
356 Farber 1980, p. 1478.
357 "*This theory of contract damages, however, does not fully correspond with reality. For instance, widespread reports of dissatisfaction with the quality of many goods and services indicate that the availability of compensatory damages does not make breach tolerable to consumers. Indeed, for many consumers, the likelihood of collecting such damages is remote, because detection of defects is often difficult, and litigation expenses often make the pursuit of damages impractical. The plight of consumers illustrates serious flaws in the mechanism for collecting compensatory damages. To the extent that every prospective plaintiff is not fully compensated, even though "compensatory" damages are awarded in every litigated case, contracts are under-enforced. Such under-enforcement produces a number of economically undesirable results, including an excessive level of breach and excessive resort to self-help remedies…*" Id, p. 1444, p. 1445.
358 Wakol 1999, p. 351.
359 Posner 2007, p. 122.
360 Eisenberg 2005, p. 1006–1008.
361 Eisenberg assumed a conversation between a buyer and a seller. If the seller says to buyer: "*In all honesty, I should tell you that although I have no present intention to breach this contract, neither do I have a present intention to perform. If a better offer comes along, I will take it and pay you expectation damages. In fact, I will begin actively looking for a better offer right after we sign this contract; let us insert a provision that recognizes I will just do that*". Most buyers will be surprised and "*would either walk away; insist on an explicit contractual provision stating that the seller has a present intention to perform and that any profit on breach and resell will go to the buyer; or demand a payment, in the form of a lower price, for the seller's right to resell.* " Id.

4.2. *Moral Concern*

For most critics, the theory of efficient breach is unjustified for ignoring the moral and ethical factors contained in contract obligations. For those critics, the efficient breach doctrine rests on an assertion by a third party (or just the fallacy of some law and economics scholars) that an immoral activity is efficient and should be encouraged just because it may produce more wealth. From a deontological perspective, an obligation of fulfilling contractual duties is embedded in a contract itself when parties conclude the contract and this obligation should be respected.[362] It is recognized that people contract not only for obtaining promises or compensation, but for accomplishing instrumental goals, such as obtaining ownership, using properties and receiving services. "*The fact that an act leads to good consequences is irrelevant if it is wrong*".[363] Thus, violating a contractual duty in order to seek for a higher surplus is an analogy to stealing a property from another person just because the thief can earn more money from using the property.[364] If the efficient breach theory can be justified for economic reasons, then stealing can also be right as long as a thief places a higher value on some goods than the owner does. Suppose *X3* purchased a TV set for € 1,000. *Z3* saw *X3*'s TV and decided that she would spend up to € 1,500 to purchase a similar one. *Z3*'s friend *Y3* knew this later. *Y3* broke into *X3*'s house and stole the TV set. Then *Y3* sold it to *Z3* for € 1,500 and returned € 1,000 to *X3*. In the end, the result is efficient and *X3* bears no loss; *Z3* obtains the TV and *Y3* gains € 500. If *Y3*'s stealing is considered to be efficient, a doctrine of so called "efficient theft" will be justified and as a result stealing will be encouraged. Moreover, facing the present global economic crisis, more and more scholars try to incorporate more virtue of ethics into law and think about how to rebuild trust, collaboration and harmony in a commercial context.[365] In this sense, the efficient breach doctrine is more to be condemned for cultivating an ethos of self-interested, short-term economic profit-making.

In addition to the moral concerns, arguments from other concerns have also been raised to attack the efficient breach doctrine. For instance, judicial attitude has also been studied so as to explain why we cannot see many cases of accepting efficient breach theory in judicial decisions.[366] Within the judicial process, as is argued, humanistic reactions and bias are engaged rather than pure economic computation. A court would not remove the moral considerations from its decision-making process.[367] In addition,

362 "*As one transactor explained, 'you want performance, not payment for non-performance. [Payment] is not fulfilling your deal.' And, as another transactor put it, 'you do not just breach and pay. This is not done.'*" Bernstein 2001, p. 1755.

363 Katz 2012, p. 787.

364 Id, p. 781.

365 Sidhu 2011, p. 360.

366 "*The theory of efficient breach fails to account for intangible human reactions, such as someone's desire to be declared the winner or to see the other party be declared the loser...However, in a courtroom the judge is face-to-face with human emotions. It is easy for academics to applaud an efficient breach in a classroom, but it is much harder for a judge to explain to the aggrieved party that society benefits from breaches that promote aggregate efficiency...this factor may contribute to the judicial rejection of efficient breach.*" Wakol 1999, p. 345.

367 Id.

the efficient breach theory is criticised for being unnecessary. Traditional scholars suggested that the existing doctrine of impracticability or impossibility can already offer sufficient excuse for a promisor's non-performance in those situations where efficient breach doctrine could apply. Namely, when "the disparity between the consequences of performance and those of breach is sufficiently great", a promisor can be exempted from his obligation and his non-performance is excusable.[368] Therefore, creation of efficient breach, as is stated, would just complicate academic theory.

5. Conclusion

In general, economists set efficiency as the criterion to evaluate people's behaviour within the ongoing contractual relationship. Efficient breach is deemed as a kind of efficient behaviour that increases society's welfare because the benefit of the breach exceeds the loss from it. Many scholars also adopt this doctrine to justify the remedy of expectation damages.

Starting from the traditional theory of efficient breach, this chapter points out that whether or not the approach of breach and compensation is efficient will depend on several correlative factors, such as specific contract forms, the social costs of breaches, the adequacy of compensation and the contract parties' risk preferences. In this sense, one cannot merely insist on the simple combination of efficient breach and expectation damages without any further analysis and investigation. In addition, the existing criticisms of the efficient breach theory are summarized in this chapter as well. The simple efficient breach theory has received various challenges and modifications since the first time when it was proposed. According to moralists, the efficiency of the result of a breach does not necessarily justify the breach since breach is essentially morally wrong. Moreover, some sociological studies have argued that people's decisions actually depend on more than economic profits. In practice, it has been found that people are more likely to be breach-averse. In addition to those concerns from the traditional legal scholars, various criticisms were raised by law and economics scholars, which also place this efficient breach theory under re-evaluation. An important argument is that breach is not the only approach that the parties will choose when it is inefficient for them to adhere to the original contract. In the situation when the performance of the original contract is inefficient, it was indicated that the parties have several alternative approaches to reaching an efficient result. For instance, they may re-negotiate their contractual relationship, or they may resort to their ex-ante arrangement. All these approaches may lead to a profit-enhancing result. Hence, breach is far from the only way to avoid performance of the contract.[369] Instead, a seller's breach and paying expectation damages is considered to be inefficient because of the under-compensation problem in expectation damages as well as the potential bias and errors involved in the damage assessment by a third party. Against this background, chapter 5 will re-evaluate whether expectation damages or any other alternative remedies will lead to an efficient result in different sales contract models.

368 Menetrez 2000, p. 880.

369 Id.

Chapter 5

ALTERNATIVE REMEDIES AND EFFICIENT BREACH

Since the legal remedy rules are able to put a price on breach,[370] then they can alter the incentives of the party who regrets entering into a contract, which will affect the probability of breach.[371] In a simple model, it is assumed that the higher the extent of the remedy, the more costly the breach and the weaker the parties' incentives to breach. According to Shavell, a high damage measure, even punitive damages measure is the best if a contract is completely drafted on the basis of the parties' rational decisions and there are no transaction costs.[372] In a completely specified contract which is established by the consensus of the parties, performance would always be efficient and a high level of remedy would give full guarantee for performance. Nevertheless, most contracts in the real-world are incomplete and transaction costs exist within transactions. In this sense, a moderate level of remedy is considered to be efficient.[373]

This chapter will answer how different contract remedy models can affect efficient breaches and efficiency when the elements of economic surplus, transaction costs, just compensation as well as risk allocation are all taken into account.[374] The question will be addressed of how different remedy rules will deal with a situation where performing the original contract is inefficient. As is mentioned in chapter 4, remedies of contract can be presented in the form of either making a person who breaches perform the contract specifically or making him pay an amount of money. Following this logic, section 1 will develop the comparison between specific performance and expectation damages. It will be structured by analysing these two types of remedies within contexts of a contract to produce a product and a contract to convey a product respectively. Subsequently, section 2 and 3 will focus on monetary remedies. Specifically, section 2 will make a distinction among different types of monetary remedies which is defined by law, including restitution, reliance damages, expectation damages and disgorgement.[375]

370 See chapter 2, section 2.2.3.

371 Mahoney 2000, p. 118.

372 Shavell 2004, p. 305–306.

373 Id, p. 306–309.

374 Some scholars also worry that efficient breach will not promote efficiency and indicate that the concept of efficient breach is incorrect because breach can never be efficient for the whole society. Hence, this chapter will both discuss the relationship between efficient breaches and remedy rules and the relationship between remedy rules and efficiency.

375 Definitions of those remedies will be provided in the section 4. 1.

Moreover, section 3 will discuss the effects of private arrangements on breach and remedies, particularly liquidated damages clauses and penalty clauses. The last question about what can be learned from the efficient breach theory will be dealt with in the final section of this chapter (section 4). In the end, section 5 will also establish a bridge between contract policy and law and economic theory.

1. Specific Performance

The typical contract remedy is manifested as monetary damages or specific performance. The former, monetary damages, is considered as the primary form of remedy in most common law countries. It requires that a breacher pays a certain amount of damages to the aggrieved party. However, in civil law countries, imposition of specific performance is more common when a breach happens. In this situation, the aggrieved party can apply to the court to have the breacher perform the specific actions.[376] In the economic theory of contract remedies, a controversy has existed for a long time concerning whether it is more efficient to grant a remedy in the form of specific performance or monetary damages.[377] Controversy, mostly, concerns the issue of under-compensation, the issue of damage estimation and the issue of people's behaviour under different remedy models. In this section, the comparison will be made on the premise where the performance cost of a contract arises or a higher outside bid occurs after a contract is signed. But before that, an introduction to the legal remedy of specific performance will be provided.

1.1. What is Specific Performance?

By referring to the remedy of "Specific performance", people always think of the remedy that requires the promisor to do what he or she promised in the contract.[378] But in legal theory, specific performance can be understood either as literal performance or equivalent performance.

1.1.1. Literal Performance & Equivalent Performance

In some situations, specific performance means to perform a contract by what is written in the contract, namely literal performance.[379] For instance, in a contract to produce goods, the producer can be forced to produce the contract-for goods personally as required by the contract. This would be applied, especially, in those cases where the performance of the promisor is unique. For instance, a painter may be required to

376 Schäfer & Ott 2004, p. 320.

377 Arguments in favour of expectation damages as the routine remedy can be found, for instance, in Barton 1996, Birmingham 1970 or Schwartz 1979. In contrast, some scholars proposed arguments against expectation damages as the routine remedy. Examples can be found in Kronman 1978, Ulen 1984 or Friedmann 1989.

378 Cooter & Ulen 2011, p. 320.

379 Shavell 2006, p. 839.

accomplish the painting as required by himself, if a remedy of specific performance is awarded. However, in some occasions, specific performance can also present itself in the form of equivalent performance.[380] Then the promisor or a third party may offer an alternative performance for what is required in the contract. Whether or not equivalent performance is possible depends on the extent to which performance can be replaced. On one hand, this form of specific performance can only occur in the contract where the promisor is not the only person who can perform. Such as in a contract to convey common goods, the seller can also ask a third party who sells equivalent products to transfer the contract-for products. On the other hand, it can only be applied to the contract concerning general goods, which can be replaced by equivalent goods in the market. But as to a contract to convey a unique product, such as a famous painting, equivalent performance may not have the same effect as that by literal performance.

1.1.2. Origin of the Dichotomy: A Liability Rule Remedy & A Property Rule Remedy

The first dimension within the legal remedy rules is through a division of specific performance and monetary damages. It is stated that this division derives from the dichotomy of liability rules or property rules, which is also referred to as the famous Calabresi-Melamed dichotomy.[381]

- **Calabresi-Melamed dichotomy**[382]: *The dichotomy of a property rule and a liability rule concerns the ways how the law can protect an entitlement. A property rule protection makes the permission of an entitlement's owner a necessary condition for transfer of this entitlement. So another person can only take the entitlement from the holder when the holder agrees (for instance, the owner sells it). If another party acquires an entitlement without the owner's permission, the law will impose a specific sanction on him, which is normally represented as an injunction, a fine or imprisonment. In contrast, a liability rule protection only requires the infringer of the entitlement to pay the owner monetary compensation. The sum of compensation will be decided by a third party, typically a court.*

Similarly, the contract expectation is treated as an entitlement that receives the law's protection. Contract law would protect the promisee's expectation by a property rule. It requires that a promisor to a contract should always comply with the contract unless he gets the permission from the promisee. If he fails to perform, the law will impose an injunction on him, normally an order of specific performance. However, the law can also offer the promisee a liability remedy, that is to say, monetary damages. That is, the promisor is free to breach if he would compensate the promisee's loss, which is based on

380 The concept of equivalent performance is used by Shavell. It is just a theoretical concept which hasn't been used in legal practice. What he calls equivalent performance would not be called specific performance in Anglo-American Law. Id.

381 Calabresi & Melamed 1972, p. 1089.

382 Calabresi & Melamed 1972, P. 1090–1093; p. 1105–1110.

the courts' evaluation.[383] In this sense, the promisee is merely granted the value that he places on the performance of the contract. Then, the difference between the remedy of specific performance and monetary damages can be summarized as:

1. Under the rule of specific performance, non-performance of a contract can only be achieved with the permission of a promisee. Conversely, if the default remedy is set as monetary damages, a promisor is free to break the contract without the agreement of the other party, as long as he decides to pay compensation.[384]
2. In the case where a promisor breaks his promise, the specific performance rule gives the promisee a right to insist on the actual (or specific) performance of the promise; but the damage rule only awards the promisee a right to claim monetary compensation.[385]
3. When the monetary damages are applied, a third impartial party (a court or an arbitration tribunal) will be involved in assessing the amount of damage compensation.

1.1.3. An Introduction to the Comparison between Specific performance and Expectation Damages

After establishing a framework of differences between specific performance and monetary damages, it is possible to develop the economic analysis with different contract models. In the first model (case 5.1), a contract to produce a product is presumed. After the contract is signed, an unfortunate contingency arises which increases the production costs. In the second model (case 5.2), a contract to convey a product is established and what may cause the seller to break his promise is a higher outsider bid. Since the intention is to compare the effects of specific performance remedy and the expectation damages, it is assumed that the goods have not been passed on to the buyer[386] and the buyer hasn't incurred any actual loss except for his expectation loss.[387]

After establishing the contract model, the comparison between expectation damages and specific performance will be developed around four major questions, namely:

1) Which rule is able to promote the creation of highest surplus?
2) Which rule is able to implement the "indifference principle"?
3) Which rule is less costly?
4) How will the risk be allocated under different remedy rules?

383 Zhou 2008, p. 4.

384 Id.

385 Calabresi & Melamed 1972, P. 1105.

386 If the property has been passed to the buyer, the rule of property law will also be involved. For instance, in a context of contracts to convey goods, we need to judge whether the outside bidder is bona fide or not. Zhou 2008, p. 14–16.

387 For instance, the buyer hasn't made any payment or reliance investment.

1.2. *Comparison in the Model of Contracts to Produce Goods*

- **Case 5.1:** *Y1 agrees to produce a car and sell it to X1 at a price of € 10,000. Suppose at the time when X1 and Y1 enter into the contract, Y1 estimates the production cost of the car will be € 5,000 but X1 estimates he can resell the car for € 15,000. Suppose two possibilities after formation of the contract. If Y1 is lucky, the* production cost *(or "PC") will not increase; but if Y1 is unlucky, the cost for producing the car will increase to € 16,000.*[388]

1.2.1. The Higher Surplus Standard

Table 7 and Table 8 show the surplus of each party when the production cost is high and when it is low. In accordance with the efficiency standard, the producer *Y1* is required to perform the contract when performance is cheap (PC = € 5,000) and to break the contract when performance is expensive (PC = € 16,000).[389]

Table 7. Surplus of Each Party if Y1 is Lucky

PC = 5,000	Y1's decision	X1	Y1	Total
No remedy	*Breach*	*0*	*0*	*0*
Specific performance	*Perform (√)*	***5,000***	***5,000***	***10,000***
	Breach	*5,000*	*5,000*	*10,000*
Expectation damages	*Perform (√)*	***5,000***	***5,000***	***10,000***
	Breach	*5,000*	*-5,000*	*0*

Table 7 depicts each party's surplus in the case when performance is cheap. Suppose *Y1* breaches. If no remedy is available or the remedy of expectation damages is applied, then *Y1* is free to break his promise and non-performance will be achieved. Besides, since nothing is produced, there is no profit shared by *X1* and *Y1* (the total surplus is 0). The only difference, however, is that there is a money transfer from the contract breaker *Y1* and the innocent party *X1* if the remedy of expectation damages is used. Therefore, if *Y1* breaches, *Y1* will suffer a surplus loss (-€ 5.000) and *X1* will obtain a surplus equal to his expectation value (€ 5,000). The producer, rationally, will choose to perform the contract rather than breach. In contrast, the specific performance rule doesn't give *Y1* an opportunity to escape his obligation without *X1*'s agreement. So *Y1* will always produce the car as agreed.

388 These two cases are modified from the cases that have been used by Cooter and Ulen. See Cooter & Ulen 2011, p. 326–331. Besides, a similar examination can be found in Eisenberg 2005, p.998–1015.

389 The currency unit is Euro in both Table 1 and Table 2.

Table 8. Surplus of Each Party if Y1 is Unlucky

PC = 16,000	Y1's decision	X1	Y1	Total
No remedy	*Breach*	*0*	*0*	*0*
Specific performance	***Perform (√)***	***5,000***	***-6,000***	***-1,000***
	Breach	*5,000*	*-6,000*	*-1,000*
Expectation damages	*Perform*	*5,000*	*-6,000*	*-1,000*
	Breach (√)	***5,000***	***-5,000***	***0***

Table 8 indicates each party's surplus in the case when performance is expensive. By the same token, if *Y1* breaches, no surplus will be shared without any remedy or with the expectation damages. However, a negative surplus of -€ 1,000 will be created if *X1* insists on producing the car or he is forced to do so. A rational producer, in this case, will probably take the breach decision or negotiate with the seller so as to avoid a larger loss (-€ 6,000). So when the performance cost is high, only the expectation damages give the promisor an incentive to break the contract freely, so as to avoid performance. If the specific performance is the routine remedy, non-performance can only be achieved through re-negotiation between *Y1* and *X1*. But if re-negotiation fails, an inefficient result will be created.[390]

To summarize, an efficient result may be created either under the remedy of specific performance or expectation damages. But the way to avoid inefficient performance is different. As to the specific performance, it gives a promisee a right to the promisor's performance, regardless of its cost. Hence a promisee has a right to compel the promisor to buy the promisee's right to performance. If the promisee asserts this right, then the promisor will be forced to perform even when the costs of performance are high.[391] So the only way to avoid costly performance is re-negotiation. In contrast, the expectation damages give a promisee a right to compensation when a contract is broken. Therefore, the promisor can avoid costly performance by breaking his promise as long as he compensates the innocent party. In this sense, under expectation damages, efficiency is achieved by encouraging efficient breach and efficient performance; while under specific performance, efficiency is realized when re-negotiation is possible.

1.2.2. The Indifference Principle Standard

As is showed in the aforementioned table 1 and table 2, no matter whether the remedy is specific performance or expectation damages, the promisor will be put in as good a position as he would have enjoyed had the promisor performed the contract (Npx = € 5,000). In this sense, both remedies may give full effect to the indifference principle ideally. But doubts arise as to the practical operation of remedies.

390 Depoorter & Tontrup 2012, p. 685.
391 Cooter & Ulen 2011, p. 327.

The comparison starts from the analysis of the case 5.1. As required, the content of *Y1*'s obligation in case 5.1 is to produce a car. The production will create an expected surplus of € 5,000 for *X1* since he can resell the car for 15,000. To ensure that *X1* will obtain the value of expectation fully, a court may require *Y1* to accomplish the production or to pay damages of € 5,000 to *X1*.

1.2.2.1. Can Expectation Damages really Fully Compensate the Promisee?

Compared to specific performance, expectation damages are questioned more often for being inadequate. It is suggested that the remedy of expectation damages fails to leave the victim indifferent between performance and compensation because every prospective plaintiff actually cannot get full compensation. The factors that may limit the scope of compensation are normally summarized as:

- **Under-compensatory damages rules:** *In contract law, several limiting doctrines have been set up to limit the scope of damage compensation. As is noted in the previous chapter, under English law, the "Hadley rule" limits the recovery to the losses that the promisor could ordinarily foresee at the time of contract formation. Besides, the "reasonably certain" rule and the "emotional damage" rule deny recovery for losses that are either uncertain or emotional. Those limiting doctrines, as is argued, have been used in a highly flexible way by courts in order to prevent recovery of damages that seem to over-compensate the promisee.*[392] *Hence, in this case, if X1 wants to get full compensation of its expected loss (5,000), he has to prove this amount of damages are foreseeable, reasonably certain and non-emotional. In this case, suppose if X1 suffers other losses beyond the scope of expectation damages. Imagine that X1 might lose a client who is assumed to buy the car that X1 wants to resell. Or breach might also cause frustration and anger. It's difficult for X1 to get fully compensated for those losses.*

- **Inaccuracy of calculation:** *Inaccurate calculation of expectation damages is deemed to be the second argument against monetary damages. This is firstly caused by the fact that the one who is going to measure the damages is a court, rather than the promisee, who posses better information than the court.*[393] *Therefore, a court may err in assessing the accuracy of a promisee's claim. This is the first reason leading to the problem of inaccurate calculation. In addition, the subjective value attached to a contract is always neglected by courts. If in this case, the purpose that X1 orders the car is to use this special car for his wedding, rather than resell it then the baseline for calculation becomes complicated.*[394] *The last point concerns unique goods, which can be produced only by the promisor. Conventionally, a court uses the baseline of "market price difference" or "lost profits" to assess the amount of compensation.*[395] *But as to the*

392 Posner 1999, p. 176.
393 Schwartz 1979, p. 277.
394 Id, p. 276.
395 Eisenberg 2005, p. 991.

standard of market price, it might grant a price below the actual value of unique goods to the promise. When the later standard is applied, it is then difficult to obtain enough information for assessing the value that a promisee places on the work. Therefore, when the subject of a contract is a unique item, awarding expectation damages can hardly realize the indifference principle[396]

- **Insolvency:** *Insolvency is another concern that is raised to criticize the compensatory remedy. In the case that the breacher is insolvent, the promisee can hardly get full compensation.*[397] *In this case, the rule of expectation damages transfers the risk of insolvency to the promisee. However, if the remedy that the promisee can obtain is specific performance, then the promisee could claim for the performance within the liquidation procedure. Therefore, it is argued that a promisee will almost invariably prefer specific performance to damages.*[398]

- **Refusal to compensate:** *The court-awarded compensation is also weak if a breacher refuses to pay damages.*[399] *In the extreme situation, suppose that the contract-breaker is threatened that he would be put in prison if he refuses to pay damages. He may still refuse to compensate the victim and choose to be imprisoned (this problem will also occur when specific performance is applied). In this sense, all the legal remedies, at some level, are optional and so is specific performance. Scholars thus summarize those types of refusal behaviour as post-breach behaviour. Under the circumstances where a contract-breaker fails to pay the full amount of the promisee's damages, he may obtain some economic gain by using the money that he should have paid. Conversely, the promisee may bear economic losses because of the delay in obtaining the payment. Hence, scholars suggest that the essential issue involved in such post-breach behaviour is how to allocate the use of the money that the breacher should have paid.*[400] *It is suggested that the monetary benefit from refusing compensation should be disgorged from the promisor who refuses to pay damages. Moreover, in order to force a breacher to make compensation, a court may take specific executive measures, such as seizing, freezing or selling the breacher's properties.*[401]

1.2.2.2. Can Specific Performance really Fully Compensate the Promisee?

Specific performance, in contrast to the monetary damages, receives less criticism concerning the problem of under-compensation. Since the purpose of specific performance

396 Mahoney 1995, p. 139.

397 Eisenberg 2005, p. 996.

398 But it depends on whether or not insurance is available as well. If the frustrated promisee could obtain full recovery from an insurance company, the worry from the insolvency problem will not exist. Id.

399 Brooks 2006, p. 572.

400 It is suggested that we should consider which party has superior investment opportunities at the time of breach. De Long 1989, p. 755–760.

401 For instance, see 中华人民共和国民事诉讼法 (Civil Procedure Law of the People's Republic of China), Article 241-Article 255.

is to have a contract-breaker satisfy his contractual obligation, there is no need to assess the expected loss of the non-breaching party. Besides, as to the unique goods which cannot be replaced in the market, the promisee's position will be untouched only if he can obtain the goods as agreed. Then it is more likely that the specific performance can fully realize the indifference principle.[402] However, there are still some doubts.

One argument is that specific performance is likely to be unsatisfactory in cases where the promisor's performance is complex. Especially, in contracts to produce goods, applying the remedy of specific performance faces more difficulties. Since a promisor's obligation in a contract to produce goods consists of a series of conducts, a reluctant promisor is more likely to commit defective performance. For instance, he may lower the standard of production or use inferior materials or take less care during the process of production. Moreover, if a promisor is forced to perform and he refuses, there is no remedy other than to imprison his body.[403] This problem caused by a promisor's refusal to perform is similar to that caused by the promisor's refusal to compensate. In this case, a promisee cannot get exactly what he expected.

In conclusion, generally, the task of fully compensating a promisee seems to be accomplished better by the rule of specific performance than by the rule of expectation damages. However, when applied to a contract to produce goods in legal practice, it is quite hard to reach a final conclusion. Compared to expectation damages which are mainly criticised for being under-compensatory, specific performance has more problems concerning operation and monitoring. Moreover, the question which type of remedy complies better with the indifference principle should still be examined in empirical studies, rather than be based on a theoretical discussion only. More practical evidence is needed in order to prove that either the under-compensation problem is much more serious in expectation damages or that execution is more problematic in specific performance.

1.2.3. The Transaction Cost Standard

In case 5.1, when the production cost is 16,000, production of the car is inefficient. As is shown in the case, it is possible to achieve an efficient result no matter whether the routine remedy is expectation damages or specific performance. The difference, however, exists in the way parties can avoid excessive performance. The rule of expectation damages allows a promisor to break his promise if he finds the performance cost is too high. In comparison, when specific performance becomes the routine remedy, the promisor can avoid inefficient performance only by negotiating with the other party ex-ante or ex-post.[404] Hence, it is necessary to compare the transaction costs of resolving a contract conflict using different approaches. Accordingly, the third baseline for comparison is the standard of transaction costs. By holding this standard, to compare the transaction costs

402 For the promisee, the under-compensatory problem will with expectation damages when the subject of the contract is unique. So he will be more likely to prefer specific performance. Kronman 1978, p. 368–369.

403 Brooks 2006, p. 571.

404 By ex-ante negotiation, the parties can opt for monetary damages as the contract relief or agree that the promisor can be exempted from performance in the situation when performance cost is high. By ex-post negotiation, the parties can also reach a mutual agreement to avoid a wasteful performance.

under the mechanisms of specific performance and expectation damages seems appropriate. A less costly remedy is assumed to be more desirable to contract parties.

As legal remedies awarded by courts, the specific performance and expectation damages share some similarities. On the one hand, both remedy types are claimed by a plaintiff in either litigation or arbitration. The plaintiff has to pay the litigation fee, hire legal counsel, suffer the loss of time, face the risk of losing the lawsuit, etc. So litigation costs will be caused no matter which remedy is applied. On the other hand, to execute legal remedies will be costly. After a contract-breaker is ordered to pay damages or to perform the contract, a court might supervise the process of execution. This may also involve time, money and energy. In the discussion below, however, attention is given more to the differences between two remedies.

First, it is assumed that the contents of the legal remedy will affect the ex-ante transaction costs (Table 3). The question is whether the ex-ante costs will increase, decrease or remain unaffected when a certain remedy rule prevails. The ex-ante transaction cost in this chapter refers to the costs involved in contract formation. As argued by some scholars, whether a legal remedy will increase or decrease the contract formation cost depends on the subject of a contract.[405] If the performance concerns unique goods, it seems that specific performance is more likely to lower the contract formation cost. The reason, given by Ulen, is that specific performance provides the promisee with a stronger guarantee of the performance. Then, for a promisee, a provision of specific performance is much more preferable. While for the promisor, he may also be willing to accept a provision like this because the chance of his receiving a more attractive third-party offer is not very high. Hence, the parties don't need to turn to a third party to offer guarantees or insurance.[406] Other things being equal, when the subject of a contract is a general item of goods, alternatives are possible. Before a contract is fulfilled, the buyer can obtain an alternative from another offer, and the producer is more likely to receive alternative bidders as well.[407] In this case, both parties prefer to retain the flexibility that comes with a monetary remedy. As a conclusion, compared to monetary damages, specific performance may increase the formation cost of contracts to produce general goods, because parties would take some formation expense to avoid specific performance.[408]

Second, the content of the legal remedy may have an effect on the ex-post transaction cost as well (Table 4). More specifically, the costs involved when a different type of remedy is applied are as follows:

- **Re-negotiation and re-negotiation costs**: *As was noted in part 2 of this chapter, transaction costs influence the way how people protect entitlements and the way of resolving contract conflicts. Without transaction costs or with low costs, contractual conflicts are mainly dealt with in the market. However, if the transaction costs are high,*

405 Ulen 1984, p. 376–379. Kronman 1978, p. 366.

406 As is noted by Ulen, the promisor is the cheapest provider of insurance against non-performance or of guarantee to performance. Id.

407 Kronman 1978, p. 368–369.

408 Id.

the market cannot always offer an efficient solution to contract disputes. Then judicial decision and supervision will make a difference. This story is applicable to the comparison between expectation damages and specific performance. Awarding expectation damages would allow a promisor to break the contract freely without the permission of the promisee. In this sense, the expectation damages can help contract parties to save the re-negotiation costs. Conversely, specific performance induces costs of re-negotiation because it forces a promisor to re-negotiate with the promisee in order to be absolved from contractual duties. Then a crucial issue is whether re-negotiations are easily achieved and whether the costs will be low.[409] *If the answer is positive, specific performance probably promotes re-negotiation eventually.*

- **Court Costs**: *The court costs refer to the costs involved in the legal procedure. Except for the normal costs of bringing a lawsuit and hiring legal counsel, some other types of costs will be necessary for making and executing legal decisions. As to the expectation damages, the major part of costs occurs in assessing the value of expectation (cost of assessment). In a case where a producer breaches, the amount of compensation is calculated as the difference between the buyer's reservation price for the performance and the contract price.*[410] *A court, then, needs to obtain sufficient information to know the buyer's reservation price. Especially, if the subject of the contract is a unique item of goods, the information cost of assessing the subject value that the promisee places on performance will be extremely high.*[411] *Comparatively, the information requirement is lower when the specific performance is ordered by the court. Because what a court needs to decide is just whether or not breach occurs. Nevertheless, the situation of executing legal relief is to the contrary. When specific performance is the routine remedy, the executing costs would be higher because it is much more difficult to monitor the conduct of performance. Moreover, this problem of monitoring would be severe when a reluctant promisor is forced to produce some goods or provide a service specifically.*[412] *However, in case 5.1, the increasing performance cost makes performance inefficient, hence, execution of specific performance becomes unnecessary. So in this section the executing cost will not be a concern.*

- **Cost of finding a substitute**: *In many cases, a promisee's purpose of transacting is to obtain the contract-for goods or services. So when a promisor breaches, the promisee*

409 Ulen 1984, p. 379.

410 As indicated in the last chapter, the reservation price is the highest price that a buyer is willing to pay or the lowest price that a seller is willing to accept.

411 Besides, some scholars also worry that the plaintiff in a contract conflict will have every incentive to exaggerate his reservation price. So he will try to obtain more evidence to prove his arguments. Ulen 1984, p. 384.

412 "Further, when the promisor's performance must be rendered over time, as in construction or requirements contracts, it is costly for the promisee to monitor a reluctant promisor's conduct. If the damage remedy is compensatory, the promise would prefer it to incurring these monitoring costs. Finally, given the time necessary to resolve lawsuits, promisees would commonly prefer to make substitute transactions promptly and sure later for damages rather than hold their affairs in suspension while awaiting equitable relied." Schwartz 1979, p. 277.

would make a substitutive transaction to realize the effect of performance that the promisor failed to render. But if a contract-breaker is ordered to perform the contract specifically, then finding substitutes becomes unnecessary for the promisee. Suppose in case 5.1, X1 has already signed a resale contract with a third party and he has to pay high damages if he fails to transfer the car on time. Then if Y1 refuses to produce the car as contracted for, and is only willing to pay compensation, X1 will probably try to find alternatives before the deadline of handing over the car. Assume, again, the car is a special one which can only be produced by Y1; the cost of finding an alternative will be extremely high. In this sense, the rule of expectation damages may cause promisees to incur a cost of finding a substitute and this would be relatively higher if the subject of the contract is unique.[413]

To summarise, when it is possible to avoid unnecessary performance costs both under expectation damages and specific performance, the difference is the costs arising out of these two rules. The ex-post costs that may arise under specific performance are mainly the re-negotiation costs; while the expectation damages, mostly, may induce the costs of assessment and the costs of finding a substitute. In order to find out which remedy is least costly, more evidence is needed to compare whether the costs of re-negotiation are higher or lower than the costs of legal assessment and finding a substitute. Furthermore, the relationship between the legal remedy rules and ex-ante transaction costs is also determined by the subject of a contract. Generally, the specific performance may lower the costs when it is a contract to produce unique goods. But when it comes to a contract to produce a general product, the expectation damages are less costly.

Table 9 shows the impact of both remedy rules on ex-ante transaction costs and table 10 indicates the ex-post costs occurring to different remedy rules.

Table 9. Impact of Remedies on Ex-ante Transaction Costs

	Specific performance	Expectation damages
For Unique goods	*Lower the formation costs*	
For General goods		*Lower the formation costs*

Table 10. Types of Ex-post Transaction Costs

		Specific performance	Expectation damages
Re-negotiation cost		(√)	
Court costs	Litigation cost	(√) *legal aid, courts ...*	(√) *legal aid, courts...*
	Assessment cost		(√) *information*
Cost of finding substitute			(√)

[413] Id, p. 275.

1.2.4. Risk-aversion

As noted above, whether or not a particular remedy rule can remove contract risks from a risk-averse party is also a criterion for judging the efficiency of that rule. A person who is risk-averse dislikes uncertainty. In a contract to produce goods, it is supposed that that the risk derives from the unexpected rising cost of production, which might influence the producer's decision of producing or not.[414] If a party is risk-averse, he is more likely to prefer a contract which guarantees him a fixed profit regardless of what production costs were realized.[415] The goal of risk removal can be realized by lowering the uncertainty of profits (or loss) that a risk-averse party can obtain. Applying this standard, case 5.1 will be analysed in detail.

First, consider that the routine remedy is expectation damages. As is showed in table 1 and 2, no matter whether the production cost is high or low, the producer has to pay damages amounting to 5,000 to the innocent buyer. In that case, the profit that the buyer may obtain is affected by neither the uncertain production cost nor by the producer's decision of breach or performance. But the risk of uncertainty is shifted to the producer. When the production cost is low (5,000), he can obtain a profit of 5,000 by performance; while if the production cost is high (16,000), then the profit he can obtain from performance is decreased to -6,000. In this case, a rational producer would prefer to break the contract and limit his risk to -5,000 (the value that the buyer placed on performance).[416] Expectation damages, thus, transfer the risk to the promisor. Therefore, the remedy of expectation damages insures the buyer against the risk of non-performance completely and also limits a producer's risk to the expected value of the other party. It will optimally allocate the contract risks when the buyer is risk-averse and the producer is risk-neutral.[417]

Then consider the opposed case. Under specific performance, the seller has to perform the contract no matter whether the performance cost is high or low. His profit or loss would be influenced substantially by the production cost. If the cost is 16,000, the producer still has to perform the contract and bears a loss of 6,000 unless he could obtain a release from the buyer through re-negotiation. But if re-negotiation fails, the producer will eventually have to bear this amount of loss.[418] In comparison, the seller's profit is unaffected by the production cost as well because he can always get the car as required. Therefore, specific performance may impose a substantial risk on the producer (promisor).

414 We only assume the risk in a contract to produce goods comes from the uncertain production cost. Hence the producer will breach when the production cost is relatively high.

415 Kornhauser 1986, p. 706.

416 Shavell 2006, p. 845.

417 "Suppose that the seller is risk-neutral but the buyer risk-averse. Expectation damages completely insure the buyer against loss so that she suffers no risk costs. The seller does not suffer any risk costs either because he is indifferent to risk. In this simple case a rule of expectation damages remains efficient." Kornhauser 1986, p. 706; Polinksy 1983, p. 434.

418 Shavell 2006, p. 845.

1.3. *Comparison in the model of Contracts to convey goods*

- **Case 5.2:** *Y2 agrees to sell an old car to X2 at a price of 10,000. Suppose at the time when X2 and Y2 enter the contract, Y2 values the car at 5,000 but X2 estimates he can resell the car for 15,000. After Y2 has signed the contract. Z2 explains that he desperately needs this car and he would pay 20,000. Suppose the car is worth 25,000 for Z2 and the highest price he would bid is 25,000.*

1.3.1. The Higher-Surplus Standard

When an alternative bidder comes into play, an efficient result is to allocate the goods to the party who can generate a higher surplus. In our case 5.2, allocating the car to Z2 will generate a higher profit of 2,000, so it is more efficient to allocate the car to *Z2*, rather than to the original buyer *X2*. Table 11 and Table 12 respectively depict each party's surplus in the cases when the remedy is expectation damages and when the remedy is specific performance.

Table 11. Surplus of Each Party under Expectation Damages[419]

		X2	Y2	Z2	Total
	Value	*15,000*	*5,000*	*25,000*	
Expectation damages	Y2 sells the car to X2	*5,000*	*5,000*	*0*	*10,000*
	Y2 sells the car to Z2	*5,000*	*10,000*	*5,000*	20,000

Table 11 depicts each party's surplus and the total surplus in the case with the remedy of expectation damages. As is shown in the table, an efficient outcome will occur only if Y2 breaks the first contract and then sells the car to Z2, whose reservation price is higher (25,000). If the seller Y2 resells the car to Z2, then the car will end up in the hand of Z2 and a total surplus of 20,000 will be created. In this case, the surplus yielded from breach will be shared among X2, Y2 and Z2. Hence, every party is better off. Y2's breach refers to what we call efficient breach. In contrast, if Y2 performs the original contract by allocating the car to X2, a less efficient result will be yielded unless X2 re-sells the car to Z2.

419 We use "*N*" to indicate the net profit, "*p*" to denote performance and "*b*" to denote breach. When Y2 performs and the car is sold to X2, each person's profit can be calculated as this: the Npx2 = 15,000 – 10,000 = 5,000; Npy2 = 10,000 – 5,000 = 5,000; Nz2 = 0; Npx2 + Npy2 + Nz2 = 5,000 + 5,000 + 0 = 10,000. If Y2 breaches and resells the car to Z3, then the net profits are calculated: Nbx3 = 15,000 – 10,000 = 5,000; Nby3 = (20,000 – 5,000) – (15,000 – 10,000) = 10,000; Nz2 = 25,000 – 20,000 = 5,000; Nbx2 + Nby2 + Nz2 = 5,000 + 10,000 + 5,000 = 20,000.

Table 12. Surplus of Each Party under Specific Performance[420]

		X2	Y2	Z2	Total
	Value	*15,000*	*5,000*	*25,000*	
Specific performance	X2 keeps the car	*5,000*	*5,000*	*0*	*10,000*
	X2 resells the car to Z3	*10,000*	*5,000*	*5,000*	20,000

Suppose in the case when specific performance applies (Table 12), an efficient result will be the outcome only when X2 resells the car to Z2, unless re-negotiations between X2 and Y2 happen and X2 agrees to transfer the car to Z2 in the name of Y2.[421] The seller Y2 is required to perform the first contract specifically, but if re-sale is possible, a total surplus of 20,000 will still be yielded and X2 can also obtain a higher surplus. However, if the buyer X2 keeps the car for himself, less profit will be induced.

From the two tables it can be observed that it is possible to pass the car to Z2 under either the specific performance or the expectation damages. In addition, realization of efficient reallocation of goods is conditional no matter which remedy is applied. That is, only under the condition when re-negotiation or re-sale is possible, the product will be reallocated to the outside bidder who comes with a higher reservation price. If the rule of expectation damages applies, the car will be transferred to Z2 only when Y2 breaches the first contract and signs another sale contract with Z2; while if specific performance applies, Z2 will obtain the car only when there is a renegotiation between X2 and Y2 or a re-sale contract between X2 and Z2. However, the possibility of efficient breach, the distribution of the total surplus, and the pathway of the individual surplus is different when different remedy rules apply.[422]

Firstly, the possibility that efficient breach takes place is higher when the remedy is expectation damages, which gives the promisor a choice between performing or breaching and paying damages. Breach is efficient if the promisor resells the goods to the outside bidder who comes with a higher reservation price and pays full compensation to the original buyer. However, when the remedy is specific performance, the possibility of efficient breach is very low. Namely, it happens only when the promisor can "bribe" the promisee to waive the right to specific performance.[423]

420 When X2 keeps the car, each person's profit can be calculated as this: the Nx2 = 15,000 – 10,000 = 5,000; Ny2 = 10,000 – 5,000 = 5,000; Nz2 = 0; Nx2 + Ny2 + Nz2 = 5,000 + 5,000 + 0 = 10,000. If X2 resells the car to Z2, then the net profits are calculated: Nx2 = (15,000 – 10,000) + (2000 – 15,000) = 10,000; Ny2 = 10,000 – 5,000 = 5,000; Nz2 = 25,000 – 20,000 = 5,000; Nx2 + Ny2 + Nz2 = 10,000 + 5,000 + 5,000 = 20,000.

421 Re-negotiation can also achieve an efficient result under specific performance. Namely, Y2 can re-negotiate with X2 to be released from the first contract; or he can ask X2 to transfer the car to the second buyer Z2. The difference between re-sale and re-negotiation is who sells the goods. If re-negotiation takes place, the one who is selling the goods is still the original seller Y2; but if re-sale happens, then the seller is the original buyer X2. A Similar case can be found in Cooter & Ulen 2011, p. 328–331.

422 Cooter & Ulen 2011, p. 328–331.

423 Schwartz 1979, p. 89.

Secondly, who will enjoy the highest share of the total surplus? It depends on the types of remedy. Under the specific performance rule, the first buyer *X2* will resell the product to the second bargainer Z2 after he obtains the car from *Y2*. In the end, *X2* will gain a total surplus of 10,000,[424] including the surplus of 5,000 that he may gain from his transaction with *Z2*.[425] But Y2 only enjoys the surplus created by the first contract, namely, 5,000 (or 10,000 – 5,000). In comparison, under the expectation damages, Y2 can choose either performing or breaching and paying damages. If Y2 breaches and resells the car to Z3, it is Y2 that keeps a higher surplus from resale after compensating X2. That is 10,000.[426] But the share X2 can enjoy from the total surplus is what he could expect from the first contract (with Y2), namely 5,000. In general, the distribution of the surplus favours the promisor when the remedy is expectation damages, but favours the promisee when the remedy is specific performance.[427]

Thirdly, the pathway of the individual surplus differs from case to case. In the case when the rule of specific performance applies, X2 enjoys a larger share in the total surplus by first contracting with Y2 and later contracting with Z2. Similarly, Y2's share in the surplus derives from his agreement with the first buyer X2. Therefore, when the rule of specific performance is the routine remedy, individual gains are obtained only through the way of private negotiation.[428] Conversely, the award of expectation damages is based on the evaluation by a third party, namely the court. For X2, what he can obtain is the court-awarded compensation of his expectation loss. For Y2, he enjoys the surplus from the second contract after compensating the first buyer. In this situation, the gains are divided both through litigation and negotiation. The contractual parties bear both the negotiation costs and the court costs (including the costs of litigation, the cost of evaluation, etc).[429]

As a conclusion, both damages and specific performance should be seen as "alternative means of achieving efficient resource allocation (the car and the surplus) in the face of different transaction costs."[430]

1.3.2. The Indifference Principle Standard

In contracts to convey properties, the ability of expectation damages to compensate a non-breaching promisee should be the same as what was discussed in section 1.2.2 for contracts to produce goods. In terms of contracts to convey goods, expectation damages are under-compensatory if a court errs in calculation or takes a strict attitude toward the scope of compensation; or if the promisor refuses to pay compensation or he is bankrupt.

424 10,000 = (15,000 – 10,000) + (20,000 – 15,000).

425 What X2 can expect from his agreement with Y2 is 5,000.

426 10,000 = (20,000 – 5,000) – (15,000 – 10,000).

427 Cooter & Ulen 2011, p. 330.

428 Ulen 1984, p. 369, p. 370.

429 The court needs sufficient information to evaluate the expected loss of a promisee. In order to convince a court of a claim, the plaintiff (normally the promisee) has to provide the court with sufficient evidence to prove the accuracy of his expected loss.

430 Ulen 1984, p. 370.

However, the capacity of specific performance to fully compensate the promisee in the context of contracts to convey goods is different than that in contracts to produce goods.

In contracts to produce goods, both specific performance and expectation damages may result in an under-compensation problem; while this may not be the case for specific performance in contracts to convey goods. This is closely related to the difference of the nature of performance between these two contract models. In contracts to produce goods, a promisor is required to finish a certain pattern of producing behaviour. However, operating and monitoring the behaviour of production involves a lot of complexities, because it needs to be determined whether or not the producer's behaviour complies with what is required in the contract.[431] This would normally not be an issue in a contract to convey a product. In case 5.2, a court will only need to decide and monitor the allocation of the car, rather than judge the adequacy of a promisor's behaviour.[432] If the car is allocated to the promisee, then the specific performance is considered adequate since the promisee will receive what exactly he expects from the contract.[433] Therefore, as for the contracts to convey property, it is easier for specific performance to realize the goal of fully compensating the victim.

1.3.3. The Transaction Cost Standard

As is shown in section 1.3.1, no matter which type of remedy is applied, it is possible to allocate the goods to the best valuable user. The differences exist in the pathway and the allocation of individual surplus. Moreover, no matter which remedy is applied, the ex-post bargaining either between the original buyer and the seller (re-negotiation)[434] or between the original buyer and the alternative buyer (re-sale) is necessary for allocating the contracted-for goods efficiently. Hence in the context of contracts to convey goods, both expectation damages and specific performance will make the parties bear the costs of bargaining.

As to other types of costs involved in the expectation damages, the analysis would be similar as for contracts to produce products. However, compared to a contract to produce a product, a contract to transfer a product ideally will involve lower execution costs, if specific performance were to be ordered. The reason, as stated previously, is that a court only need to check the location of the contracted for goods so to judge whether or not the performance is compliant.

1.3.4. Risk-aversion

In the context of a contract to convey a property, the risk derives from the possibility that an alternative bidder may come along before delivery has occurred, thus inducing the

431 Shavell 2006, p. 845–846.

432 Id., p. 849–850.

433 The court will use its power to achieve compliance. If the seller refuses to transfer the property, an injunction can be ordered by the court.

434 In Shavell (2006), the author only considered the situation of re-sale. But to realize an efficient resource allocation, the seller can also try to persuade the buyer to release him from his obligation and then he can sell the goods to the third party. Shavell 2006, p. 849.

seller to breach.[435] A risk-averse party, as is indicated, would prefer a certain return that is unaffected by the risk. To be more specific, the risk-averse party would prefer a certain amount of surplus which will not be affected no matter whether the outsider comes with a higher bid or a lower bid. Expectation damages will guarantee that the original buyer gets a certain surplus amount to the value of his expectation. Take case 5.2 as example. In this case, the original buyer X2 will get 5,000 (or 15,000 – 10,000). However, since the risk arises from a third party's bid, calculation of the buyer's net profit is affected by whether or not the buyer could find the third party and transact with him.[436] 1) If the buyer could not re-sell the car to the outsider, then his net profit is calculated as the amount of damages that he will obtain (5,000). In this case, expectation damage insures the buyer against the risk of non-performance. Moreover, the seller's return is the surplus left after subtracting the amount of expectation compensation from the total surplus that he obtains in the alternative transaction. Besides, the total surplus the seller obtains from a transaction is the discrepancy between the contract price and the value he places on the contract-for good. So the higher the alternative bid is, the larger the amount of surplus that the seller could retain after breach. For instance, in case 5.2, an outsider (Z2) bids a price of 20,000. So the seller Y2 can obtain a surplus of 10,000 by breaking the first contract and re-selling the car to Z2. Other conditions being equal, if the alternative bid is 12,000, then the seller Y2 can only retain a surplus of 2,000 (or 12,000 – 5,000 – 5,000) after he breaks the original contract and compensates X2. Therefore, expectation damages shifts the risk to the seller. The seller is forced to assess who is the highest bidder in order to increase his total surplus. He will sell the goods to the outside bidder if his bidding is high so as to increase the seller's surplus, otherwise sell it to the initial buyer. This would optimally allocate the risk if the buyer is risk-averse and the seller is risk-neutral.[437] 2) If the buyer could find the third party and re-sell the product to him, then the buyer's profit would be the surplus that he could obtain from re-selling the product to the third party (the difference in the market price, namely 20,000 – 10,000 = 10,000). The buyer's surplus, in this case, depends on the possibility of re-sales and the third party's bid; while the seller has to pay a fixed amount of damages. Therefore, expectation damages will allocate risks optimally when the buyer is risk-neutral and the seller is risk-averse.[438]

Specific performance, in contrast, guarantees that the seller can obtain a certain surplus amount to the surplus he could obtain from the original sale. This can be explained as follows: Specific performance requires the seller to transfer the goods to the original buyer no matter whether or not an alternative bidder comes into play. So the surplus that the seller could obtain would be fixed as 5,000 (or 10,000 – 5,000) after he signed the first contract. As for the buyer, however, he bears the risk arising from an alternative higher bid. The higher the alternative bid is, the higher the return that the

435 Polinksy 1983, p. 428.

436 Id, p. 434.

437 Id.

438 "*Suppose now that the buyer would have had the same access to the third party as the seller. Then the buyer would be put in the position he would have been in had the third party come along and he, the buyer, had resold the goods to the third party at the higher offer.*" Id.

buyer can obtain from re-sale. In this sense, specific performance shifts the probabilistic opportunity to make additional profit from the seller to the buyer.[439] It is the buyer who is required to decide whether or not to re-sell the product to an outside bidder. It will optimally allocate the contract risk only when the buyer is risk-neutral and the seller is risk-averse.[440]

1.4. *Result of Comparison: Will Breach be Optimal to Promote Efficiency?*

1.4.1. Approaches to Achieve an Efficient Result

Summarizing the above, both in contracts to produce products and in contracts to convey products, it is possible to achieve an efficient result at a final stage no matter which remedy rule is taken. In the end, the unnecessary performance costs can be saved or the goods can be re-allocated to the best user. The difference exists in the pathway of achieving this result.

When expectation damages are set as the routine remedy, a promisor can choose either breaching and paying damages or re-negotiating to avoid inefficient performance or allocate the goods to the outside bidder whose reservation price is much higher. However, under specific performance, the realization of non-performance of an inefficient contract can only be achieved under the condition of bargaining (re-negotiations or re-sales). The conclusion derived from this comparison is that expectation damages offer the promisor more flexibility to get rid of the contract which he considered inefficient.

1.4.2. Efficient Remedy and Efficient Breach

In both contractual contexts, the possibility that efficient breach will take place is higher when expectation damages are the routine remedy. However, the answer to whether or not the combination of expectation damages and breach will be chosen by a seller would be different if the context of a contract changes.

1.4.2.1. Contracts to Produce Goods

Our primary conclusion is that in contracts to produce goods (or provide a service), expectation damages are generally more preferable to specific performance for preventing inefficient performance. 1) As is indicated, the expectation damages offer a producer the option to choose breaching and paying compensation or re-negotiating so as to prevent inefficient performance. While under specific performance, inefficient performance can only be prevented through negotiation. 2) Practising specific performance might be complex because performance concerns a certain pattern of behaviour. This might create an under-compensatory problem if the promisor who is compelled to perform is

439 Shavell 2006, p. 849.
440 Polinksy 1983, p. 435.

unwilling to do so. 3) Expectation damages insure the buyer against the risk of non-performance and limit the producer's risk to an amount equal to the buyer's expected loss; conversely, specific performance will impose the risk on the producer and creates a possibility that the producer may suffer a huge loss.

Our second conclusion is: efficient breach would happen conditionally in contracts to produce goods. The conditions are: 1) the routine remedy is expectation damages and a producer is able to breach freely as long as he compensates the buyer. 2) The buyer can obtain full recovery of his expectation loss. This would be possible only when the goods are general goods, or in another word, replaceable goods. On the one hand, the buyer may place less subjective value on general goods; on the other hand, an available market price can be a guide for evaluating the buyer's expectation. So the under-evaluation problem may not be severe when it comes to general goods. In addition, it is easy for the buyer to obtain a substitution from the market. 3) Re-negotiations are unavailable or more costly. There are several reasons to explain a failure in renegotiation. In some cases, for instance, where one party has a predominant position and stronger bargaining power, people may dislike re-negotiation.

1.4.2.2. Contracts to Convey Goods

One conclusion is: in contracts to convey goods, specific performance is generally more preferable for allocating the contract-for goods. This is explained by four reasons. First, as to contracts to convey goods, re-sale or re-negotiation will be necessary for re-allocation no matter whether the routine remedy is expectation damages or specific performance. Second, practising specific performance is not complex because it only concerns the location of the goods. In contrast, expectation damages would create an under-compensation problem. Third, both expectation damages and specific performance will create a bargaining cost. However, the cost of practising expectation damages would be relatively higher than that of practising specific performance. In addition, specific performance may encourage people to lower the contract-formation costs by encouraging efficient contracting. Fourth, specific performance shifts the risk to the buyer, but won't make him suffer an uncertain loss.

The probability of efficient breach, however, is lower in contracts to convey property. Even under the remedy of specific performance, efficient breach may still rarely take place. As is noted, an efficient breach will take place only if the seller re-sells the contract goods directly to a third party. But this is very unlikely. If the contract goods are general, the third party would not bid a much higher price for getting them from the seller. However, if the subject of the contract is a unique item, then re-sale from the first buyer to the alternative buyer is cheaper because there is no need to involve court costs.

2. Monetary Remedies Defined by Law

As noted in the previous section, when a breach occurs, the court can either award specific performance or a monetary remedy. In section 1 of this chapter, the monetary remedy was constructed by two categories of remedies, namely, party-designed remedies and legally-defined remedies. The party-designed remedy mainly refers to liquidated damages which are specified by the parties at the time of contract formation. Under the remedies defined by law, the court may choose among different measurements to decide the amount of money that a contract breaker should pay to the non-breaching party. The most common measurements recognized by law are the rules of restitution, reliance damages, expectation damages and disgorgement. In this section, an analysis will be developed on how breach and efficiency will be influenced under the monetary remedies defined by law.

2.1. *An Introduction to Restitution, Reliance Damages and Disgorgement*

Traditional legal studies focused on different interests of the promisee that are protected by law and thus categorized three major types of legal damages rules. They are expectation damages, reliance damages, and restitution.[441] Those three types of damage rules are awarded because a party in a contract suffers from a certain amount of loss. Besides, another remedy which would also be used by a court is disgorgement which is based on the profits rendered by breach.[442] Before the comparison between those types of remedies is made, a brief introduction to each of them will be given.

2.1.1. Definition

Relying upon a promise, a promisee may engage in some behaviour, such as transferring profits to the promisor or making some investments which will change his position. If the promisor breaks the contract, the promisee's investments will be rendered useless and the promisee may suffer from a loss of restitution interest or reliance interest. To deal with those situations, a court may award restitution or reliance damages. By restitution, the court will force the promisor to return the value he obtained from the non-breaching party.[443] Restitution applies, for example, in a case when a buyer has already made a payment before the seller breaks his promise. Then the buyer can ask for his money back. The purpose of this remedy is to reverse the transfer that took place and to prevent the promisor from getting unjust enrichment at the expense of the promisee. The other damage refers to reliance damages, which require the promisor to pay damages to the plaintiff for the purpose of undoing the harm which is caused by his reliance on the defendant's promise.[444] By awarding reliance damages, the law is aimed to put the promisee in as good a position as he was in before the promise was made.[445]

441 Fuller & Perdue 1936, p. 53–57; Fransworth 1970, p. 1147–1149.

442 Siems 2003, p. 30.

443 Note as to the definitions of different remedies, that there is some conflict concerning the boundary between restitution and disgorgement. In some literature, such as Mc Kendrick (2003), the concept of restitution is used to describe transferring the profits that a breacher gained from his behaviour to the innocent party. In contrast, many scholars, for example Fox (2001), Siems (2003) and Kull (2006), define the concept of restitution as returning something back to the owner of it. As was indicated in Siems (2003), the word of "'*re'stitute" – in latin "restituere" – means that "you have to give it back to the claimant and would not gained by him or her"*. Siems (2003), p. 28.

444 Fuller & Perdue 1936, p. 53–57; Cooter & Ulen 2011, p. 318–319.

445 Id.

Another type of monetary remedy, named as disgorgement, is to disgorge the benefit obtained by the contract breaker. Unlike other damages, disgorgement deals with the profits realized by a party in breach, rather than the loss suffered by a non-breaching party.[446] So disgorgement does not have a compensatory character. In traditional legal study, disgorgement is based on a principle that one should not gain by one's wrong. Therefore, profits obtained by an injurer should be eliminated. Commentators who consider a breach to be wrong would suggest stripping the party in breach of all gain if the gain obtained by him exceeds the injured party's loss.[447] In economic theory, however, disgorgement is awarded for the purpose of deterring undesirable behaviour. If a perfect disgorgement remedy is awarded, a defendant will have to hand over all the profits from his behaviour and will achieve no gain from this type of behaviour.[448] Hence this type of behaviour is rendered worthless to the defendant and he has no incentive to do so.

2.1.2. Effects of Damages Rules

In order to understand different remedy rules well, let us look at the effect of each rule. As is suggested, the court uses different rules to undo the effect of either the breach or the promise on one or both parties.[449] For instance, by awarding either expectation damages or specific performance, the court wants to realize the effect of full compensation. Ideally, either the expectation damages or specific performance should put the non-performing party in as good a position as he would have enjoyed had the contract been performed. Hence the effect of breach on the promisee would be counteracted. Similarly, disgorgement makes the promisor hand over all the profits yielded from breach so that the breach would become worthless for the promisor. Disgorgement hence undoes the effect of breach on a promisor. The other two types of damage rules, however, may create an effect as if there were no promise or no contract at all. Damages of reliance undo the effect of promise on a promisee, because the discrepancy in the promisee's position which is caused by a promise will be compensated. By obtaining perfect reliance damages, the promisee will be indifferent to either breach or "no promise".[450] While restitution makes the promisor return the profits that he has obtained from the other party and thus undoes the effect of the promise from the promisor's perspective. "No promise" offers a baseline for computing damages when either restitution or reliance damages are applied. Accordingly, in order to reach a state as if there were no promise, courts normally award restitution or reliance damages when the contract is rescinded or terminated.[451] Table 13 gives an overview of counter-factual effects realized by different damages.

446 Smith 1995, p. 122.
447 Fransworth 185, p. 1341.
448 Cooter & Ulen 2011, p. 319–320.
449 Brooks 2006, p. 577–578.
450 Cooter & Ulen 2011, p. 311.
451 Kull 2006, p. 569.

Table 13. Effect of Different Damage Measures

		Counterfactual state	
		No breach	No promise
Relative	Promisee	*Expectation*	*Reliance*
Party	Promisor	*Disgorgement*	*Restitution*

2.2. *Comparison among Different Damage Rules' Abilities to Achieve Efficiency*

Generally a contract should be performed according to the agreement between the contract parties so as to maximize social welfare. However, from an economic perspective, one can hypothesize two occasions where non-performance turns out to be efficient because non-performance may save the cost of performance or increase the total profit. These two situations were analysed within two different contract contexts respectively in section 3 of this chapter. In a contract to produce a product, the major problem caused by the increased performance costs is whether or not the producer should take a certain type of behaviour, namely, whether or not he should perform the contract specifically. In contrast, in a contract to convey a product, the question caused by an outside bid is whether or not the seller should transfer the product to the outsider and how to allocate the total benefit among the buyer, the seller and the outsider. There are several choices to allocate the profits. The buyer may ask for rescission of the contract and claim for restitution or reliance damages. Or the law may award the buyer an amount of benefit equal to his expectation loss or the surplus obtained by the seller from breach. In order to give a better clarification, this section will be developed only around a case concerning a contract to convey a product.

- **Case 5.3.** *Y3 agreed to sell an old car to X3 at a price of 10,000. Suppose at the time when X3 and Y3 entered the contract, Y3 valued the car at 5,000 but X3 estimated he can re-sell the car for 15,000. After the formation of the contract, X3 made the payment of 10,000 and invested 200 which is non-refundable in renting a parking place. Before the car is conveyed to X3, Z3 comes to Y3 and explains that he desperately needs this car. Suppose the price that Z3 is willing to pay is 12,000 if the value of the car is 13,000 or 20,000 if the value of the car is 21,000 for him.*[452]

There are four types of measurements for deciding the amount of compensation. Then we may calculate the net profit that X3 could have when each remedy applies: 1) Restitution: Y3 has to return what he has obtained from X3 (10,000). But note the return of 10,000 will not increase X3's net surplus because he is the original person who owned this amount of money. In this sense, X3 finally got -200 left since the investment of 200 is non-refundable.[453] 2)

[452] This case is modified from what has been used by Brooks in his "The Efficient Performance Hypothesis". Brooks 2006, p. 579.

[453] In this sense, the expenditures of 200 is a sunk cost that has already been incurred and cannot be covered. The cost of 200 will be consumed by one of the party, no matter whether the promisor Y3 will compensate X3 for this part of loss or not.

Reliance damages: The amount of damages that X3 may obtain should be able to put X3 in a position as if there were no promise. The court would require Y3 to return X3's upfront payment of 10,000 and to compensate X3's loss of 200 in reliance on the promise.[454] Then X3 suffers no loss and obtains no gain. 3) Expectation damages: X3 will obtain damages equal to his value of performance (15,000) and his net profit in the end is 4,800. 4) Disgorgement: The court will ask Y3 to hand over all the profits that he obtains from breaking the contract, namely 17,000 or 15,000. Thus, X3 will get a surplus of 6,800 or 14,800.

Table 14 shows each party's surplus if the seller Y3 breaches and the outsider Z3 offers a low bid of 12,000; while table 15 shows each party's surplus when Z3 has a high bid of 20,000.

Table 14. Each Party's Surplus when Z3 Bids a Low price[455]

	X3	Y3	Z3	Total
Value of the car	*15,000*	*5,000*	*13,000*	
Restitution	*-200*	*7,000*	*1,000*	*7,800*
Reliance damages	*0*	*6,800*	*1,000*	*7,800*
Expectation damages	*4,800*	*2,000*	*1,000*	*7,800*
Disgorgement	*6,800*	*0*	*1,000*	*7,800*

Table 15. Each Party's Surplus when Z3 Bids a High Price[456]

	X3	Y3	Z3	Total
Value of the car	*15,000*	*5,000*	*21,000*	
Restitution	*-200*	*15,000*	*1,000*	*15,800*
Reliance damages	*0*	*14,800*	*1,000*	*15,800*
Expectation damages	*4,800*	*10,000*	*1,000*	*15,800*
Disgorgement	*14,800*	*0*	*1,000*	*15,800*

Compare these two situations. When the outsider Z3 values the car at 21,000 and offers a high bid (20,000), allocating the car to him will create a total surplus of 15,800 and will be efficient. In contrast, when the outsider Z3 places a low value (13,000) on the car and

454 Brooks 2006, p. 580.

455 When restitution applies, Nbx3 = -200 – 10,000 + 10,000 = -200; Nby3 = (12,000 – 5,000) + (10,000 – 10,000) =7,000; Nz3 = 13,000 – 12,000 = 1,000. When reliance damages apply, Nbx3 = -200 – 10,000 + 12,000 = 0; Nby3 = (12,000 – 5,000) + (10,000 – 10,200) = 6,800; Nz3 = 13,000 – 12,000 = 1,000. When expectation damages applies, Nbx3 = -200 – 10,000 + [(15,000 – 10,000) + 10,000] = 4,800; Nby3 = (12,000 – 5,000) – [(15,000 – 10,000) + (10,000 – 10,000)] = 2,000; Nz3 = 13,000 – 12,000 = 1,000. When disgorgement applies, Nbx3 = -200 – 10,000 + [(12,000 – 5,000) + 10,000] = 6,800; Nby3 = 12,000 – 5,000 – [(12,000 – 5,000) + (1000 – 1000)] = 0; Nz3 = 13,000 – 12,000 = 1,000.

456 When restitution applies, Nby3 = 20,000 – 5,000 – (10,000 – 10,000) = 15,000; Nz3 = 21,000 – 20,000 = 1,000. When reliance damages applies, Nby3 = 20,000 – 5,000 – (10,000 – 10,200) = 14,800. When expectation damages applies, Nby3 = 20,000 – 5,000 – [(15,000 – 10,000) + (10,000 – 10,000)] = 10,000. When disgorgement applies, Nby3 = 20,000 – 5,000 – [(20,000 – 5,000) + (10,000 – 10,000)] = 0.

comes with a low bid (12,000), allocating the car to X3 rather than Z3 will be more efficient. However, a promisor has no incentive to calculate the total surplus that his behaviour will generate for the society. His decision of breach or performance may not be socially optimal. Rather, a promisor cares about how much surplus he will obtain for himself and would make decisions for his own sake. In case 5.3, what Y3 could obtain from performing his contract with X3 is 5,000. Assume Y3 is a rational person. Hence, Y3 will perform the first contract when breach creates a surplus lower than 5,000 for him, but break the contract when breach creates a surplus higher than 5,000.

If reliance damages or restitution applies, Y3 will breach no matter whether the outsider Z3 values the car more and offers a high bid or he values the car less and offers a low bid. What Y3 can obtain (7,000 or 6,800 when Z4 bids low and 15,000 or 14,800 when Z3 bids high) after breaching and paying damages is always higher than what he could obtain from performing the first contract (5,000). In this sense, either restitution or reliance damages is insufficient to deter inefficient breach. Moreover, since the baseline for computing damages is "no promise", either reliance damages or restitution is insufficient to counteract the effect brought about by breach. The promisee, hence, could not get full compensation covering his expectation loss.

Disgorgement, nevertheless, may create an over-deterrence effect. Depriving the person who breaches the contract of all the gains, makes breach worthless, thereby undermining a promisor's incentive to breach efficiently.[457] This doesn't mean, however, disgorgement will necessarily cause over-performance of contract and decrease social welfare. Efficient allocation of the car will be achieved under the condition that ex-post re-negotiation is available.[458] Assume that disgorgement applies, even though the seller Y3 knows that all the profits he could obtain from breach might be disgorged to X3, he would offer to compromise with X3 rather than perform the original contract reluctantly. If X3 accepts, a compromise about profit allocation will be made between X3 and Y3.[459] In this sense, even if disgorgement applies, Y3 may still be able to pursue a more profitable opportunity and the total surplus will be the same as what is created under expectation damages.

As is shown in the two tables above, it seems only expectation damages are consistent with the efficient breach doctrine and will induce high-surplus behaviour. On the one hand, it legitimizes efficient breaches[460] and creates possibilities for a promisor to take efficient breach provided he compensates the promisee. On the other hand, this rule limits the promisor's compensation to the promisee's expectation loss. Hence the promisor is allowed to keep the premium from the breach after he compensates the other party's loss.[461] In this way, a promisor is motivated to choose breach only if he could still earn a

457 Zhou 2008, p. 3–5.

458 Smith 1995, p. 134.

459 The party will settle for some amount between the expected value of the promisee (5,000 in case 5.3 when outside bidding is 20,000) and the profit gained by the promisor from breach (15,000 in case 5.3). For a promisee, he would accept some amount which is higher than his expectation vale, while a promisor will only agree to give up a lower amount of profit than what he can obtain from the opportunity with the outsider. Id.

460 Zhou 2008, p. 3–5.

461 De Long 1989, p. 739.

surplus after compensating the promisee. Nevertheless, this conclusion is still doubtful. The premise set in case 5.3 is that a promisor faces a more profitable opportunity after he has signed a sale contract. Even if expectation damages apply, an efficient result will be created only when the promisor Y3 and outsider Z3 could sign a contract successfully. Then, one may ask why an outsider Z3 is willing to bid a much higher price to induce Y3's breach. If the product is general goods, then Z3 could easily obtain a similar one in the market. If the goods are unique, Z3 could still negotiate with the promisee X3 and try to buy the product directly from the promisee. If Z3 values the product more than X3 does, he would be willing to bid as high as possible to get the product from X3. This analysis is similar to that in section 1.3. In this sense, the expectation damages will not be better than disgorgement or specific performance in inducing efficient allocation of resources.

3. Contract Damages Stipulated by the Parties

Another remedy which is being debated in the literature is the stipulated damages which are set by the parties at the time when they enter a contract. Generally, the stipulated damages fall into two categories.[462] Those damages which are reasonably stipulated by the parties, based on their estimation of the true losses, refer to liquidated damages (or called compensatory damages). Usually, a liquidated damages clause specifies an amount of damages that are equal to or lower than the actual harm caused by breach.[463] The other category concerns penalty (or called punitive damages) that are deliberately over-compensatory by the parties. To note, the concept of penalty is used only in the context where the parties deliberately stipulate damages much higher than the losses they could predicted ex-ante. So if the stipulated damages are reasonably computed ex-ante, but turn out to be higher than the actual losses ex-post, they are still placed in the category of liquidated damages.[464]

In different legal systems, courts take different attitudes towards stipulated damages. Courts in common law countries such as in the US and UK, normally distinguish penalty from liquidated damages and withhold the enforcement of a penalty clause. Courts in civil law countries, in contrast, take a lenient attitude toward penalty clauses. Rather than setting a penalty clause aside, courts may be willing to enforce it or lower the amount of damages.[465] In law and economics studies, scholars have been holding conflicting opinions

462 Some scholars divide the stipulated damages into three categories. Except for liquidated damages and penalty, another damages stipulated by contract parties ex-ante refers to "under-liquidated damages". By definition, under-liquidated damages refers to the damages which are designated lower than the parties' estimation of true loss. In this chapter, the concept of under-liquidated damages will not be used, but to put this concept into the category of liquidated damages. De Geest 2000, p. 141, p. 156.

463 Cooter & Ulen 2011, p. 321; De Geest 2001, p. 141.

464 Rea differentiated between the damages stipulated unreasonably ex-ante and damages stipulated reasonably ex-ante but deemed unreasonable ex-post. For more discussion, see Rea 1984, p. 150–166.

465 In legal practice earlier than 1980, evidence shows that some courts in the US are quite sceptical to enforce all the stipulated damages. Strict judicial scrutiny has been applied to party-designed damages. Liquidated damages are enforceable in courts only when they comply with two conditions. First the liquidated damages are consistent with the just-compensation principle or there is no evidence of unfairness or other bargaining abnormalities. Second, the possible damages which might result from

toward liquidated damages and penalty for a long time. In this section, there will first be an overview of the debate and then a focus on the relationship between efficient breach and liquidated damages and penalty. The emphasis will be placed on the question, whether or not efficient breach will be promoted under the mechanism of damage stipulation.

3.1. Debates over the Efficiency of Liquidated Damages and Penalty Clause

Generally, there are two groups of opinions concerning the party-stipulated damages.

3.1.1. A Distinguishing Model

One idea is to distinguish penalties from liquidated damages and treat them differently. Liquidated damages which have been stipulated not to exceed the reasonable estimation of real loss are accepted as being efficient. Those damages that are set extremely high ex-ante so as to deter breach are considered as unfair and inefficient. Thus it is proposed that damages which have been set much higher than the expected losses deliberately should be identified as penalties and deemed non-enforceable. There are at least four major economic reasons for supporting liquidated damages:

- **Liquidated damages avoid ex-post valuation difficulties:** *Awarding legally defined damages is grounded on a court's estimation of damages caused by the breach. However, there are several factors preventing a court from awarding accurate compensation. Lack of information, difficulties in assessing subjective value, kinds of under-compensatory rules in law (for instance, the "Hardly rule" or "reasonable causation rule") and a non-breaching party's overstatement of losses, etc., increase the possibility of legal error or under-compensation or over-compensation problems.*[466] *Since the parties possess more information than courts do, ex-ante damage stipulation by parties is more efficient than ex-post damage computation by courts. It is cheaper for parties to specify their own preferences and subjective values in liquidated damages clauses.*[467] *In this sense, an ex-ante agreement on contract damages eases a court's burden of assessment and decreases the uncertainty in ex-post estimation of damages.*

- **Liquidated damages function as an efficient insurance mechanism:** *A liquidated damages clause, to some extent, can be viewed as a mechanism for retaining money*

the breach must be uncertain and difficult to estimate. Goetz & Scott 1977, p. 558–562; Cooter & Ulen 2011, p. 321; Eisenberg 1995, p. 225, p. 226.

466 "When the buyer perceives that he will suffer a loss as a result of a breach of contract but realizes that the actual amount of the loss will be difficult to prove, he may wish to specify the damages at the time that the contract is signed. There is no incentive for him to overstate the loss because this would add to the contract price ... After a breach, the victim has an incentive to exaggerate his loss, and the cost of negotiating a settlement or going to trial is high when losses cannot be easily be measured ... " Rea 1984, p. 159.

467 Liquidated damages may not eliminate the problem of legal error. For instance, a court may take some normal liquidated damages as penalties and hence refuse to enforce them. De Geest 2001, p. 145; Moreno 2009, p. 13–14.

that has been deposited or paid under the contract.[468] *If a promisor accepts those liquidated damage clauses, it is considered that he agrees to make a payment in an insurance contract. In this way, an innocent promisee who is vulnerable to breach obtains a kind of insurance against the promisor's breach.*[469]

- **Liquidated damages save transaction costs:** *It is assumed that liquidated damages provisions will save the costs of litigation and the costs of legal error.*[470] *Of course, drafting a liquidated damages clause may also induce negotiation costs. But the parties may compare the costs of damage stipulation and the costs of legal damages. In fear of bringing contract conflicts to courts, parties may design liquidated damages clauses, according to which the parties may settle their future conflicts in a less costly way by themselves. In this sense, a liquidated damage clause is able to decrease the volume of litigation. Moreover, even if a contract dispute enters a court, it is easier for the court to award damages based on the liquidated damages provisions drafted by the parties than on the assessment of the court. Or, those existing provisions provide some evidential value in the trial.*[471] *In this way, the courts may also decrease their error in computing expectation damages.*

- **Enforcement of liquidated damages promotes efficient contracting:** *The last point to justify liquidated damages is derived from the concern of motivation. On the one hand, if a condition that the law can always provide perfect damage measures is satisfied, then damage stipulation is costly and unnecessary. However, individual's preferences are homogenous and people would prefer to negotiate their own damage clauses, for instance, out of concern for protecting privacy and avoiding disclosure of their private information (such as reservation price) to a court.*[472] *On the other hand, people's preferences and subjective values are assumed to be expressed in the amount of damages that they specify in their contracts. Under the condition that those liquidated damages are enforceable, the parties are motivated to assess the possible loss and decide how to allocate future risks by themselves. By ex-ante estimation, the parties may consider the transaction as risky and decide to stop contracting or choose to enter the contract and allocate the future risks. Within the process of negotiation, the higher the amount stipulated by the parties, the higher the price that the promisor will require the promisee to pay.*[473] *If courts void those stipulated clauses, it may create unnecessary judicial interference with a negotiated business transaction.*[474]

468 Di Matteo 2001, p. 634.

469 Cooter & Ulen 2011, p. 321, 322.

470 Goetz & Scott 1977, p. 578.

471 Di Matteo 2001, p. 634.

472 This is related to an issue of protecting parties' secret interests in contract. As is proposed by Ben-Shahar and Bernstein, "the use of the liquidated damages provision decreases the likelihood that a repeat-dealing relationship, with its associated relationship-specific efficiency gains, will end if a dispute arises. Because the dispute will not require either party to reveal its reservation price, the parties at least have the opportunity to resume dealing on their former terms". Ben-Shahar and Bernstein 2000, p. 1902–1904.

473 "The debtor will require compensation for his additional prevention costs and for the additional risk he has to insure." De Geest 2001, p. 144.

474 Di Matteo 2001, p. 682.

Penalty clauses, in contrast, are criticized for being inefficient. Early studies focused on penalty clause's super-compensatory nature and cared about the effect of damage stipulation on breach and performance of a contract.[475] Starting from this point, economists also discussed the impacts of penalties on other behavior of the parties. The major reasons for opposing penalties are summarized as:

- **Penalties will hamper efficient contracting**: *1) when drafting a liquidated damages provision, the parties have to exchange information about each other's performance ability and consider all the possible damage cases that might occur in order to compute a reasonable amount of damages. Unlikely, penalty clauses can be less costly because the parties can just choose the highest amount so as to ensure that the contract will be performed. Accordingly, if penalty clauses are enforceable, the parties may be prevented from exchanging information efficiently. 2) Another point is that a penalty clause can be used as a signal for a promisor's reliability and capacity.*[476] *It is self-evident that the heavier the sanction imposed on breach, the lower chance that the promisor will breach. So a promisor might be willing to offer a heavy sanction on his non-performance in order to convince the promisee of his creditability and win the opportunity of a trade. This signal function may create an adverse selection problem.*[477] *If a promisee cannot obtain enough information to assess the risk from transacting with different promisors, one promisor's acceptance of penalty clauses is a signal of a high level of reliability.*[478] *In this case, a bad entrepreneur might win the chance of contracting if he is willing to accept penalty provisions, while those good traders who prefer real damage computation are excluded. 3) Inefficiency may also be created because people might sign a contract with penalty clauses having made a cognitive error.*[479] *In Eisenberg's argument, a cognitive error probably occurs when people merely focus on their intention to perform or underestimate the likelihood of breach.*[480]

475 Goetz & Scott 1977; Posner 1977.

476 The signaling function of penalty clauses has been first articulated by Posner in 1977. Afterwards, more scholars accepted this idea. For more discussion, see Posner 1977, p. 93; Rea 1984, p. 156–160; Aghion & Hermalin 1990.

477 De Geest 2001, p. 153.

478 Rea 1984, p. 156.

479 De Geest 2001, p. 147, 148.

480 Eisenberg raised several reasons to explain the cognitive biases. For instance, "*with bounded rationality, contracting parties will normally find it relatively easy to evaluate proposed performance terms, such as subject matter, quantity, and price. In contrast, at the time the contract is made it is often impracticable, if not impossible, to imagine all the scenarios of breach ...*" Besides, three other reasons may contribute to the problem of cognitive biases. "*The availability heuristic may lead a contracting party to give undue weight to his present intention to perform, which is vivid and concrete, as compared with the abstract possibility that future circumstances may compel him to breach. Because a contracting party is likely to take the sample of present evidence as representative of the future, he is apt to overestimate the extent to which his present intention to perform is a reliable predictor of his future intentions. Because actors have faulty telescopic faculties, a contracting party is likely to overvalue the benefit of the prospect of performance, which will normally begin to occur in the short term, as against the cost of the prospect of a breach, which will typically occur, if at all, only down the road. Because actors tend to underestimate risks, a contracting party is likely to underestimate the risk that a liquidated damages provision will take effect.*" Eisenberg 1995, p. 227, p. 228.

Hence, even without fully understanding the possibility and severity of the actual damages, a promisor will accept a penalty clause and sign the contract. Some scholars call this problem "sign without reading". Without careful stipulation, a breaching party's business will be totally ruined and the promisee will get enriched in the case that a contract is broken.

- **Penalties will give promisees an incentive to induce breach:** *if a stipulated damage clause has an over-compensatory nature, a moral hazard problem might occur. This idea was first raised in 1970's.*[481] *As is indicated, in the situation where a contract contains penalty clauses and the promisee can influence the probability of breach, this promisee has incentives to induce the promisor to break the contract in order to profit from the breach. De Geest used an example to illustrate this moral hazard problem. He imagined a construction contract with a penalty clause indicating that a promisee can obtain damages of 1,001,000 from the builder if the construction is delayed. If the promisee could estimate the actual loss that he will suffer from delay is just 1,000, then he will do everything to hinder the builder's performance in order to obtain the damages stipulated by the contract (1,001,000).*[482]

- **Penalties will increase the cost of legal error:** *According to this argument, since penalties are much harsher than liquidated damages, the consequences of erroneously enforcing a penalty are worse.*[483] *Similar articulation can be found in the literature on criminal law when capital punishment is being debated. There is a risk of legal error in the judicial procedure. For instance, a court normally makes its decision based on the evidence provided by the litigants involved in the case. Then a legal error might happen if the proof raised by an innocent defendant is insufficient. This innocent defendant might be erroneously sentenced to death.*

- **Penalties will create an inefficient entry problem:** *By making a hypothetical analysis of the relationship between penalties clauses and market competition, some scholars have criticized penalty clauses for their negative influence on competition. It is argued that the parties who have written penalty clauses in their contract may exercise monopoly power over other potential partners within the market. Imagine a sales contract requiring the buyer to pay an extremely high amount of damages to the seller in the case he breaches. The buyer will breach only when an external seller can compensate him for what he has paid to the original seller. In this case, the cost of a penalty is transferred to all the other potential competitors.*[484]

481 De Geest 2001, p. 149; Goetz & Scott 1977, p. 588; Clarkson, Miller & Muris 1978, p. 368–372.

482 De Geest 2001, p. 149.

483 Id.

484 "*When individuals choose their own damages (i.e. liquidated damages), they do not generally select compensatory damages. Parties to a contract must divide the product of that contract in some way. For symmetry, we assume that they split the surplus from the contract equally. This surplus equals the excess of the sum of values to the individuals of having the new contract over the sum of values of their previous positions plus the damages they must pay. Because the surplus depends on damage payments, an individual who breaches can, in effect, get his new partner to share the burden of the damages he pays to his old partner. In this way, a pair of individuals in a contract exerts some monopoly power over potential partners...*" See: Diamond & Maskin 1979, p. 284.

3.1.2. A Unified Model

The other idea is to treat liquidated damages and penalties equally. Scholars in favour of this idea argue against regulating penalty clauses in contracts and proposed to eliminate legal interference with stipulated damages. They suggest that penalty clauses should also be enforceable. The reasons are:

- **Penalty clauses will promote efficient contracting:** *In the eyes of some scholars, if penalty clauses are enforceable, people are encouraged to contract efficiently rather than inefficiently. Those scholars proposed several arguments to refute the opposite idea. 1) Penalty clauses are considered to be the result of the parties' rational stipulation. Ulen indicates this idea explicitly by stating that "there is every reason to believe that they will stipulate the most efficient remedy, considering all the parties."*[485] *If parties agree on a penalty clause, this is the choice made by the parties and this choice is better than the decision deriving from a court's estimation. 2) Penalty clauses have a cautionary function, which will encourage parties to carefully assess the feasibility of performance and consequence of non-performance when signing on a contract.*[486] *According to this argument, the problem of cognitive error in negotiations is over-stated. Rather than signing without reading, parties are more likely to make reasonable estimations and decisions based on some cost-benefit calculations.*[487] *In this sense, the result of considering a penalty clause enforceable is that careless behavior will be discouraged in the contracting process.*[488] *Moreover, judicial error is argued to be much more a threat than the problem of cognitive error. If a court appears to be subject to cognitive bias or to be over-confident about its ability to assess the loss, this court will make an erroneous judicial decision.*[489] *3) The worry about penalty clauses' signaling function is re-examined. Good entrepreneurs, as argued, are more willing to signal their above-average ability to accomplish the contracts than bad entrepreneurs. A good entrepreneur is willing to accept a penalty clause if he thinks the value of this contract exceeds the risk he has to bear by doing so. In contrast, a bad entrepreneur will be sacred by having to pay high damages and would be less likely to accept a penalty clause. Therefore, the signaling function of penalty clauses, as is stated, can help traders to distinguish good partners from bad partners.*[490]

- **Penalty clauses will internalize the risks in the contract:** *Another argument against regulating penalty damages clauses is derived from the insurance function of damages stipulation. In a commercial context where people don't have enough information about other traders, they need some factors with which to estimate whether it is worth trading with a potential contract party. Damages stipulation, generally offers this kind of warranty which internalizes the risk of searching for contracting parties. Moreover, parties can*

485 Ulen 1984, p. 356.
486 Walt 2011, p. 181–182; 190–192.
487 Wilkinson-Ryan 2010, p. 646.
488 Dematteo 2001, p. 685.
489 Walt 2011, p. 201.
490 Id, p. 196–198.

make risk-arrangement through punitive damages clauses. If a promisor is risk-preferring and a promisee is risk-averse, a high amount of damages could best shift the risk of non-performance from the promisee to the promisor.[491] *Especially when non-compensable interests are involved in a contract, "a penalty clause may represent the best effort of the parties to allocate risk."*[492] *At the same time, the party which bears a risk of paying penalty damages would require a higher price to cover any increase in the cost of performance.*[493]

- **The moral hazard problem will not be serious:** *The argument that a problem of moral hazard is induced by penalty damages has been refuted as well. As is argued, a promisor will be very cautious when he is aware that he has to pay a large amount of damages in the case of breach. In this situation, the promisee can hardly affect the possibility of breach.*[494] *Another point to be noticed is that the parties would also take the promisee's future behavior into account when negotiating over a penalty clause. Thus, they may agree on some precautions so as to lower the risk that the promisor has to bear, such as a reduction in the damages.*[495] *In this sense, it is unnecessary to exaggerate the worry about moral hazard caused by penalty clauses.*

- **Regulating penalty clauses creates unnecessary costs:** *The scrutiny on stipulated damages, however, may create unnecessary costs. In the case that the court needs to exercise separate rules for stipulated damages, administrative costs are increased. A court might wrongly take a damage provision which both parties initially considered as beneficial as a penalty under insufficient proof or inaccurate assessment.*[496] *This complexity of rules, according to some scholars, might also add complexity to the process of contract formation and dispute solution. For instance, Mattei (1995) argued that the insuring party (promisor) will be more likely to bring out litigation so as to void the penalty provisions.*[497] *Therefore, it is suggested that instead of avoiding penalty clauses, courts should pay more attention to clauses that are drafted under necessity, by mistake or fraudulently.*[498]

491 *"If the seller is risk neutral and the buyer is risk averse, it is beneficial to both parties for the seller to insure the buyer...Damages in excess of full compensation would not appeal to a risk-averse buyer because he would face an unwanted variation in his income, depending on whether the product failed. He would not wish to pay a higher price for the product...If the buyer is risk-preferring, a clause that specified damages in excess of losses would provide an opportunity to gamble..."* Rea 1984, p. 152.

492 Wilkinson-Ryan 2010, p. 644.

493 *"When the promisee demands a "penalty clause," the promisor will agree only if the price is increased sufficiently to cover any increase in the cost of performance."* Kornhauser 1986, p. 720.

494 De Geest 2001, p. 149.

495 Kronman & Posner 1979, p. 224, p. 225.

496 *"But, since it seems plausible that commercial contractors act largely in their "rational" self-interest, it is likely that both parties initially saw a benefit even in a clause which a court later terms a penalty."* See: Kornhauser 1986, p. 720.

497 *"The insuring party in default will have an incentive to litigate, hoping the court will declare the penalty clause void, rather than buying itself out of the contract by bribing the other party. Coasian negotiations do not occur in the presence of unclear property rights."* See: Mattei 1995, p. 432.

498 Di Matteo 2001, p. 694.

As is shown, the central issue embodied in the debate concerns the justifications for penalty clauses (or punitive damages) in contract law. Besides the ideas in favour of or against punitive damages, an alternative perspective is taken to view this question. As is suggested, penalty clauses should be divided into efficient clauses and inefficient clauses, rather than be viewed as efficient or inefficient as a whole.[499] Thus, those damage clauses which are judged as efficient should be enforceable, while inefficient penalty clauses should be deemed non-enforceable. Generally, either penalties or liquidated damages specified in a contract are viewed as the parties' rational response to the uncertainty arising in the on-going contractual relationship. So those clauses would be efficient and enforceable. However, some criteria are established so as to exclude the penalty clauses which are inefficient. For instance, a penalty clause designed in a purely punitive manner is deemed as inefficient. Di Matteo (2001) gave an example showing the difference between an inefficient penalty clause and an efficient penalty clause (Table 16).[500] In his illustration, a penalty clause included in a contract which is formed under a premise of unfairness and inefficiency only has the purpose of punishing the weaker party and enriching the other party. In this case, this clause should not be enforceable.

Table 16. The Hypothesis of an Efficient Penalty Clause

Basic condition	*Suppose a production contract. Assume contract price is set as 1000 and the production cost is 800. If the parties agree on a penalty of 200 for non-performance, then the producer will require to increase the price of contract to 1050 (1000 plus the 50 premium).*
An inflationary market (market price increases)	*The penalty clause is a reasonable reaction to uncertainty. If the market price increases to 1251, the seller can retain 1 (1251 – 1050 – 200) after compensating the buyer.[132] In this case, the seller would prefer to breach.*
A deflationary market (market price decreases)	*The penalty clause only has a punishing nature. The market price may decrease to 900 or even a lower level. The buyer can clearly estimate that performance is inefficient and any breach from the seller's perspective is non-opportunistic. In this case, the penalty is clearly designed merely for punishment.[133]*

3.2. *Will Damage Stipulation Enhance Efficiency?*

This section will only examine the relationship between penalty clauses and efficient breach and fit this topic into the context which was proposed in section 2. The premise of analysis is that the penalty clauses have been agreed on by the parties voluntarily. Thus if there is necessity, duress or any other problem with the negotiation process when the

499 Id, p. 675.

500 Id, p. 695–700.

501 Since the market price of the product increases, it is still profitable for the producer to produce the product. If the producer breaches by selling the product to a third party at the market price, then he has to compensate the seller for his expected loss plus 200 as the fine.

502 Di Matteo 2001, p.695–700.

parties are drafting the penalty clauses, then the problem concerns another issue about contract validity. The following arguments will be presented:

3.2.1. Damage Stipulation and Efficient Breach

For those who worry that penalty clauses will induce over-performance, the worry is based on the super-compensatory nature of punitive damages. In Goetz & Scott's theory, a promise who is subject to damages clauses that are used as a deterrent to breach or as security for full performance will inevitably undertake an inefficient performance. Suppose after a contract is formed, it turns out that performance of the contract is inefficient because of changed circumstances, a promisor will still not break it in fear of paying penalty damages.[503] Instead, a promisor is motivated to take undue precaution in order avoid the burden of paying penalty damages.[504] This idea has been incorporated into some courts' opinion in the USA. It is expressed in *Leasing Serv. Corp. v. Justice & Childers* (1982): "*contractual terms fixing damages in an amount clearly disproportionate to actual loss seek to deter breach through compulsion and have an in terrorem effect: fearing severe economic loss, the promisor is compelled to continue performance, while the promisee may reap a windfall in excess of his just compensation*".[505]

For those people who criticize the idea that penalty clauses will deter efficient breach, their critique is based on two reasons:

I.Traditional compensatory damages are always insufficient to fully compensate the loser (normally the promisee). Section 1.2.2.1 in this chapter has given several statements about the under-compensatory problem under expectation damages. Moreover, a court's verification of breach and compensation depends on several factors, such as the possibility of litigation, the evidence raised by a victim party and so on. Thus the possibility and level of full compensation is lowered. Then over-breach or inefficient breach might be caused under traditional ex-post compensatory damages because promisors are not always held liable for their breach. It is suggested that an optimal damage measure should be greater in amount than the actual loss in order to deter inefficient breach.[506] Besides, damages which are designed to be greater in amount than expectation damages may be closer than the actual loss that a non-breaching party suffers when other costs like litigation costs or non-monetary losses are included.

II. Evidence from behavioural studies shows that people are more likely to breach when liquidated damage clauses or even penalty clauses have been attached to contracts. There are some behavioural experiments about the relationship between people's non-cooperative behaviours and penalties.

503 Goetz & Scott 1977, p. 561, p. 562, p. 586, p. 587.

504 Goetz & Scott 1980, p.

505 673 F.2d 70 (2d Cir.1982), cite from Di Matteo 2001, p. 677.

506 Craswell 1999, p. 2223; Polinsky & Shavell 1998, p. 874.

- **Day-care Centre Study:** *in 1998 Gneezy and Rustichini made the famous study of the "day-care centre" in Israel.*[507] *They researched the relationship between a penalty and the possibility that parents pick up their children late. A result was found that the number of late-coming parents increased significantly after a monetary fine was attached to the behaviour of coming late.*[508] *As is explained, the introduction of a fine may remove the non-market nature that actors place on being late. Actors are willing to treat a fine as a price for being late and no guilt or shame will be attached to the act of buying a commodity.*

- **Sick-leave Case:** *A Similar conclusion was reached in the Wilkinson-Ryan observation of the sick-leave case in the Boston Fire Department from 2001 to 2002. It was shown that the total number of sick days was increased dramatically after the Boston fire department explicitly allowed 15 sick days per year.*[509] *In Wilkinson-Ray's illustration, fire-fighters felt more obliged to show up when the sick time had been unlimited in the previous system, while they felt less guilty to miss work when an explicit rule about sick-leave has been published.*

- **The cases of Party Rental and IT Seminar:** *Another experiment was conducted by Wilkinson-Ryan under two contractual contexts. In these two contexts, he asked the participants to act as a promisor (a landlord or an IT firm) and assumed a promisee (a tenant: the Wilsons or a client: a temp agency).*[510] *In each context, he presumed a third party who is willing to offer a higher price for the performance of the promisors and*

507 Gneezy & Rustichini 2000, p. 1–17.

508 Id, p. 8.

509 *"In December of 2001, the Boston Fire Department changed its sick-leave policy to allow 15 sick days per year. The previous system had allowed unlimited sick time, and the new rule was part of an initiative to bring professional management tools to the department. In 2001, firefighters took a total of 6432 days. In 2002, the total number of sick days rose to 13,431 – more than double the previous year."* Wilkinson-Ryan 2010, p. 635.

510 Wilkinson-Ryan gave two case scenarios to the 200 participants involved. The Party Rental scenario is set as follows: "*Please imagine that you own a small restaurant, which you sometimes rent out for private parties. The Wilsons want to rent your restaurant for a party. Similar venues cost about $2000. For you, the event is pure profit, since you would normally be closed anyway. You settle on a price of $1000 for the night and sign a basic contract... The contract also includes the following clause: If the restaurant becomes unavailable or unusable for any reason, Mr. and Mrs. Wilson will be compensated...Two weeks before the Wilsons' party, a famous rock band calls to ask if they can rent your place out for the night the Wilsons have booked...the band is willing to pay much more than usual... Given that you have to pay the Wilsons $1000, what is the smallest amount the band could offer such that you would accept their offer?*" In the "IT Seminar" case, subjects read the following: "*Please imagine that you own a small technology consulting firm. One of the things your firm does is provide trainings to businesses on different computer applications. You have recently been called by a temp agency to train a group of temporary workers...The agency has been hired to do a week-long filing project for a local law firm, and the firm has offered them an extra $2000 if the workers can use this program. You charge $1000 for the training...The contract also includes the following clause: If either party to this contract is unable or unwilling to fulfil his obligations, he will be required to compensate the other party ... A week before you are scheduled to start the training, an out-of-town client calls to ask you to run a seminar for them. ... Given that you have to pay the temp agency $1100, what is the smallest amount the out-of-town client could offer such that you would accept that job?*". Wilkinson-Ryan 2010, p. 655–658.

examined under what price the participants are willing to breach. A "willing-to-accept" figure (WTA) is used to represent the price that people would accept to breach. He assumed that someone is more willing to breach if his WTA figure is lower.[511] *As was shown, the WTA figure is lower when a penalty (not too high) is attached to the contract; while higher when the condition of penalty or liquidated damages is not satisfied.*

As is shown in all those experiments, people's behaviour becomes more strategic and self-interested when the punishment of uncooperative behaviour (late coming, sick-leave, or re-rent) has been clarified.[512] The reason is given as: social norms concerning a specific action do exist and control this behaviour. In the examples above, picking up the children on time, showing up at work and performing contracts are morally right in most people's intuition. Those moral norms often affect people's decision making.[513] However, this effect on behaviour can be diminished by explicitly creating a fine, which will change people's "perception of the environment" and reduce their "internal motivations for cooperation".[514] People are willing to interpret the fine as the price for self-interested behaviour and do not feel ashamed to buy this behaviour.[515] Apply this doctrine to penalty clauses. If there is no clear rule, moral intuition plays an important role in the decision-making process. People view the obligation of performance as a moral obligation even when they know they might pay compensation if they breach. So they are held by the text that they have agreed on in the contract. However, a more clear incentive structure may decrease people's moral aversion to breach and be more lenient with uncooperative behaviour (for instance, breach). When there is an explicit and real penalty for non-cooperation, actors are more likely to deny social norms and be self-seeking. At the same time, people think paying a high amount of damages will lead to less reputation loss and hence they feel less guilty if they break contracts.[516] In this sense, creation of penalty clauses will eventually encourage people to take the decision of efficient breach, rather than deter breach.

3.2.2. Concerns about Transaction Costs

Another dimension to examine whether or not a breach is efficient and socially desirable is to estimate the costs of breach under a system of remedy. The costs probably aroused under a penalty clause are presented as the costs of ex-ante negotiation, the costs of dispute settlement and the reputation costs of breach.

First, to negotiate over damage measurement, parties will try to estimate all the possible contingencies arising after the formation of the contract and to understand each

511 If someone requires less monetary incentives to breach, then he is more willing to breach. Id, p. 659.

512 Smith, Houser, Xiao & McCabe 2008, P. 522, p. 523.

513 An important resource of moral norms derives from people's interpretation of justice and fairness. "*People may want to act fairly and perhaps more importantly, they want to be seen to act fairly, especially among non-strangers.*" Sunstein, 1997, p. 1186.

514 Smith, Houser, Xiao & McCabe 2008, p. 523.

515 Id.

516 Wilkinson-Ryan 2010, Id, p. 664. Dematteo 2001, p. 705.

other's preferences and capacity to accomplish the contract. Adequate information is necessary for making this assessment and hence ex-ante transaction costs are increased.[517]

Ex-ante negotiation over the damage measure, however, may lead to a decrease in the ex-post costs of dispute settlement because the parties are likely to settle their dispute before the trial phase.[518] With an explicit amount of damages specified in a contract, the promisor is more willing to breach and pay damages as required when the performance cost turns out to be too high or there is a more lucrative opportunity after the formation of a contract. The promisor's cost of the decision of breach in those situations would not be high and the costs of legal estimation and the costs of litigation are awarded. There are two reasons to explain this. I) the penalty price set in the contract would in reality normally not be unduly disproportionately higher than the promisee's actual losses,[519] so a promisor will not really pay an extremely high amount of damages. As is explained in some literature, as long as a competitive market exists or the bargaining parties are well informed, the parties have no rational motivation to contract for *supra*-compensatory remedies.[520] For the promisor, he does not want to bear the risk of paying a penalty. Besides, a promisee has no incentive to force the promisor to accept the penalty as well, because the contract price will be higher if the promisor risks paying a penalty. II) Damage stipulation removes the uncertainty of predicting damages when a promisor is deciding whether or not to breach. According to the efficient breach doctrine, a breacher must still earn a surplus after breaking the contract and compensating the innocent party. So a breaching party has to determine the amount of monetary compensation that he should pay and he will be discouraged to breach efficiently if he is uncertain about the costs of breach.[521] This uncertainty problem is quite common if parties only count on judicial decisions which are made under the ex-post evaluation of a third party.[522] Nevertheless, this worry of uncertainty can be diminished by ex-ante damage stipulation.

517 De Geest 2001, p. 146.

518 Dematteo 2001, p. 634.

519 Id, p. 690.

520 "*Promisees would not contract for supra-compensatory remedies when they act in competitive markets or bargain under conditions of full or asymmetric information. In the former two cases, promisees cannot engage in strategic behaviour, but rather earn an exogenously determined share of the gains from trade. Hence, promisees prefer the contractual damage measure that maximizes these gains. The optimal measure restricts the promisee to his expectation interest. In the last case, promisees can engage in strategic behavior but nevertheless do not prefer supracompensatory remedies. This is because a promisee would have to pay for this preference, and so would gain nothing by pursuing it...*"Schwartz 1990, p. 382, p. 383. "*With a competitive entrant, the buyer and seller not only have an incentive to sign a socially efficient contract, but can also achieve the first best using a relatively simple stipulated damage contract that sets damages equal to the efficient expectation damage.*" Spier & Whinston 1995, p. 198.

521 The result of litigation is quite random so that it is hard for a promisor to accurately predict the amount of damages that he is going to pay after breaking the contract. For instance, judges might err in calculating the damages.

522 "*Even when judges do not misunderstand basic ideas, we must take their interpretation of facts on faith. Judges' reasoning can be evaluated only against the canned facts described in the opinion, which themselves are the result of a fact-finding process that does not inspire confidence. Parties can reasonably believe that given the varying sophistication of trial judges, lawyers, and juries, the accidents of discovery, the varying credibility of witnesses, the vagueness of the law, and so on, that the chance of winning a breach of contract suit is pretty much random.*" Posner (B) 2000, p. 758.

Moreover, the reputation loss estimated by a promisor decreases if he is willing to pay a *supra*-compensatory amount of damages. As is indicated by behavioural literature, by showing the willingness of sharing the surplus generated by the breach with the promisee, a promisor can still maintain his reputation and keep on cooperating with the promisee.[523]

To summarize, except for creating the costs of ex-ante negotiation, the existence of a penalty clause will generally decrease the costs of making and implementing a decision of efficient breach.

3.2.3. Risk Allocation through the Damage Stipulation

It is well recognized that parties could allocate contract risks through damage stipulation and transferring a risk is cheap when the parties can arrange it through free negotiations.[524] Section 3.4 of chapter 4 has indicated that the choice of a contract remedy will make sense only if at least one of the parties is risk-averse.[525] An efficient remedy should be able to lower the risk that a risk-averse party bears. In this section, there will be an inference from the hypothesis that at least one of the contract parties is risk averse. To improve the analysis, we only presume the case in which a seller breaches.[526]

I) If the seller is risk-averse, the seller would prefer a kind of damage payment which will guarantee him a fixed profit which is unaffected by either the performance cost or any outsider's offer.[527] The seller would not agree to any damage measure that is higher than the expected loss suffered by the buyer. Hence, the parties will not draft a penalty clause in their contract.

II) If the seller is risk neutral, it might be possible that the seller would accept a penalty clause. If the seller is risk-preferring, then a penalty clause offers him an opportunity to gamble. He would accept a penalty clause because he sees a great profit in the contract opportunity or in the increase of contract price. In contrast, the buyer may hope to get insured against breach and require a damage payment which is higher than his expected losses when he is risk-averse. The more risk-averse the buyer is, the higher amount of damages he would require.[528] If those assumptions are put into specific contractual contexts, Then in the case where risks arise from a third party's bid, the parties have no incentive to draft an extraordinary high amount of punitive damages. If the product is general goods which are replaceable within the market, then the buyer can easily find an alternative and would not agree to pay a high amount of contract price in order to make the seller accept a penalty clause. If the product is unique, "*any tendency for the buyer to*

523 Dematteo 2001, p. 705.

524 Polinsky 1983, p. 436. "*Extending this analysis to liquidated damages clauses, such clauses are risk allocation devices that are freely entered into by the parties. The risk of under or over-liquidation is allocated to one of the parties. One party is assured of a minimum level of recovery; the other party is assured a maximum level of liability. In contracts between commercial entities, the courts should not tamper with such allocations.*" Dematteo 2001, p. 683.

525 Every remedy has the same effect on risk-allocation if both of the contract parties are risk-neutral.

526 So the concepts of promisor, breacher and seller will be used in the same sense.

527 Kornhauser 1986, p. 706.

528 The risk-averse buyer is willing to pay a premium in advance so as to shift the risk to the seller. So he would accept to pay a higher amount of contract price.

assume price risk will be offset by the fact that the seller is in the better position to locate other buyers".[529] A seller who has an advantageous position would not agree to an unreasonably high damage payment. In another contractual context where risks arise from uncertain production costs, the possibility of assuming a risk-preferring seller is low. There are few examples in the commercial context where gambling is the motivation for a seller to accept unreasonably high damages when he is uncertain about the production cost.

To sum up, a more desirable damage payment that contract parties would draft in their contract would not be extremely high when the parties take their respective attitude toward risks into consideration. It is more likely that the amount of damages will always be reasonable under ex-ante stipulation of contract parties. In Polinsky's observation, a damage payment stipulated by parties will always allocate contract risks optimally because the parties will agree on a damage payment which allocates risks according to their "relative aversion to risks".[530]

This section has examined the monetary remedies. It firstly compared expectation damages with other legal damages.[531] Within the monetary remedies defined by law, both restitution and reliance damages are calculated upon the baseline where there is no contract. These two types of damages will be insufficient to fully compensate the non-breaching party and thus may induce over-breach but may not induce over-reliance investment. In contrast, both expectation damages and disgorgement have an advantage of deterring inefficient breach. But as to the ability to induce efficient breach, disgorgement deprives a breaching party of all the profit that can be obtained from breach and thus may deter breach, unless the parties renegotiate successfully and enter into an agreement to allow breach. Afterwards, this section has examined the monetary damages that are stipulated by contract parties. Damages that are stipulated by parties have advantages in inducing rational decisions, precluding conflicts or costly litigation and allocating risks. From theoretical inference, efficient breach will be promoted if contract parties have stipulated damage clauses explicitly ex-ante.

4. Implications from Efficient Breach Doctrine

Early proponents of efficient breach focus on the doctrine's contribution to shaping contract law and remedy rules. They asked: what should the rules of contract law be so as to promote efficient breach? But the significant gap between the theoretical hypothesis and legal realities put those early findings in jeopardy.[532] After almost 40 years' controversy, the topic of efficient breach has currently almost lost its attraction in the normative construction of contract rules.[533] Since 2000, more literature has raised radical

529 Rea 1984, p. 152.

530 Polinsky 1983, p. 436.

531 Strictly speaking, disgorgement is not a kind of damages or compensation which is based on the victim party's loss.

532 Id, p. 334.

533 "*Despite the attention it still garners, almost no economically oriented scholars adhere to the simple theory of efficient breach. In fact, it's been almost forty years since any serious scholar defended the simple*

attacks against this doctrine and suggested putting an end to it.[534] Faced with all kinds of questions from both economic and non-economic arguments one might ask whether or not the efficient breach doctrine is still useful in modern study of contract law.

The practical issue motivating scholars to develop the efficient breach theory is to find an optimal solution to the situation where circumstances have changed after contract formation and so performing the original promise may decrease welfare.[535] Even if our perspective to the contract formation stage changes, we may agree that the parties have to consider how they are going to deal with the possible risks arising from the on-going contractual relationship. People would not enter a contract had both of them already known that performing the contract would decrease their welfare. But in a world with positive transaction costs and incomplete contracting, some risks are beyond parties' stipulation. Hence parties might find a contract which they had initially considered as efficient becoming inefficient. So solutions are still needed if there is no ex-ante arrangement about these unexpected events. Of course, it has to be admitted that breach is one among a number of optimal solutions in all circumstances where performing the original contract is considered economically inefficient. The aim of efficient breach theory is not merely to discharge a promisor from his contractual obligation by making him pay money in place of specific performance.[536] Instead, re-negotiations and ex-post cooperation are considered much more preferable in dealing with uncertainty and risks arising after the conclusion of contracts. Under this premise, the doctrine of efficient breach opens a window for evaluating contractual behaviour and assessing legal remedies in a wider perspective. There are at least three implications that can be inferred from the efficient breach doctrine.

Firstly, one contribution of the efficient breach doctrine is to draw the line between an efficient performance zone and efficient breach zone, on the basis of cost-benefit analysis. In this chapter, it is suggested that the border between efficient breach zone and efficient performance zone should be drawn with the consideration of performance cost. As is shown, efficient breach doctrine works better in the model of contracts to produce goods, while it happens at a relatively lower probability in the context of contracts to convey goods. The result that the efficient breach doctrine is applied differently in these two contract models is explained by the performance cost aspect. Even for the contract to produce goods, the possibility that efficient breach takes place is low if the risk of non-performance arises from an outside bidder who is willing to pay a higher price for the goods to be produced. For the same reason, efficient breach may take place in the context of contracts to deliver goods in relation to unexpected performance costs. In this sense, it is preferable

theory outside of a first-year Contracts course. Most contract theorists, however, have paid little attention to subsequent work in the area." Klass 2013, p. 2.

534 Sidhu 2011, p. 360.

535 Katz 2012, p. 780.

536 Some scholars try to defend the efficient breach theory by treating it as "an alternative way of discharging one's duties under the contract." It is argued that: "*the term 'efficient breach' is actually a misnomer, because paying money in place of specific performance, if the promisor finds it advantageous to do so, is entirely consistent with the best understanding of the parties' agreement. Thus it is not a breach at all, but rather an alternate way of discharging one's duties under the contract... we might equivalently (and perhaps more clearly) speak of 'efficient performance' or 'efficient cancellation option' or 'efficient rescission' and if there is no breach of promise, then there can be no promissory wrong.*" Id, p. 785.

to integrate the first model of efficient breach which is based on the explanation of performance cost into the structure of law. By differentiating an efficient performance zone (or inefficient breach zone) and an efficient breach zone (or inefficient performance zone), this doctrine causes a re-think over that behaviour which either falls into the efficient breach zone or into the efficient performance zone. A promisor should be motivated to take the optimal level of performance rather than be strictly bound by the obligation to perform when it is economically inefficient to do so. In order to realize this, the law should be shaped in a way that, on the one hand it facilitates the promisor to base his act on the prospective profit and cost of this act, and on the other hand enables the promisee to realize his expected benefits in a cost efficient way. Moreover, another interesting topic arousing quite a lot of discussion in law and economics refers to "opportunistic breach". A breach is deemed as opportunistic when "one-party attempts to reap the benefit of the bargain without bearing the agreed-upon cost".[537] We may want the law of contract to discourage this type of breach and consider depriving the actor of all the benefits he could obtain from the opportunism.

The second lesson to be learned from the efficient breach theory is that remedies for breach may have multiple influences over all aspects of transactions. Other than to motivate a single breach-or-perform decision, remedies will influence resource allocation, transaction costs, risk-allocation, contract re-negotiation or even the price in the relative market. By realizing this, one can better understand how to balance contract remedies with one specific goal. For instance, it is possible to evaluate whether a whole system of remedies for breach may promote performance, negotiation or risk allocation. As is known, the ultimate goal of contract remedies which constitute an important part of contract law is to help parties to better achieve their individual preferred aims and realize welfare maximization. However, this final goal can only be achieved through the realization of every specific task.

The last point to be inferred from the efficient breach doctrine concerns freedom in contracting. As is noted, breach and compensation is the second-best tool for welfare maximization on many occasions. A more desirable approach to guiding people to behave efficiently is derived from private negotiation. After all, contract parties are better than courts or legal scholars at assessing their own preferences and working for their own welfare. They know more about how to deal with risks in their transactions, which kind of breaches are clearly efficient and should be priced rather than punished, through which remedy they can avoid inefficient breach more cheaply and so on.[538] We want the law to facilitate parties' ex-ante and ex-post contracting. Therefore, legislators should carefully design the default remedy rules, because they may have either a negative or positive effect on free contracting.[539] Moreover, the most important point is to diminish mandatory rules in contract law and give parties more freedom in choosing their own remedies or settle their disputes. For example, courts should reduce interference with liquidated damage clauses. Rather than scrutinize the amount of damages stipulated by contract parties, a more preferable way for courts is to evaluate the formation process of those clauses.

537 Klass 2013, p. 10.

538 Id, p. 24.

539 For more discussion, see Depoorter & Tontrup 2012.

5. Conclusion

This chapter compares the capacities of different remedies to promote efficiency in cases where unexpected contingencies have altered the utility of a contract which used to be efficient at the time when it was concluded. In the context where a seller breaches a contract to convey goods, specific performance provides a better solution than monetary compensation to enhancing efficiency under the consideration of fully compensating the buyer, lowering transaction costs as well as allocating risks. In such a context, efficient breaches occur in a very limited scope, irrespective of whether the subject of the contract concerns general goods or unique items. However, under another contract context, concerning goods to be produced, the story of efficient breach is applicable based on the explanation of unexpected performance cost. Performance of a contract is inefficient if the cost of performance increases to such an extent that it exceeds the profits to be obtained by the promisee from the contract. In such a case, the remedy of expectation damages offers the promisor more solutions to achieve non-performance. Moreover, the risk of non-performance is moved from a buyer to the seller without making the seller bear uncertain costs.

Within the category of monetary damages defined by law, expectation damages work better than other forms of damages on motivating efficient performance and efficient breach. In comparison, reliance damages as well as restitution create insufficient incentives for the promisor to perform the contract, since these two types of remedy are based on a promisee's economic position before the contract was made. Disgorgement goes to another extreme and deters breach by eliminating all the profit to be obtained by a promisor from the breach. However, what is found to be optimal in enhancing efficiency regarding an inefficient contract is a remedy based upon an ex-ante or ex-post agreement by contract parties. Hereby, it is suggested that the law should encourage such an agreement, for instance by diminishing obstacles to negotiations.

Applying the findings in this chapter to legal analysis, chapters 6, 7 and 8 will put the analysis into the background of specific legal systems, including English Law, Chinese Law and European Union Law, respectively. The purpose of the analysis is to assess whether or not the efficient breach theory can be promoted by the remedy rules in these three systems. To be more specific, the premise set in the whole research is based on the structure of commercial sales contracts, in which both of the parties are assumed to be equal rational maximisers of their own welfare. In order to make this assessment, the questions to be answered within each legal system will be shaped into two major categories, including the remedy system as well as a general application of the efficient breach doctrine in sales contracts.

This research will take the following issues into consideration within each legal system: 1) How does the law deal with situations when a contract falls into the efficient performance zone and the efficient breach zone respectively? 2) What is the default remedy for a seller's breach of contract in each legal system? 3) What is the general attitude of each system towards monetary damages, especially, party-designed remedies? 4) Is it possible for efficient breach to take place in specific cases? Afterwards, chapter 9 will compare the capacities of these three legal systems to promote performance, and non-performance, as well as re-negotiations.

Chapter 6

EFFICIENT BREACH AND EUROPEAN UNION CONTRACT LAW

European contract law, in its definition, may be understood in a broad sense, including the rules of contract law at many different levels, such as the international, the European and the national levels.[540] A rule of European contract law may follow from international conventions, for instance, the "UN Vienna (Sales) Convention" (or the "CISG")[541] or from the general principles recognized in the contract law of Member States. However, discussion about efficient breach in this chapter will be developed within a narrow scope of European law. In this thesis, the concept of European contract law only refers to the substantive contract law at the European level, namely, rules of sales contract law based on the achievements of Europeanization. This chapter will particularly focus on three European contract law instruments: the Principles of European Contract Law, the Draft Common Frame of Reference and the Common European Sales Law. At the beginning of this chapter, an introduction to the process of Europeanization in Private Law and Contract law will be provided (section 1). Afterwards, section 2 will indicate the general remedy rules within EU contract law concerning the application of specific performance, damages rules as well as party-agreed damages. The goal of this section is to answer the question of whether EU law can motivate people to perform the contract in an efficient way or not. Application of the efficient breach model with regard to performance cost will be analysed in section 3, particularly concerning how EU law deals with a contract which has fallen into the zone where strict performance is inefficient. However, application of efficient breach has its limitation within the scope of EU law measures, in relation to the nature of EU law as well as the characteristics of cross-border transactions (section 4). In section 5, an economic analysis will be provided, examining a seller's incentives to perform and to breach within EU law. Section 6 concludes.

540 Beale, Fauvarque-Cosson, Rutgers, Tallon & Vogenauer 2010, p. 4.

541 The Vienna Convention on the International Sale of Goods (1980), so far, has been ratified by 74 countries. Among European Union countries, only the United Kingdom, Portugal, Malta and Ireland have not accepted it.

1. An Introduction to European Union Sales Contract Law

1.1. Europeanization of Private Law and Contract Law

Since the 1980's, a large number of academic or political documents have appeared at European level, purporting to support the creation and operation of an internal market within Europe. This goal of shaping a common market with free movement of goods, people, capital and services[542] has been stated clearly in both the "Treaty Establishing the European Community (Articles 14, 94 and 95 TEC)" and the "Treaty on the Functioning of the European Union (Article 26, 114 TFEU)",[543] which provided a legal basis for Europeanization measures in the field of contract law.[544] Accordingly, the European countries have been witnessing a process of Europeanization in multiple dimensions. The European Union members promote the legislative harmonisation by adopting measures

542 Traditionally, the reason for creating a European contract law is to reduce the transaction costs involved in cross border trades. This is also one of the strongest reasons for promoting the Europeanization of contract law. A different idea is to keep Europe open up to local elements. For instance, Heirbaut & Storme 2011 argues: "something else to keep in mind is that flexibility and openness made the old Ius Commune successful. It was always a blend of local and European elements...as such it embraced unity in diversity long before that became the motto of European Union". *See* Heirbaut & Storme 2011, p. 32.

543 Article 14 (2) of TEC: "2. The internal market shall comprise an area without internal frontiers in which the free movement of goods, persons, services and capital is ensured in accordance with the provisions of this Treaty." Article 94 of EC: "*The Council shall, acting unanimously on a proposal from the Commission and after consulting the European Parliament and the Economic and Social Committee, issue directives for the approximation of such laws, regulations or administrative provisions of the Member States as directly affect the establishment or functioning of the common market.*"Article 95 of EC: "*... The Council shall, acting in accordance with the procedure referred to in Article 251 and after consulting the Economic and Social Committee, adopt the measures for the approximation of the provisions laid down by law, regulation or administrative action in Member States which have as their object the establishment and functioning of the internal market. 2. Paragraph 1 shall not apply to fiscal provisions, to those relating to the free movement of persons nor to those relating to the rights and interests of employed persons. 3. The Commission, in its proposals envisaged in paragraph 1 concerning health, safety, environmental protection and consumer protection, will take as a base a high level of protection, taking account in particular of any new development based on scientific facts. Within their respective powers, the European Parliament and the Council will also seek to achieve this objective...*"Article 26 TFEU: "The Union shall adopt measures with the aim of establishing or ensuring the functioning of the internal market, in accordance with the relevant provisions of the Treaties. 2. The internal market shall comprise an area without internal frontiers in which the free movement of goods, persons, services and capital is ensured in accordance with the provisions of the Treaties..." Article 114 TFEU: "*1...The European Parliament and the Council shall, acting in accordance with the ordinary legislative procedure and after consulting the Economic and Social Committee, adopt the measures for the approximation of the provisions laid down by law, regulation or administrative action in Member States which have as their object the establishment and functioning of the internal market...6. The Commission shall, within six months of the notifications as referred to in paragraphs 4 and 5, approve or reject the national provisions involved after having verified whether or not they are a means of arbitrary discrimination or a disguised restriction on trade between Member States and whether or not they shall constitute an obstacle to the functioning of the internal market...*"

544 Twigg-Flesner 2008, p. 27.

(EU measures), which take the form of a Regulation or a Directive.[545] The Courts at both EU and national level, such as the Court of Justice of the European Union (CJEU)[546] and the European Court of Human Rights (ECHR)[547], contributed to the process of Europeanization by creating case law or applying and interpreting the European norms.[548] In addition, legal scholars contributed with a considerable amount of activities to the Europeanization of law, for instance, by doing comparative studies of national law and finding the general principles and rules for a common European Law, etc.

With respect to private law, efforts have been made in order to create a Common European Private Law. An obvious feature of this Europeanization is that the general contract law and sales law which share a more technical character than other branches of civil law have been at the centre of attention.[549] In the early 1980s, the Commission on European Contract Law (called the "Lando-Commission" after its chairman and founder Ole Lando) was established, which represented one of the first steps of Europeanization of contract law.[550] In 1989, the European Parliament passed a resolution calling for the start of the preparation of a "Common European Code of Private Law",[551] which was reiterated five years later.[552] Almost at the same time, the Lando-Commission published the first part of the "Principles of European Contract Law (hereinafter: PECL)"[553], based mostly on a comparative approach. The second and third part of the "PECL" came out in

545 The legislative measures are normally accomplished in a way: "*a European measure which sets out a specific result, but leaves it up to individual member states to choose the 'form and methods' (Article 248EC[Article 228 TFEU]) as to how this result can be achieved in national law.*" Twigg-Flesner 2010, p. 3.

546 The CJEU was established in 1952 and has its location in Luxemburg. It consists of three courts: the Court of Justice, the General Court (created in 1988) and the Civil Service Tribunal (created in 2004). The CJEU deals with three missions, including: reviewing the legality of the acts of the institutions of the European Union; ensuring that the Member States comply with obligations under the Treaties, and interpreting European Union law at the request of the national courts and tribunals. For more information, see the official website: http://curia.europa.eu/jcms/jcms/Jo2_6999/.

547 The ECHR was set up in 1959 and has its basis in Strasbourg. It rules on individual or State applications alleging violations of the civil and political rights set out in the European Convention on Human Rights. See www.echr.coe.int/Documents/Court_in_brief_ENG.pdf.

548 For instance, Article 234 of EC and Article 267 of TFEU indicate the role of CJEU. "*The Court of Justice of the European Union shall have jurisdiction to give preliminary rulings concerning: (a) the interpretation of the Treaties; (b) the validity and interpretation of acts of the institutions, bodies, offices or agencies of the Union; Where such a question is raised before any court or tribunal of a Member State, that court or tribunal may... request the Court to give a ruling thereon... .*"

549 As is indicated by Chirico (2010): "*The specific focus on contract law, rather than on the whole of private law, is probably the consequence of the perceived more "technical" character of the contract branch of civil law, as compared not only to family or labour law, but also to neighbouring areas of civil law such as property law and extra-contractual liability/tort law. In such fields, policy considerations play a more obvious role and may render a Europe-wide agreement more difficult to reach...*" Chirico 2010, p. 11–12.

550 Zelst 2008, P. 4.

551 Resolution of the European Parliament on action to bring into line the Private Law of the member state, [OJ 1989 C 158/400].

552 Resolution of the European Parliament on the harmonization of certain sectors of the Private Law of the member states, [OJ 1994 C 205/518].

553 See: Lando & Beale 1995.

1999 and 2003 respectively.[554] Moreover, in reaction to the second resolution issued by the European Parliament,[555] the European Council in Tampere in 1999 reached a conclusion, expressing the common desire of creating a "greater convergence in Civil Law".[556] Following this step and the adoption of the "Consumer Sales Directive (the "CSD 99/44/EC")" in 1999, the European Commission took increasing activities for promoting the realization of "A common European private law".

In July 2001, the first communication on contract law was issued by the European Commission and it was followed up by successive subsequent communications. One important event was the publication of the second communication in 2003, *A More Coherent European Contract Law, An Action Plan* (the "Action Plan"),[557] in which the measure of a "Common Frame of Reference (CFR)" was raised by the commission.[558] As indicated, the Commission announced the funding of the project of CFR, which is aimed at improving the quality and coherence of European contract law.[559] In addition, the "Action Plan" also suggested a review of the Union *acquis* in the area of Consumer contract law, which afterwards led to the issuance of a proposal for a Directive on Consumer rights in 2008.[560] After publishing this action plan, the European Commission and Parliament submitted a number of resolutions on the matter. In 2009, a final outline edition of the "Draft Common Frame of Reference (hereinafter: DCFR)"[561] containing

554 See: Lando & Beale 2000; Lando et al 2003.

555 In the second resolution, the Parliament called for convergence of particular sectors of private law, while also arguing for the commencement "*on the possibility of drawing up a Common European Code of Private Law*" which is "*essential to the completion of the internal market*". [OJ 1994 C 205/518].

556 Presidency Conclusion, Tampere European Council, 15, 16 October 1999, SI (1999) 800, heading in front of no 28ff; COM (2001) 398 final no 4.

557 COM (2003).

558 Beside the "CFR", an optional instrument was mentioned as a measure in the Action Plan. The Commission wrote: "92. *The Commission will examine whether non-sector-specific-measures such as an optional instrument may be required to solve problems in the area of European contract law. It intends to launch a reflection on the opportuneness, the possible form, the contents and the legal basis for possible action of such measures. As to its form one could think of EU wide contract law rules in the form of a regulation or a recommendation, which would exist in parallel with, rather than instead of national contract laws. This new instrument would exist in all Community languages. It could either apply to all contracts, which concern cross-border transactions or only to those which parties decide to subject to it through a choice of law clause. The latter would give parties the greatest degree of contractual freedom. They would only choose the new instrument if it suited their economic or legal needs better than the national law which would have been determined by private international law rules as the law applicable to the contract.*"

559 Section 62 of the Action Plan indicates three objects of the "CFR": "*First...providing for best solutions in terms of common terminology and rules... The second objection... achieving a higher degree of convergence between the contract laws of the EU Member States and possibly appropriate third countries...Thirdly, the Commission will base its reflections on whether non-sector-specific measures such as an optional instrument may be required to solve problems in the area of European contract law on the common frame of reference.*"

560 Proposal for a Directive of the European Parliament and of the Council on Consumer Rights, COM (2008) 614.

561 Von Bar et al 2009.

principles, definitions and model rules of private law was presented to the European Commission by a network of research groups.[562]

The creation of the DCFR is probably one significant step toward a greater harmonization of European Contract Law and it put this issue into another stage.[563] The next step was the European Commission's publication of a Green Paper on "policy options for progress towards a European Contract Law for consumers and businesses",[564] in which a number of options on "how to strengthen the internal market` by making progress in the area of European Contract Law" were set out.[565] The Green Paper put forward the production of the "Common European Sales Law",[566] which was passed by the European Commission in October 2011 as an optional instrument for cross-border transactions in Europe. However, given the fact that the digital market is developing rapidly, the Common European Sales Law is considered to be an insufficient instrument and hence has been withdrawn by the European Commission via its work Program for 2015. Moreover, the European Commission intends to adopt a modified proposal in order to boost e-commerce in the Digital Single Market.[567] This is not the last word on the subject of the Europeanization of contract law, but a movement into dealing with the

562 A joint collaboration called "Common Principles of European Contract Law (CoPECL) Network of Excellence" was established in 2005 in order to accomplish the undertaking of creating the "CFR". Among this network are 150 legal scholars from all the European Union member states and legal experts from a number of research groups (the major ones are the "Study Group" and the "*Acquis* Group"). The "Study Group (the 'Study Group on a European Civil Code')" is a network of academics, from across the EU, conducting comparative law research in private law in the various legal jurisdictions of the Member States. Their aim is to "*produce a codified set of Principles of European Law for the law of obligations and core aspects of the law of property.*" The "*Acquis* Group", founded in 2002, currently consists of more than 40 legal scholars from nearly all EC Member States. It "*targets a systematic arrangement of existing Community law which will help to elucidate the common structures of the emerging Community private law. For this purpose, the Acquis Group primarily concentrates upon the existing EC private law which can be discovered within the acquis communautaire. The research of the Acquis Group will be published as 'Principles of the Existing EC Contract Law'* ". More information about the research groups involved in the drafting of European Contract Law can be found in the website www.copecl.org/, which lists out all the research groups and the websites of the "Study group" and the "Acquis Group" respectively (www.acquis-group.org/ and www.sgecc.net).

563 McKendrick 2012, p. 9.

564 COM (2010) 348 final.

565 "1...*The purpose of this Green Paper is to set out the options on how to strengthen the internal market by making progress in the area of European Contract Law, and launch a public consultation on them.*" See: COM (2010) 348 final.

566 COM (2011) 635 final. The CESL is comprised of three main parts: a Proposal for a Regulation (hereinafter: Prop. CESL), Annex I to the Regulation consisting of the contract law rules (hereinafter: CESL) and Annex II containing a Standard Information Notice.

567 On December 16th of 2014, the European Commission adopted its Work Programme for 2015 and set out the actions the Commission intends to take over in 2015. One action to be taken by the European Commission is to withdraw or modify 80 proposals after examining around 450 proposals. It is intended to use a new proposal to replace the COM/2011/0635 Common European Sales Law. See European Commission, A New Start: European Commission work plan to deliver jobs, growth and investment. The analysis of European Union contract in this thesis is developed on the basis of COM/2011/0635.

problems in cross-border contracts by legislative measure. Besides the aforementioned instruments, more legislations and actions have been launched at the European level.[568]

So far, a large variety of documents concerning European Contract Law have appeared at the EU level, including, for instance, the "PECL" (1994), the "Acquis Principles", the "CSD (the Consumer Sales Directive) 99/44/EC" (1999), the "DCFR" (2009), and the CESL (2011). The achievements in the Europeanization of Private Law until now, on the one hand, have focused on the areas of contract law and sales law (esp. consumer contracts)[569] in relation to commercial activities which have been of central importance in the legal unification agenda. On the other hand, those achievements have been presented as several different types of measures including soft law, directives, and regulations. In section 1.2, a framework of EU sales contract law will be presented.

1.2. *Structure of EU Sales Contract Law*

Featured as a multi-level structure, EU sales contract law in the current stage includes two major resources. One is binding rules of contract law, which are mostly derived from national law, international conventions (for instance, CISG which applies by default whenever the parties have not opted out of it) and legislative measures by the European Union (principally referring to regulations, directives and decisions).[570] Besides, the other source of EU contract law comes from non-binding rules or soft law,[571] aiming at improving the consistency and quality of EU legislation.[572] Examples are official "toolbox" rules, recommendations or publications of the results of the Expert Group.[573] Those soft laws also provide resources for legislations, judgments and contract drafting. Table 17 shows a framework of EU contract law.

Among those resources which may shape the structure of cross-border commercial sales within the EU, contract law instruments based on the recent evolution of

568 For instance, in between August and December of 2012, the "public consultation through a Green Paper on the delivery of parcels", the Communication on "Protecting businesses against misleading marketing practices and ensuring effective enforcement" and "Global Recalls Portal" (which will help government regulators, consumers and businesses search for information on consumer product recalls across the world), etc. have been passed by the European Commission. Delfino 2013, p. 90.

569 An obvious feature is that the Consumer Rights Directives constitute the major part of contract law issued at the European level. The major directives regarding consumer contracts are: the Doorstep Selling Directive (85/577 EEC), the Directive on Distance Selling (97/7EC), The Package Travel Directive (90/314/EEC), the Timeshare Directive (94/47/EC), the Unfair Contract Terms Directive (93/31/EEC), the "Directive (98/6/EC) on Consumer protection in the indication of the prices of products offered to consumers", the Consumer Sales Directive (99/44/EC), the Directive on injunctions for the protection of consumer's interests (98/27/EC) and the Distance Marketing of Financial Services (2002/65/EC). Keirse 2011, P 43–44.

570 Beale, Fauvarque-Cosson, Rutgers, Tallon & Vogenauer 2010, p. 3–4.

571 Soft law is normally used to describe those rules "*laid down in instruments which have not been attributed legally binding force as such, but nevertheless may have certain (indirect) legal effects, and that are aimed at and may produce practical effects*". As to the concept of soft law, see Senden 2004, p. 111–112.

572 COM (2010) 348 final, p. 7.

573 Id; McKendrick 2012, p. 9.

Europeanization will be targeted as the subject in this chapter. The discussion will be limited to the PECL, DCFR and CESL.

PECL: Principles of European Contract Law are one of the most famous rules of soft law drafted by the "Lando Commission". Based on comparative research, the PECL provides a set of model rules for guiding "*the interpretation and development of the national legal systems in Europe and thus pave the way towards a gradual assimilation of these systems*".[574] In this sense, it works as a source of inspiration in creating contract laws by national or European legislators as well as in drafting standard terms and conditions by contracting parties.[575]

DCFR: Similar to the PECL, the DCFR is based on scholarly endeavours. However, as is indicated in the text of the DCFR, this text is also assumed to serve as "a draft for drawing up a 'political' Common Frame of Reference (CFR)" which was first called for by the European Commission's "Action Plan" of 2003. In this sense, the DCFR was supposed to be acknowledged by the European Community. The content of the DCFR contains "principles, definitions and model rules", covering the areas beyond contract law such as in book I (General Provisions), book V (Benevolent Intervening in Another's Affairs), book VI (Non-Contractual Liability Arising out of Damage Caused to Another) and book VII (Unjustified Enrichment), etc. In relation to sales contracts, Book III (Obligations and Corresponding Rights) and Book IV Part A (Specific Contracts and the Rights and Obligations Arising from Them: Sales) shape the basic structure of rules.

CESL: Unlike the PECL and the DCFR, the CESL was launched by the European Commission as a regulation that introduces an optional instrument for European firms and consumers. As is stated, the CESL could be chosen by the parties as the law regulating their contracts and thus works as an alternative to national law. Besides, rather than setting general rules of private law or contract law, the CESL only covers contracts for the supply of goods to be manufactured or transferred and contracts for the supply of digital contents, as well as the service contracts related to the sales contracts.[576] Emphasis in the CESL is placed specially on offering a specific, largely protective sales regime for consumers and small and medium sized entrepreneurs ("SME"),[577] for whom negotiations about the applicable law are less possible.

574 The work of "PECL", to some extent, is similar to the codification of the UNIDROIT Principles on International Commercial Contact (PICC). Both of them are meant to "formulate systematic rules on cross-border transactions by in part codifying adopted principles of international contracts, and in part developing new rules". Moss 2011, p 148; Jansen & Zimmermann 2008, p. 505–506. Zimmermann 2009, p. 481–482.

575 Beale 2011, p. 118.

576 Art 5 of the proposed regulation designed to give effect to the CESL (Prop. CESL).

577 The discussion of the CESL in this thesis is based on the COM/2011/0635, which was published in October 2011. The CESL has made a clear differentiation between a trader and a consumer. As is given in art 2 of the proposed regulation designed to give effect to the CESL (Prop. CESL), a trader means any natural or legal person who is acting for purposes relating to that person's trade, business, craft,

Until now, although the Europeanization of Contract Law is still at the early stage of development, the large variety of EU contract law measures has formed a blueprint of EU contract law. This framework, including mixed resources of binding rules and soft rules may provide the parties involved in cross-border sales with optional instruments to structure their contracts. For those commercial sales with a cross-border dimension, businesses may have access to more options of applicable laws to their contractual relations in addition to national laws. Moreover, businesses may also draw inspiration from standard provisions provided by those European Union instruments when drafting their contract terms.

Table 17. Resources of EU Contract Law

Binding Rules of ECL	Primary law:		TEU, TFEU, Charter of fundamental rights
	Secondary law: (Article 288. TFEU)	Regulations	**CESL**
		Directives	
		Decisions	
	Judicial practice of the CJEU		
	General Principles		
	International Agreements		CISG
Non-binding Rules	Recommendations and Opinions		
	"Tool box" for the legislator		Commission Act[39]
			Inter-institutional Agreement[40]
	Publication of the results of the Expert Group		**PECL**
			DCFR

or profession. A 'consumer' means any natural person who is acting for purposes which are outside that person's trade, business, craft, or profession. In addition Art 7 of Prop. CESL defines a small medium sized enterprise as "a trader which (a) employs fewer than 250 persons; and (b) has an annual turnover not exceeding EUR 50 million or an annual balance sheet total not exceeding EUR 43 million, or, for an SME which has its habitual residence in a Member State whose currency is not the euro or in a third country, the equivalent amounts in the currency of that Member State or third country."

578 As is pointed out in the Green Paper COM (2010) 348 final:

"[t]he Commission could adopt an act (e.g. a Communication or Commission Decision) on European Contract Law to be used as a reference tool by the Commission to ensure the coherence and quality of legislation. The Commission would use the "toolbox" when drafting proposals for new legislation or when revising existing measures."

579 A "Tool-box" could also be an inter-institutional agreement. This kind of agreement is created between "the Commission, Parliament and Council to make consistent reference to its provisions when drafting and negotiating legislative proposals bearing on European Contract Law." *See id.*

2. General Rules about Sales Contract, Breach and Remedies

One crucial concept stressed in this research refers to "breach". However, instead of using the concept of "breach", the EU instruments adopt the terminology of "non-performance to include any failure to perform a contractual obligation, no matter whether or not this failure is excused.[580] Cases of breach might be presented either as a business seller's breach or a consumer buyer's breach. This section will only provide the basic structure of a seller's breach and a buyer's remedies indicated in the EU law. According to the efficient breach theory, the remedy system should facilitate the promisor to base his act on the expected profit and cost of this act as well as enable the promisee to realize his expected interest in a cost efficient way. Based on this assumption, the purpose of this section is on the one hand to analyse EU law's capacity to shape a seller's incentive to perform the contract and on the other hand to examine whether EU law provides a cost efficient way to protect the expected benefit of a promisee.

2.1. Sales Contract

In contrast to the PECL, both the DCFR and the CESL have drawn a set of separate rules governing what is defined as sales contracts.[581] Moreover, the scope of the sales contract has been extended to covering contracts for the supply of goods to be manufactured or produced.[582] The PECL, in contrast, are drafted as general rules of contract law for the European Union and it applies to types of contracts other than sales contracts.

2.2. Seller's Breach and Buyer's Remedy in General

After a contract is concluded, both parties have the obligation to comply with it. A seller has to deliver the goods, transfer the ownership of the goods and the goods should be in conformity with the contract.[583] Basically, two major types of "non-performance" are indicated, including the situations where a seller fails to deliver the goods ("non-

580 The term of "non-performance" instead of "breach" has been used in PECL, as well as subsequent European soft law texts. See Chapter 8 (Non-Performance and Remedies in General') PECL; Book III-1:101 DCFR; and Annex I, chapter 1, Article 8.2, Chapters 11 ('the buyer's remedies') and 13 ('the seller's remedies') CESL.

581 Article 2 Reg CESL: "'sales contract' means any contract under which the trader ('the seller') transfers or undertakes to transfer the ownership of the goods to another person ('the buyer'), and the buyer pays or undertakes to pay the price thereof; it includes a contract for the supply of goods to be manufactured or produced and excludes contracts for sale on execution or otherwise involving the exercise of public authority." DCFR IV.A.–1:202: "A contract for the "sale" of goods is a contract under which one party, the seller, undertakes to another party, the buyer, to transfer the ownership of the goods to the buyer, or to a third person, either immediately on conclusion of the contract or at some future time, and the buyer undertakes to pay the price."

582 Article IV.A.–1:102 DCFR: *"A contract under which one party undertakes, for a price, to manufacture or produce goods for the other party and to transfer their ownership to the other party is to be considered as primarily a contract for the sale of the goods."*

583 Article IV.A.-2:101 DCFR; Article 91 CESL.

delivery") or the goods delivered are not in conformity with the contract ("non-conformity"). Breach of an obligation is the condition for awarding consumer remedies. In the case of breach, a buyer is provided with a set of standard remedies which are available in the PECL, DCFR and CESL.[584] As is indicated, a buyer may require: 1) performance (including specific performance, repair or replacement); 2) withhold the buyer's own performance; 3) terminate the contract; 4) declare a price reduction; or 5) claim damages (Table 18).

The application of remedies depends on the specific case of breach. When it comes to non-delivery, there is in principle no strict hierarchy among these five major types of remedies. Without exception, the PECL (Article 8:101), DCFR (Article III. – 3:101) and CESL all state that the aggrieved buyer may resort to "any" of the remedies provided by them. It means that a buyer may choose the remedy which is most preferable to him as long as the prerequisites for this remedy have been satisfied. But there is no priority of claim for specific performance or damages. The rule is different when it comes to non-conformity where priority is placed on specific performance that is present as a cure. Within the EU measures, a distinction between business contracts and consumer contracts has been made in relation to the application of remedies.[585] An important feature implied in commercial sales where both the seller and the buyer are professional business men, is that a buyer's choice of remedy is subject to cure by the seller. Article 106 (2) has indicated the priority of cure in business contract specifically. As is shown in the PECL (Article 8:104), DCFR (Article 3:202) and CESL (Article 109), a seller whose early tender was not in conformity with the contract may make a new and conforming tender within the time allowed for performance or cure the defect at its own expense even after the time allowed for performance. (Table 18)[586] The buyer may not directly terminate the contract unless the non-conformity constitutes fundamental breach.[587] This is the normal case in commercial sales. In this sense, the buyer's cure is treated more like the right of a seller rather than merely the remedy of a buyer.

584 Article 106(1), (3), CESL.

585 But in the consumer contract, a consumer buyer has great freedom in choosing remedies. He may require the seller to either repair the defects in the goods he received or change the defective goods into conforming goods. More importantly, the consumer is able to turn down any offer by the seller to cure so as to require price reduction, damages or termination of the contract immediately. The application of the remedy is at the consumer's choice. Furthermore, Article 114 of CESL and Article IV.A.–4:201 of DCFR adds that consumers may terminate the contract even when the lack of conformity is not fundamental, enhancing a consumer's free choice of remedies.

586 There are also some limits to the buyer's cure, which will be shown in section 4.

587 For instance, DCFR lists out the conditions for terminating contracts, which are indicated in Article. III.–3:502: Termination for fundamental non-performance; Article. III.–3:503: Termination after notice fixing additional time for performance; Article. III.–3:504: Termination for anticipated non-performance; and Article. III.–3:505: Termination for inadequate assurance of performance. Situation in consumer contracts is different, where a creditor may resort to termination unless the non-performance is insignificant.

Table 18. Articles in EU Contract Law regarding a Buyer's Remedy[588]

PECL	*8:101: Whenever a party does not perform an obligation under the contract and the non-performance is not excused under Article 8:108, the aggrieved party may* resort to any of the remedies *set out in Chapter 9.* *8:104: A party whose tender of performance is not accepted by the other party because it does not conform to the contract* may make a new and conforming tender *where the time for performance has not yet arrived or the delay would not be such as to constitute a fundamental non-performance.*
DCFR	*III.-3:101: (1) If an obligation is not performed by the debtor and the non-performance is not excused, the creditor may* resort to any of the remedies *set out in this Chapter.* *III.-3:202: (1) The debtor* may make a new and conforming tender *if that can be done within the time allowed for performance.*
CESL	106: *(1) In the case of non-performance of an obligation by the seller, the buyer* may do any of the following: *(a) require performance, which includes specific performance, repair or replacement of the goods or digital content, under Section 3 of this Chapter; (b) withhold the buyer's own performance under Section 4 of this Chapter; (c) terminate the contract under Section 5 of this Chapter and claim the return of any price already paid, under Chapter 17; (d) reduce the price under Section 6 of this Chapter; and (e) claim damages under Chapter 16.* *(2) If the buyer is a trader: (a) the buyer's rights to exercise any remedy except withholding of performance* are subject to cure by the seller *as set out in Section 2 of this Chapter; and (b) the buyer's rights to rely on lack of conformity are subject to the requirements of examination and notification set out in Section 7 of this Chapter.* *109(1): A seller who has tendered performance early and who has been notified that the performance is not in conformity with the contract may make a new and conforming tender if that can be done within the time allowed for performance.*

The remedies can be cumulative. It means that a buyer may either choose between one and the other remedies or resort to more than one remedy in the same case. Both the PECL and the DCFR especially emphasize that the non-breaching party's right to damages cannot be cancelled when he resorts to any other remedies. However, a party cannot resort to two or more than two remedies at the same time if the remedies chosen by him are incompatible with each other (Table 19). For example, termination of contract is compatible with damages but incompatible with specific performance. Hence, if a buyer chooses to terminate a contract, it means the bond created by the contract will be brought to an end and he cannot ask for repair or replacement anymore but he is still able to claim for damages.

Table 19. Cumulation of Remedies under EU Contract Law

PECL	*8:102: Remedies which are not incompatible may be cumulated. In particular, a party is not deprived of its right to damages by exercising its right to any other remedy.*
DCFR	*III.-3:102: Remedies which are not incompatible may be cumulated. In particular, a creditor is not deprived of the right to damages by resorting to any other remedy.*
CESL	*106 (6): Remedies which are not incompatible may be cumulated.*

588 The underlined parts show: 1) the buyer's free choice of remedies; 2) the seller's right to cure. This chapter will always underline the part showing the similarities and differences in the languages expressed by these three EU measures.

2.3. *Damages rules*

As to the damages rules, the PECL, DCFR and CESL all include a separate part (Section 4 of the PECL; Section 7, Book III of the DCFR or Part VI of the CESL) covering the issue of damage measurement, types of damages and conditions for damages. A non-breaching buyer is entitled to damages for his losses that are caused by breach.[589]

2.3.1. General Measurement of Damages

Following the traditional doctrine of damages, EU contract law also sets the aim of damages as compensatory. More specifically, it aims to compensate a non-breaching party's expectation loss and to make him indifferent to breach and performance of the contract. As is indicated, the scope of damages should be able to put a creditor as nearly as possible (the underlined parts) into the position in which he would have been had the contract been duly performed (Table 20).

Table 20. The Rule of Expectation Damages in EU Contract Law

PECL	9:502: *The general measure of damages is such a sum as will put the aggrieved party* as nearly as possible *into the position in which it would have been if the contract had been duly performed. Such damages cover the loss which the aggrieved party has suffered and the gain of which it has been deprived.*
DCFR	III.–3:702: *The general measure of damages for loss caused by non-performance of an obligation is such sum as will put the creditor* as nearly as possible *into the position in which the creditor would have been if the obligation had been duly performed. Such damages cover loss which the creditor has suffered and gain of which the creditor has been deprived.*
CESL	160: *The general measure of damages for loss caused by non-performance of an obligation is such sum as will put the creditor into the position in which the creditor would have been if the obligation had been duly performed,* or, where that is not possible, as nearly as possible into that position. *Such damages cover loss which the creditor has suffered and gain of which the creditor has been deprived.*

The way of damage calculation is specified in relation to whether or not there is a substitute transaction (Table 21). If a creditor has arranged an alternative transaction to reasonably replace the original transaction, he could recover the shortfall between the value of what would have been payable under the terminated contract and the value of what is payable under the substitute transaction.[590] In contrast, if there is no alternative transaction, then the creditor's loss from non-performance is generally measured by the discrepancy between the contract price and the market price at the time when the creditor terminates the contract. Or if the creditor has arranged an unreasonable alternative transaction, then the market price rather than the alternative contract price should be considered. One example of an unreasonable transaction is the case in which the buyer could have

589 Article 9:504 PECL; Article III. 3:701 DCFR and Article 159 CESL.
590 Article 164, 165 CESL.

bought the substitute directly after he found out the existence of breach but he made an unreasonable delay in buying the substitute which was in fact more expensive.[591] According to the damages rules in European Contract law, what should be referred to for calculating the buyer's damages is the market price rather than the substitutive contract price. It is the buyer's unreasonable behavior (delay) that has contributed to his paying a higher price than the market price. However, a question might arise with regard to the way of damage assessment when the market price is higher than the alternative contract price. Suppose a buyer has arranged an alternative transaction for a price of 120 that is higher than the contract price (100) and lower than the market price (150). What he can recover is 20 (the difference between the contract price and the price of the alternative transaction) rather than 50 (the difference between the contract price and the market price), because the rule of market price can be precluded in this occasion. As is shown, the PECL, DCFR and CESL all try to entitle a creditor to his real loss rather than to motivate the creditor to make best possible substitute transaction. In addition, there is no specific rule dealing with how to calculate the damages in the circumstances when neither an alternative transaction nor the current price is available.

Table 21. Market Price or Alternative Price in EU Contract Law

PECL	9:506: *Where the aggrieved party has terminated the contract and has made a substitute transaction* within a reasonable time and in a reasonable manner, *it may recover the difference between the contract price and the price of the substitute transaction as well as damages for* any further loss *so far as these are recoverable under this Section.* 9:507: *Where the aggrieved party has terminated the contract and has not made a substitute transaction but* there is a current price *for the performance contracted for, it may recover the difference between the contract price and the price current at the time the contract is terminated as well as damages for any* further loss *so far as these are recoverable under this Section.*
DCFR	*III.-3:706: A creditor who has terminated a contractual relationship* in whole or in part *under Section 5 and has made a substitute transaction* within a reasonable time and in a reasonable manner *may, in so far as entitled to damages, recover the difference between the value of what would have been payable under the terminated relationship and the value of what is payable under the substitute transaction, as well as damages for* any further loss. *III.-3:707: Where the creditor has terminated a contractual relationship* in whole or in part *under Section 5 and has not made a substitute transaction but* there is a current price *for the performance, the creditor may, in so far as entitled to damages, recover the difference between the contract price and the price current at the time of termination as well as damages for* any further loss.

591 The comment of the DCFR provides another example in which the alternative transaction made by the creditor is significantly different from the original transaction.

O supplies a small car on hire to H for three weeks at a rent of € 1000 a week. The car breaks down at the end of the first week while H is on holiday, and as no other small car is available H terminates the contractual relationship with O and hires a large luxury car from another firm for the remaining two weeks at a rent of € 5000 a week. H's damages for extra rental charges will be restricted to the additional cost, if any, of hiring the nearest available equivalent of the original car in size and value.

See DCFR, p. 959.

CESL	*164: A creditor who has terminated a contract* in whole or in part *and has made a substitute transaction* within a reasonable time and in a reasonable manner *may, in so far as it is entitled to damages, recover the difference between the value of what would have been payable under the terminated contract and the value of what is payable under the substitute transaction, as well as damages for* any further loss. *165: Where the creditor has terminated the contract and has not made a substitute transaction but* there is a current price *for the performance, the creditor may, in so far as entitled to damages, recover the difference between the contract price and the price current at the time of termination as well as damages for* any further loss.

2.3.2. Limits on Damages

Several limits and conditions, however, have been set out on the expectation measure as well.

Firstly, without any exception, the famous "Hadley rule" or "Foreseeability rule"[592] has been incorporated into the EU instruments (Table 22). A debtor is only liable for losses that he did foresee or could be expected to have foreseen when the contract was concluded, as a possible consequence of his breach.[593] In economic theory, the "Hadley rule" is grounded on information explanation.[594] The debtor is assumed to make decisions based on his information about the benefit from and cost of his behavior. When the losses that are recoverable are limited to the amount that a debtor did foresee at the time of contract formation, the creditor would be motivated to disclose the information relating to his potential losses from non-performance. Besides, the information disclosed by the creditor ideally may facilitate the debtor to calculate his liability from non-performance which is equal to the other party's expectation loss and to make rational decisions concerning contract formation, price negotiation or precautions against non-performance. Assimilation of the "Hadley Rule", to some extent, is in accordance with the optimal reliance theory as well. The creditor is provided with incentives to take behavior in relation to the debtor's reasonable expectation since only the costs incurred by that behavior are recoverable. However, both the PECL and the DCFR have set exceptions if the non-performance was intentional, reckless or grossly negligent (Table 22). In this situation, the non-performing party's liability will not be restricted to the damage that he has foreseen or could be expected to have foreseen. However, two questions have been neglected by both the PECL and the DCFR. First, neither of them has indicated the scope of damages to be paid by the party who breaches a contract intentionally if the foreseeability rule is excluded. Should he compensate all the losses that are directly or indirectly caused by the

592 As is explained in Chapter 3, the "Hadley Rule" originated from the famous English case Hadley v Baxendale. In this case, the defendant delayed in delivering the plaintiff's crankshaft to an engineer for repair and thus the plaintiff suffered loss of profits. In the end, the judge held:

> *"[I]t follows, therefore, that the loss of profits here cannot reasonably be considered such a consequence of the breach of contract as could have been fairly and reasonably contemplated by both the parties when they made this contract."*

See [1854] 156 E.R. 145 p.152.

593 Article 161 CESL.

594 Ogus 2008, p. 141–143.

breach? Will a court apply the rule of disgorgement and make the breacher transfer all the profits created by his breach to the victim? The official comments on Article III.–3:703 of the DCFR gave an example indicating a case where a breach exposes a non-breaching promisee to heavy liability to a third party.[595] In this case, the breacher has to compensate the cost of the liability incurred by the promisee. But this does not clearly define the scope of damages for intentional breaches. Another question that is ignored by both the PECL and the DCFR is the definition of "intention".[596] Does an intentional breach indicating that the actor has bad faith or he merely knows he is breaching a contract? In the case regarding a breach of contract, it is difficult to describe the subjective status of the breacher, because a breach always presents itself as a state of affairs that a contract is broken.[597] As to those cases, it is difficult to determine the scope of damages merely based on a breacher's subjective intention. In order to answer the above questions, more explanations should have been made regarding the relationship between intentional and foreseeable losses.[598]

Table 22. The Foreseeability Rule

PECL	*9:503: The non-performing party is liable only for loss* which it foresaw or could reasonably have foreseen at the time of conclusion of the contract *as a likely result of its non-performance,* unless the non-performance was intentional or grossly negligent.
DCFR	*III.–3:703: The debtor in an obligation which arises from a contract or other juridical act is liable only for loss which the debtor* foresaw or could reasonably be expected to have foreseen at the time when the obligation was incurred *as a likely result of the non-performance,* unless the non-performance was intentional, reckless or grossly negligent.
CESL	*161: The debtor is liable only for loss which the debtor foresaw or could be* expected to have foreseen at the time when the contract was concluded *as a result of the non-performance.*

Another condition for awarding expectation damages is the causal relationship between non-performance and loss (Table 23). The commentary under Article III.-3:701 of the DCFR provides a basic standard to evaluate the causation between the non-performance and the loss. As is required, the creditor can only recover the losses that would not have

595 DCRF, p. 948.
"A contracts with B to construct and erect stands for a major exhibition at which leading electronic firms will display their equipment, hiring the stands from B. A week before the exhibition is due to open A demands a substantial increase in the contract sum. B refuses to pay, pointing out that A's failure to complete the remaining stands will not only cost B revenue but expose B to heavy liability to an exhibitor, C, which intended to use the exhibition to launch a major new product. A nevertheless withdraws its workforce, with the result that C's stand is not ready in time and C claims substantial compensation from B. A's breach being intentional and with knowledge of the likely consequences, the court has to award B an indemnity in respect of its liability to C, even though A could not reasonably have foreseen the magnitude of such liability at the time it made its contract with B. The same may be done even if A was not aware of the serious consequences for B of the intentional breach."

596 "Adjectives like "knowing" and "intentional" (and their adverb forms, "knowingly" and "intentionally") are most easily applied to specific action."

597 Craswell 2009, p. 1502–1504.

598 Van Kogelenberg 2013, p. 110–112.

occurred without the failure in performance.[599] In addition, the debtor is exempted from compensating the loss to the extent that the creditor contributed to the non-performance or its effects (the rule of contributory negligence), or the creditor omitted reasonable steps to reduce the loss (the rule of mitigation).[600]

Table 23. The Contributory Negligence Rule and the Mitigation Rule in EU

PECL	*9:504: The non-performing party is not liable for loss suffered by the aggrieved party to the extent that the aggrieved party contributed to the non-performance or its effects.* *9:505: (1) the non-performing party is not liable for loss suffered by the aggrieved party to the extent that the aggrieved party could have reduced the loss by taking reasonable steps.*
DCFR	*III.-3:704: The debtor is not liable for loss suffered by the creditor to the extent that the creditor contributed to the non-performance or its effects* *III.-3:705: (1) The debtor is not liable for loss suffered by the creditor to the extent that the creditor could have reduced the loss by taking reasonable steps.*
CESL	*162: The debtor is not liable for loss suffered by the creditor to the extent that the creditor contributed to the non-performance or its effects* *163: (1) the debtor is not liable for loss suffered by the creditor to the extent that the creditor could have reduced the loss by taking reasonable steps.*

With regard to the types of loss that are recoverable, the attitude of the CESL is different from that of the other two EU instruments (Table 24). Both the PECL and the DCFR have allowed creditors to claim for damages covering their non-pecuniary losses. But within the CESL, not all types of loss are recoverable. Art 2 of Reg. CESL specifies the losses that are recoverable by limiting them to economic loss and non-economic loss in the form of physical pain and suffering. What is more, other forms of non-economic loss such as impairment of the quality of life and loss of enjoyment are precluded from recovery with emphasis.

Table 24. The Term Loss in EU Contract Law

PECL	*9:501: (2) The loss for which damages are recoverable includes: (a)* non-pecuniary loss*; and (b) future loss which is reasonably likely to occur.*
DCFR	*III.-3:701 (3): "Loss" includes economic and non-economic loss. "Economic loss" includes loss of income or profit, burdens incurred and a reduction in the value of property.* "Noneconomic loss" includes *pain and suffering and* impairment of the quality of life.
Reg. CESL	*2 of (c) 'loss' means economic loss and non-economic loss* in the form of pain and suffering, excluding other forms *of non-economic loss such as* impairment of the quality of life and loss of enjoyment.

[599] III.-3:701 of DCFR.

[600] Article 162, 163, CESL.

2.4. *Agreed Damages: Liquidated Damages and Penalty Clauses*

The DCFR takes a similar attitude towards party-designed damages as the PECL does, while the CESL does not address the issue concerning this (Table 9). Generally, liquidated damages or penalty clauses are allowed in the contracts according to either the PECL or the DCFR. If the parties have agreed upon a certain amount of damages for non-performance, the agreement will be valid and enforceable. It is common for contract parties to specify the sum to be paid for non-performance as higher than the creditor's expected loss or the real loss. The court should award the larger damages stipulated by the parties disregarding the smaller real-loss suffered by the creditor in the case where there is non-performance. But where the sum of damages is smaller than the real loss, it is at the creditor's choice whether to sue for actual loss or for the damage agreed by the parties.[601] In this sense, a moderate penalty is accepted.

The PECL and the DCFR's attitudes toward party-designed remedies, to some extent, are in accordance with their awards for non-economic or non-pecuniary losses. In practice, if the buyer has placed non-pecuniary value on the contract, it is normally quite difficult to make a correct assessment at the ex-post stage. An ex-ante stipulated damage that reflects the contractual parties' expected value can decrease the problem of either error calculation or under-compensation in awarding expectation damages.[602] As long as the process of damage stipulation is based on equal bargaining power and symmetric information, the increased cost that a debtor bears will be reflected in the contract price as well. The creditor may not be willing to pay the increased price if he thinks it is cheaper for him to deal with the subjective element in the loss by other means or if his subjective value of the contract is insignificant. What is more, ex-ante stipulation of damages provides the creditor with explicit information about his liability for non-performance. The debtor may alter his investment in the precaution against breach in proportion to his cost of liability for non-performance. If properly assessed, damage stipulation will create appropriate incentives for efficient performance and efficient breach.

As is mentioned, neither the PECL nor the DCFR, however, allow unreasonably high penalties. According to Article 9:509(2) of the PECL or Article III.-3:712(2) of the DCFR, excessively high penalties are subjected to a reduction by the court (Table 25). On the one hand, the benchmark for damage control is grounded on the actual loss from non-performance and "the other circumstances". In the circumstances where the agreed damages are extremely disproportionate to the creditor's actual loss, the damages stipulation is judged as unreasonable even if it was reasonable at the time of contract conclusion. But there is no reference to the terminology of "the other circumstances" that is adopted in the PECL and the DCFR. The aim of the damage stipulation control, as is mentioned in the

601 The comment on Article III.-3:712 indicates: "Where, however, the contract specifies merely the minimum sum payable by the debtor, the creditor may recover a higher figure if the loss exceeds the minimum sum. In this case the creditor may elect to sue for damages at large instead of invoking the provision for agreed damages".

602 Harris & Ogus & Phillips 1979, p. 581.

comments of the DCFR, is to preclude those stipulations which are abusive in their effect.[603] In other words, the fact that the stipulated amount is larger than the real loss from non-performance is merely an indicator of abusive stipulation. The other circumstances, in this sense, may cover other facts related to abusive stipulation in the process of damage negotiation, such as information asymmetry, necessity and so on. Rather than denying penalty clauses, the DCFR and the PECL choose to regulate abusive stipulations. Hence, punitive damages that are only for punishment or for deterring breach are prohibited.

When unreasonable damage agreements are recognized by the court, the court has the power to reduce the amount of damages to a reasonable amount. As is shown, "*this power of the court has a limit: it should respect the intention of the parties to deter default and therefore should not reduce the award to the actual loss.*"[604] In other words, the court should not directly invalidate those unreasonably penalties and impose expectation damages on the debtor who has broken the contract. Rather, the court is required to make the damage assessment from the parties' perspective and decide on a sum to be payable for non-performance that the parties would agree on.

Table 25. Liquidated Damages in EU Contract Law

PECL	*9:509: (1) Where the contract provides that a party who fails to perform is to pay a specified sum to the aggrieved party for such non-performance, the aggrieved party shall be awarded that sum irrespective of its actual loss. (2) However, despite any agreement to the contrary the specified sum may be reduced to a reasonable amount where it is* grossly excessive *in relation to* the loss resulting from the non-performance and the other circumstances.
DCFR	*III.–3:712: (1) Where the terms regulating an obligation provide that a debtor who fails to perform the obligation is to pay a specified sum to the creditor for such non-performance, the creditor is entitled to that sum irrespective of the actual loss. (2) However, despite any provision to the contrary, the sum so specified in a contract or other juridical act may be reduced to a reasonable amount where it is* grossly excessive *in relation to* the loss resulting from the non-performance and the other circumstances.

3. Application of the Efficient Breach Model

After a general introduction to the remedy system adopted in the EU contract law instruments, this section will attempt to incorporate the economic story of efficient breach into the EU law. As shown in the previous section, one intriguing topic in the discussion of efficient breach theory arises from the situations where breach of the contract will be more efficient than performing the contract. Applying the economic surplus standard, a contract may either fall into the efficient breach zone or into the efficient performance zone after its formation. According to economic theory, contract law should aim to optimize the contracting parties' incentives to take efficient actions, or, to facilitate their abilities to

603 The comment under Article III.-3:712 states: "Since the purpose is to control only those stipulations which are abusive in their effect, the court's reducing power is exercisable only where it is clear that the stipulated sum substantially exceeds the actual loss."

604 DCFR, p. 978.

maximize welfare from transactions.[605] Based on this cognition, it is assumed that contract law should be able to help the contracting parties to avoid strict performance of a contract when it falls into the efficient breach zone but encourage performance otherwise. In this section, the general attitude taken by EU law towards efficient breach will be discussed.

3.1. Rules in the efficient Performance Zone

According to economic theory, actors engage in contracting in order to enhance their wealth. Hence the law should motivate the parties to comply with their agreement. Accordingly, breach of a mutually agreed contract should be avoided unless performing the contracts will decrease social welfare. Within a trade, the seller, to a large extent, is motivated to comply with the contract consciously, by either the intention of earning money or his moral consciousness of keeping promises, or the mechanism of reputation established in the market, where a bad actor might be boycotted.[606] Moreover, legal rules may encourage performance in the efficient performance zone by, for instance, imposing obligations on the contracting parties and creating remedy rules for a non-breaching party which may increase the cost of breach and alter a promisor's incentive to breach. The idea of encouraging the performance of those contracts within the efficient performance zone has also been adopted in EU measures.

3.1.1. Specific Performance, Substitutive performance

A general issue stressed in relation to the efficient performance zone concerns the application of specific performance.

General provisions have been set entitling a buyer to the claim of performance, including claiming specific performance, repair or replacement of the goods. Basically, if a seller fails to deliver the goods or the goods delivered are not in conformity with the contract, the buyer may ask for delivery, repair or replacement unless some specific conditions are satisfied.[607] However, there is a time limit to the creditor's claim of specific performance. It is supposed that an unreasonable delay in requesting specific performance may increase the cost of performance and make performance become difficult for the debtor. In order to motivate the creditor to make the claim in time, both the PECL and the DCFR deprive the creditor of his right to performance if the claim is made after a reasonable period of time[608] since he became aware of the non-performance (Table 26).

605 Schwartz & Scott 2003, p. 544.

606 Schäfer & Ott, 2003, p. 277.

607 Section 3.4 will discuss the exceptions to the claim of specific performance.

608 With regard to the "reasonable period of time", neither DCFR nor PECL has set any specific standard. It is the debtor that should prove that the delay in requesting performance was unreasonably long. The comment of DCFR states: "*the reasonable period of time is to be determined in view of the rule's purpose. In certain cases, it may be very short, e.g. if delivery can be made out of the debtor's stock in trade. In other cases it may be longer.*" DCFR, p. 854.

Table 26. Unreasonable Delay in Requesting Specific Performance under EU Contract Law

PECL	*9:102(3) The aggrieved party will lose the right to specific performance if it fails to seek it within a reasonable time after it has or ought to have become aware of the non-performance.*
DCFR	*III-3:302(4): The creditor loses the right to enforce specific performance if performance is not requested within a reasonable time after the creditor has become, or could reasonably be expected to have become, aware of the non-performance.*

The PECL and the DCFR, nevertheless, put priority on substitute performance (Table 27).[609] When reasonable substitute performance can be made without significant cost, it is required that the creditor should resort to a substitute transaction rather than to insist on specific performance. Consider the way of damage calculation if a creditor has made a reasonable substitute transaction after terminating the contract. As is mentioned in section 2.2, the creditor is able to recover the discrepancy of the price that is payable between the broken contract and the alternative contract. In order to motivate the creditor to choose substitute performance, Article III.-3:302 (5) of the DCFR deprives the debtor of the damages for the increased losses that have been caused by the debtor's insistence on specific performance if a substitute transaction is less costly. In addition, Article 9:102(2) of the PECL directly deprives the creditor of his right to specific performance in the situation where he can reasonably obtain substitutive performance from another source. But the PECL has not indicated the consequence of a creditor's insistence upon specific performance. The enforcement cost provides a strong argument for the DCFR's support of substitute performance. Compared to substitute performance, specific performance incurs the cost of enforcement that will be increased provided the debtor refuses performance or delays performance intentionally.[610] If the debtor is reluctant to perform, it becomes difficult to monitor and force the performance. Hence, the cost of enforcing specific performance is moved to the creditor and the "*creditor's threat of claiming specific performance may not be credible*".[611] Other than the explanation of enforcement cost, another argument for substitute performance is that it involves the "same efficiency issues as specific performance" does when the creditor has made a specific investment. For example, assume that a company bought a piece of equipment for producing widgets and he has already made other arrangements for his business, such as buying raw materials and accepting orders. If the seller of the equipment fails to deliver the product, the buyer's specific investment will be wasted. In this situation, specific performance and substitute performance share the same character in avoiding

609 De Geest 2010, p. 131–132.

610 Id. It is argued that "*the choice of remedy in the performance zone is largely a matter of administrative cost*". For a non-motivated promisor, supervising the enforcement of specific performance is quite difficult and he can easily refuse to perform.

611 If the creditor is entitled to make a choice between the claim for specific performance and damages, the creditor still needs to bear the cost of enforcement in his choice. As is argued by Lando & Rose (2004): "*if one cannot realistically impose very high sanctions on the defendant, and the plaintiff carries the cost of enforcement, it may become unattractive to claim specific performance, and such claims may become to few to make it worthwhile to design the system to be ready to enforce specifically.*" Lando & Rose 2004, p. 485.

the waste of resource and achieving efficiency. Moreover, computation of expectation damages is avoided when substitute performance is arranged. Empirical studies observed that substitute performance is routinely enforced by courts and sought by plaintiffs in practice as well.[612] In addressing this issue, both the DCFR and the PECL consider substitute performance as the first remedy that is prior to specific performance. In contrast, the CESL only takes the substitute transaction as the benchmark for evaluating expectation damages.

Table 27. Substitutive Performance in EU Contract Law

PECL	*9:102(1): The aggrieved party is entitled to specific performance of an obligation other than one to pay money, including the remedying of a defective performance.* *9:102(2): Specific performance cannot, however, be obtained where: ...... (d): the* aggrieved party may reasonably obtain performance from another source.
DCFR	*III.-3:302: ...(5) The creditor cannot recover damages for loss or a stipulated payment for nonperformance to the extent that the creditor has increased the loss or the amount of the payment* by insisting unreasonably on specific performance *in circumstances where the creditor* could have made a reasonable substitute transaction without significant effort or expense.

3.1.2. A Grey Zone

Within the efficient performance zone, the PECL, DCFR and CESL have all recognized a situation where performance of a contract has become more onerous but the surplus from performance is still assumed to be totally higher than that from non-performance under the heading of "Change of Circumstances". There are two types of contingencies which may cause an added burden in performance, namely, an increase in the cost of performance or a decrease in the value of what is to be received by a seller. Nevertheless, the seller's obligation to perform the contract in general will not be affected if the extent to which performance becomes more onerous is not great. In this sense, if a seller refuses to deliver the goods as required or delivers defective goods merely on the grounds of a minor difficulty in performance, the buyer may still claim for remedies including requiring performance (Table 28).[613]

612 Lando & Rose (2004) provided evidence that "*specific performance is in fact a rare remedy in Denmark, Germany and France, and under CISG, when performance requires actions to be undertaken*". Rather, evidence showed that "*cover purchase is empirically more relevant than specific performance; cover purchases are routinely enforced and sought by plaintiffs in all of the three countries, and also under CISG*". Lando & Rose 2004, p. 475–480, p, 485.

613 More discussion about this will be present in the section 3.4.1.

Table 28. The Rules regarding the Grey Zone in EU Contract Law

PECL	**6:111:** *(1) A party is bound to fulfil its obligations even if performance has become more onerous, whether because the cost of performance has increased or because the value of the performance it receives has diminished.*
DCFR	*III.–1:110: (1) An obligation must be performed even if performance has become more onerous, whether because the cost of performance has increased or because the value of what is to be received in return has diminished.*
CESL	*89:(1). A party must perform its obligations even if performance has become more onerous, whether because the cost of performance has increased or because the value of what is to be received in return has diminished.*

3.2. *Rules in the Efficient Breach Zone*

Following the theory of efficient breach, a contract falls into the efficient breach zone when an unexpected contingency arises so that the performance of the contract will create less profit than the breach does. As noted in section 2, either a drastic increase in performance cost or an extremely high bid by a third party may bring a contract into the efficient breach zone. In the efficient breach zone, performance of the original contract should be prevented so as to avoid economic waste and to enhance the total welfare that the contract parties obtain. Two questions will be stressed in this section. What rules have been adopted by European Union law to deal with a contract that falls into the efficient breach zone? How does European Union law deal with the situations when the contract is in the efficient breach zone.

3.2.1. Unexpected Contingencies in EU Contract Law

The EU law provides three examples where a seller's obligation to perform will be influenced, implicitly responding to the doctrine of efficient breach. They are: Excused Non-performance, Change of Circumstances and Impossibility or Impracticability.

Firstly, following the Vienna Convention, the EU measures have provided the doctrine of Excuse,[614] referring to an impediment which is beyond the non-performing party's control and that party could not be expected to have taken the impediment into account at the time when the contract was formed, or to have avoided or overcome the impediment or its consequences (Table 29).[615] This situation is also covered by the civil law principle of *Force Majeure*.[616] The requirements for recognizing *Force Majeure* can be

614 Article 8:108(1) PECL 1999, Article III.– 3:104(1) DCFR 2008 and Article 88(1) CESL are practically identical to Article 79 (1) CISG.

615 Article 88(1) CESL.

616 The principle of *force majeure* originated in the French Civil code of 1804. Article 1148 provides that "*There is no occasion for any damages where a debtor was prevented from transferring or from doing that to which he was bound, or did what was forbidden to him, by reason of force majeure or of a fortuitous event.*" Besides, the UNIDROIT PICC, the term *force majeure* has been also used as the title for Article 7.1.7, which covers the "*impediment beyond the non-performing party's control and the party could*

traced back to the previous documents that the EU measures are based on. For example, the ICC *Force Majeure* Clause 2003 sets out that: 1) the impediment must be out of the debtor's control, or, not fall in the sphere of risk of the debtor; 2) it must have been unforeseeable at the time of contract formation; and 3) it or its consequences must have been unavoidable. It lists some typical events that are amount to impediments, such as war, natural disasters or acts of terrorism. In addition, the commentary on Article III.-3:104 of the DCFR provides some examples to show when an obstacle should be recognized as an insurmountable impediment that is outside of the debtor's control and could not been taken into account by the debtor. As is shown, an unexpected strike in the nationalised company which distributes natural gas can be recognized as out of the control of a debtor who only heats its furnaces with gas.[617] Or, an earthquake is also considered as an impediment since it is insurmountable or irresistible unless the debtor can build a virtual fortress. In those cases, "one cannot expect the debtor to take precautions out of proportion to the risk",[618] hence, the impediment or its consequences cannot be overcome or avoided and strictly performing the contract is basically impossible.

Table 29. The Conditions for Excuse in EU Contract Law

PECL	Article 8:108: *(1) A party's non-performance is excused if it proves that it is due to an impediment* beyond its control *and that it* could not reasonably have been expected *to take the impediment into account at the time of the conclusion of the contract, or to have* avoided or overcome *the impediment or its consequences.*
DCFR	*III.-3:104: (1) A debtor's non-performance of an obligation is excused if it is due to an impediment* beyond the debtor's control *and if the debtor* could not reasonably be expected *to have* avoided or overcome *the impediment or its consequences. (2) Where the obligation arose out of a contract or other juridical act, non-performance is not excused if the debtor could reasonably be expected to have taken the impediment into account at the time when the obligation was incurred...*
CESL	*88: A party's non-performance of an obligation is excused if it is due to an impediment* beyond that party's control *and if that party* could not be expected *to have taken the impediment into account at the time of the conclusion of the contract,* or to have avoided or overcome *the impediment or its consequences.*

Another situation where a debtor's duty to perform is affected refers to what is included in the provision of change of circumstances (Table 30). As is noted in 3.1.2, a debtor's

not reasonably be expected to have taken the impediment into account at the time of the conclusion of the contract or to have avoided or overcome it or its consequences". There are also other terms to describe similar supervening events that make contract performance impossible. For instance, the English law principle of frustration or German law principle of impossibility. In many situations, those terms are used interchangeably, except for some subtle difference. For instance, the English principle of frustration has a broader meaning, including that "*which renders the contract something radically different from that which was in the contemplation of the parties*". Article 7.1.7 UNIDROIT principles; Mazzacano 2011, p. 38–45; Beale, Fauvarque-Cosson, Rutgers, Tallon & Vogenauer 2010, p. 1106; Schwenzer 2012, p. 469–471.

617 DCFR, p. 809.

618 De Geest 2010, p. 128. DCFR, p. 810.

obligation of performance is normally untouched even if the cost of performance has increased or the value to be received has decreased so that to perform the contract is onerous. In general, the debtor is required to bear the cost of performance and the risk of any increase in the performance costs.[619] Nevertheless, the exception exists when there is "an exceptional change of circumstances", which is governed by Article 6:111(2) of the PECL, Article III.–3:104(2) of the DCFR and Article 89(1) of the CESL.[620] An exceptional change of circumstances makes performance excessively onerous, because the cost of performance has increased or the value of what is to be received in return has diminished to a large extent. Hence, whether an impediment amounts to an exceptional change of circumstances or not depends on the extent to which that performance has become more onerous. However, the articles haven't drawn a clear line between the situation where "performance becomes more onerous" and the situation where "performance becomes excessively onerous". The terminologies adopted in those EU measures refer to "excessive onerosity" and "an exceptional change of circumstances", which are ambiguous. The task of distinguishing an exceptional change of circumstances from simple changes in the surrounding conditions of a contract is left to judges in individual cases. Another name that has been used by some scholars to denote this situation is "hardship".[621] In contrast to *Force Majeure*, performing the original contract is only excessively onerous, but physically possible when the principle of "change of circumstances". It might be a great fluctuation of price in the material market that raises the seller's costs of production greatly, for instance, by 200%.[622] In such a situation, producing the commodity as required by the contract is still possible, but the increased costs will consume all the profits that may be created by the contract and thus performance of the contract is economically inefficient. Except for "being exceptional", the rule of "exceptional change of circumstances" will apply only when three more prerequisites are satisfied. It is required that the change of circumstances should: 1) occur at the time after conclusion of the contract; 2) its possibility or scale could not have been taken into account by the debtor and; 3) the risk of it has not been assumed by the aggrieved party or cannot reasonably be regarded as having been assumed. Apply those conditions to a consumer contract. Changes of circumstances in relation to matters within the area of professional expertise may normally be precluded from the scope of change of circumstances. As a professional, the business seller is considered to have assumed or should have assumed risks arising out of his profession.[623]

619 Article 7:112 PECL states: "*each party shall bear the costs of performance of its obligations.*" Article III.–2:113(1) DCFR also provides: "*the costs of performing an obligation are borne by the debtor.*"

620 In contrast, the CISG, upon which both the PECL and the DCFR were raised, has not established a separate article dealing with change of circumstances, but only Article 79 includes all the contingencies that lead to exemption. As is indicated by Schwenzer 2012, the approach taken by the CISG is more preferable, because it is difficult to draw a clear line between *force majeure* and exceptional change of circumstances. Schwenzer 2012, p. 470.

621 Mac Queen 2012, p. 300; Magnus 2012, p. 251; Schwenzer 2012, p. 470. In order to avoid confusion, this thesis will not use the term hardship under the context of EU contract law.

622 Schwenzer 2008, p. 715–717.

623 This has been clearly stressed in the commentary of DCFR.

Table 30. The Conditions for an Exceptional Change of Circumstances in EU Contract Law

PECL	*6:111(2): If, however, performance of the contract becomes* excessively onerous *because of a change of circumstances, the parties are bound to enter into negotiations with a view to adapting the contract or terminating it, provided that: (a) the change of circumstances occurred* after the time of conclusion *of the contract, (b) the possibility of a change of circumstances* was not one which could reasonably have been taken into account *at the time of conclusion of the contract, and (c) the* risk *of the change of circumstances* is not *one which, according to the contract,* the party affected should be required to bear.
DCFR	*III.-1:110(2): If, however, performance of a contractual obligation or of an obligation arising from a unilateral juridical act becomes* so onerous *because of* an exceptional change of circumstances *that it would be manifestly unjust to hold the debtor to the obligation a court may ... (3) Paragraph (2) applies only if: (a) the change of circumstances occurred* after the time when the obligation was incurred, *(b) the* debtor did not at that time take into account, *and could not reasonably be expected to have taken into account, the possibility or scale of that change of circumstances; (c)* the debtor did not assume, *and cannot reasonably be regarded as having assumed,* the risk *of that change of circumstances; and (d) the debtor has attempted, reasonably and in good faith, to achieve by negotiation a reasonable and equitable adjustment of the terms regulating the obligation.*
CESL	*89 (1): Where performance becomes* excessively onerous *because of an* exceptional change of circumstances, *the parties have a duty to enter into negotiations with a view to adapting or terminating the contract... (3). Paragraphs 1 and 2 apply only if: (a) the change of circumstances occurred* after the time when the contract was concluded; *(b) the party relying on the change of circumstances* did not at that time take into account, *and could not be expected to have taken into account, the possibility or scale of that change of circumstances; and (c) the* aggrieved party did not assume, *and cannot reasonably be regarded as having assumed,* the risk *of that change of circumstances.*

In addition to the provisions of excuse due to an impediment and change of circumstances, which are included in the general chapter on obligations and remedies, what should be mentioned as well is the rule that puts forward exceptions to the remedy of specific performance (Table 31). Three cases are recognized where a buyer cannot require specific performance. The first case refers to a situation where performance of the contract is impossible or has become unlawful. Without any exception, the PECL, DCFR and CESL all require that specific performance cannot be enforced when performance becomes impossible. Another situation where specific performance cannot be requested is when the burden or expense of performance becomes disproportionate to the benefit that the buyer would obtain. Those two situations are recognized in relation to the traditional German contract law theories of impossibility and impracticability[624] and they have been both incorporated in all the three EU measures.[625] The third exception to specific

624 As to the "impossibility principle", it covers not only physical impossibility, but also legal impossibility. However, more information about when and how performance should be judged unlawful cannot be found in CESL. It leaves us to wonder which law should be applied to make this judgement. For instance, will performance of a contract be rendered unlawful if it violates mandatory rules in the national laws and regulations? See Feltkamp & Vanbosselе 2011, p. 897.

625 The doctrine of impossibility is used in German law in BGB §275(1) and called "*Unmöglichkeit*". German law has distinguished different categories of impossibility, such as initial impossibility and

performance exists in the contracts where performance would be of a personal character. But the CESL does not mention this situation.

The standard for assessing when performance of a contract becomes impractical (or uneconomic) is based on the comparison between the costs of performance and the benefit that a buyer will obtain. It is analogous to the requirement for the situation where efficient breach arises because of an unfortunate contingency. Performance of a contract is rendered impractical if the cost of performance exceeds the benefit that the buyer can obtain from it. In other words, an impractical contract may fall into the efficient breach zone where performance of the contract is inefficient. In contrast to the provisions of *force Majeure* and change of circumstances, the articles concerning impossibility or impracticability have not set any prerequisite for the cause of impossibility or impracticability. Hence, even if a situation of impossibility or impracticability is induced by some events that are expectable or controllable to the seller, the buyer still cannot ask for specific performance.

Table 31. Restrictions to Specific Performance in EU Contract Law

DCFR:	*III.–3:302(3) Specific performance cannot, however, be enforced where: (a) Performance would be unlawful or impossible; (b) Performance would be unreasonably burdensome or expensive; or (c) Performance would be of such a personal character that it would be unreasonable to enforce it.*
CESL	*110(3), "Performance cannot be required where: (a) performance would be impossible or has become unlawful; or (b) the burden or expense of performance would be disproportionate to the benefit that the buyer would obtain."*
PECL	*9:102(2) Specific performance cannot, however, be obtained where: (a) performance would be unlawful or impossible; or (b) performance would cause the debtor unreasonable effort or expense; or (c) the performance consists in the provision of services or work of a personal character or depends upon a personal relationship, or......*

To summarize, situations where a sales contract may fall into the efficient breach zone have been recognized by EU law. With regard to the type of contingency rendering a contract economically inefficient, EU law only accepts unfortunate contingencies which have increased a seller's cost of performance or decreased the benefit that the seller may obtain in return. The general qualification for this type of contingency is based on a cost-benefit rule of comparing the cost or burden of performance and the cost incurred by non-performance. A contract falls into the efficient breach zone only when its performance becomes impossible or is excessively costly. As a result, the seller's obligation of performance will be influenced. Nevertheless, it is assumed that a contract will still stay at the performance zone if the non-performance is motivated by the higher surplus yielded from contracting with a third party. Even if a third party bids a price that is much

subsequent impossibility, objective impossibility and subjective impossibility, and temporary impossibility and definitive impossibility and applied different rules to different categories. In addition, BGB §275 (2) also stipulates a situation where performance of a contract requires excessive expenses and efforts. In those situations, the obligor may refuse performance. See BGB §275, see also Beale, Fauvarque-Cosson, Rutgers, Tallon & Vogenauer 2010, p. 855–886, p. 1102–1106.

higher than the highest price offered by the buyer, the seller's obligation of performance will not be affected and he must perform his obligation as required by the contract.[626]

3.2.2. Reactions to Contracts within the Efficient Breach Zone

When a contract falls into the efficient breach zone, there are two basic conditions for qualifying the seller's breach as an efficient breach. First of all, the law should not force the seller to perform the contract so that the seller is able to make a free choice between breach, performance or offer to negotiate. Moreover, the buyer should not be worse off on account of the seller's non-performance. This would be possible if the buyer's expectation interest is protected through the award of expectation damages.[627] Then questions arise: whether the priority is to put to breach or renegotiation; whether non-performance is allowed or not; and if so, whether the aggrieved buyer is entitled to the claim of expectation damages or not.

Concerning the situation of *Force Majeure*, EU law follows the traditional doctrine by exempting the seller from liability for non-performance. A permanent impediment[628] will extinguish the seller's obligation to perform the contract, at the same time extinguishing any reciprocal obligation of the creditor as well (Table 32). Therefore, the creditor cannot claim for specific performance anymore and he also does not have to fulfil the reciprocal obligation.[629] Moreover, the general rules concerning the buyer's remedy have added information on the effect of excuse by extending excuse to damages claims and performance claims.[630] Other remedies remain available to the buyer. In the case of *Force majeure*, a buyer may still withhold his payment, claim price reduction or terminate the contract except for requiring specific performance and damages.

An obligation of notification is imposed on the party who is unable to perform.[631] After the seller is aware or could be expected to have been aware of an impediment, he has to notify the buyer of this impediment and its effect without any undue delay. It is also indicated that the party who has violated the duty of notice is held liable for any damages incurred from his failure to notify.

626 Article 89(1) CESL.

627 Zhou 2008, p. 3–4.

628 If the impediment is only temporary, the excuse will only have effect for the period during which the impediment exists. However, if the delay in performance amounts to fundamental breach, the impediment may still be treated as a permanent impediment.

629 "*It may happen that the extinguished obligation of the debtor is just one of several obligations under a contract and that performance of the remaining obligations has become valueless to the creditor as a result of the extinction of the one obligation. In such a case the creditor will have the option of terminating the whole contractual relationship for fundamental nonperformance.*" DEFR, p. 812.

630 Magnus 2012, p. 251.

631 Article 8:108(3) PECL; Article III.-3:104: (5) DCFR; Article 88(3) CESL.

Table 32. Consequence of *Force Majeure* in EU Contract Law

PECL	*8:101(2): Where a party's non-performance is excused under Article 8:108, the aggrieved party 416 may resort to any of the remedies set out in Chapter 9 except claiming performance and damages.* *9:501: (1) The aggrieved party is entitled to damages for loss caused by the other party's non-performance which is not excused under Article 8:108.*
DCFR	*III.–3:101: (2) If the debtor's non-performance is excused, the creditor may resort to any of those remedies except enforcing specific performance and damages......* *III.-3:104: (4) Where the excusing impediment is permanent the obligation is extinguished. Any reciprocal obligation is also extinguished. In the case of contractual obligations any restitutionary effects of extinction are regulated by the rules in Chapter 3, Section 5, Subsection 4 (Restitution) with appropriate adaptations.* *III.–3:701: (1) The creditor is entitled to damages for loss caused by the debtor's nonperformance of an obligation, unless the non-performance is excused.*
CESL	*106(4): If the seller's non-performance is excused, the buyer may resort to any of the remedies referred to in paragraph 1 except requiring performance and damages.* *159(1): A creditor is entitled to damages for loss caused by the non-performance of an obligation by the debtor, unless the non-performance is excused.* *Obligation to Inform.*

Rather than directly allowing non-performance, both PECL and CESL have imposed a duty to re-negotiate explicitly on the contract parties in the case of hardship (Table 33). As is set in Article 6:111: (2) of PECL and Article 89(1) of CESL, when performance becomes excessively onerous, the parties have the obligation to enter into negotiations in order to adapt or terminate the contract. Furthermore, it is indicated in the PECL and the CESL that if the parties fail to reach an adaptation or termination of the contract within a reasonable time, a court or arbitral tribunal can do so.[632] PECL has carried this idea of encouraging re-negotiation further, by bringing the duty of good faith as well as the obligation to re-negotiate together and specifying the consequences of the failure to re-negotiate. Article 6:112(2) entitles the aggrieved party to damages for his loss caused by the other party's refusal to negotiate or by the other party's breaking off negotiations contrary to good faith and fair dealing. However, the imposition of the obligation to re-negotiate and the award of liability for failure to negotiate have been criticized a lot for being undesirably complicated and heavy. When there is a conflict of interests, realization of negotiation is costly and burdensome.[633] Unlike the PECL and the CESL, the DCFR does not explicitly impose any obligation on the parties to renegotiate.[634] Rather, Article

632 Feltkamp & Vanbossele 2011, p. 891; Schwenzer 2012, p. 471.

633 On consultation of the PECL, "this technique was criticized by some stakeholders as being undesirably complicated and heavy. It was pointed out, for example, that a creditor in an obligation might be acting in a fiduciary capacity and might be placed in a difficult situation of conflict of interests if obliged to negotiate away an advantage. " DCFR, p. 738.

634 The comment of DCFR expressly articulates that: "*It does not impose an obligation to negotiate but makes it a requirement for a remedy under the Article that the debtor should have attempted in good faith to achieve a reasonable and equitable adjustment by negotiation. There is no question of anyone being forced to negotiate or being held liable in damages for failing to negotiate*". DCFR, p. 739.

III.-1:110(2)(d) of the DCFR makes the request for re-negotiation as the pre-condition for its application (Table 33). After hardship occurs, a court will interfere only if the debtor has attempted to reach negotiation with the creditor reasonably and in good faith. Conversely, an unjustified refusal to re-negotiate would prevent the application of Article -1:110, but would not lead to sanctions.[635]

Two general restrictions are set in relation to the adjustment of the contract by a court or arbitral tribunal. First of all, the court or arbitral tribunal cannot decide to adjust the contract directly after unexpected circumstances occur. Only if the parties cannot negotiate successfully within a reasonable time and one of the parties makes a request to the court or arbitral tribunal for a solution, the court may adapt or terminate the contract.[636] Secondly, the content of the court's adaption is restricted. In the texts of the PECL, DCFR or CESL, there is no order of preference between termination and adaptation of the contract. Nevertheless, the court is bound when choosing either to terminate the contractual relationship or alter the content of the contract. In the PECL and the DCFR, the court is required to make the adaptation to the threshold where benefits and costs in the new circumstance are distributed reasonably and equitably. With regard to the CESL, it requires that the adaptation should be made from the perspective of the contracting parties, namely, it should be "in accordance with what the parties would reasonably have agreed at the time of contracting if they had taken the change of circumstances into account."

In brief, neither the PECL nor DCFR nor CESL has expressively disallowed specific performance of the original contract. However, the clarification of the parties' duty to re-negotiate as well as a possible adjustment of the contract to the hardship implicitly interferes with any direct claim for specific performance or expectation damages by the buyer.

Table 33. Obligation to Re-negotiate in EU Contract Law

PECL	6:111: *(2) If, however, performance of the contract becomes excessively onerous because of a change of circumstances*, the parties are bound to enter into negotiations *with a view to adapting the contract or terminating it ... (3) If the parties* fail to reach agreement within a reasonable period, *the court may: (a) end the contract at a date and on terms to be determined by the court; or (b) adapt the contract in order to distribute between the parties in a just and equitable manner the losses and gains resulting from the change of circumstances.* *In either case, the court may* award damages *for the loss suffered through* a party refusing to negotiate or breaking off negotiations contrary to good faith and fair dealing.

[635] If it is the debtor that created an unjustified refusal, Article III-1:110 DCFR will be excluded. However, if it is the creditor that refuses to re-negotiate or breaks off re-negotiations contrary to good faith, then Article III.-1:103 about the general rules on good faith will apply. The creditor might be prevented from "exercising or relying on the rights and remedies arising from the non-performance of the contract by the debtor, e.g. specific performance and damages". Uribe 2011, p. 211.

[636] MacQueen 2012, p. 301.

DCFR	*III.-1:110: (2) If, however, performance of a contractual obligation or of an obligation arising from a unilateral juridical act becomes so onerous because of an exceptional change of circumstances that it would be manifestly unjust to hold the debtor to the obligation a* court *may: (a) vary the obligation in order to make it reasonable and equitable in the new circumstances; or (b) terminate the obligation at a date and on terms to be determined by the court. (3) Paragraph (2) applies only if: ... (d)* the debtor has attempted, *reasonably and in good faith,* to achieve by negotiation *a reasonable and equitable adjustment of the terms regulating the obligation.*
CESL	*89: (1) ... Where performance becomes excessively onerous because of an exceptional change of circumstances, the parties* have a duty to enter into negotiations *with a view to adapting or terminating the contract. (2): If* the parties fail to reach an agreement *within* a reasonable time, *then,* upon request *by either party* a court may: *(a) adapt the contract in order to bring it into accordance with what the parties would reasonably have agreed at the time of contracting if they had taken the change of circumstances into account; or (b) terminate the contract within the meaning of Article 8 at a date and on terms to be determined by the court.*

In addition to the rules of excuse and change of circumstances, the seller may also defend against a buyer's performance claim, resorting to the rule of impossibility or impracticability (Table 34). As is provided by either the PECL or DCFR or CESL, performance cannot be required if it is objectively impossible or legally impossible or if it incurs excessively high costs or burdens. Implicitly, application of exceptions to performance which is based on the balance between costs and benefits should be applied to two other forms of performance, namely, repair and replacement. If cure is impossible or the cost or burden of cure exceeds what a buyer can benefit from it, the seller may decline the buyer's request of cure. Nevertheless, a debtor is not exempted from his liability for damages when performance is impossible or impracticable. This has been expressly included in the PECL (Article 9:103) and the DCFR (Article III-3:303). Although the CESL does not specifically mention that a creditor's right to damages is unaffected by the exclusion of specific performance, this information can be inferred from Article 159 implicitly.[637] As is shown, a creditor is entitled to any damages for loss caused by non-performance of an obligation by the debtor, with the only exception in the situation where the rule of *force majeure* applies and the debtor's non-performance is excused.

Table 34. Unavailability of Specific Performance in EU Contract Law

PECL	*9:102:(2) Specific performance cannot, however, be obtained where: ......* *9:103: The fact that a right to performance is excluded under this Section does not preclude a claim for damages. The Breacher should pay damages unless performance is impossible and he is excused.*
DCFR	*III.-3:302(3): Specific performance cannot, however, be enforced where:......* *III.–3:303: The fact that a right to enforce specific performance is excluded under the preceding Article does not preclude a claim for damages.*
CESL	*110: (3). Performance cannot be required where:......*

637 Article 159 CESL: "*(1). A creditor is entitled to damages for loss caused by the non-performance of an obligation by the debtor, unless the non-performance is excused.*"

4. Limits of Efficient breach in EU Law

To conclude, efficient breach is possible in a legal framework where a seller will not be forced to perform the contract specifically and the buyer will not become worse off because of the non-performance if the contract falls into the efficient breach zone. This framework of efficient breach within EU law is composed by the rules of *force majeure*, hardship, impossibility and impracticability and remedies. Within this framework, efficient non-performance from which the surplus is greater than that from strict performance is possible. In contrast, EU law does not allow breach when it comes to the model of outsider bidding. So if there is another higher bid after the conclusion of the contract, the seller still has to deliver the product to the original seller rather than make the performance or breach decision based on the different buyer's bids. However, there are two basic factors that may limit the application of efficient breach doctrine in EU contract law.

4.1. EU Measures as Optional Instrument Cross-border Sales

In the context of Cross-border Sales, parties have autonomy in choosing the applicable law governing their contract law. But what can be chosen as the applicable law is only legally-binding law. Non-state law, such as PECL, PICC or DCFR will only work on cross-border contracts by, for instance, being incorporated into cross-border contracts as contract terms if they have been chosen by the parties; or being included in national legislation. But those instruments cannot be chosen as the applicable law that substitutes national law directly.[638] In this sense, if national law imposes a higher standard requirement for performance and requires performance in the circumstances where non-performance may be recognized as efficient according to EU contract law, the seller still has to comply with the contract. With regard to CESL, it functions as an optional European Contract Law instrument that can be chosen by parties in their contractual relations as an alternative to the existing national law for a cross-border contract. As optional instrument, CESL's applicability depends on whether or not it is attractive to parties engaging in cross-border transactions and whether or not it will be chosen by the parties.

4.2. Dispute Resolution

The way of dispute resolution may also matter. As to the way of avoiding specific performance, a seller may not choose to break the contract unilaterally but to reach a settlement. For instance, he may offer to make a new tender, reduce the price or return the money paid by the buyer back. From the standpoint of a buyer, he is also willing to choose the dispute resolution that is less costly, either simpler or less time-consuming. In terms of cross-border transactions, the cost involved in suing a foreign company is huge

[638] Moss 2011, P. 156–159.

and the application of law is complicated. Therefore, what might be preferable to the buyer is to reach a settlement with the seller, by either price reduction or termination of the contract and getting the money back rather than go to the court and sue for monetary damages if the cost of litigation is taken into account.

5. Economic Analysis

5.1. The Seller's Incentive to Perform

In accordance with the law and economics doctrine, EU law generally encourages performance of the contract that the parties have agreed on. The remedy system established in the EU measures provides a strong incentive for the seller to comply with the contract unless the contract falls into the zone where non-performance is allowed. Most importantly, an aggrieved buyer is entitled to the claim for specific performance in the case that the seller breaks the contract. Besides, performance may also be motivated through the award of expectation damages. Within the context of EU measures, an aggrieved buyer to a contract is entitled to compensation for his expectation damages. In this sense, the seller is induced to take the other party's expectation benefit into account and is supposed to make a comparison between his profit from breach and the other party's expectation interest from performance. The seller is supposed to break the contract only when he thinks he can still make a profit from breach after compensating the buyer's expectation losses. The law should assist the seller to make a correct assessment as far as is possible. On the one hand, the benchmark for assessing damages should be clear; and on the other hand the seller should be able to obtain sufficient information relating to the buyer's expectation as well as the possibility of paying damages. Accordingly, rules are established in order to facilitate the assessment of damages and motivate information disclosure, such as the rules on limiting expectation damages including the "Hardly rule" and the "causation rule". However, the "Hardly rule" will be excluded if the breach is intentional or grossly negligent and as a result the breacher will be exposed to a larger amount of liability.

Both PECL and DCFR have accepted liquidated clauses and allowed party-designed damages which are even higher than the actual loss from non-performance. But damages that are stipulated purely for punishing breach are not allowed and the court may alter it to a reasonable extent. This is largely in line with what is inferred from the analysis about the capacity of damage stipulation to motivate efficient performance and efficient breach. As is suggested, an explicit amount of damages that are stipulated upon agreement reflects the parties' expected value, especially covering the subjective values which are difficult to be assessed ex-post. If properly assessed, liquidated damages will promote welfare maximization. However, the CESL does not specially provide a separate provision on liquidated damages or penalties. This is to a certain extent caused by the nature of the contracts to which the CESL applies. As is mentioned by Article 7 of the Prop. CESL, the CESL applies only if the seller is a trader or if all the parties to a contract are traders but at least one of those parties is a small or medium-sized enterprise ('SME').[639] In such a

639 Article7 Prop. CESL.

contract context, the seller might take a better position than the buyer and may not accept any penalty clause that is disadvantageous to him. For this reason, the CESL has not designed any particular provision on a liquidated damage clause or penalty clause. Instead, the CESL places its emphasis on unfair contract terms which are used more frequently by the party who takes an advantageous position in a sale contract.[640] In this sense, liquidated damages clauses according to the CESL are subject to the rules on unfair contract terms.

5.2. *The Seller's Incentive to Breach*

In drawing the line between efficient breach and efficient performance, the EU measures basically adopted a cost-benefit analysis. Two basic situations are addressed where a seller's obligation to perform will be affected. The first one refers to the circumstances where performance is impossible, which might be caused either by an unexpected, uncontrollable and unavoidable impediment or by a general impediment. The other situation where performance is still possible but burdensome is purely judged on the basis of the balance of cost and benefit of performance.[641] For example, a pre-condition set for the rule on "change of circumstances" is that a debtor's obligation to perform will be deterred when performance not only becomes more onerous but excessively onerous.[642] Specific performance is generally not allowed if contracts fall into the efficient breach zone where performance is impossible or impracticable. With regard to the issue of damages, whether or not the buyer is able to obtain damages depends on the cause of non-performance. In principle, a buyer is still entitled to damages when he is not able to claim for specific performance of the contract. However, where the non-performance is caused by an impediment that the seller did not expect and for which he did not assume the risk, the procedure of renegotiation should be invoked. Furthermore, if this kind of unexpected impediment is uncontrollable and unavoidable or could not be overcome by the debtor, the creditor cannot ask for damages because non-performance is excused. In other words, the idea implied in the damages rule is to correlate the possibility of damages to the allocation of risk. The debtor who assumed the risk of impediment is made to take the risk and pay damages to the other party. If the seller is risk neutral, he is indifferent to risk and should assume the risk of non-performance after the conclusion of the contract. By awarding expectation damages, the law removes the risk of non-performance from the buyer and transfers it to the seller. Nevertheless, non-performance will be excused in the circumstances where the seller has not assumed the risk.

640 Article 85 CESL.

641 With regard to the obligation that involves personal character, enforcing and monitoring specific performance is costly.

642 In this situation, adaptation of the contract is suggested to re-allocate the cost incurred by the supervening circumstances. However, "*it is not correct that any costs resulting from the supervening circumstances must be fairly shared by the parties, but only those costs that can be considered to be beyond the 'limit of sacrifice', i.e. the threshold where performance has not only become 'more onerous', but 'excessively onerous'* " Uribe 2011, p.213.

More importantly, cooperation and re-negotiation is generally encouraged within the efficient breach zone. Some special obligations or rules have been established in order to promote communication and cooperation between contract parties. On the one hand, the debtor who has been influenced by a *force majeure* event is under an obligation to inform, upon which the other party may understand the situation and take responding measures without any delay. For instance, the creditor may negotiate with the debtor to either adapt or terminate the contract or to arrange a substitute sale in order to reduce the loss incurred by non-performance. On the other hand, re-negotiation is recommended if an unexpected situation occurred. The PECL and the CESL directly put forth the parties' duty to negotiate within a reasonable time and the possibility of a court or an arbitral tribunal's adjustment of the contract in the light of hardship. If a party refuses to re-negotiate or breaks off re-negotiation in bad faith, he is liable for the increased loss suffered by the other party according to the CESL. However, imposing an obligation to re-negotiate and allowing a court's adjustment of the contract also gets some criticism from scholars. For instance, as is pointed out, "allowing the court to directly interfere in the content of a contract is a serious challenge to the principle of party autonomy and the *pacta sunt servanda* rule".[643] Moreover, creation of a duty to negotiate and a mandatory re-negotiation period is accused of being unnecessary. The reason, as is given, is that the parties already have a strong incentive to re-negotiate and settle disputes because settling is cheaper than going to court.[644] Nevertheless, the imposition of an obligation to re-negotiate will just interfere with the parties' freedom in choosing between re-negotiation or going to trial directly.[645]

6. Conclusion

Influenced by the European continental law tradition, the PECL, DCFR and CESL all place an emphasis on performance of contracts that have been concluded by voluntary agreements and pay great attention on how to fully protect a promisee's expectation in a contract. This is especially indicated in the CESL that primarily applies to consumer contracts as well as to contracts involving small to medium sized enterprises.[646] Accordingly, an aggrieved promisee is able to make a free choice among five major types of remedies[647] provided by those EU law measures, in particular the choice of specific

643 Feltkamp & Vanbossele 2011, p. 891.

644 De Geest 2010, p. 132–133.

645 Id. *"(T)he likely effects of a duty-to-re-negotiate are usually (a) that court decisions are delayed, because when a party comes to the conclusion that settlement is not possible (for instance, because parties have different expectations as to what the court will decide, so that there is no 'settlement range'), she still has to wait until the mandatory re-negotiation period is over before going to court; and (b) that parties are obliged to play a you-quit-first game in which they have to try to make the other party leave the negotiation table first, so that the other one is held responsible for the failure of the negotiations."*

646 The limitation of the CESL to B2B relationships where at least one of the businesses was an SME was present in the original proposal for a CESL, but was later deleted before the CESL was withdrawn.

647 All the three EU law measures provide five major types of remedy that are available to an aggrieved promise, including withholding performance, termination of contract, specific performance, price reduction as well as monetary damages.

performance (including reparation and replacement). However, both the PECL and the DCFR have restricted the promisee's free choice of specific performance when he is able to obtain substitutes without significant effort or expense. Moreover, the idea of protecting an aggrieved promisee is also indicated in the rules of expectation damages established in the PECL, DCFR as well as CESL. On the one hand, all these three EU law measures base the assessment of expectation damages either on the current market price of the goods at the time when the aggrieved promisee terminates the contract or on the substitute price when the promisee has made a substitutive transaction after the breach. As a result, the aggrieved promisee is free to choose whether or not to make substitutive transactions as well as choose the timing point for damage assessment according to his interest. On the other hand, with regard to the losses that are recoverable, all the three EU law measures hold a broad concept of losses that also includes non-pecuniary losses in the form of physical pain and suffering.[648] In terms of liquidated damage clauses as well as penalty clauses, the EU law measures adopt a lenient attitude and generally respect the parties' agreement. Instead of defying the validity of penalty clauses, both the PECL and the DCFR only reject damage clauses which stipulate an excessive amount of damages.

Performance of a contract is restricted by particular EU sale law rules in relation to unexpected contingencies as well. This is to a certain extent consistent with the efficient breach model with regard to increased unexpected performance costs, which cause contracts to fall into the efficient breach zone. When drawing the border of the efficient breach zone, EU law measures all place an emphasis on a grey zone where the performance cost has increased but not to an excessive extent. In the grey zone, the seller still has to comply with the contract by performing his obligations. A contract might fall into the efficient breach zone only if the intervening event is exceptional. According to EU law, if an unexpected contingency amounts to a *force majeure* or an exceptional change of circumstances or other event that has rendered performance impossible or impracticable, the aggrieved party may not directly require specific performance. In the case of a *force majeure*, non-performance of a contract is achieved by discharging both of the parties from the contract as long as the party affected by the *force majeure* does not bear the risk of it. In comparison, if a change of contract circumstances is excessive or exceptional, the case is more complicated. Instead of directly declining specific performance of the contract, the EU law measures generally impose an obligation of re-negotiation in such a case. It is required that the parties should attempt to re-negotiate with each other with a view of adapting the contract to the new circumstances. The PECL has even indicated a liability of paying damages if a party to a contract maliciously violates the obligation to re-negotiate. Moreover, a court may adapt the contract by modifying or terminating it if the parties fail to reach a successful re-negotiation.

648 The PECL and the DCFR have not specified the types of non-pecuniary losses that are recoverable. It can be understood that mental losses or losses of enjoyment should also be recovered according these two EU law measures. However, CESL has explicitly excluded the recoverability of the impairment of the life quality and enjoyment. *See* Article 9:501 PECL; Article III.–3:701 DCFR (3); Article 2 of (c) Prop. CESL.

To conclude, the EU contract law measures generally show a great respect for contract parties' freedom and try to protect the parties' benefit from the contract based on a free agreement. Moreover, the idea of lowering the cost of executing contract remedies has been incorporated into the remedy system of EU law as well. In those aspects, EU law is consistent with the requirements of the efficient breach theory. In terms of the way of achieving efficiency within the efficient breach zone, what is favored by EU law is re-negotiations and cooperation instead of the approach of breaching a contract. However, the fact that EU law places the priority on substitute performance increases the possibility that a seller may choose to breach a contract and pay monetary damages. The application of efficient breach, in the real world, is restricted by some practical factors in relation to the limited use of the current EU law measures as well as the features of cross-border transactions. Under the present premise, EU contract law is still under development. Within the three EU law measures, the PECL as well as the DCFR work as soft law measures which will not directly be applied to specific contracts and the CESL is an optional instrument which is applicable only if it is opted into by contract parties. In most cases concerning transactions within the EU, it is still the national sales laws that affect the contractual relationship. Moreover, within cross-border transactions, the parties are more likely to choose alternative dispute resolutions instead of going to a court and resorting to legal remedies offered by EU law if the costs of each approach are taken into account.

Chapter 7

EFFICIENT BREACH AND RE-NEGOTIATION IN ENGLISH SALES LAW

According to law and economics theory, contract law should facilitate transactions and hence promote welfare maximization. In the absence of complete contracts, it is necessary for the system of remedy rules to shape the parties' incentives to make efficient contracts ex-ante and to act optimally after the contract has been concluded. Accordingly, contract remedy techniques, such as techniques to encourage accurate evaluation, to promote efficient precaution, to avoid performance when it is inefficient to do so and to optimally allocate future risks are desirable. Moreover, contract law may also include particular rules dealing with risks that fall out of the scope of a contract. This chapter will apply the theory of efficient breach to English sales law by analysing its remedy rules and rules in relation to unexpected risks. After a basic introduction to English sales law in section 1, section 2 of this chapter will provide the framework of a buyer's remedies, including the remedy of specific performance, monetary damages and remedies stipulated by contract parties. Afterward, section 3 will analyse the English doctrines of frustration and hardship, which deal with contracts falling into the efficient breach zone. An economic analysis of English law will be made in section 4 in order to examine to what extent a seller is motivated to adhere to the contract as well as to analyse the role of party-autonomy in dealing with breach and performance of commercial sales contracts. Section 5 will conclude.

1. Introduction to English Sales Law

What we call English sales law mostly refers to the modern law of sales which dates from the end of the 19th century.[649] Before the Sales of Goods Act 1893 (hereinafter SGA 1983),[650] the law of sales basically consisted of common law[651] and a few

649 Brown 2001, p. 243–44.

650 The entire title of the Act was "An Act for codifying the law relating to the Sale of Goods 1893". It came into force on January 1894. *See* Id, at. 243.

651 In the early English practice, the law of sales contract started with a "covenant (conventio, agreement)". Actions may be brought to the royal courts, called "covenant" concerning breaches of the sales agreement. The plaintiff began his action by a *praecipe* writ, aiming to make the defendant keep the agreement. Later, this claim was declined by English judgments, which prefers to award damages

enactments[652] applying to the general aspect of contracts. Originally, it was the criminal statutes, for instance, rules prohibiting "the use of false measures...or the adulteration of food" that regulated sales transactions[653] and actions on sales were majorly based on deceit, relating to fraud or breaches of express warranty.[654] But from the late 18th century, actions with a contractual basis in the form of *assumpsit*[655] started to be separated from the form of claim in deceit, and breach of "implied warranty" started to be recognized by the court.[656]

In 1889, the time of codification of sales law started, bringing out the Sales of Goods Bill which was presented by Sir Mackenzie Chambers.[657] This Bill was later modified and became the Sales of Goods Act 1893 which was one of the most important parts of English commercial law[658] in that period. The distinguishing feature of the SGA 1893 was that it provided a network of rules arising from a large amount of unsystematic judicial decisions for commercial sales transactions.[659] Moreover, it laid down the basis for the

instead. In the early time, judges required a document under the defendant's seal as the requirement for proving the existence of the agreement and any absence of a sealed agreement might entitle the plaintiff to nothing. *See* Beatson 2010, p. 10–16.

652 E.g., the Statute of Frauds (1677) ss 15, 16; the Statute of Frauds Amendment Act 1828 s7; Mercantile Law Amendment Act 1856 ss 1, 2. SGA 1893 s60 repealed all those enactments. *See* Mackay 2005, p. 16–18.

653 McKendrick 2010, p. 200.

654 The justification of the seller's liability was considered as that he had made a false statement deceiving the buyer to sign the contract. The seller is only liable for his explicit expression of warranty. This has been confirmed in the case of *Chandelor v. Lopus*, 79 Eng. Rep. 3 (K.B. 1603) ("[F]or the bare affirmation that it was a bezar-stone, without warranting it to be so, is no cause of action: and although he knew it to be no bezar-stone, it is not material; for every one in selling his wares will affirm that his wares are good, or the horse which he sells is sound; yet if he does not warrant them to be so, it is no cause of action, and the warranty ought to be made at the same time of the sale") and even been cited in *Oscar Chess Ltd v Williams* 1 ALL ER 325 (1957).

655 The landmark is the case of *Stuart v Wilkins*, 99 Eng. Rep. 15 (K.B. 1778). Afterwards, "assumpsit" replaced deceit altogether as the remedy for non-fraudulent breach of warranty." *See* McKendrick 2010, at. 203.

656 But the reorganization of implied warranty was still difficult between from the 18 century to the 19 century. Even in the late 19th Century, breaches of contract were still treated as torts. For instance, in the case of *Hyman v Nye*, the judge Lindley stated that the defendant (a jobmaster, who lent a carriage, a pair of horses, and a driver to the plaintiff) was not liable for the injury caused by a broken bolt in the underpart of the carriage because there is no evidence showing that the injury was attributed to the defendant's fault. Id, *see* also *Hyman and Wife v Nye & Sons*, (1880–81) L.R. 6 Q.B.D. 685.

657 The Sale of Goods Bill 1889 was raised up from the sales law for England and Wales. In 1888, Sir Mackenzie Chalmers made the draft and Lord Herschell introduced it to the House of Lords. In 1889, the Bill was modified and re-introduced again, with assimilation of some law of Scotland. But there were still many questions concerning its applicability in Scotland. Rodger 1992, p. 581.

658 Since the second half of 19th Century, England witnessed a mass work of codification of commercial rules, including the Joint Stock Companies Act 1844, the Limited Liability Act 1855, the Bills of Exchange Act 1882, the Bankruptcy Act 1883, the Factors Act 1889, the Partnership Acts 1890 and 1980 as well as the Marine Insurance Act 1906. Omar 2007, p. 236.

659 An important aim of the English sales law at this period was to facilitate purely commercial sales, where both parties are commercial traders (sales of materials from a manufactory to a business company) with equal bargaining power. Moreover, a sale was defined as a "consensual contract" so that parties would be able to exclude or modify most of the provisions by SGA 1979 as they want. *See* the SGA 1979, s 55; *see* also Brown 2001, p. 244; *see* also Bridge 2009, p. 5.

later Sales of Goods Act 1979 (hereinafter SGA 1979) which also accepted minor amendments, repeal and changes and finally replaced the SGA 1893.[660] The process of codification of English sales law has been continued by several amendments to the SGA 1979, including the Insolvency Act 1985, the Sale of Goods (Amendment) Act 1994, the Sales and Supply of Goods Act 1994, the Sale of Goods (Amendment) Act 1995 and the Sale and Supply of Goods to Consumers Regulation 2002.[661]

So far, modern English sales law presents a hybrid system, originating from two major branches. The first branch refers to what we call primary law, consisting of common law, parliament acts (e.g. SGA 1979, SGA 1994 and SGA 1995), European Directives and a number of other statutory provisions promoting the interpretation and development of the SGA.[662] The second branch contains various commercial customs and academic works (e.g. leading textbooks in the field),[663] which are not binding but may offer inspiration for legal judgments.

Among those sources of English sales law, the SGA (including its amendments) and case law make up the most important part. However, the SGA 1979 cannot be considered as an independent and complete system, but it needs to be interpreted and complemented by other resources, such as the Common Law[664] or the Law

660 See Mackay 2005, p. 16.

661 The Sale and Supply of Goods to Consumers Regulation 2002 was aimed at implementing the European Union Directive 1999/44/EC of 25 May 1999 on Certain Aspects of the Sale of Consumer Goods and Associated Guarantees. But the problem with implementation is the EU consumer directive has only been incorporated in to the SGA act rather than be transferred into a separate consumer sales enactment. As a result, complexity may arise in applying the law. *See* 99/44/EC, OJ L171, 7/7/99; *See* McKendrick 2010, p. 205–06; *See* also Mackay 2005, p. 17.

662 Adams & Macqueen 2010, p. 3.

663 Only those academic works that are considered to be authoritative in that field will be referred to by the court. Slapper & Kelly 2011, p. 143 ([T]he courts, however, will look at the most eminent works by accepted experts in particular fields in order to help determine what the law is or should be. See for example, the citation of Shetreet's Judges on Trial, and De Smith, Wolf and Jowell, Judicial Review of Administrative Action, in Lord Browne-Wilkinson's decision in Re Pinochet (1999...).

664 With regard to the relationship between the SGA and the Common Law, there were different ideas in the early time when the SGA had just come into being. One is an optimistic attitude towards the independence of SGA itself. This idea is stated by Lord Herschell in the case of *Bank of England v Vagliano Bros*:

> *"I think the proper course is ... to examine the language of the statute and to ask what is its natural meaning, uninfluenced by any considerations derived from the previous state of the law, and not to start with inquiring how the law previously stood...If a statute, intended to embody in a code a particular branch of the law, is to be treated in this fashion, it appears to me that its utility will be almost entirely destroyed... The purpose of such a statute surely was that on any point specifically dealt with by it, the law should be ascertained by interpreting the language used instead of... by roaming over a vast number of authorities in order to discover what the law was, extracting it by a minute critical examination of the prior decisions, dependent upon a knowledge of the exact effect even an obsolete proceeding such as a demurrer to evidence."*

He, moreover, addressed that citation of a previous case should only be needed in exceptional situations, for instance where the text was unclear or it had adopted a term of art which could be only clarified from the previous decisions. This indication, as is recognized, led to "two divergent judicial approaches to its interpretation", including to seek the meaning of the text itself and to look at the earlier cases dealing with the same situation. See A decision on the Bills of Exchange Act 1882, *Bank of England v. Vagliano Bros* [1981] A C 107, 144–5; *see* also Adams & Macqueen 2010, p. 4; *see* also Bridge 2009, p. 6.

Merchant[665] or other important statutory provisions.[666] This has been confirmed by s 62 (2) of the SGA 1979.[667] Moreover, as is shown, the SGA 1979 has limitations in its application as well. On the one hand, it only codified rules in relation to sales contracts,[668] but omits general rules of contract law, such as rules dealing with the validity of contract or interpretation of contract terms.[669] On the other hand, neither the SGA 1979 nor the SGA1893 have made a distinction between different types of Sales, but only focused on the type of sales contracts pre-occupying England between the 19th and 20th century, representing small commodities sales or sales of industrial materials between commercial parties.[670] Nevertheless, sales contracts in English practice have become more complex since the late 20th century. Especially, a large number of sales transactions are taking place in more complex commercial forms, such as the sales based on financing techniques[671] or the sales with forward delivery terms that involve transferring documents.[672] Besides, sales between private parties or between retailing business and individual consumers have also gained more significance in the modern times, arousing re-examination of, for example, the rules about implied terms as well as the term "merchantable quality".[673] In addition, the efforts in the Europeanization of Private Law have provided new sources to the

665 The law merchant designates a sum of usages and customs derived from commercial practices from time to time. In modern times, most of them take the form of standard form clauses and can be opted out by the agreement between the contractual parties. Many of them still have a great impact on the common law. *See* Bridge 2009, p. 11.

666 For instance, the Unfair Contract Terms Act 1977.

667 SGA 1979, s.62 (2) states:

> *[T]he rules of the common law, including the law merchant, except in so far as they are inconsistent with the provisions of this Act, and in particular the rules relating to the law of principal and agent and the effect of fraud, misrepresentation, duress or coercion, mistake, or other invalidating cause, apply to contracts for the sale of goods.*

668 SGA 1979 contains seven parts, including: Part I. Contracts to Which Act Applies; Part II. Formation of the Contract; Part III. Effects of the Contract; Part IV. Performance of the Contract; Part V. Rights of Unpaid Seller against the Goods; Part VI. Actions for Breach of the Contract and Part VII. Supplementary.

669 *See* Mackay 2005, p. 17–18.

670 As is shown by s1(1), SGA 1979 applies to contracts of sale of goods made on or after (but not to those made before) 1 January 1894. *See* also Adams & Macqueen 2010, p. 6; *see* also Bridge 2009, p. 2; *see* also Brown 2001, p. 244.

671 For instance, hire purchase came into being for the purpose of encouraging consumers to acquire on credit rather than on cash. If the consumer fails to keep up the payment, the seller is able to repossess the products.

672 An example is the transfer of security in the stock market.

673 In reaction, for instance, the 1994 Sale and Supply of Goods Act amends the traditional rules of warranty and damages based on express contract terms relating to the description, quality and fitness of goods for selling. S.1(1) and (2) of the 1994 Sale and Supply of Goods adds that:

> *[F]or the purposes of this Act, goods are of satisfactory quality if they meet the standard that a reasonable person would regard as satisfactory, taking account of any description of the goods, the price (if relevant) and all the other relevant circumstances... (2) In section 15 of that Act (sale by sample) in subsection (2) (c) for "rendering them unmerchantable" there is substituted "making their quality unsatisfactory"...*

English sales Law as well, such as Directive *1997/7/EC*[674] on the protection of consumers in respect of distance contracts or the European Union's Draft Common Frame of Reference 2008.

Table 35 shows the basic sources of English Sales Law.[675]

Table 35. Sources of English Sales Law

<table>
<tr><td rowspan="9">Primary Law</td><td rowspan="5">Statutory Law</td><td rowspan="5">SGA 1979</td><td colspan="2">Amendments(1994, 1995)</td></tr>
<tr><td rowspan="4">Other Statutory</td><td>Factors Act 1889</td></tr>
<tr><td>Unfair Contract Terms 1977</td></tr>
<tr><td>Unfair Contract Terms Regulation 1999</td></tr>
<tr><td>...</td></tr>
<tr><td rowspan="2">Common Law</td><td colspan="3">Case Law: Pre-1893 cases & cases after 1893</td></tr>
<tr><td colspan="3">Rules of Equity:</td></tr>
<tr><td>Customs</td><td colspan="3">Law Merchant:</td></tr>
<tr><td>EU Directives</td><td colspan="3">1999/44/EC
1997/7/EC ...</td></tr>
<tr><td>Secondary law</td><td>Books & Articles</td><td colspan="3">Books of Authority
Leading casebooks
Key articles</td></tr>
</table>

2. General Rules about Sales Contract, Breach and Remedies

In this section, the general rules regarding breach and remedies in English sales law will be presented in order to analyze the role of remedy rules in affecting people's behavior after the conclusion of a contract. To make the analysis more precise, this section will be grounded on the scenario that a seller breaches a sales contract in a general form.

2.1. Sales Contract

Apparently, s2(1) SGA tries to limit the scope of its application by indicating the two basic elements of sales, namely, transfer of ownership and monetary consideration.[676] In this sense, transfer of ownership is regarded as the primary message embedded in sales, no matter whether the subject of the sale exists or not; or is specified or not (See table 2).

674 Directive 97/7/EC of the European Parliament and of the Council of 20 May 1997 on the protection of consumers in respect of distance contracts. 97/7/EC, OJ L144, 4/6/97 implemented by SI 2000/2334.

675 For the actual scope of commercial sales, this chapter will just focus on the SGA and the common law.

676 SGA 1979 makes a difference between a sale and an agreement to sell. For the term of an agreement to sell, it is merely "the description of the contract at the executory stage". When one party breaks the agreement and the other party can only bring out action in personum. In contrast, a sale is the "actual conveyance of the goods". If a sale is broken, the non-breaching party can also claim for the specific goods. See Bridge 2009, p. 56.

Other sales related contracts, including pledge, hire-purchase or service contracts are ruled out of the scope of the sales contract.

In terms of remedying an aggrieved buyer in sales contracts, the English sales law does not specify an abstract category of remedies in response to different forms of breach.[677] Rather, the remedy rules of the SGA are presented as a mixed system, consisting of both contract rules and property rules, such as the rules about the unpaid buyer's real rights.[678] In general, the main English sales law remedies include monetary compensation, specific performance and injunction.[679] Besides, the common law rules and commercial usage compliment this system, catering for different concrete commercial purposes of sales contracts, including sub-sales, rent-out, self-use and so on. The purpose of either sub-sales or self-use directly influences the interpretation of the buyer's expectation and the choice of a certain type of remedy.

Table 36 shows some typical forms of commercial sales in modern society.[680]

Table 36. Typical Forms of Commercial Sales in English Law

the seller transfers or agrees to transfer the property in goods to the buyer for monetary consideration (price)

sale		Agreement to Sale	
Existing or not		Specified or not	
Existing Goods	Future Goods/ Forward Selling	Specific Goods (SG)	Uncertain Goods
		An undivided share in SG	

...

Purpose of the Buyer			Finance the sales			
Sub-Sale (chain sale)	Self Use	Lease	Conditional Sales	*Sales related agreement*		
				Pledge	*Hire-purchase*	...

...

2.2. *Seller's Breach and Buyer's Right to Specific Performance*

After a contract has been concluded, the primary obligation for the seller is to deliver the goods as required by the contract. However, within the remedy system of English sales law, the remedy of specific performance belongs to equitable measures and courts have

677 In contrast, in statutes law system, a general rule about breach and remedies is provided by the statute.

678 Unpaid seller's right in lien, right to stoppage in transit and right to resale.

679 Injunction, in English Law includes two forms, namely a mandatory injunction (to take positive behaviour to undo a breach committed in the past) and a negative injunction (to take a negative attitude against breaching certain behaviour). An example of a mandatory injunction is to remove a building built in breach of a restrictive covenant, while a negative injunction example is typically indicated as a post-employment non-competitive obligation or an obligation to keep privacy. Rowan 2012, p. 30–1.

680 Rowan 2012, p. 21.

wide discretion to decide whether or not to make an offer of specific performance.[681] In English law practice, this remedy is granted on a rare basis.[682] Many reasons were given by English scholars to justify the English courts' reluctance to grant specific performance. For example, some think that, to enforce the discretionary equitable remedies of specific performance and injunction is to impose physical constraints on the promisor's person and it would incur high compliance cost and administration cost.[683] Conversely, a monetary award can be achieved without "constant supervision" and in many situations would be adequate for the injured party because then he could use this money to buy the replacement in the market.[684] Or it is stated that by enforcing specific relief, the court would infringe on the individual liberty of the breaching party.[685] More importantly, the historical development of English law adds to the undesirability of enforcing specific performance, which was presented as an order by the chancellor that an injurer should do something or stop doing something. But the common law courts basically only awarded monetary equivalence as they thought money was always equivalent to contractual undertakings.[686] When a claimant could not obtain sufficient relief from the common law court, he could turn to the court of chancery which acted according to "conscience" and "fairness". Moreover, the violation of the Chancellor's command was always severe (the defendant could be put in prison or awarded fines) so that this kind of equitable relief was always considered unnecessary and developed in very limited occasions. Those reasons, to some extent, explain why specific performance and injunctions have been granted only when the courts consider doing so is just and necessary.[687]

The inadequacy of damages is one of the most important reasons for a court to exercise the equitable remedy of specific performance. Normally, attachment of consumer

681 In English law, equitable remedies for breach of contract also include injunctions. Different from specific performance, an injunction is usually an order by a court restricting the breach of a pure negative promise by the seller. In this thesis, the scenario under discussion is that a seller breaches a contract in a general way, e.g. he refuses to deliver the goods as required. Therefore, this thesis does not consider remedies in the form of injunctions. Bridge et. al. 2010, p. 1115, 1116.

682 Adams & Macqueen 2010, p. 558.

683 For more discussion regarding the difference between specific performance and monetary damages, see chapter 5, section 1.

684 If both damages and specific performance are sufficient to protect the commercial expectation interest of the buyer, the court would always elect the damages for one reason that the remedy of damages is assumed to be less costly. *See* Harris 2005, p. 167.

685 Smith 2004, p. 422.

686 After the Norman Conquest of England, the King's Court became the common law court and did not enforce obligations but only monetary compensation. The court of chancery, however, was influenced by canon law and had to take "fairness", "conscience" and "morality" into consideration when exercising its discretions. Harris 2005, p. 166–7; Rowan 2012, p. 32.

687 Jones & Goodhart 1996, p. 1. There are more reasons why the specific performance is not accepted in the common law courts. For example, it is argued that awarding specific performance would have a negative impact on the ex-post negotiation as the injured promisee would commit oppressive conduct against the breaching party. Or it would be undesirable to have the contract parties keep on performing their contractual undertakings because of the breakdown of their reliance and contractual relationship. As is stated by Lord Hoffmann, the parties are forced to stay together in a continuing hostile relationship. *See* Rowan 2012, p. 35; *see* also *Co-operative v Argyll* [1998] AC 1 (HL).

surplus[688] or commercial uniqueness to the sales is assumed to be the prerequisite for granting specific relief.[689] In most commercial sales transactions, the court refused specific performance for the reason that the goods indicated in the contract possessed no special characteristics and the commercial buyer's interests is the exchangeable value of goods which can be converted into a certain amount of money. This has been confirmed in the case of *Société des Industries Métallurgiques SA v Bronx Engineering Co Ltd* (the machine is available in the market) and the case of Cohen v Roche (the buyer intended to re-sell it at a profit).[690] In other cases, for instance in the case of *Behnke v Beda Shipping Co Ltd*,[691] there was no alternative vessel available in the market so that the buyer would suffer irrecoverable loss if he could not obtain the ship mentioned in the contract, the court finally issued an order of specific performance.

The SGA has also assimilated the rule of uniqueness of goods into section 52.[692] As is stated, specific performance applies when a contract involves "specific" and "ascertained goods" as well as that the court thinks it is necessary to award it upon the application of the plaintiff. S.61 further provides the meaning of specific goods as "goods identified and agreed on at the time a contract of sale is made".[693] The case concerning specific performance in sales of "specific and ascertained goods" is normally presented as, for example, sales of land[694] or purchasing a unique item or antiques.[695] But in judicial

688 The concept of "consumer surplus" is based on the idea that "the subjective value of something to the individual may sometimes diverge from its value as represented by the market price." For instance, if one person can buy a product at 100£ which he is willing to pay a maximal amount of 150£, then 50£ is the consumer surplus. In the market, the consumer seeks individual use of the product that he intends to buy. The difference between the market price of a product and the value that a consumer places on this product is consumer surplus. Harris 2005, p. 168–170.

689 Id, p. 167–8.

690 In the *Société des Industries Métallurgiques SA v Bronx Engineering Co Ltd* case, the goods involved were a large machine weighing over 220 tons and worth more than £ 270,000. However, the court still awarded monetary damages even though it would take the buyer 9 to 12 months to obtain a substitute and the delay in obtaining the machine would incur substantial consequential loss. [1975] 1 Lloyd's Rep 465 (CA); Cohen v Roche [1927] 1 KB 169.

691 [1927] 1 KB 649.

692 SGA 1979, S 52:

1) *In any action for breach of contract to deliver specific or ascertained goods the court may, if it thinks fit, on the plaintiff's application, by its judgment or decree direct that the contract shall be performed specifically, without giving the defendant the option of retaining the goods on payment of damages.*
2) *The plaintiff's application may be made at any time before judgment or decree.*
3) *The judgment or decree may be unconditional, or on such terms and conditions as to damages, payment of the price and otherwise as seem just to the court.*
4) *The provisions of this section shall be deemed to be supplementary to, and not in derogation of, the right of specific implement in Scotland.*

693 SGA 1979, S. 61.

694 As is explained, "Each plot of land is regarded as being unique and irreplaceable. As a result, damages for the breach of such contracts will seldom be adequate". See the case of *Sudbrook Trading Estate Ltd v Eggleton* [1983] 1AC 444 (HL).

695 There are some cases where the courts granted specific performance because the goods to be delivered were recognized as unique, special and unreplaceable. For instance, the case of *Thorn v Commissioners of Works and Public Buildings* concerned special stones from Old Westminster Bridge and the case *George v Ascot Supreme Ltd.* involved the supply of a luxury horsebox needed for summer evening and

practice, the cases where the court has accepted specific performance are also extended to such as a long-term contract for supply of future goods (e.g. future supply of oil in the case of *Sky Petroleum Ltd v VIP Petroleum Ltd*)[696] and complex sales agreements in the form of a franchise agreement or an exclusive distributorship agreement[697] (e.g., sole agent for reselling wine in the UK in the case of *Evans Marshall & Co v Bertola SA*[698]). In those cases, the courts generally exercised the "inadequacy test" to decide whether or not specific performance should be awarded. Many factors, such as the buyer's reason for purchase, the unavailability of market equivalence and the remoteness of losses have been taken into account in those cases. Moreover, when deciding whether or not damages are sufficient to compensate for the buyer's loss, the court may also consider other practical factors, including the seller' insolvency,[699] the buyer's previous claim,[700] the supervision cost[701] and so on. But what is confirmed by the court is that the remedy of specific performance is unlikely to be granted if doing so would incur undue hardship to the defendant.[702]

horse shows. See *Thorn v Commissioners of Works and Public Buildings* [1863] 32 Beav. 490; *George v Ascot Supreme Ltd* [2002] EWHC 1978 (Q.B.).

696 In this case, the buyer's businesses largely relied on the seller's supply of oil and at that certain period to find substitutive oil in an over-excited oil market was impossible. Although the case also covered future suppliers of oil which did not exist, the court still granted an injunction against the seller's breach on the grounds that monetary damages would be insufficient. [1974] 1 WLR 576.

697 Bridge 2009, p. 736–7.

698 In this case of *Evans Marshall & Co v Bertola SA* [1973] 1 W.L.R. 349, M Co., the English wholesale wine company, signed an agreement in 1951 with B Co., a Spanish company producing and shipping sherry, to the effect that M Co. should become B Co.'s sole agents in England for five years. After five years, that agreement was extended until 1986. In 1972, the ownership of B Co. was changed into the hands of another Spanish company who alleged that M Co.'s carrying out of their obligations was unsatisfactory and purported to appoint I Co. in replace of M Co. In this case, the plaintiff, M Co. sued for injunctions against B Co. and I Co. In the end, injunctions were awarded by the court for two reasons: 1) breach of the exclusive clause would harm the plaintiff's goodwill and trade reputation; 2) it is difficult to ascertain the economic loss suffered by the plaintiff. In another case of *Land Rover Group Ltd v UPF (UK) Ltd* [2002] EWHC 3183 (Mercantile Court), the court also granted specific relief. This case concerns the sale of a chassis to be used in the buyer's manufactory business. The buyer had invested heavily in the seller's premises and the seller also had invested a lot in its production of the chassis. The court decided that there was a fiduciary duty to act in good faith in this contractual relationship and monetary damages would be insufficient because it could not secure the continuing supply of the chassis which is the pre-condition for the buyer to manage his manufactory business. *See* also Yorio 2012, p.16–10.

699 For instance, suppose the seller has become insolvent after he obtained the payment but before the delivery. The court would grant specific performance by allowing the buyer to take the goods out of the seller's estate. By being entitled to a right to the goods, the buyer is given a priority over other unsecured creditors. Harris 2005, p. 185–6.

700 If the buyer previously has sued for terminating the contract and claimed for damages, he is bound by his original claim and not allowed to change his words by resorting to specific relief again. See *Meng Leong Development Pte Ltd v Jip Hong Trading Co Pte Ltd* [1985] AC 511.

701 If the cost of monitoring the breaching party's compliance is very high, the court might also reject to grant specific performance.

702 More discussions will be made in Section 3.

2.3. *Damage Rules*

As is noted, if the seller breaks the contract, the routine remedy that will be issued by the court is damages so as to compensate for the buyer's loss. This has been confirmed in a series cases and also by the S. 51 (2) of the SGA 1979.[703]

2.3.1. Compensation and the Measurement of Loss

2.3.1.1. The Prima Facie Rule

The first question that English courts are faced with is the measurement of damages. In principle, the courts accept the rule of "expectation damages" by entitling the aggrieved buyer to the amount of damages that he expected to recover. But it might sometimes be difficult for the injured party to prove the amount of expectation loss he has suffered; in which case, the court may also allow him to make the substitute choice of claiming reliance loss. For instance, in the case of *McRae v Commonwealth Disposals Commission*, what the court awarded to the buyer was the purchase price paid and the expenditure wasted in reliance of the promise.[704]

The subsequent issue following the concern of damage measurement is how to calculate the injured party's losses caused by breaches. The market price rule[705] has been generally applied by the courts as the *prima facie* rule,[706] in order to quantify the buyer's loss from breach in those contract breach cases where a relevant market does exist.[707] The logic is simply stated as: the rule of expectation damages is aimed to put the aggrieved party in the position that he would enjoy had the contract been performed, hence the value of this position, naturally, should be ascertained by the market price at the time and the place of the due performance.[708] To be more specific, the *breach date rule* is taken to fix the time for ascertaining the market price.[709] If the seller fails to deliver the goods, the buyer's loss is evaluated as the difference between the contract price and the current market price of the goods at the time the product should be delivered or if no time was fixed, at the time of the refusal.[710] Or if the seller delays delivery of the goods, the buyer would be able to recover

703 SGA 1979, S. 51 (2):

> *[T]he measure of the damages is the estimated loss directly and naturally resulting, in the ordinary course of events, from the seller's breach of contract.*

704 In this case, the plaintiff made an offer to buy a wrecked oil tanker provided by the defendants. In the end, it was proved that the tanker did not exist and never had existed. The high court of Australia held that the plaintiffs were entitled to recover the expenditure that they invested in looking for the tanker. See *McRae v Commonwealth Disposals Commission* [1952], 84 C.L.R. 377; Similar case is *CCC Films v Impact Quadrant Films*, [1984] 3 All ER 298.

705 S 51 (3). The market price rule has been firmly established in Scottish law and English law.

706 Bridge 2009, p. 782–83.

707 For deciding whether or not there is available market for measuring the value of the product, see *Dunkirk Colliery Co v. Lever* (1878) 9 ChD 20, CA.

708 Brown 2001, p. 694.

709 Bridge 2009, p. 783.

710 Mackay 2005, p. 215–16, 218.

the difference between the market price of the goods at the time when they were delivered and the due time when they ought to be delivered.[711] Or In the case where the seller delivers defective goods, the buyer may recover the price difference of the defective product and the conforming product.[712] It is noticed that the market price of the goods in those situations is fixed at the time when the goods (or the conforming goods) ought to be delivered[713] or the time when the goods (or the defective goods) were delivered. Accordingly, finding an appropriate date for market price assists the seller to obtain information about the buyer's expected loss when it comes to the time for him to sign the contract and to perform the contract (See Table 37). Nevertheless, the "breach date" rule in English practice is applied with a lot of flexibility. For example, the case law modified the "breach date rule" when it comes to the situation where the contract has not expressly indicated a date for delivery and an anticipatory breach occurs.[714] As is provided in the important case of *Tai Hing Cotton Mill Ltd v Kamsing Knitting Factory*,[715] the delivery should be made within a reasonable period and the damages are based on the market price at the due delivery date.[716] What's more, according to the prime facie rule, the price of the goods is fixed at the time when they should be delivered rather than when the buyer makes the damage claim, the buyer is encouraged to make the damage claim or other precautions in order to diminish his loss, after he realizes the fact of breach, without delay.[717]

Table 37. Timing Point for Assessment in English Law

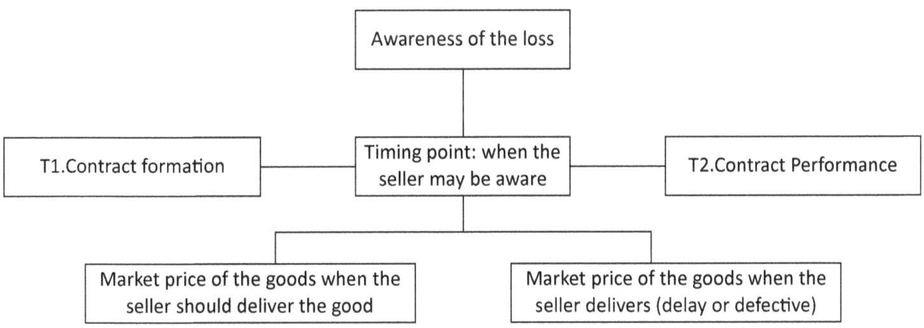

711 Mackay 2005, p. 221.
712 SGA 1979, S. 53 (3); Mackay 2005, p. 227.
713 To evaluate whether an available market exists or not and the market price of the product at the time when the seller is required to deliver puts forth to a further question, namely, whether or not the loss that the plaintiff claims would be within the contemplation of the parties. Mackay 2005, p. 216.
714 If an anticipatory breach happens, the breach date rule will not be applicable.
715 [1979] AC 91.
716 Adams & Macqueen 2010, p. 533.
717 Such a rule does not apply in the case of defective performance. In cases where the goods delivered by a seller contain defects, the buyer usually will not find out the defects until he receives the goods. Therefore, if the goods delivered by the seller are not inconformity with the contract, the buyer's expected loss will be calculated by reference to the time when the buyer, by reasonable diligence, could find out the defects. Treitel 2003, p. 960–961. This was put forth to the rule of mitigation principle, which will be discussed in section 2.3.2.

To be noted, the market price rule is merely a *prima facie* rule, which would be far less sufficient when complicated factors are considered in the specific cases. Questions specifically arise in the situations where the buyer has made substitute goods or where there is no market price.

2.3.1.2. Substitute Transaction

If there is an available market and thus a market price for the product at the date of breach can be ascertained, it is assumed that awarding damages referring to market price is desirable. As is explained, the market price rule is able to motivate the aggrieved party to buy the products at that price in the available market if necessary although actually he might not have done so.[718] In this sense, the market price rule still prevails even though the buyer has bought substitute goods in the market at more or less than the market price, because it is argued the price of the substitute purchase is the result of the bargaining power of the buyer rather than the result of breach.[719] If the actual purchase price is higher, higher damages will still be ruled out because it might be held that the buyer should and could have bought the goods at the market price unless the buyer had to conduct such a purchase for mitigating his loss from the breach.[720] But if the actual purchase price is lower, an exception case (*Pagnan & Fratelli v Corbisa Industrial Agropacuaria Ltda*) does exist where the court reduced the damages awarded to the buyer.[721]

Generally, English law has not adopted the "substitute transaction rule" which has been commonly accepted in other legal systems,[722] although exceptions may be made if

718 Brown 2001, p. 692–93.

719 Suppose the injured buyer, after breach bought the substitute goods at a lower price. The logic for awarding higher damages with reference to the market price at the time of breach is:

> *[I]t could not be argued that B's opportunity to buy at the low price arose solely as a consequence of S's breach; in fact, S has delivered the contract goods, B would still have been able to buy the low-priced goods in the available market.*

Brown 2001, p. 693.

720 The rule of mitigation will be cited in relation to such a case. Section 2.2.2 will provide more discussions. Id; *see* also Adams & Macqueen 2010, p. 535.

721 In the case of *R Pagnan & Fratelli v. Corbisa Industrial Agropacuaria Limitada*, the aggrieved buyer, rather than buy substitute goods from the market, decided to buy the same goods (but with defective quality) from the breaching seller at a lower price than what they agreed in the settlement. This price is even lower than the original price and the market price. The buyer, afterwards, resold the product and reaped a profit covering his loss in the original contract. The Court of Appeal held that the second contract was the continuous dealing of the original contract and thus awarded the buyer only nominal damages.

722 For instance, Article 2–712 of the Uniform Commercial Code in the USA provides that the price of the substitute goods should be taken as the basis for the assessment of the damages. Similarly, Article III 3:706 of the DCFR states that an aggrieved creditor who has terminated a contractual relationship and made a substitute transaction within a reasonable time and in a reasonable manner may recover the difference between the value of what would have been payable under the terminated relationship and the value of what is payable under the substitute transaction. Adams & Macqueen 2010, p. 535.

there is no relevant market price for the goods.[723] In this sense, after the fact of breach occurs, the buyer runs the risk that the market price might rise or fall if he has not bought the substitute goods immediately.[724] Since the price of substitute goods would not make any difference in deciding the amount of damages, a risk-averse buyer is on the one hand motivated to make the substitute purchase as soon as possible if he predicts an increase in the market price so as to reduce his own loss from breach; but on the other hand he would prefer to delay the substitute purchase if he witnesses an decrease in the market price in order to reap a profit from the fall of market price. For example, suppose a breach case in which the contract price of the product (M) was stipulated as 8,000£ and the price of the M in the market at the breaching date (Jan 1st) is 10,000£. In any case, the buyer is entitled to a fixed amount of damages (2,000£) according to the market price rule. Therefore, a rational buyer should buy the substitute immediately as long as he expects M is getting more expensive in the market. In contrast, he would prefer to wait until the price of M reaches its lowest point if he expects it is decreasing. Nevertheless, in the circumstances where the price of M fluctuates erratically so that prediction is difficult, the buyer bears the risk of paying either a high price or low price for the substitute goods. Furthermore, a reasonable delay in making substitute goods will actually happen if the aggrieved buyer plans to negotiate with the breaching seller rather than accept the fact of breach and arrange substitution on the exact day on which the breach takes place. In this sense, a more preferable approach, suggested by this chapter, is to allow the "substitute transaction rule".

2.3.1.3. Cost of Cure

Beside the topic of "substitute price", another issue that has also aroused controversy within English courts is the "cost of cure". Discussion of the "cost of cure" always takes place in the cases where the actual goods delivered by the seller contain defects or non-conformities. The question for the court in such cases is whether or not the expenditure on curing the defective product should be considered when calculating damages. The effect of cure, in fact is to make the aggrieved buyer obtain what he has expected from the contract. In this sense, it is a particular form of specific performance.[725] However, the English court takes a cautious attitude towards recovery of cost of cure as well. In the case of *Ruxley Electronics and Construction Ltd v Forsyth*,[726] the maximum depth of the swimming pool constructed by the promisor is 1 foot less than what was agreed, but the actual depth of the swimming pool has already met the requirements for swimming and diving. In this case, curing the defect will cost £21,000. The House of Lords refused to award damages that are based on the cost of curing the defect. It was held that the cost of reconstructing the swimming pool was more costly than the potential benefit that the promisee could enjoy from increasing the depth of the swimming pool. Thus cure was considered to be unreasonable and the cost of cure should not be considered as the basis

723 A more detailed discussion about the exceptions to the "market price" rule can be found in section 2.3.1.4 of this chapter.

724 Brown 2001, p. 693.

725 Rowan 2012, p. 111.

726 [1996]AC 344 (HL).

for damage calculation. However, the *Ruxley* case has not absolutely refused recovery of the cost of cure. The reason for refusing to base damages on the cost of cure, as is stated by Lord Jauncey is that such an award of damages has exceeded the scope of compensatory damages.[727] If remedying the defective performance is larger than the difference of the value between the defective product and a conforming product, the award of the cost of cure is considered to be unreasonable.[728] It is argued that by awarding damages based on excessive costs of cure the aggrieved promisee may obtain a financial windfall beyond his expected loss.[729] In contrast, reasonable expenditure on curing breach is generally recoverable. SGA 1979 refers a defective performance to "a breach of warranty" and repeats the rule of compensatory damages in the case of breach of warranty. As is included in section 53, the buyer's expected loss is "prima facie the difference between the value of the goods at the time of delivery to the buyer and the value they would have had if they had fulfilled the warranty."[730] Therefore, in the cases of defective performance, recovery of cost of cure in English law is subject to the rule of compensatory damages.

2.3.1.4. Available Market Does not Exist

Another question arises in the situation where there is no available market for measuring the buyer's expected loss. When deciding the amount of damages, common law accepts several indicators to determine the buyer's loss. One important indicator is the loss of profit that the buyer may generate out of the products that he receives from the original sales contract. For instance, in the case where there is no available market price but the buyer has re-sold the goods, the re-sale price may be treated as "the evidence but not conclusive evidence" for the buyer's loss.[731] This story could be similarly applied to the

727 In the *Ruxley* case, Lord Jauncey stated:

> *"Damages are designed to compensate for an established loss and not to provide a gratuitous benefit to the aggrieved party, from which it follows that the reasonableness of an award of damages is to be linked directly to the loss sustained. If it is unreasonable in a particular case to award the cost of re-instatement it must be because the loss sustained does not extend to the need to re-instate."*

728 Rowan 2012, p. 112.

729 There are more explanations have been given for holding reasonableness as the requirement for recovering cost of cure. For instance, according to the explanation of "undue hardship", awarding excessive costs of curing the breach that are disproportionate to the benefit to be obtained from cure would create undue hardship to the promisor. Webb 2006, p. 63, 64.

730 SGA 1979, S.53.

731 Whether or not the sub-sale price conclusive evidence for assessing the loss of the profit of the buyer depends on several factors, such as the time when the contract of sub-sale is made. In the case of *France v Gaudet*, the plaintiff bought 100 cases of champagne and entered another sale for reselling that champagne to a third party. Afterwards, the seller refuse to deliver the champagne as agreed and it was impossible to find similar champagne of that quality. The court supported the plaintiff and entitled him to the damages equivalent to the difference between the price in the original contract (14s per dozen) and the sub-sale price. However, in the *Arpad*, the buyer bought a cargo of Romanian wheat in August 1930 and made a sub-sale contract directly after that. The actual delivery of the wheat took place in January 1931 and in between the period of August 1930 and January 1931 the price of similar wheat decreased a lot. The court held that the resale price could not be considered as satisfactory evidence of the buyer's expected loss because the resale price "made at a date far removed from the date of the breach of contract have to be neglected". *See France v Gaudet* [1871] L.R. 6 Q.B. 199; *see also* The Arpad [1934] P189 at 212, per Greer LJ.

hire-out case in which the profits that a buyer expects from the hiring period could be taken as the evidence for calculating damages as well. Another indicator of the buyer's loss is derived from the case where there is no available market but the buyer could purchase or has purchased the nearest available equivalent to the contract goods or the buyer could arrange other measures to meet the seller's breach.[732] In those cases, the buyer's cost in finding alternative measures is taken into account by the courts in assessing the value of the goods at the time they should be delivered. This rule can be applied either when the buyer bought the goods for sub-sale or for self-use.[733] For instance, in the case *Hinde v Liddell*, the aggrieved buyer immediately bought the nearest equivalence at a higher cost after the seller failed to deliver 2,000 shirts as promised. The court supported the plaintiff's claim for recovering the increased costs in obtaining substitutes since the buyer's extra investments in substitutes are reasonable.[734]

2.3.2. Restrictions to Damages

As is indicated, S 51(2) of the SGA 1979 provides that the buyer's recoverable losses are limited to the amounts that, directly and naturally resulted, in the ordinary course of events, from the seller's breach. The concepts of "directly and naturally resulted" as well as "in the ordinary course" are closely related to the common law principles for limiting the buyer's damages, including the buyer's duty to mitigate his loss (Mitigation Rule),[735] the losses contributed by the buyer (Contributory Loss Rule)[736] and the remoteness of the losses (Hadley Rule).[737]

732 For instance, the buyer may order the manufacture of the substitute goods. *See Sealace Shipping Co. Ltd v. Oceanvoice Ltd*, The Alecos M [1991] 1 Lloyd's Rep. 120.

733 But to note, if the buyer bought the goods for sub-sale at a profit, it is very likely that this part of profit would be offset against the cost of obtaining the substitute goods when the court is assessing the buyer's damages if the subsequence sale rose out of the breach. This has been confirmed in the case of *Erie County Natural Gas and Fuel Co Ltd v Samuel S. Carroll* [1911] A.C. 105. The court held that:

> *"The prima facie inference to be drawn from a document printed in the record is that $75,000 was the amount of it[cost of procuring substitute gas supply]...The Plaintiffs...have only sued for the damages caused to them by the temporary deprivation of the gas. They have got the substituted article, identical in description and quality, have used it, and have failed to shew that it has not in the result been obtained by them free of cost. They are therefore, according to the principles established by the authorities already cited, only entitled to nominal damages."*

734 *Hinde v. Liddell* (1975) L.R. 10 Q.B. 265.

735 The rule of mitigation is interpreted in two basic messages. First, the injured buyer bears the responsibility to take reasonable steps to minimize his loss, otherwise he is not entitled to the damages caused by his failure to mitigate. (*Payzu Ltd v Saunders* [1919] 2 K.B.581, C.A.) Second, the injured buyer's mitigating behaviour should be reasonable and he is not entitled to the amount of damages that are beyond the reasonable extent. It also means that the buyer's benefit or cost exceeding the reasonable extent should be subtracted from the recoverable scope. (*British Westinghouse Electric & Manufacturing Co Ltd v Underground Electric Rlys Co Ltd* [1912] A.C. 673).

736 If the losses suffered by the non-breaching party are partially caused by his own behaviour, the amount of damages paid by the breacher will be reduced. The extent of reduction depends on the extent the non-breaching party contributes to his loss. See also chapter 6, section 2.3.3.

737 The rule of Hadley was established in the case *Hadley v Baxendale* [1854] 9 EX 341 and authoritatively stated in the cases *Koufos v Czarnikow Ltd* (The Heron II) [1969] 1 A.C. 350. It was established that the

2.3.2.1. Damage Limitation Rules

These three principles share some similarities in their economic rationales. Basically, the contract parties are motivated to diminish economic waste[738] and thus reduce the social costs of transactions through a series of cooperative behaviour. On the one hand, the buyer is motivated to disclose sufficient information concerning his expected loss at the stage of contract formation, to take due care in supporting the performance by the seller at the stage of performance and to take reasonable steps to minimize his loss after the breach takes place.[739] On the other hand, the limitation rule helps the seller to predict his liability from non-performance and to make a cost-benefit analysis of his own behaviour. The seller is exempted from the losses which he could not foresee and losses caused by the buyer's activities (faults or unreasonable mitigating behaviour) or by the buyer's failure to take reasonable mitigation. Moreover, under the premise of commercial sales, the standard of the reasonable business person has been frequently cited even though the application of the limitation rules varies from case-to-case. For instance, in the process of "remoteness" test, the remoteness of the loss depends on whether or not this type of loss is derived from the circumstances that the seller has or would reasonably have adequate knowledge.[740] The English courts may deny the buyer's claim for the losses that are considered too remote according to a reasonable business man. Or in the mitigation case, the injured buyer's mitigation obligation is only extended to the scope that a reasonable business person would accept. In the case of *James Finlay & Co Ltd v NV Kwik Hoo Tong Handel Maatschappij*,[741] the buyer (Finlay & Co. is a company carrying on business as merchants in India and elsewhere with a house in London) had made an agreement with Indian sub-purchasers after he signed the first contract, but the seller (merchants in Java dealing in the sale and shipment of sugar) made a delayed delivery and the sub-purchaser refused to accept the belated delivery. The buyer accordingly declined to bring any action against the sub-purchasers to compel them to take goods which were not in accordance with the contract. The court supported the buyer and held that the buyer is not bound to the obligation to mitigate because doing so "in the ordinary course of business" would in fact ruin their credit in India.

The combination of those restriction rules produce an effect of testing whether or not the buyer is entitled to a certain amount of damages in any special circumstance, no

loss is compensable if the plaintiff has informed the defendant at the time of contract formation of the circumstances in which this loss would be incurred. Sometimes, the courts may also use other language to describe the "Hadley Rules", such as the "foreseeability rule" or "contemplated as a not unlikely result". Mackay 2005, p. 218; *see* also Furmston 2000, p. 171.

738 Rowan 2012, p. 146.

739 See Rowan 2012, p. 146 ([T]he injured promisee should be required to be pro-active in preventing his losses from accumulating, thereby reducing the overall burden to society of legally compensatable losses.).

740 Heron II (1969). Furmston 2000, p. 171.

741 [1929] 1 K.B 400, C.A. It is held that:

> *[A] person is not obliged to minimize damages on behalf of another who has broken his contract, if by doing so he would, as I think might have happened here, have injured his commercial reputation by getting a bad name in the trade.*

matter whether there is an available market price or not, whether the buyer has arranged substitutes or other loss-reducing measures or not. But what has been discussed frequently concerns the case involving the buyer's specific purpose of buying the goods.[742]

2.3.2.2. Sub-sales Case

Basically, the buyer's loss of profit from the sub-contract is unrecoverable as long as it is remote.[743] Apply this rule to the sub-sale case. If there is an available market price, the basic rule is that sub-sale price should be disregarded in assessing the buyer's damages. But there are also some exceptions where the sub-sales price is referred to in determining the buyer's damages. One type concerns the cases involving specific goods for sub-sale where the parties have stipulated terms in the original sales contract for re-sale by the buyer.[744] Another type is where the goods ought to be delivered to the sub-purchaser on the same day when they are to be delivered to the original buyer and the sub-sale is within the seller's contemplation. In these situations, the sub-sale price will become the clue for the buyer's loss only if the original seller could expect that the buyer would be unable to fulfil the contract of sub-sale if he could not fulfil the first contract.[745]

2.3.2.3. Purchase for Self-use

When the goods are purchased for self-use by the buyer, the *prima facie* rule is still the rule of market price. However, in legal practice, the court might take a different form of damage calculation. One possibility is that the buyer is required to take mitigating steps, for instance to buy a substitute when the seller fails to deliver the goods and there is an available market for finding a substitute, or simply to have the goods modified or repaired and recover the costs of modification when the goods that he received are defective.[746]

The complicated case, however, is where the product to be delivered is a profit-earning property and the question concerns the recoverability of the buyer's loss of profit from

[742] A buyer may expect to use the specific goods for operating business, such as for manufacturing in his factory; or the buyer may intend to re-sell the products in retail business.

[743] It is assumed that the parties will not naturally contemplate that the goods bought by the buyer are for sub-sale. *See* Mackay 2005, p. 217.

[744] In the arbitration between Re R & H Hall and W H Pim (Junior) & Co Ltd, the buyer agreed to buy a specific cargo of corn from the seller for re-sale. The seller failed to deliver and the market price of this kind of corn fell. The House of Lords decided that the difference between the re-sale price and the contract price should be granted as the buyer's damages even through there was an available market price for the corn. The reason is given that the parties had already estimated the buyer's forthcoming loss if the seller failed to deliver the cargo of corn. [1928] All ER Rep 763.

[745] Another important case is *Wertheim v Chicoutimi* (1911), in which the seller delayed to deliver the product. In this case, the court referred to the higher price (65£ a ton) that the buyer re-sold in the market after he received a delayed delivery. The price of the product when they ought to have been delivered was 70£ and the market price at the time when they were actually delivered was 42.6£. The court refused to award the difference between 70£ and 42.6 £ but decided to refer to the higher price of 65£ a ton because the court considered that the difference between 70£ and 65£ was the actual loss that the buyer suffered. *See Wertheim v Chicoutimi* [1911] AC 301.

[746] *See* Adams & Macqueen 2010, p. 545–546.

using this product.[747] The court's attitude towards the buyer's trade profit varies in special situations. In the case of *Victoria Laundry (Windsor) Ltd v Newman Industries Ltd*,[748] the seller was supposed to deliver a boiler on 5 June 1946 but actually he delivered it on 8 November. The buyer (a launderer) claimed compensation for his loss of trade profit between this period for the reason that the boiler was used to expand his business. In this case, the court supported the buyer's claim for the loss of profit that he would have earned had he received the boiler on time but declined the buyer's claim for profit from a lucrative trading opportunity. As is explained, recovery for trading profits is possible only if the parties have manifestly intended to secure this[749], on the ground of the "Hadley rule". Conversely, trading profits generated from any other novel or unusual use of the product which is beyond the contemplation of the seller cannot be secured. However, the situation is different in the cases which relate to defective performance because it is always difficult for the aggrieved buyer to prove his loss of trading profit. For example, in the case of *Cullinane v British 'Rema' Manufacturing Co Ltd*,[750] the buyer rejected the goods because of the defects. The court only awarded the buyer the return of money payment plus his wasted expenditure for the reason that the buyer could not quantify his loss of profit in an evidentiary way.

2.4. *Agreed Remedy: Liquidated Damages and Penalty Clauses*

As is indicated, the remedy rules of English contract law are largely based on the compensatory goal. Accordingly, in terms of party-negotiated damages, the principle is that only liquidated clauses are enforceable, while penalty clauses are not.[751] According to the English court, a liquidated damage clause refers to a damage clause based on a genuine estimate of the possible loss resulting from the breach at the time when the contract is concluded. In contrast, penalty clauses are merely designed to put pressure on the promisor to perform the contract rather than to compensate the creditor and they are not based on the probable loss of the injured creditor.[752] Once a damage clause is recognized as a penalty clause, the English courts will disregard it and just follow the regular course of damages assessment. Nevertheless, English law only regulates against penalty clauses which put forth excessively high damages. The enforceability of a damage clause will not be affected if the sum set by it has been proved to be lower than the expected loss.[753]

In order to judge whether a sum payable for breach amounts to a penalty or not, the English court will consider the meaning behind this amount which depends on several

747 *See* Brown 2001, p. 707.

748 [1949] 2 K.B. 528.

749 Similar cases are Cory v Thames Ironworks and shipbuilding Co Ltd [1868] LR 3 Q.B. 181; Steam Herring Fleet Ltd v VS Richards & Co Ltd [1901] 17 T.L.R. 731.

750 [1954] 1 Q.B. 292.

751 *See* Rowan 2012, p.173; *See* also Furmston 2000, p.175–176.

752 Rowan 2012, p. 184–85.

753 If the sum of compensation is lower than the expected loss of a plaintiff, the term in fact is regarded as liability limiting clause and it will only be regulated by the rule of unfair terms.

factors rather than any expression by the parties.[754] So the court may decide a term to be punitive even though this term is stipulated under the name of "liquidated damages", as long as it is recognized to be pressurising and unreasonable.[755] To be noted, the amount of damages stipulated by a contract clause is one, but not the decisive factor for the courts to determine whether this clause amounts to a penalty or not. A court might judge that an exaggerated and excessive amount of damages is punitive, provided it is manifestly and obviously disproportionate to the expected loss of the aggrieved party at the time of contract formation.[756] For instance, a contract term stipulating £1 million for the failure to deliver goods worth £100 is likely to be treated as a penalty in the absence of evidence to the contrary. In addition, the court might presume a clause to be punitive and invalid if

754 Lord Dunedin, when giving a speech in the case of Dunlop Pneumatic Tyre Co. Ltd. v. New Garage & Motor Co., stated several guidance notes for distinguishing penalty clauses and liquidated clauses. *See* [1915] A.C. 79, at. 86:

> "*... I shall content myself with stating succinctly the various propositions which I think are deducible from the decisions which rank as authoritative: –*
> *Though the parties to a contract who use the words 'penalty' or 'liquidated damages' may prima facie be supposed to mean what they say, yet the expression used is not conclusive. The Court must find out whether the payment stipulated is in truth a penalty or liquidated damages. This doctrine may be said to be found passim in nearly every case.*
> *The essence of a penalty is a payment of money stipulated as in terrorem of the offending party; the essence of liquidated damages is a genuine covenanted pre-estimate of damage.*
> *The question whether a sum stipulated is penalty or liquidated damages is a question of construction to be decided upon the terms and inherent circumstances of each particular contract, judged of as at the time of the making of the contract, not as at the time of the breach.*
> *To assist this task of construction various tests have been suggested, which if applicable to the case under consideration may prove helpful, or even conclusive. Such are:*
> - *It will be held to be penalty if the sum stipulated for is extravagant and unconscionable in amount in comparison with the greatest loss that could conceivably be proved to have followed from the breach.*
> - *It will be held to be a penalty if the breach consists only in not paying a sum of money, and the sum stipulated is a sum greater than the sum which ought to have been paid ...*
> - *There is a presumption (but no more) that it is penalty when 'a single lump sum is made payable by way of compensation, on the occurrence of one or more or all of several events, some of which may occasion serious and others but trifling damage'.*
>
> *On the other hand:*
> - *It is no obstacle to the sum stipulated being a genuine pre-estimate of damage, that the consequences of the breach are such as to make precise pre-estimation almost an impossibility. On the contrary, that is just the situation when it is probable that pre-estimated damage was the true bargain between the parties.*"

755 In practice, contracting parties sometimes may attempt to shield a term which is actually intended to deter breach from the scrutiny of the court by using the terms of "liquidated damages". For instance, in the case of Duffen v Fra Bo Spa, the parties negotiated damages of £ 100,000 as the liquidated damages. Moreover, the contract itself provides a clause that "by way of liquidated damages, which sum is agreed by the parties to be a reasonable pre-estimate of the loss and damage which the agent shall suffer on termination of this agreement". In the end, the court decided the sum of stipulated damages is punitive because there is no evidence showing that the breach of this contract would give rise to such a high amount of loss. Duffen v FRA Bo Spa (No 2) [2000] 1 L. R. 180. (This is not a sales contract case, but an agent contract).

756 For instance, see the case of Dunlop Pneumatic Tyre Co. Ltd v New Garage & Motor Co. [1915] A.C. 79.

it provides a single lump sum payable for a number of events in relation to different degrees of breach. One example is a damage stipulation for non-delivery on the same level as for relatively minor breaches, such as a delay in providing the specification for the products. It is held that this type of damage stipulation is penal because it is general, indefinite and deviates from the reasonable estimation of potential loss.[757] However, a more lenient attitude towards party-designed damages presents in the modern English law as a result of commercial development. The significant evidence is shown as the court's acceptance of stipulated damages that are large but not oppressive.[758] A recent trend in commercial contracts indicates that the courts are more willing to respect the agreement by commercial parties. As is stated, the discrepancy between the agreed sum and common law damages are no more than a guide for judicial scrutiny.[759] Hence even if the stipulated amount is larger, a damage clause may still be enforceable, as long as the sum is not unreasonable based on the equal bargaining power of the parties and this sum is commercially justified.

Beyond liquidated damages, the parties-designed remedies in a broader sense also include clauses providing remedies in relation to such as specific performance,[760] cost of curing breach measures and disgorgement of interest. The practice of this kind of clause goes in the same direction as the concrete remedy which it has put forth. For example, the specific performance clause is treated as specific relief and has to go through the scrutiny of the court on the enforceability of specific performance. The result is that this

757 This opinion is stated in the early case of lease contract. For instance in the case of *Lord Elphinstone v. Monkland Iron and Coal Co.* [1886] 11 A. C. 332, 342, Lord Watson said:

> *"[W]hen a single lump sum is made payable by way of compensation on the occurrence of one or more or all of several events, some of which may occasion serious and others but trifling damage, the presumption is that the parties intended the sum to be penal, and subject to modification."*

The court confirmed this idea in the later *Willson v Love* [1896] 1 Q.B. 626.

> *"[I]t seems on the one hand to be generally admitted that where, among various stipulations covered by one sum, whether called a penalty or liquidated damages, is included a stipulation for payment of a smaller sum of money, that is a case of penalty and not liquidated damages; on the other hand it is stated that, where the damages caused by a breach of a contract are incapable of being ascertained, the sum made by the contract payable upon such a breach is to be regarded as liquidated damages. "*

Another example arose in the case of Ford Motor Co v Armstrong [1915] 31 TLR 267 (CA).

758 The important cases are *Philips Hong Kong Ltd v The AG of Hong Kong* [1993]61 BLR 41 (PC) (construction contract); *Murray v Leisureplay plc* [2005] EWCA Civ 963 (CA) (employment contract); *Tullett Prebon Group Ltd v El-Hajjali [2008] EWHC 1924* (QB) (employment contract); *M&J Polymers Ltd v Imerys Minerals Ltd* [2008] EWHC 344 (QB) (sales contract); *Azimut-Benetti Spa v Healey* [2011] 1 Lloyd's Rep 473 (QB) (sale of yacht).

759 *Murray v Leisureplay plc* [2005] EWCA Civ 963 (CA), 69–76.

760 A typical specific relief term may provide that the contracting parties agreed in the event of breach, one party could have the right to the specific enforcement of the contract or an injunction as long as specific enforcement is still possible. In the case of *Société des Industries Métallurgiques SA v Bronx Engineering Co*, the parties have written down a clause intended to give rise to specific enforcement if a breach takes place. Mr. Justice Boreham refused to continue the ex parte injunction. The court, on appeal held, that

> *(1)[A]n assumption would be made in B's favour that they would succeed in showing at the trial a breach of contract by S. Therefore the issue was whether a decree of specific performance of the contract would be granted at the trial; (2) on the evidence the machine was readily obtainable in the market upon placing an order and damages were a sufficient remedy and B was not entitled to a decree of specific performance.*

[1975] 1 Lloyd's Rep 465 (CA).

kind of specific relief clauses can only find limited space in real judicial decisions.[761] By the same story, courts are more likely to enforce the contract clauses, which have indicated the cost of curing breach as long as they are treated as the a genuine estimate of the promisee's possible loss.

3. Application of the Efficient Breach Model regarding Unexpected Contingencies

In law and economics theory, contracts that are based on voluntary agreement are welfare-maximizing and thus offer the economic basis for contract enforcement. Unlike the civil law tradition, English sales law treats specific performance only as an exceptional remedy and takes the compensation of expectation damages as its default remedy. In this sense, the seller always has incentives to breach as long as he can earn more after breaking the contract and compensating the buyer.

However, this hypothesis needs to be supported by more analysis in specific efficient breach models. The first model, as is indicated in chapter 5 concerns the scenario where performing the original contract leads to economic waste because of its increasing costs or its decreasing value. This type of scenario is closely related to the matter about unexpected contingencies arising after the formation of the contract and before the conclusion of the performance.

In English sales law, the terminology concerning unexpected contingencies refers to frustration and hardship. In legal doctrine, rules in relation to these two concepts are essentially a matter of risk allocation. In the early time, common law only accepted the frustration principle by forming a bundle of judicial decisions. Following commercial developments, English law also assimilated the hardship principle into the common law rule. This section will provide the attitude of English sales law towards the efficient breach model in relation to unexpected contingencies. Some basic issues will be addressed in this section regarding how English law draws the boundary of non-performance and whether such a boundary is in accordance with the boundary of the efficient breach zone or not as well as the corresponding rules on behaviour falling into the efficient breach zone. The goal is to test whether or not the English rules in relation to unexpected contingencies have provided a seller with sufficient incentives to prevent wasteful performance as well as to take optimal precautions against inefficient breach.

3.1. English Law Doctrines in Relation to the Efficient Breach Zone

It is assumed that a contract may fall into the efficient breach zone if performance of the contract will decrease the welfare created by the contract. Suppose that the cost of performance has increased or the benefit of performing has decreased, leading to an imbalance between the cost and benefit of performance. This is the typical threshold for efficient breach. This section provides the pre-conditions for the application of the rule of frustration and hardship.

761 Rowan 2012, p. 212.

3.1.1. Frustration

The English concept of frustration describes some exceptional situations where the contract is rendered "radically different" from what has been contemplated by the parties.[762] Lord Radcliffe made the classical statement about this term as:

> *"Frustration occurs whenever the law recognises that without default of either party a contractual obligation has become incapable of being performed because the circumstances in which performance is called for would render it a thing radically different from that which was undertaken by the contract. Non haec in foedera veni. It was not this that I promised to do... There must be as well such a change in the significance of the obligation that the thing undertaken would, if performed, be a different thing from that contracted for."*[763]

The operation of this rule normally involves events such as those making the contracts "physically or legally impossible. In practice, the law governing frustration of the contract consists of SGA rules, common law rules and the rules in the Law Reform Act (Frustrated Contracts) 1943.[764] To summarize, a contract is frustrated if the following events have taken place:

3.1.1.1. The goods have perished

Perishing of the goods is one typical event giving rise to frustration of the contract. This rule can be traced back to the early Taylor principle established in the case of *Taylor v Caldwell*.[765] As is stated in the judgment of Blackburn J.:[766]

> *"The principle seems to us to be that in contracts in which the performance depends upon the continued existence of a given person or thing, a condition is implied that the perishing of the person or thing shall excuse the performance."*

Later the Taylor principle was also incorporated in to the SGA. Section 7 of the SGA 1979 provides:

762 Beale et al 2010, p. 1106.

763 *Davis Contractors Ltd v Fareham U.D.C.* [1956] AC 696, 728–729.

764 An Act to amend the law relating to the frustration of contracts was enacted 5 August 1943. The full text can be found in: www.legislation.gov.uk/ukpga/1943/40/pdfs/ukpga_19430040_en.pdf.

765 This is a lease case. Caldwell (defendant) agreed to rent his music hall to Taylor (plaintiff) for £700 a day for holding four concerts in June, July and August of 1861. But the music hall was burned to the ground by a fire on 11 June 1861, just one week before the first concert. The plaintiffs sued for damages for the Caldwell's failure to provide the music hall. Both of the parties had not included any clause allocating the risk in the contract. The court decided that the both of the parties are discharged from the contract because the Music Hall had ceased to exist, without default of either party. The plaintiffs were excused from taking the gardens and paying the money and the defendants were excused from performing their promise to give the use of the Hall and Gardens and other things. *See Taylor v Caldwell* [1863] EWHC J1 (QB), 122 ER 309, 3 B & S 826.

766 Id.

> *"Where there is an agreement to sell specific goods and subsequently the goods, without any fault on the part of the seller or buyer, perish before the risk passes to the buyer the agreement is voided"*

In the usual case, the seller bears all the risk and should be liable if the goods perish before the risk is passed. This is the *prima facie* rule on contract risk allocation.[767] However, a contract is frustrated if it falls into the scope of S7. To be more detailed, Section 7 provides the following information as the pre-condition for its application.

1) Perishing of Specific goods. The first pre-requisite that section 7 would apply is that the goods perished are specific goods. In contrast, if the perished goods are uncertain or generic, the seller will be required to find another from the seller's existing stock of goods or identical goods in the market.
2) The buyer doesn't bear the risk. If the buyer, according to the contract or risk sharing rule (section 18 or section 20)[768] bears the risk of the contract, then he still has to pay the price whatever happens to the goods.

767 Section 20 provides the prima facie rule about the risk. As is stated:
20.-(1) Unless otherwise agreed, the goods remain at the seller's risk until the property in them is transferred to the buyer, but when the property in them is transferred to the buyer the goods are at the buyer's risk whether delivery has been made or not.
(2) But where delivery has been delayed through the fault of either buyer or seller the goods are at the risk of the party at fault as regards any loss which might not have occurred but for such fault.
(3) Nothing in this section affects the duties or liabilities of either seller or buyer as a bailee or custodier of the goods of the other party.
So in the normal case, if the goods perished and it is at the seller's risk, the seller still has to find substitute goods and he cannot ask for payment until he delivers the goods. A failure to deliver the goods as required may invoke the seller's liability. See Bridge 2009, p. 181.

768 Section18 of SGA 1979:
Unless a different intention appears, the following are rules for ascertaining the intention of the parties as to the time at which the property in the goods is to pass to the buyer. (Rule for Ascertaining Intention)
Rule 1.-Where there is an unconditional contract for the sale of specific goods in a deliverable state the property in the goods passes to the buyer when the contract is made, and it is immaterial whether the time of payment or the time of delivery, or both, be postponed.
Rule 2.-Where there is a contract for the sale of specific goods and the seller is bound to do something to the goods for the purpose of putting them into a deliverable state, the property does not pass until the thing is done and the buyer has noticed that it has been done.
Rule 3.-Where there is a contract for the sale of specific goods in a deliverable state but the seller is bound to weigh, measure, test, or do some other act or thing with reference to the goods for the purpose of ascertaining the price, the property does not pass until the act or thing is done and the buyer has notice that it has been done.
Rule 4.-When goods are delivered to the buyer on approval or on sale or return or other similar terms the property in the goods passes to the buyer:
1) *when he signifies his approval or acceptance to the seller or does any other act adopting the transaction;*
2) *If he does not signify his approval or acceptance to the seller but retains the goods without giving notice of rejection, then, if a time has been fixed for the return of the goods, on the expiration of that time, and, if no time has been fixed, on the expiration of a reasonable time.*

3) Neither the buyer nor the seller is at fault. Another pre-condition for triggering the Frustration rule is that none of the parties can be blamed for contributing to the existence of the supervening event. The court would refuse to apply the frustration rule if the alleged event is actually caused by the fault of either party.[769] Instead, the court may hold the party, through whose fault the frustrating event has occurred, liable.[770] Preclusion of self-induced frustration has been confirmed by the English court as an important rule deriving from the rationale that nobody could benefit from his own fault.[771] The rule of "Self-induced Frustration" is followed by the question of how to understand the meaning of fault. By section 61, fault is defined as "wrongful act or default"[772], without referring to negligent conduct. In terms of whether negligent conduct can amount to self-induced frustration or not, common law tried to provide an answer. As is stated, "the fact that a party in breach of the contract or the tortuous duty of care would preclude the operation of the frustration rule".[773] It is further proposed that defining self-induced frustration depends on whether or not the frustrating event was foreseeable and within the reasonable control of the party seeking to rely on the doctrine.[774] In this sense, any event caused by tortuous negligence should, by its very nature be foreseeable and within the reasonable control of the party concerned.

Section 7 of the SGA only deals with the problem when it comes to the perishing of specific goods. But common law has encouraged the frustration rule by approving this

> *Rule 5.-(1) Where there is a contract for the sale of unascertained or future goods by description, and goods of that description and in a deliverable state are unconditionally appropriated to the contract, either by the seller with the assent of the buyer or by the buyer with the assent of the seller, the property in the goods then passes to the buyer; and the assent may be express or implied, and may be given either before or after the appropriation is made.*
> *(2) Where, in pursuance of the contract, the seller delivers the goods to the buyer or to a carrier or other bailee or custodier (whether named by the buyer or not) for the purpose of transmission to the buyer, and does not reserve the right of disposal, he is to be taken to have unconditionally appropriated the goods to the contract.*

769 Phang 1992, p. 296.

770 If it is the seller whose behaviour has caused the perishing of the goods, he should be liable for damages for non-delivery. In contrast, the faulty buyer is required to pay the price as agreed and to bear the loss of the goods. Bridge 2009, p. 180.

771 The rule that no one can benefit from his own fault has been confirmed in many cases. For instance in the case of *Alghussein Establishment v Eton College* (a Lease contract), the appealing court held that:

> *"[T]he well-known rule of construction, that there was a presumption that a party to a contract could not be permitted to take advantage of his own wrong as against the other party, applied, in the absence of an express provision to contradict the presumption, as much to a party who sought to obtain a benefit under a continuing contract on account of his breach, as it did to a party who relied on his breach to avoid a contract and thereby escape his obligations."*

See [1988] 1 W.L.R. 587. Similar cases are *Francis Milton Gibson v J T Allen Agency* [1965] W.Y. 51 407 P.2d 708 and *Cheall v. Association of Professional Executive Clerical and Computer Staff* [1983] 2 A.C. 180.

772 Section 61(1) SGA1979.

773 *J Lauritzen AS v Wijsmuller BV (The Super Servant Two)* [1990] 1 Lloyd's Rep. 1.

774 Phang 1992, p. 298.

rule in more cases, for instance in the case where it is illegal for the seller to proceed with the contract.

3.1.1.2. Illegality of the Contracts

Another case for the operation of the frustration principle concerns obstacles to performance which are caused by legislative or administrative interference. The English court started to apply the Frustration principle in a supervening illegality case at the end of the 18th century.[775] It was held that the contract is frustrated if the performance was legal when the contract was formed but has been rendered illegal because of a subsequent change of law.[776] In the early time, the English court recognized that only a change of English law would invoke the application of the frustration principle.[777] But this rule became more lenient afterwards. Since the late 19th century, the application of this doctrine was also extended to cases involving foreign law or government behaviour.[778] An example is the case where the government has imposed restrictions on the export or import of goods. For instance, in the case of *McMaster & Co Ltd v Mc Euen & Co Ltd*,[779] an English company bought goods from a foreign company and an export licence was necessary for accomplishing the contract, which had been realized by both of the parties. The contract was held frustrated later on the grounds that the parties failed to obtain the export license.

3.1.1.3. Events covered by Force Majeure Clauses

In commercial practice, it is quite common for business parties to include *force majeure* clauses so as to protect the parties from unexpected contingencies arising after the contract formation. Those clauses, typically put forth a list of events, such as strikes, war, bad weather, government activities and the like, upon which the parties are discharged. Take the *force majeure* clause in the GAFTA as an example.[780] Article 19 provides the

775 The early cases of supervening illegality typically concerned shipping contracts with an exporting or importing character. For instance, in Hadley v Clarke, the English government laid an embargo on the defendant and deterred the carriage. The contract was held frustrated since the performance of the contract was rendered illegal. See Hadley v Clarke [1799] 101 E.R. 1377.

776 Wladis 1987, p. 1599.

777 For instance, in the case of Splidt v Heath, it was a contract for sales of hemp to be shipped to Russia. The Russian government seized the hemp to be delivered to the buyer and the buyer brought out a lawsuit. In this case, the seller was held liable because the contract had not been frustrated. [1809] 170 E.R.1080.

778 The early case where the frustration principle was adopted to the cases in relation to government intervention refers to the case of Baily v. De Crespigny [1869] 4 L.R. 180 (Q.B.). Besides, the case of Ford v Cotesworth [1870] 5 L.R. 544 (Q.B.) opened the gate for the adoption of the frustration principle with regards to foreign law cases.

779 [1921] S.C. (HL) 24. Another similar case is AV Pound & Co Ltd v M W Hardy & Co Inc [1956] AC 588.

780 Form 100 of the Grain and Feed Trade Association is a standard form contract for the shipment of feeding studs in bulk provided by the Grain and Feed Trade Association which is based in London. Article 19 provides the rule under *force majeure* events:

standard *force majeure* clause, in which a seller is excused from liability for a delay in shipping the goods as long as he has taken due steps to inform the buyer.[781] Sometimes, the *force majeure* clauses may also indicate different solutions other than bringing the contract to an end. For instance, the seller might be given more time for delivery or might be provided with alternative means of delivery in the case of certain interrupting events.[782]

When interpreting the *force majeure* clauses, the courts normally take a strict and narrow attitude. Even if the events included in the *force majeure* clauses occur, the seller might still be held liable if he would have been able to perform the contract, for example, by shipping earlier or by finding substitutes in the market.[783]

3.1.1.4. Other Impossibilities

The fundamental rationale for the English frustration rule is that the "condition or state of facts basic to the contract" has ceased or failed to occur.[784] It does not matter whether it is a physical impossibility or a legal impossibility, the frustration principle only applies when the impossibility has destroyed the basis that the contract relies on. Based on the early Taylor principle, English Common law developed the frustration rule by extending it to the cases where the performance is still possible but the "underlying purpose of the contract is frustrated" provided that the unexpected event occurs before the risk and property has passed to the buyer.[785] This is established as what is called the Krell

Sellers shall not be responsible for delay in shipment of the goods or any part thereof occasioned by any Act of God, strike, lockout, riot or civil commotion, combination of workmen, breakdown of machinery, fire, or any cause comprehended in the term "force majeure". If delay in shipment is likely to occur for any of the above reasons, the Shipper shall serve a notice on Buyers within 7 consecutive days of the occurrence, or not less than 21 consecutive days before the commencement of the contract period, whichever is the later. The notice shall state the reason(s) for the anticipated delay.
If after serving such notice an extension to the shipping period is required, then the Shipper shall serve a further notice not later than 2 business days after the last day of the contract period of shipment stating the port or ports of loading from which the goods were intended to be shipped, and shipments effected after the contract period shall be limited to the port or ports so nominated.
If shipment be delayed for more than 30 consecutive days, Buyers shall have the option of cancelling the delayed portion of the contract, such option to be exercised by Buyers serving notice to be received by Sellers not later than the first business day after the additional 30 consecutive days. If Buyers do not exercise this option, such delayed portion shall be automatically extended for a further period of 30 consecutive days. If shipment under this clause be prevented during the further 30 consecutive days extension, the contract shall be considered void. Buyers shall have no claim against Sellers for delay or non-shipment under this clause, provided that Sellers shall have supplied to Buyers, if required, satisfactory evidence justifying the delay or non-fulfilment.

781 GAFTA 100, however, has not indicated the consequences of the failure to notify. In legal practice, any failure to notify the other party of the *force majeure* event is treated as breach and the party who failed to make the notification is held liable for compensating the other party's loss. See Tradax Export SA v Andre & Cie SA [1976] 1 Lloyd's Rep. 416; See also Bridge 2009, p. 190.

782 Furmston 2000, p. 98–9.

783 Adams & Macqueen 2010, p. 352–3.

784 Wladis 1987, p. 1608.

785 Živković, 2013.

Principle.[786] In the contract of sales of goods, the court would sometimes extend the application of the frustration principle to the uncertain goods, provided there is a loss or destruction of an irreplaceable object which is the necessary and only source for accomplishing the performance.[787] A typical example is illustrated in relation to the unforeseen bad harvest of farming products. In the case of *Howell v. Coupland*,[788] the seller agreed to sell 200 tons of potatoes that would be grown on his specified land. However, the land only produced 80 tons of potatoes because of disease. In the end, the defendant is held excused since the subject of the contract could not come into existence so that the sales contract was frustrated. Another example which has been referred to frequently in the literature concerns the outbreak of wars. In the case of *Re Badische Co Ltd*,[789] the court held that the contract was frustrated due to the outbreak of war. As was given by the court, both of the parties had realized that the goods could only be obtained from Germany although the goods were uncertain at the time of the contract formation. Therefore, the war blocked the availability of obtaining this source and frustrated the contract.

As is shown, the key element for the English law to apply the frustration principle is that the foundation of the contract has been altered by the supervening event and this is beyond the reasonable foresight and control of the both parties.[790] The operation of such a principle relies on the assumption that some elements are essential to the continued existence of a contract, such as the existence of a subject-matter and the legality of the contract. Therefore, changes of those fundamental elements will lead to a result that the contract be completely altered and performance is pointless.[791] In this sense, the common law rule of frustration of contract purpose should include a larger range of events than the civil law doctrine of force-majeure as long as these unexpected events would render the contract fundamentally different from the parties' expectation. However, the frustration principle is still cited rarely in judicial practice and it has to go through strict scrutiny by the court.

786 The Krell Principle was established in the famous case of Krell v Henry in relation to the postponement of Edward VII's coronation. In this case, the defendant rented a flat from the plaintiff at one side of the route of the processions. However, the coronation in the end was postponed for the reason that Edward suffered from appendicitis. The defendant thus refused to pay the rent as promised. The contract was held frustrated. In this case, Lord Justice Vaughan Williams stated "if the contract becomes impossible of performance by reason of the non-existence of the state of things assumed by both contracting parties as the foundation of the contract, there will be no breach of the contract...". This was later recognized as the Krell Principle. See Krell v Henry [1903] 2 K.B. at 749.

787 Wladis 1987, p. 1603. Adams & Macqueen 2010, p. 351.

788 *Howell v. Coupland* [1876] 1 Q.B.D. 258 (C.A.).

789 [1921] 2 Ch 331.

790 If the contract is performed, it would be significantly different from the contract intended for. Beale et al 2010, p. 1115.

791 Firoozmand 2007, p. 176.

3.1.2. Hardship

Beside the concept of frustration, English law also includes the concept of hardship, describing a situation where execution of the contract would be much more onerous owing to changed circumstances arising after the conclusion of the contract. Normally, the terminology of hardship would apply in two types of linguistic contexts.

The first case refers to the concept of hardship, and is still within the scope of the frustration principle, namely the case where unexpected events have arisen rendering the contract fundamentally different from what was envisaged by the parties when they entered into the contract. When deciding whether an event amounts to frustration of the contract or merely a hardship in performance, the court would ask: whether performing the contract is impossible (legally impossible or physically impossible) or physically possible but costly and whether the burden of performance is assumed by the parties. A contract would not be frustrated if it is just more onerous to perform the contract and the seller should assume the risk of the contingency. In *Tsakiroglou & Co Ltd v Noblee & Thorl GmbH*,[792] delivery of the Sudanese ground nuts had become very onerous because of the closure of the Suez Canal. In order to provide the goods as agreed, the seller had to ship them via the Cape of Good Hope to reach Europe and this route is much longer and more costly. The seller refused to perform the contract on the ground that the closure of the Suez Canal was so dramatic that the contract was frustrated. This claim was declined by the court for the reason that the risk of carriage should be assumed by the seller according to their contract. What happened is simply a fluctuation of the freight price and that did not alter the contract fundamentally. As is shown, in the test of "frustration", the object is the contract itself, but not the contract cost.

The second scenario is hardship; hardship is also cited in relation to the refusal of specific performance by the courts. For instance, in the case of a sale of a house or land, the court may grant specific performance on a quite regular basis but exceptionally withhold it when it causes difficulty.[793] In the early case of *Wedgwood v Adams*,[794] the court indicated this point by addressing the necessity of balancing the specific relief and monetary damages in a sales contract of land. In this case, Lord Langdale MR stated that specific performance should be generally granted in the sale of land unless it is highly unreasonable to do so. When explaining the meaning of "highly unreasonable", he stressed that the court should in the particular case balance the convenience of different remedies. In the later cases afterwards, although the court did not cite the concept of "hardship" directly, it was noticed that the fact that the cost of performance to the breaching party was wholly disproportionate to the benefit to the aggrieved party, would enable the court to decide that the specific relief order was unreasonable.[795] Moreover, if the specific performance order would make a third party suffer from hardship, the court

792 [1962] AC 93.

793 Beale et al 2010, p. 885–6.

794 [1843] 49 E.R. 958.

795 *Tito v Waddell* (No 2) [1977] CH 106.

may also decline it.[796] Nevertheless, the concept of hardship is still bound to a strict interpretation. As is indicated in the case of *Francis v Cowcliffe*,[797] the mere financial difficulty suffered by the default party would not invoke the rule of "hardship". The only exception is where performance of the contract would cause extreme financial misfortune or incapacitating illness to the promisor. To summarize, in both situations, performance of the contract is still possible, but the increased performance cost or the decreased value of the contract makes it extremely onerous to perform the contract.

3.2. *Rules in the Efficient Breach zone*

In English law, it is well-established that specific performance of the contract will be refused by the court in any case where performance of the contract is impossible or the result of performance would lead to great hardship. Meanwhile, any efforts insisting on specific performance by the buyer in the case of hardship would be deemed as the evidence for his violation of the mitigation rule. As a result, the buyer could not ask for compensation for the extra cost incurred by unreasonably insisting on performance. Moreover, in most cases, monetary damages rather than specific performance is established as the only remedy. The amount of damages, as is noted in section 2.2.1 is the value of the buyer's expectation. This is in accordance with the economic waste doctrine that specific performance should be prevented when the cost of performance is disproportionate to the welfare improvement.[798] But to be more specific, the fact that the contract has been frustrated would lead to a different effect.

In cases where the contract has been frustrated, the basic principle is that the parties are discharged from the contract. Section 7 of SGA 1979 states that the agreement is "voided" if perishing of the goods takes place. So the seller is excused from the duty to deliver and the buyer is not required to pay the price.[799] If the buyer has already paid the price, he would also be able to claim it back. The frustration in the common law rules takes the same consequence as this. The perishing of specific goods was considered to be the evidence for a "total failure of consideration".[800] In the famous *Fibrosa* case, the court confirmed this logic. In this case, the seller was supposed to manufacture some machinery and deliver it to the buyer but the contract was frustrated before the undertaking was finished. The seller was required to return all the payments to the buyer although he argued that he had incurred large expenses in performing the contract. The exception is

796 This is recognized in the case of Thames Guaranty Ltd v Campbell. In this case, a husband without informing his wife sold their matrimonial house. The court refused to grant specific performance for the reason that to implement the sale of the house will deprive the innocent wife of her home. [1985] Q.B. 210 (C.A.).

797 [1976] 33 P & CR 368 (CH).

798 De Geest 2012, p. 32.

799 Mckendrick 2010, p. 285.

800 See Fibrosa Spolka Akcyjna v Fairbairn Lawson Combe Barbour Ltd [1943] AC 32. Another case is Logan v Le Mesurier which happened even earlier. A raft of red pine timber which had been assumed to be sold to a buyer in Quebec was destroyed in a storm. The court allowed the buyer to claim his payment of money back after deciding the contract was frustrated. [1847] 6 Moo PC 116.

where the contract is partially frustrated. Since the buyer is still able to keep the benefit of the remaining part of the contract, he can only claim a refund of the payment to the extent that the contract has been frustrated.[801] This is also within the meaning of S.7. However, the S7 stops here and excludes the consequence of other frustrating events beyond the perishing of goods, such as wars, government interference and so on. The Frustrated Act, however, complements the SGA concerning those events.

4. Economic Analysis

An important feature in English Contract law is that the common law provides a dynamic system which is open for new problems and challenges. Beyond the sales law and the traditional hypothetical models of efficient breach, case law brings various challenges to this topic. The questions under all these cases bring us back again to the question that arises from the efficient breach model: should economic efficiency become a vital factor for the judgment of contract cases?

4.1. A Seller's Incentive to Perform

As is shown, in general the remedy rules in the English Sales Law cater for protection of the parties' expectation interest. With regard to its attitude towards breach, a central topic illustrated by the current remedy system is to deter breach and to compensate the aggrieved buyer's expectation loss. In exceptional cases, particularly when the breach is very serious or outrageous, punitive damages are even awarded by the courts.[802] The rationale, as is stated, is that English Law does not want efficient breach, but it wants efficient contracting and prefers no breach at all. Any breach is deemed as a waste of contracting. Therefore, as long as the contract has been concluded, the parties should be motivated to perform it. In order to motivate efficient contracting, English law provides a bundle of corresponding rules. For instance, it accepts liquidated damages which facilitate pre-estimation of damages by the parties. In addition, the market price rule and the foreseeability rules enable ex-ante information searching and assist contract parties to estimate each other's expected surplus. Additional evidence of respecting contract expectation is that the courts frequently adopt the test of "contract expectation" to decide whether or not a party is discharged when exercising the frustration rules.

The real effect derived from the contract remedy system, however, is that the remedy rules in the sales law are lenient to the seller. Firstly, the system of remedies seeks to compensate the aggrieved party and hence it only imposes a limited burden on a defaulting party. Obviously, specific performance is rarely granted. But the remedy of compensatory damages, as is pointed out, "only deters breach to the extent that an

[801] For instance, if the seller has to deliver 100 articles of goods and half of them have been destroyed by a frustrating event, then the contract is partially frustrated and the seller is exempted from the obligation to deliver the destroyed part. Meanwhile, the buyer still has to pay for the 50 articles. *See* Adams & Macqueen 2010, p. 55–6.

[802] Edelman 2001, p. 545.

alternative use of the contractual resources does not enable the promisor to make a profit which exceeds the compensable loss suffered by the premise."[803] In this sense, the seller still has a significant chance of escaping the contract when he thinks it worthwhile. Secondly, the operation of remedies rule is largely in accordance with the economic rationale for efficient breach. In order to make a rational decision, the seller must have a clear idea about the other party's expectation from the contract. What the buyer expected is the discrepancy between the contract price and his expected value (v-p)[804] and it is presented in different forms if the buyer has different purposes for buying. Apparently, judges in England have noticed this by exercising different methods of damage assessment (market price rule, substitute price rule and loss of profit rule) in reaction to whether the goods are bought for self-use, re-sale or other profit-earning activities. In this sense, the remedy rules have opened a window for efficient breach to take place. Thirdly, the binding ability of a contract is abated when it comes to expectation damages. The concern of risk-allocation has been taken into account as well in a way that the risk-averse seller is exempted from liability in the course of unexpected uncertainties. This is in accordance with the model of efficient breach in relation to unexpected contingency.

4.2. *A hypothetical Case: the Forward Issue*

Let us analyse a hypothetical case under the English Sales Law. Suppose that a supervening event happening at the warehouse of Y destroyed all the products that Y needs to deliver to X and it is impossible or extremely onerous for Y to make the performance.

The first scenario is that this is a risk beyond the control of Y, such as an earthquake. In this situation, if the frustration rule applies, then the non-performance is discharged and no liability for damages will be incurred. Since in the circumstances of frustration events, the seller does not assume the risk and he cannot prevent the occurrence of this event or its impact on performance.[805] The second scenario is that Y can still control the risk, for instance of an outbreak of fire, at a lower cost than X does. In this case, specific performance cannot be required but Y still has to pay damages. Assume that what caused the perishing of the goods is a fire taking place at Y's premises incurred by his deliberate or negligent behaviour. In this case, we can hardly assert that this is generally an efficient breach case.[806] Hence, it is assumed that one important determinant for whether Y's failure to perform is efficient or not is whether Y is required to take precaution against the risk or not. Apparently, if Y sets fire to his own property or Y is grossly negligent in letting the fire break out, his non-performance should be regarded as inefficient.

As is shown in this case, the real problem is how to deter inefficient breach in the form that the seller assumes the risk but is at fault in causing the hardship. In law and economics, it is assumed that fault (deliberate or negligent) is recognized in the case where the expected cost from the supervening event is larger than the expected cost of

803 Rowan 2012, p. 190.
804 Schwartz & Scott 2008, p. 1610.
805 The cost of preventing an earthquake is extremely high.
806 Eisenberg 2004, p. 55–62.

preventing it (possibility of risk × expectation loss < precaution cost).[807] In this sense, for example, failure to install a fire alarm in fire sensitive premises provides evidence of the seller's fault because the possibility of the outbreak of a fire and the potential loss is large. This draws us, to some extent, back to the legal rules about self-induced frustration. The English sales law would preclude the operation of the frustration principle in relation to self-induced frustration cases, which also include the situation where one party was negligent in causing the frustrating event. This is the primary rule. Hence, the breaching seller who failed to perform has to pay expectation damages to the buyer. Nevertheless, general hardship in any case will not excuse the seller from contract liability, because he is assumed to take the risk of the intervening event (the fire occurs at his premises) as well as that the goods are generic.[808] In this sense, even if the seller has taken sufficient precautions and is innocent with regard to the outbreak of the supervening events, what he has to pay is still the expectation damages of the buyer according to English law. As is indicated in this example, the remedy rules in the English sales law have not made a distinction between an innocent breach and a breach with fault. It also shows that the English remedy rules in fact provide weak incentives for the seller to perform the contract. Furthermore, what is still open for discussion in future research is the necessity of introducing punitive damages into contract law.

4.3. *Controversy over the Introduction of Punitive Damages*

Since the 20th century, there has been another trend, inaugurated by scholarship endeavour, supporting the introduction of punitive damages into contract law. A radical idea is to distinguish deliberate breaches and involuntary breaches and to award punitive damages in all the deliberate breach cases.[809] Hence, only those involuntary breaches (e.g. breaches in the case of hardship) are acceptable and all the deliberate breaches (e.g. self-induced hardship) should be punished through punitive damages that are much higher than any potential or actual losses suffered by the non-breaching party. However, a more moderate idea is that the deliberate nature of a breach should not be the only prerequisite for awarding punitive damages, but only a relevant consideration. With regard to the amount of damages, it is suggested that all the profits that a breacher has obtained should be disgorged to the non-breaching party. In this sense, the promisor will be prevented from committing those outrageous breaches since he has no profit through

807 The law and economics theory would provide some guidance for deciding whether the seller is at fault or negligent or not. For instance, we may apply the Hand formula to make the assessment.

808 As is indicated already, the basic rule for the remedy rule in relation to sales of generic goods is that the market price would provide the aggrieved buyers sufficient compensation. With this monetary value granted to the buyer, he can always go to the market and obtain the alternatives.

809 MC Bride 1995, p. 369; MC Bride 1995, p. 175. Deliberate breach, according to MCBride, refers to a situation, where:

> *[a]given defendant, willingly breaches a common law obligation when three things hold together:*
> *(I)He must have performed an action.*
> *(II)He must have been aware at that time that action could be described in a certain way.*
> *(III)An action described in that way is wrongful.*

breach. For instance, in *Experience Hendrix LLC v PPX Enterprises Inc*, Gibson LJ proposed a gain-based award of damages on account of the breacher's deliberate actions.[810]

Some English lawyers have addressed the question of when to allow punitive damages in contract law. They suggest that punitive damages should be awarded in the outrageous breach case, even if it has been very rarely used until now, for example only in insurance contracts (Whiten v Pilot Insurance Co).[811] They argued that the operation of the punitive damages should be expanded, especially in commercial society, in order to maintain proper business practice. But a difficulty does exist concerning how to draw the line between the breaches which should be punished and other types of breaches which should not. Two opinions are proposed: 1) As is suggested, deliberate action is one consideration for granting punitive damages in contracts. But it is still difficult to distinguish deliberate breaches which should incur punitive damages, and other deliberate breaches which do not qualify to be fined (Breach for higher profits). 2) Bad-faith breach should be punished. It is suggested that deliberate breaches should fall into two categories, including efficient breaches and opportunistic breaches. Punishment should only be directed at breaches which amount to "oppression, exploitation of the predicament of the other party, wilful lack of diligence and failure to cooperate."[812] However, traditional English lawyers still take a conservative attitude. It is suggested that English contract law historically operated without regard to blame. Therefore, if a breach of contract is deliberate or committed in bad faith, it might constitute a tort as well and the injurer should bear liabilities according to tort law.

5. Conclusion

In the classic economic theory, it is suggested that contract law should be structured in such a way that efficient breaches (i.e. those increasing social welfare) would be promoted and inefficient breaches would be deterred. This is known as the efficient breach theory. Nowadays, more and more suspicion and criticism have been raised against the so-called simple efficient breach model. However, it is proposed that the doctrine of efficient breach has its theoretical significance for shedding light on how to design and assess contract law. Moreover, this theory leads to a wider topic about how to shape the parties' incentives to make efficient contracts ex-ante and to behave optimally ex-post in the absence of self-motivation and complete contracts. Accordingly, contract remedy techniques, such as techniques to encourage accurate evaluation, to promote efficient precaution against breach, to avoid wasteful performance and to optimally allocate future risks, are desirable. Under the context of English sales law, this chapter tests whether or not a seller has been provided with sufficient motivation to act efficiently and to what extent adhering

810 "[N]o doubt deliberate breaches of contract occur frequently in the commercial world; yet something more is needed to make the circumstances exceptional enough to justify ordering an account of profits." [2003] EWCA Civ 323.

811 *Royal Bank of Canada v W Got Associates Electrical Ltd* [1999] 3SCR 408.

812 Rowan 2012, p. 181.

to the contract by the seller is required. Two basic issues are addressed. On the one hand, this chapter critically examines the rules about the buyer's remedy in the English sales law from the perspective of economic theory. As shown, the remedy system in the sales law is lenient to the seller since it seeks compensation for the aggrieved party and hence only imposes a limited burden on the defaulting seller. On the other hand, this chapter also applies the specific efficient breach model to English law in relation to an unexpected contingency. In general, the rules in English sales law are largely in line with the doctrine of efficient breach. However, the *prima facie* rule of compensatory remedies offers the sellers insufficient motivation to take optimal precaution as well as to avoid inefficient breach.

Chapter 8

APPLYING THE EFFICIENT BREACH DOCTRINE TO CHINESE COMMERCIAL SALES LAW

As China is becoming more active in the global economic market, the development of Chinese Law has also gained more and more attention from both policy makers and scholarship. Special emphasis has been placed on the rules in relation to business activities and market regulation. Against this background, this chapter will show how the Chinese sales law motivates a seller to perform contracts as well as to what extent the economic theory of efficient breach is embodied in Chinese law. At the beginning of this chapter, a general introduction to Chinese sales contract will be provided. Afterwards, section 2 will discuss the basic rules on the seller's breach as well as the buyer's remedy. Specific issues such as the Chinese concept of "continuing performance" as well as the rules concerning monetary damages and liquidated damages will be included in section 2. As will be shown, China has established the basic rules on expectation damages in the newly enacted Contract Law (1999) by some provisions similar to those in other civil law legislations and international documents. However, the supplementary rules adopted in judicial practice have modified this type of damages. Application of efficient breach in a specific model will be structured in section 3. In section 4 of this chapter, an economic analysis of remedy rules in Chinese Law will be developed. At the end of this chapter, section 5 will provide a conclusion to the question how Chinese law motivates a seller in a sales contract to perform and breach

1. Introduction to Chinese Sales Law

Although the law of sales contracts in China is mostly discussed in recent decades, the concept of contract has existed in Chinese civil society for a long time. The concepts of "Agreement" and "Contract" in China have their origins in the ancient term of "Qi Yue".[813] In the early dynasty of "West Zhou" (1046–771 BCE), "Qi Yue" was used to make

[813] In Chinese history, there are many equivalent concepts to the term of "contract". A contract may be referred to "Qi Yue", "He Tong (和同)", "He Tong (合同)" "Qi Ju", "Pan Shu", etc. However, the most common terminologies that have been used are "Qi Yue" and "He Tong". As was explained in "Shuo Wen Jie Zi" (说文解字) which was edited as the first dictionary in China by the famous linguist "Shen Xu" in the East Zhou dynasty, "Qi" is similar to "Yue", namely, agreement and people used "Qi" in order

an agreement between private parties.[814] As is recorded in the "Rites of Zhou", a written form of agreement ("Zhi Ji")[815] should be adopted in sales and this written contract was deemed important, as the "certificate of the agreement" or "Qi Ju".[816] This tradition of conducting formal transactions in a written way has been kept in Chinese civil society from dynasty to dynasty, particularly when it came to trades of land or other important materials for agricultural production.[817] Generally, customs or common usages and the Confucian traditions[818] constituted the main source of "law", regulating "Qi Yue", which is different from the term "contract law" in Europe.[819] According to many Chinese scholars, one of the most important norms people had to comply with is that

to conduct transactions. Another concept of "He Tong" has been adopted in the modern Chinese legislation that will be discussed in the following part of this section. See Xu 2001, p. 592. (契，大约也…"易"，后世圣人易之以书契…).

814 In the "West Zhou" dynasty, "Qi Yue" has three major forms, namely, "Fu Bie (傅别)", "Zhi Ji (质剂)" and "Shu Qi (书契)". When two private parties engaged in a loan, what they used is called "Fu Bie". In this process, the loaner and the loanee had to write their agreement on a piece of cloth, tear it into two parts and each party should get one part of it so as to prove the existence of their relationship. When conflicts arose, the two parties would bring both parts of cloth together and thus re-create the written agreement. However, when it came to a loan between the government and a private party, they used a formal written document called "Shu Qi" to record the loan. In contrast, "Zhi Ji" is the form of concluding sales contracts. When it came to sales of slaves, oxen and horses, the parties had to use a long "Zhi". In contrast, a short "Zhi" is used for sales of small things. Liu (刘云生) 2000, p. 24; see also He (贺卫方) 1992, p. 95. Zheng (郑显文) 2003, p. 58.

815 "Zhi Ji (质剂)" in the Zhou dynasty was normally used in mortgage, pledge and sales. At that time, "Zhi Ji" were mostly made of bamboo and took different forms when different products were sold. The "Rites of Zhou" states: people use "Zhi" which is larger and longer to sell slaves and livestock while "Ji" that is smaller and shorter is used to sell iron and jewellery. Id.

816 In ancient China, the written "Zhi Ji" was called as "He Tong", which was not exactly the same as the term of "Qi Yue". Rather, "He Tong" was a form of "Qi Yue" and it worked as the symbol, proving the existence of the agreement. After "paper" was invented in ancient China, the contracting parties wrote "He" and "Tong" on the paper and each party got the part with either "He" or "Tong" on it. "He Tong" was made of these two parts of paper and indicated the existence of the agreement between these two parties. However, this difference between the concepts of "He Tong" and "Qi Yue" has been narrowed down in the modern literature and many scholars used these two concepts in the same way. He (贺卫方) 1992, p. 25–26. Zhang 2006, P. 25.

817 China in the ancient time was largely based on agriculture. Resources for production, such as land, cattle or slaves were very important and valuable properties. One can hardly find that trades of those valuable properties were not made in the written way. The last dynasty of Chinese feudal society is the Qing dynasty. Mac Cormack 1985, p. 53.

818 Confucianism tradition is regarded as the origin of moral norms in China. It is based on the hypothesis that people are born with a good heart and they should be educated and enlightened to behave with good intentions. A contract is thus considered as a tool that discourages sin and bad intentions and forces people to keep promises.

819 An important element of Chinese traditional culture is moral norms (Rate or Li), which might be presented in different forms and played different roles in the process of trade. On the one hand, it imposed a general obligation of good faith (different from good faith in Europe) on the parties and on the other hand it required people to avoid conflicts and to solve all problems in a harmonious way. Nevertheless, national law plays a less important role in shaping the contractual relationship and people's obligation to a contract. Hereby, China had not established a system of contract law rules or techniques, which somehow exist in Europe, regarding the formation of a contract, contract interpretation, breach and remedies. See Huo (霍存福) 2005, p. 44. MacCormack 1985, p. 17–18.

"agreements are legally binding law"[820] and agreements create obligations between parties[821] which has been found written on the deeds (contracts for sales of land) dated back to the Han Dynasty.[822] Thus, the obligor is subject to the obligee's claim and is liable for what he owes to the obligee.[823] In order to ensure the performance of "Qi Yue", parties would include self-help rules, such as rules regarding "Jian Zheng Ren (a witness)",[824] "Bao Ren (a guarantor)",[825] "Zhai Wu Di Ya (a mortgage or pledge)"[826] or

820 In Chinese ancient times, the term of "law" was normally used in the same meaning as "Xing (刑)", namely "penalty" or "punishment". See Xin (信春鹰)1999, 313.

821 In ancient China, emphasis of law was placed on "obligation". The reason for this, as is explained by Chinese scholars, is that the old China was established upon a strict hierarchy in which the emperor was positioned at the top. Therefore, the whole society was under the control of the emperor and obliged to the central power. Wang 1997, p. 4–8.

822 The term "Min You Si Yue Ru Lv Ling"(agreements are legally binding law) was found on a number of deeds (Mai Di Quan or contracts for sales of land) dated back to the Han dynasty. In tombs dated back to the Han dynasty, Chinese archaeologists found a large number of deeds, which were carved on stones. These deeds usually stipulated the names of the contract parties, the guarantors, the objects and so on. Moreover, many of them included a clause indicating that "agreements are binding laws". Although those deeds were virtual and intended to be used in sacrifice activities, most Chinese scholars think that the contents of those deeds reflect how Han people made real estate contracts in that period. In Tun-huang, scholars also found this type of deeds which are considered to be from the Tang dynasty. The evidence regarding Chinese "Qi Yue" can be found in Chinese literary works as well. For instance, Wang Guowei (Wang Kuo-wei or王国维) in his "Guan Tang Ji Lin" mentioned that it was a tradition for Chinese people to write a term "Ru Lv Ling" or "Ji Ji Ru Lv Ling" or "Ru Tian Di Lv Ling" in a "Qi Yue" or a "Fu Zhou (Taoist Charms)" in order to indicate the effectiveness of the "Qi Yue" or "Fu Zhou". By indicating the binding effect of a "Qi Yue", the parties would show their willingness to perform the "Qi Yue". For more information about contracts in ancient china, see Zhang (张晋藩) 1985; Zhang (张传玺) 1991; Li (李显冬) 2007; Huo (霍存福) 2008.

823 China has a concept of "Zhai" which came from the Roman concept of "Obligatio". It stands for the relationship between two particular parties. Within this relationship, one party is entitled to claims against the other party, while the other party is liable to him. Wang 2001, p. 13–14. Zhang 2006, p. 26.

824 A "Jian Zheng Ren" is a person who witnesses the process of a trade and who should later monitor the performance of a "Qi Yue". In Chinese ancient times, it was quite often that a trade of an expensive property (e.g lands, houses or farms) was made between two parties from one small community and both of them were already familiar with each other. A person who was elder and respected in this community would always engage in the process of making "Qi Yue". Sometime, a "Jian Zheng Ren" was an officer from an authority so that both of the parties would realize the importance of performing the "Qi Yue". Normally, a "Jian Zheng Ren" had an independent position and he should check if the property to be sold was in accordance with the "Qi Yue" or not and if the terms of "Qi Yue" were fair or not. In case of disputes arising, the "Jian Zheng Ren" may also become the mediator. See Li (李晓英) 2003, p. 88; Zheng (郑显文) 2003, p. 56; Zeng (曾宪义) 2009, p. 38.

825 Bao ren is too some extent similar to "a guarantor" in the modern times. If a debtor could not perform a "Qi Yue", a Bao ren would be held jointly liable for non-performance. See Li (李晓英) 2003, p. 88.

826 By "Zhai Wu Di Ya", a debtor (or purchaser) could raise money or credit in order to guarantee his payment. Such a mechanism could be traced back to the "Qin" dynasty. The loan might be secured on the debtor's properties (houses, land, slaves, cattle, etc.) or the labour of the families (children or wife) or sometimes the debtor himself. In some situations, the creditor might take possession of the debtor's property and would only return it when the "Qi Yue" (or loan) was performed. Or the debtor might keep possession of his property, but the creditor would sell the property or own the

"Cong Qi Yue (accessory contracts)".[827] Official Laws (lü or ling) in most situations, however, did not interfere with a "Qi Yue" unless a "Qi Yue" concerned the benefits of the state.[828] During the Tang dynasty (618–907 AC), the official law (Tang Code) for the first time stipulated some rules regarding "Qi Yue" in a relatively systematic way. For instance, the "Zha Lv" of the Tang code included several rules regarding for example the form of the "Qi Yue", the punishment for non-performance and restrictions to loans. As was required by the Tang code, people should make written contracts and go to an authority to register the trade and to obtain a certificate (Shi Quan); otherwise the parties will both be punished.[829] In addition, the punishment for breach of "Qi Yue" is harsh and it normally took the form of a criminal penalty.[830] For example, the Tang code also stipulated that if the products such as fabric sold by the seller contained defects or shortages, the seller should be beaten or whipped.[831] Such rules had been kept in the "laws" of the following dynasties. However, there are also many Chinese scholars holding that criminal liabilities in fact had not been used frequently in practice, but merely been staying in the laws laid on by the government. Instead, "Qi Yue" according

property had the "Qi Yue" not been performed. If it was the wife, daughter or son of the debtor or the debtor himself that had been used to secure the loan, the families or the debtor might become the creditor's slave in case of non-performance. See Li (李晓英) 2003, p. 90; Huo (霍存福) 2005, p. 49–51.

827 "Cong Qi Yue" was similar to "liquidated damages" which would be paid had the performance not been made on time. For instance, in a bamboo slip from the Han dynasty found in Gansu, Chinese scholars found some paragraphs indicating that a fine should be paid in case of delay in performance and the total fine to be paid by a debtor depended on the length between the day when the performance was made and the due time when performance should be made. See Li (李晓英) 2003, p. 90.

828 For instance, in many dynasties, the state had special rules regarding the interest rate on loans in order to keep loan interest not too high. In some dynasties, the state was even forbidding people to charge interest on loans, since usurious profits were inconsistent with the policy of "Zhong Nong Yi Shang (encouragement of agriculture and discouragement of business)". "Wei Shu (history of Wei dynasty)" indicates that, "Zhu You Gong Si Zhai Fu, Yi Qian Yi Shang, Ju Wan Yi Huan, Xi Jie Jin Duan, Bu De Zheng Zhai", which means the emperor of "Wei" dynasty ordered that no one can charge interest on loans. However, such a rule was not very common in Chinese history. Another issue that is closely related to the state's concern is the problem of sales of human beings. In many cases, a debtor might transfer a slaver to the creditor in replacement of performance, if he could not perform the "Qi Yue". However, China used to forbid sales of "Liang ren (normal persons who were not slaves) in many dynasties ". For more discussion about the relationship between national laws and private "Qi Yue", see Huo (霍存福) 2005; Huo (霍存福) 2008.

829 The original words used in the Tang Code are "Zhu Mai Nu Bi, Ma Niu Tuo Luo Lü, Yi Guo Jia Bu Li Shi Quan, Guo San Ri Chi San Shi, Mǎi Zhe Jian Yi Deng". It means that in case a buyer of slaves or cattle has not gone to the government for registration, the buyer should be beaten with a whip for 30 times and the seller should also get punishment, but in a less harsh way. See Zeng et. (曾宪义) 2000, p. 166.

830 As is commonly accepted, traditional Chinese civil law was structured on a mixed system, including both civil rules and criminal rules. The criminal law served as the backup of the whole legal system and criminal penalties played a role in forcing people to comply with the law. Zhang(张晋藩) 1999, p. 7–8; Han (韩世远) A 2011, p. 23–24.

831 According to "Tang Lv Shu Yi" (Tang Code), if the seller sells a defective product or delivers less than agreed, he should be beaten with a rod; if the seller delivers a sick slave or animal, he is regarded as a liar and should be whipped. Similar rules existed in the Qing Dynasty as well. Han (韩世远) A 2011, p. 23–24.

to Chinese scholars plays an important role in preventing litigation[832] and in most situations conflicts arising around a "Qi Yue" were solved via mediations rather than via the state.[833]

After the end of the second war and the Chinese civil war (1946–1949),[834] the new People's Republic of China (hereinafter the PRC) was established and China entered a new era of development. In that period, the central government which was taken over by the Communist Party (hereinafter the CPC) adopted Chairman Mao's "Plain Paper" idea[835] and attempted to revive the Chinese economy by accomplishing various mandatory economic plans. On the one hand, the old laws and regulations including those enacted by the former Nationalist government were eliminated[836] and a new constitution was adopted, empowering the National People's Congress (hereinafter the NPC) as the central legislative institute in China.[837] On the other hand, sales and commerce were restricted[838] and all the goods and serves were distributed and

832 In the "Zhou Rate", it has been pointed out that contracts could make people to trust each other and hence avoid lawsuits. See Huo (霍存福) 2008, 63.

833 The mediator sometimes might be the "Jian Zheng Ren" of a "Qi Yue" who is a local old person ("Li Lao") respected by the people from a community. In some situation, the mediator might also be an officer who worked at the local government. According to a Chinese historian "Huang Zongzhi", two thirds of all disputes were solved either via mediations or negotiations in the Qing dynasty. See Zeng (曾宪义) 2009, p. 39.

834 The Chinese civil war broke out between the Nationalist party which was chaired by Dhiang Kai-shek and the Communist party led by Mao Zedong (Chairman Mao). After the Civil war, the Nationalist party was expelled from the mainland of China and the communist party took over the nationalist party's position in the central government of China.

835 The idea of "Plain Paper" originated from the economic model of the former Soviet Union. Early in 1951, Chairman Mao raised the proposal to establish the Chinese Planned economy within 10 years. In 1952, China drafted the first five-year plan, which was executed between 1953 and 1957. There were several reasons explaining the rise of this idea at that time. One of the most important ones, as is stated, derived from the necessity of consolidating the power of the new central government. Moreover, the emphasis of economic recovery was placed on industry, agriculture and manufacturing and it was easier for the central government to gather capital, resources and labour as well as the support from other Soviet Union countries. Mao also indicated that the economic plan was necessary at that period for China to transit into a socialist country. A "plan paper" was important for China to follow the track of reaching its expected economic goal. Zhu (朱佳木) 2007, p. 3–6.

836 In 1949, the Communist Party started the process of tidying up the old laws and published the Directives on the Abolishment of the Code of Six Laws and the Establishment of Judicial Principles in the Liberated Areas in Feb. Xin (信春鹰)1999, p. 325–327.

837 On September 20 of 1954, the 1st NPC meeting took place in Beijing and it promulgated the 1954 Constitution of the People's Republic of China. In this constitution, the NPC was empowered as the central legislative institute. However, the Chinese government and its internal institute were empowered to create administrative rules that actually played an important role in the Chinese civil and commercial society. The 1954 constitution also proposed a project of drafting the Chinese Civil Code. In 1956, the first draft of the "Chinese Civil Code" was completed, including General Principles, Ownership, Obligatio (Zhai) and Inheritance. But this process was finally aborted in 1957. To be noted, the 1954 the Constitution had been replaced by the 1982 Constitution and what China currently uses is the 1982 Constitution.

838 Trades and contractual agreements, however, should be made among the public agencies, state-owned enterprises and cooperatives. This was confirmed in an Administrative Document ("Provisional Methods on Contractual Agreement Made between Government Agencies, State Enterprises, and Cooperatives") issued by the Commission of Finance and Economy within the Administration Council

allocated according to the government's plan rather than according to the market.[839] This situation lasted until 1979, when the new policies of "Open Door" and "Economic Reform" were proposed by the new generation of leaders.[840] The idea of a "Planned Economy" started to give way to a "Market Economy", leading to the re-establishment of a new legal system in which civil and commercial law were considered important for supporting the "Economic Reform". During the period from 1979 to the end of the 20th century, massive laws and regulations were enacted at the national level in relation to the economy and the market.[841] Through a succession of legislative activities by the NPC, a diversified sales law system was created, consisting of several important pieces of contract law and general principles.[842] In 1981, China enacted the Economic Contract Law (hereinafter ECL)[843] dealing with the sale, construction and other business relationship between legal persons.[844] Three years later, the Foreign Economic Contract Law (hereinafter FECL)[845] was enacted covering the contractual relationship

(later it was replaced by the State Council) in 1950. In contrast, trades and transactions between private parties were inhibited. Mo 2006, p. 3.

839 During the period between the 1950s and 1970s, the concept of contract did exist but only as an economic tool for carrying out the state's plans. For instance the Central Committee of the CPC and the Administration Council jointly issued the "Notice on Strictly Implementing the Procedure of Basic Construction and Economic Contracts" in 1962. Besides, in 1963, the National Economic Committee issued an "Interim Regulation on Contract for Ordinary Industrial and Mineral Products". These regulations have been cancelled afterwards. Zhong & Yu 1999, p. 3.

840 The new generation of leadership was established in the Third Session of the Eleventh Congress of the Communist Party in 1979. Led by Deng Xiaoping, the central government began to reflect on the old policies and the suffering incurred in the Cultural Revolution. The state started to seek "a significantly more decentralized, market-oriented and incentive-based economy" and an integration into the global market. See Chen 2002, p. 155.

841 According to the data gathered by Chinese scholars, more than 300 laws and regulations were published from 1979 to 1982 by the NPC and by the State Council. More than two thirds of the legislation concerned the issues of economic development and market management. Xin (信春鹰) 1999, p. 348–349.

842 There were also a number of administrative regulations promulgated by the State Council or its ministries in order to interpret and implement the ECL. Zhong & Yu 1999, p. 5.

843 中华人民共和国经济合同法 [The Economic Contract Law of the People's Republic of China] was adopted at the 4th Session of the 5th NPC on December 13, 1981, and took effect on July 1, 1982. It was annulled in 1999. Full text of ECL can be found at: www.lawinfochina.com/display.aspx?lib=law&id=18&CGid.

844 As is stated in Article 2 of ECL:

> The economic contract is an agreement between legal persons specifying their mutual relations, rights and obligations in order to realize certain economic aims.

In Chinese academic literature, legal persons are mostly referred to as corporations and partnerships and thus exclude natural persons. However, the ECL was amended in 1993 and its scope of application was extended to other economic organizations, individual business households ("Ge Ti Hu") and lease-holding rural households (Nong Cun Cheng Bao Jing Ying Hu). Chen 2001, p. 159.

845 中华人民共和国涉外经济合同法 [Law of the People's Republic of China on Economic Contracts Involving Foreign Interest] was promulgated by Order No. 22 of the President of the People's Republic of China on March 21, 1985, and took effect on July 1, 1985. It was annulled in 1999 as well. Full text can be found at: www.lawinfochina.com/display.aspx?id=55&lib=law&SearchKeyword=&SearchCKeyword.

between Chinese enterprises[846] and foreign enterprises (or other economic organizations). Two other significant legislative activities followed between the years 1986 and 1987. In the year 1986, the General Principles of Civil Law (hereinafter referred to GPCL)[847] were published, first adopting the term of "Contract (or "He Tong")"[848] and stipulating the basic principles of contract.[849] In 1987, the NPC enacted the Technology Contract Law (hereinafter TCL)[850] dealing with the innovation and the transfer, the consultation as well as the service of technology.[851] What is more, another achievement was China's signature of the CISG in 1981 and ratification of it in 1986.[852] In the early decades after the new PRC was born, the development of law was slow and most activities within China mainly served for the consolidation of the state and recovery of the economy. Until the 1980s, a raw framework of contract law which was aimed to facilitate the market economy was gradually being shaped.

846 Before the enactment of Chinese Corporation Law, the concept of enterprise was used including corporations, partnerships, economic organization, etc. As is stated in Article 1 of FECL:

> *This law is formulated to expand economic co-operation and technological exchange with foreign countries and to promote the joint establishment, on the principle of equality and mutual benefit, by foreign enterprises and other economic organizations or individuals and Chinese enterprises or other economic organizations of Chinese-foreign contractual joint ventures within the territory of the People's Republic of China.*

847 中华人民共和国民法通则 [The General Principles of Civil Law of the People's Republic of China] was adopted at the 4th Session of the 6th NPC, promulgated by Order No. 37 of the President of the People's Republic of China on 12 April 1986, and it took effect on 1 January 1987. Full text can be found at: www.npc.gov.cn/englishnpc/Law/2007-12/12/content_1383941.htm.

848 Before the GPCL, the term used in China was "Economic Contract." Han 2011, p. 33. As is provided in Article 85:

> *A contract shall be an agreement whereby the parties establish, change or terminate their civil relationship. Lawfully established contracts shall be protected by law.*

849 The GPCL includes nine chapters in total, in which 17 articles dealing with contracts. It also covers issues such as the basic principles of civil law, the natural person and legal persons, civil juristic acts, civil right, civil liability and so on.

850 中华人民共和国技术合同法 [The Law of the People's Republic of China on Technology Contracts] was adopted on 23 June 1987 by the 21st Session of the Standing Committee of the 6th NPC. However, it was annulled together with ECL and FECL in 1999. The full text of the TCL can be found at: www.lawinfochina.com/display.aspx?id=1177&lib=law&SearchKeyword=&SearchCKeyword=.

851 As is stated in Article 2 TCL:

> *This Law applies to contracts made between legal persons, between legal persons and citizens, and between citizens, which establish civil rights and obligations in technical development, technology transfer, technical consultancy and technical service. It does not apply, however, to contracts in which one party is a foreign enterprise, other foreign organisation or foreign individual.*

As is shown, both the ECL and the FECL would not be applied to natural persons while the TCL allowed individuals to conclude technological contracts. However, only the FECL applied to those contracts involving foreign enterprises and both the ECL and the TCL regulated domestic contracts.

852 The Vienna Convention on the International Sale of Goods was created by the United Nations Commission on International Trade Law and was signed in Vienna in 1980. China signed the convention on 30 September 1981. By 1 January 2014, there are 80 countries that signed the convention. In general, the CISG applies to contracts between parties from different countries but it supplements the Chinese contract law and prevails if there is inconsistency between Chinese law and the convention. See Han (韩世远) A 2011, p. 33; See also Mo 1999, p. 217; See also: www.uncitral.org/uncitral/en/uncitral_texts/sale_goods/1980CISG_status.html.

Nevertheless, the co-existence of the ECL, FECL, TCL and a bundle of other administrative regulations on contracts posed many complexities, inconsistences and ambiguities in the application of the law,[853] which led to the call for a unified contract law.

The publication of the 1999 Uniform Chinese Contract Law (in Chinese referred to as "He Tong Fa", hereinafter CCL)[854] brought an end to the situation where multiple systems of contract law co-existed and opened the door for the modern development of Chinese contract law. The CCL contains 23 chapters and 428 articles dealing with the general rules of contract, 15 specific types of contract[855] and 1 supplementary rule concerning the validity of the CCL.[856] The sales contract is treated as one of the most important and common contracts and it covers the largest number of articles among those 15 types of contracts.[857] Even until now, according to many Chinese legal scholars,[858] the CCL is still deemed as a successful achievement which has been inspired by the civil law tradition and by international conventions.[859] Moreover, after the

853 There were many conflicts, ambiguities and overlaps among the ECL, the FECL and the TCL. For instance, with regard to the scope of application, the ECL, the FECL and the TCL dealt with different types of contract and pointed to different legal aspects. Both the ECL and TCL regulated the domestic contracts but the ECL only applied to contracts between legal persons. Another example of conflict is the liability rule adopted in each law. As indicated in Article 29 of the ECL, the ECL took the rule of negligence liability so that the contract breaker was only liable if his breach was based on fault. However, the FECL adopted a strict liability rule in Article 19. Moreover, both the ECL and the FECL mixed the concepts of "Economic Contract" and "Contract".

854 The drafting of a unified contract law started in 1993 by the Standing Committee of the NPC and in January of 1995 the first draft was completed and sent to the Legislative Affairs Commission by legal scholars from 12 universities. After several times of modification, revision and requests for opinions, the commission finished the final draft of Contract Law of the People's Republic of China and submitted it to the NPC. On March 15th, 1999, the CCL was adopted at the 2nd Session of the 9th NPC and promulgated by Order No. 15 of the President of the PRC. The Full text of the CCL can be found at: www1.lawinfochina.com/display.aspx?lib=law&id=6145.

855 These 15 types of contract, which are also called "You Ming He Tong (the named contract), were considered being used most frequently in practice, such as the loan contract, lease contract, financial lease contract, technology contract, transportation contract and construction project contract. According to Article 124 of the CCL, for the other types of contract which are not listed in CCL, the general rules and the rules of the most similar contracts could be applied as reference. Zhang 2006, 11–12. Jiang 1996, p. 245–246.

856 Article 428 took effect on October 1st, 1999 and it repealed the ECL, FECL and TCL.

857 There are 46 articles in chapter 9 under the title of "Purchase and Sale Contract".

858 Han (韩世远) A 2011, p. 34; Cui (崔建远) 2010, p. 11–14.

859 For example, the CCL adopted the structure of civil legislation from the civil law tradition. It contains chapters on general principles of contract law and chapters dealing with specific contracts and this structure is quite similar to that in the civil law legislations such as the German Civil Code (BGB). Moreover, some articles are drafted in consistence with the CISG. Examples are Article 17 (Withdrawal of Offer) and Article 18 (Revocation of Offer) in the CCL, which are similar to Article 15(b) and 16(a) of the CISG. Besides, China after accepting the CISG has, to a very limited scope, borrowed some common law concepts, such as the term "Anticipatory Breach (Article. 94, Article 108)". Han (韩世远) B 2011, p. 9–10.

establishment of the CCL, the Supreme People's Court of the PRC (hereinafter the SPC) published several important pieces of judicial interpretation which have the force of law and which facilitate the application of the CCL.[860] So far, a relatively unified legal system on sales contracts has been established which is largely based on the 1999 CCL and the GPCL and supplemented by the Supreme Court's interpretations, administrative law and regulations. This system provides the basic framework for general sales[861] and is presented as a hierarchy. Within this system, the new CCL is deemed to be the main body of Chinese contract law, while the GPCL is relatively considered as a "stand-by law" which serves as a "gap-filling" law.[862] Table 38 shows the source of sales contract law in China.[863]

860 Interpretations in China can be divided into legislative interpretations, judicial interpretations and administrative interpretations. According to Article 27 of the"最高人民法院关于司法解释工作的规定[Provisions of the Supreme People's Court on the Judicial Interpretation Work]" which was issued by the SPC in 2007, the judicial authority refer to law and the related judicial interpretation. In this sense, judicial interpretation is regarded as having the same force of law within the judicial process. However, only the SPC has the power to provide a binding interpretation. There are several types of judicial interpretations. When the SPC makes a response to questions in a specific case raised by a trial court, this kind of interpretation is called "Letters of Reply (Jieda, Dafu, Pifu, Han or Fuhan)". Letter of reply is normally short and only points to a certain case. Another type of interpretation is called Opinions (Yijian) or Notices (Tongzhi) or Measures (Banfa) or Provisions (Guiding). This type of interpretation is drafted by the SCP itself (or sometimes together with the Supreme People's Procuratorate) and is aimed to interpret specific law or provisions. Moreover, the SCP may also publish model cases in order to show samples for inexperienced judges to consult. In theory, it is considered that the published cases are not binding. Chen (陈春隆) 2003, p. 24. Li 1997, p. 95–100; Han 2011(韩世远), p. 17–20.

861 According to Article 123 of the CCL, if there are other statutes stipulating relative rules in relation to a specific type of contract, those rules should be applied. For instance, with regard to consumer sales, China has the "Law of the PRC on Protection of Consumer Rights and Interests" which entered into force in 1994.

862 Chen 2008, p. 450.

863 Han (韩世远) A 2011, p. 16–21.

Table 38. Sources of Sales Contract Law in China[864]

Binding law	Civil and Commercial Law	***GPCL***	*Article84–88 Contract right*
			Article111–115 Breach of Contracts
		CCL	*Article 1–129 General rules on Contracts*
			Cha. 9. Art 130–175 Sales Contracts
		Other: Guarantee law Auction Law...	
	Judicial Interpretation	*Interpretation of Some Questions Relating to the Contract Law I (1999), II (2009)*[53] (hereinafter Interpretation of the CCL)	
		Guiding Opinions of the SPC on Several Issues concerning the Trial of Cases of Disputes over Civil and Commercial Contracts under the Current Situation (2009)[54] (hereinafter Opinions on Contract Law)	
		Interpretation of Issues Relating to the Interpretation of Law Arising from the Adjudication of Sales Contracts Disputes (2012)[55] (hereinafter Interpretation over Sales Disputes)	
	Administrative law and regulations		
	International Convention		CISG
Soft law	Regulations (Gui Zhang), Ordinances(Tiao Li) & Orders (Ming ling) by administrative department[56]		*eg. Administrative Ordinance on transaction of Urban Real Estate in Xuzhou*
	Model cases issued by the SPC [57]		
	Usages and customs: Guanxi		

From the introduction to the development of Chinese sales contract law, three major features of Chinese sales law can be generated. First, the form and function of sales law have changed. As shown above, in Chinese history, most rules on sales contracts were

864 Special attention should be paid to those types of contract law which have been emphasized in bold. However, the focus of this chapter is placed only on the binding law within China. Cultural factors or moral issues, which nevertheless are essential in defining the Chinese law, fall outside the scope of this chapter.

865 合同法司法解释[Interpretation over the CCL] Volume I was promulgated by the SPC on December 19, 1999 and volume II was promulgated on April 24, 2009.

866 合同指导意见 [Guiding Opinions] was promulgated by the SPC on July 2009 with the document number of No. 40 [2009].

867 买卖合同司法解释[Interpretation over Sales Disputes] was promulgated by the SPC on May 10, 2012.

868 These types of documents are normally issued by the specific departments of the State Council or local governments or local People's Congress. They normally point to a specific issue such as transaction of real estate or environmental issues and this type of document does not have legal binding power in the trial. The court may take them as a reference in making decisions. Han (韩世远) A 2011, p. 20.

869 For example, the National Judges' College published a book under the name of "Chinese courts decisions for 2012: sales contract disputes" in February 2012. Another famous case book is called "Sales Contract Disputes, judicial rules and discretion" which was edited by a judge (Langliang Tian) of the SPC in 2012.

presented as either administrative commands or criminal rules or customs and were aimed at regulating the state by imposing obligations and liabilities.[870] In contrast, the role of modern contract law has been switched to facilitating the market economy by protecting private rights and interests.[871] On the one hand, the modern Chinese sales law contains less regulation and is being accepted as a legal basis for judicial discretion.[872] On the other hand, several modern contract law principles have been assimilated into the new contract Law,[873] such as the principle of freedom of contract,[874] the principle of good faith[875] as well as the principle of "*pacta sunt servanda*".[876] Second, there is a trend in Chinese legal history that criminal liability and administrative liability was being precluded from sales contract law[877] and the system of civil liability is being established.[878]

870 In Chinese feudal society, most rules on sales were customs or common usages. Although the state might also issue some binding rules regulating sales contracts, most rules took the form of criminal law or public regulation. Liang (梁慧星)2010, p. 85.

871 Articlel of CCL provides that the goal of this law is to protect the legitimate rights and interests of the parties to contracts, maintaining the social-economic order and promoting the socialist modernization. According to some scholars, however, the CCL "remains to contain provisions of state-plan-related contract". For instance, Article 38 of the CCL still refers to the goal of implementing a mandatory plan of the state. Zhang 2006, p. 13. Article 38 provides:

> *Where the state has, in light of its requirements, issued a mandatory plan or state purchase order, the relevant legal persons and other organizations shall enter into a contract based on the rights and obligations of the parties prescribed by the relevant laws and administrative regulations.*

872 To some extent, the existence of contract law also restricts the judge's discretion in a way that the judges have to make judicial decisions according to the law rather than based on administrative orders. Han (韩世远) A 2011, p. 34.

873 In terms of contract law principles, there are several different ideas. In some literature, it is considered that the new CCL also contains the principle of equality (Article 3 CCL), the principle of fairness (Article 5 CCL), the principle of public order and social ethics (Article 7 CCL) and the principle of fostering transactions. Han 2011, p. 36–44. Wang & Xu 1999, p. 9–33.

874 Article 4 CCL:

> *The parties shall, pursuant to law, have the right to enter into a contract on their own free will, and no unit or person may unlawfully interfere.*

875 Article 6 CCL:

> *The parties shall abide by the principle of good faith in exercising their rights and performing their obligations.*

876 Article 8 CCL:

> *A legally executed contract has legal binding force on the parties. The parties shall fulfil their obligations as contracted, and may not arbitrarily modify or terminate the contract.*

877 As is noted, the sales rules issued by the public authority in the Chinese feudal society were predominantly criminal rules. In addition, some sales rules before the publication of the CCL in the new China (after 1949) chose both criminal liability and administrative liability as the consequence of breaches of contracts. For example, Article 32 of the ECL provided:

> *If, due to the fault of one party, an economic contract cannot be performed or cannot be fully performed, the party at fault shall be liable for breach of the contract; if both parties are at fault, in accordance with the actual conditions, each party shall be commensurately liable for breach of the contract that is due to its fault.*
>
> *If an individual is directly responsible for dereliction of duty, malfeasance or other unlawful conduct that gives rise to a major accident or severe losses, he shall be investigated for economic and administrative responsibility, and even criminal responsibility.*

878 This will be explained in section 2.

Thirdly, the traditional customs, usages and moral norms have been playing a significant role in shaping the system of sales rules and have sometimes been even more important than the written law. A well-known example is the role of "guan xi" which is essential for Chinese commercial society. As a special relationship or connection or network, a "guan xi" consists of a "mutual obligation", "reciprocity" and "personal affection"[879] which may decide the way and content of the on-going relationship between traders.[880] In addition, according to China's traditional moral norms, a person who always keeps his promise is considered to be honest and reliable. In addition, it was strengthened at the time of the centrally planned economy that the state mandatory plans must be carried out.[881] In this sense, breach of contract in the Chinese legal system, is generally considered to be immoral and condemnable.

2. General Rules on Sales Contracts, Seller's Breach and Buyer's Remedies

2.1. Sales Contracts and Buyer's Remedies in General

As indicated in section 1, the main rules on Chinese sales law are provided by the 1987 GPCL, 1999 CCL and by the relative judicial interpretation. In the CCL, there is one separate chapter (Chap. 9 CCL) dealing with the contract of sales under the title of "Purchase and Sale Contract".

Article 130 of the CCL states that a "purchase and sale contract" is a contract whereby the seller transfers his ownership of the targeted matter to the buyer and the buyer pays the price for this.[882] In this sense, sales contracts in Chinese law only cover those contracts involving visible and certain goods,[883] while the other contracts concerning goods to be manufactured belong to Contracts of Hired Works or Contracts of Construction Projects which are defined separately in chapter 15 and 16 of the CCL.

After the conclusion of a sales contract, the seller is obliged to transfer the products and their ownership as well as to provide a warranty against any defect.[884] The fact of a

879 Pattison & Herron 2003, p. 484; Matheson 2006, p. 374.

880 Unlike the concept of contract in other countries, the term contract in China indicates the beginning of the business relationship. In this sense, there is great flexibility in the content and the method of the contract. Especially when the "guan xi" between the parties is close and intimate, the parties would modify and revise their contact easily in their on-going relationship.

881 At that period, many contracts were made under the state plan in between state enterprises. Wang 1992, p. 18; Zhu 2005, p. 1146.

882 Article 130 CCL.

883 If there are other relative laws or statutes dealing with sales contracts, those laws or statutes should apply. For instance, Article 7 of the "Auction Law" states that if some goods are forbidden to be traded within the market according to law or administrative regulation, those goods cannot be auctioned. Cui (崔建远) 2010, p. 383.

884 According to Chinese legal theory, the seller has to guarantee that the goods delivered by him do not contain any defect and there is no third party claiming right over the goods. Id, p. 386–401.

seller's breach (violation of his obligation)[885] is the pre-condition for triggering the application of the buyer's remedies[886] according to both the GPCL (Article 106, Article111) and the CCL (Article 107), which provides the general rules regarding breaches and contract liabilities.[887], Article 111 of the GPCL and Article 107 are written as follows:

Article.111 GPCL: If a party fails to fulfil its contractual obligations or violates the terms of a contract while fulfilling the obligations, the other party shall have the right to demand fulfillment or the taking of remedial measures and claim compensation for its losses.

Article.107 CCL: Either party that fails to perform...shall bear the liability for breach *of contract by continuing to perform the obligations, taking remedial measures, or compensating for losses.*

If the seller breaches the contract, he should bear the liabilities in the form of continuing to perform his contractual obligations, taking remedial measures or compensating for the buyer's losses. As explained in Chinese literature, the different forms of contract liability mentioned by Article 111 of the GPCL and Article 107 of the CCL above are referred to as remedies of continuing performance,[888] reparation, replacement and return[889] as well as monetary compensation. Furthermore, the application of contract remedies depends on the specific form of breach. In the situation where a seller refuses to deliver the goods or is delayed in delivering the products according to the contract, the other party is able to request specific performance or monetary damages or to directly terminate the contract if the purpose of the contract is frustrated by the seller's breach.[890] If the goods delivered by a seller contain defects, the buyer may also require the seller to cure the defects or reduce the price for the goods.

What is considered to be a great progress of the modern Chinese contract law is that the aggrieved party has been given freedom in choosing the remedies provided by contract law.[891] In contrast, the emphasis and priority of previous Chinese contract legislation was placed on a strict enforcement of contracts before the 1990s. The reason, as is explained by some Chinese scholars, is that contracts in the past were aimed at implementing state plans rather than fostering transactions and other market activities.[892]

885 There are four major situations where a contract has been broken by the promisor. The promisor might be unable to fulfil his obligation, or be unwilling to perform or be delayed in performance. Another form of breach exists in the circumstance where a party has performed the contract but his performance contains a defect.

886 According to Chinese legal scholars, there are two ways of dealing with breaches of contracts in the law. The law may set different rules on breaches according to either the causes or the forms of breach or the remedies that are available to the aggrieved party. What has been adopted by the CCL is the later approach. Cui (崔建远) 2010, p. 285–286.

887 Article 111 GPCL; Article 107 CCL.

888 For more detailed discussion on "continuing performance", please see section 2.2.

889 These three types of remedies in essence belong to the remedy of specific performance.

890 Article 94 CCL.

891 Hsu 2007, p. 255.

892 For example, Article 11 of the Economic Contract Law of China required that:

Economic contracts that concern economic dealings in products or projects under a mandatory state plan must be concluded in accordance with state-issued targets; if at the time of signing the parties cannot reach an agreement, the matter shall be handled by both parties' superior authorities in charge

As China has been transformed into a socialist market economy, state plans are no longer consistently emphasized.[893] Alternatively, the goal of modern contract law has been switched into protecting the contract parties' rights and facilitating a socialist market economy.[894] Accordingly, the specific embodiment of this goal is that the non-breaching party has more flexibility in choosing the remedies available to him. If the seller violates his contractual obligations, the buyer could resort to either continuing performance, or monetary damages or any other remedial measures according to his own preference.

2.2. *Continuing Performance*

Both the GPCL and CCL have adopted the term "continuing performance" to indicate the remedy of making the breaching party continually perform the contract as agreed by the state.[895] Some Chinese literature may also call this kind of remedy "compelled performance" or "enforced performance".[896] The purpose of continuing performance is to have the contract specifically implemented so that the promisee could obtain what he is entitled to according to what has been agreed upon at the time of contract formation. In this sense, the continuing performance is referred to as specific performance, which has the same meaning as that in Europe as well.[897] For this reason, the concept of specific performance will be used in this chapter in the same sense as continuing performance.

2.2.1. The priority of Continuing Performance

As mentioned in the previous section, the CCL has changed the position of specific performance by making it an optional remedy. Article 110 provides the rule of specific performance of the non-monetary obligation. Article 110 of the CCL holds:

If either party fails to perform non-pecuniary debt or fails to perform non-pecuniary debt as contracted, the other party may demand performance...

It is stated that if one party fails to perform the non-monetary obligation or his performance fails to satisfy the requirement of the contract, the other party may request the breaching party to perform. In a sale contract, the non-breaching buyer is able to require the breaching seller to deliver the goods according to the contract and the state authority will protect this kind of request. In this sense, the court cannot decide to award specific performance directly without a request by the aggrieved party. Some scholars summarize that the new Chinese contract remedy system is transformed gradually from

of planning. Economic contracts that concern economic dealings in products or projects under an indicative state plan shall be concluded after taking account of state-issued targets and the actual conditions of the units involved.

Accordingly, contract parties are required to strictly comply with their economic contracts. Zhang 2006, p. 297.

893 Kornet 2010, p. 7.

894 Article 1 CCL.

895 Cui (崔建远) 1992, p. 169.

896 Cui (崔建远) 2010, p. 313; Han (韩世远) 2011, p. 600.

897 Zhang 2006, p. 296–297.

punitive into compensatory.[898] However, specific performance is still deemed as an important way of implementing contracts, which purports to ensure that the non-breaching party is able to obtain what he could expect from the contract.[899]

First of all, the prevailing position of specific performance is indicated by the principle of "*Pacta Sunt Servanda*" or "Sanctity of Contract", which was established in Article 8 of the CCL as one of the basic principles in Chinese contract law.[900] As is required, once a contract is legally formed, it has legal binding force on the parties and should be executed properly and completely.[901] As a result, contract parties are required to take their legally binding contract seriously and cannot violate, modify or terminate it arbitrarily. This principle was re-confirmed and mentioned many times in the CCL. For instance, Article 60 states that contract parties should not only perform their contract obligation, but should also make the performance in a complete and proper way.[902] Besides, it is required that a legally binding contract cannot be modified or terminated arbitrarily without the other party's agreement.[903]

The priority of specific performance in Chinese contract Law is also manifested in the rules over some practical issues on the enforcement. The civil procedure law (hereinafter CPL)[904] provides the rules on the measures of executing specific performance. The most common way of execution is to directly force the seller to transfer the properties and the ownership by the executive authority (Chinese courts).[905] In order to facilitate execution, the courts are empowered, according to different circumstances, to seize,

898 Id.

899 Cui (崔建远) 2010, p. 601.

900 The principle of "Pacta Sunt Servanda" may also be referred to as "Observant of Contract". The core idea of this principle is that "contract should be honored and respect". In Chinese ancient time, it was already commonly held that "agreements should be treated as law".

901 Article 8 CCL. "*A legally executed contract has legal binding force on the parties. The parties shall fulfill their obligations as contracted, and may not arbitrarily modify or terminate the contract.*"

902 Article 60 CCL provides:

(1) The parties shall fulfil fully their respective obligations as contracted. (2)The parties shall observe the principle of good faith and fulfill the obligations of notification, assistance and confidentiality in accordance with the nature and aims of the contract and trade practices.

Article 60 encourages the contract parties to take a complete and proper approach to fulfil their contract obligation. It means the parties should take the other party's convenience into account when fulfilling the contract obligation. Hence, the promisor should choose a proper time, place and method when performing the contract. Chinese scholars also refer Article 60(1) to the rule of "proper performance". The problem is this kind of article established in the CCL only suggests that contract parties should take proper performance. However, there is no rule in the CCL indicating the legal consequences of improper performance. Cui (崔建远) 2010, p. 126.

903 Article 94 provides the conditions for terminating a binding contract. Han 2011, p. 44.

904 The 中华人民共和国民事诉讼法 [Civil Procedure Law of the People's Republic of China] was adopted at the Fourth Session of the Seventh National People's Congress on 9 April 1991. It was amended according to the Decision on Amending the Civil Procedure Law of the People's Republic of China which was passed at the 30th Meeting of the Standing Committee of the 10th National People's Congress on 28 October 2007. The second amendment of the civil procedure law took place according to the decision concluded at the 28th Meeting of the Standing Committee of the 11st National People's Congress on August 31st, 2012.

905 According to Article 229 of the Chinese civil procedure law, the people's courts at each level have the authority to execute judicial decisions.

freeze, seal up or transfer the properties that are subject to execution.[906] In sales of real estates, the courts are authorized to compel the breaching party to leave the land or house or require the registration office to assist with the registration of transfer.[907] In addition to the direct execution, there is an indirect way of execution stipulated by the CPL. That is, the courts try to execute judicial decisions by imposing psychological pressure on the breaching party. The breaching party will be compelled to perform his contractual obligation by the threat of paying interest or being restricted of his personal freedom or even bearing criminal liability.[908] Moreover, Chinese law also includes a kind of alternative execution, which is similar to the concept of "substitutive performance" in the PECL, the DCFR and the CESL.[909]

2.2.2. Alternative Execution in Chinese Law

Alternative Execution (Ti dai lü xing),[910] in Chinese law is stipulated in the Chinese Civil Procedure Law and the Supreme Court's interpretation as a substitute for enforcing specific performance.[911] Article 252 of the CPL holds:

> *If the person subjected to execution fails to perform acts specified in a judgment or written order or any other legal document according to the execution notice, the people's court may carry out compulsory execution or entrust the task to a relevant unit or other persons, and the person subjected to execution shall bear the expenses thus incurred.*

As shown in Article 252 of the CPL, alternative execution takes place when the obligor fails to accomplish the acts according to the judicial decision. In this situation, the court may authorize a third person or the plaintiff to carry out the execution and make the obligor bear the cost incurred by the execution. Nevertheless, substitutive execution only applies to the obligation that could be accomplished by a third party.[912] If the obligation

906 Article 241–251 CPL.

907 Article 250, Article 251 CPL.

908 Article 114 CPL; Article 253 CPL. Article 253 states:

> *If the person subjected to execution fails to fulfil his obligations with respect to pecuniary payment within the period specified by a judgment or written order or any other legal document, he shall pay double interest on the debt for the belated payment If the person subjected to execution fails to fulfil his other obligations within the period specified in the judgment or written order or any other legal document, he shall pay a charge for the dilatory fulfilment.*

909 Han (韩世远) A 2011, p. 604–605.

910 In some literature, Article 252 is referred to as "Ti Dai Lv Xing" (substitutive execution or alternative execution). Qiao (乔宇) 2011, p. 10.

911 Article 252 CPL. A similar provision can be found in the "Provisions of the Supreme People's Court on Several Issues Concerning the Judicial Enforcement of People's Courts' Decision." According to Article 60, for those acts that can be accomplished by a third party, the court may ask the third party to take execution and make the obligor bear the costs by doing so.

912 Wang(王洪亮) 2012, p. 107.

required by the judgment is personally related and the obligor refuses to be persuaded to assist in its execution, the court may impose criminal punishment on him.[913]

As a result of alternative execution, the obligee is able to obtain what he is entitled to according to the judgment and the obligor is required to bear the cost of performance. Suppose a scenario where a defendant (seller) refuses to enforce the judgment and an alternative execution takes place. If the non-breaching buyer has been allowed by the court to make an alternative purchase, the court will later make the defendant pay the value of the price difference between the original contract and the alternative contract. By this means, the obligee is able to obtain what he is entitled to according to the judgment and the obligor is required to bear the cost of performance. In this sense, alternative execution is similar to the concept of substitutive performance in Europe, which sometimes might also be referred to as cover purchase.[914] For instance, according to some empirical studies in Germany and France, if an aggrieved buyer has conducted a cover purchase after he learned the fact of breach, he is normally allowed to recover the costs of making the cover purchases.[915] Besides, in the European Union instruments, such as in the CESL, it is held that: "A creditor who has terminated a contract in whole or in part and has made a substitute transaction within a reasonable time and in a reasonable manner may … recover the difference between the value of what would have been payable under the terminated contract and the value of what is payable under the substitute transaction, as well as damages for any further loss".[916]

Substitutive performance and the Chinese concept of alternative execution included in the CPL, however, belong to different categories of enforcement mechanisms. To summarize, the differences between these two concepts lie in at least three facets. Firstly, in China, substitutive execution in Chinese Law is stipulated by the procedural law as a special way of judicial execution. The plaintiff or the third party is authorized to carry out what is included in the judgment. Substitutive performance in the European law is the alternative of specific performance which merely relies on the aggrieved buyer's alternative purchase. Secondly, in China it is the court who decides that the judicial decision should be carried out by the alternative party and the costs should be borne by the defendant. Hence, a definite judgment provides the legal base for substitutive execution. In contrast, substitutive performance in European law is also referred to as "cover purchase" which is "routinely enforced and sought by the plaintiff".[917] Thirdly and most importantly, substitutive performance in European law is grounded on the economic logic of enforcement cost. In the context of enforcing specific performance, high administrative costs would be incurred to establish a series of administrative

913 Id.

914 For instance, Lando & Rose (2004) used the concept of "cover purchase" to denote substitutive performance. See Lando & Rose 2004, p, 476–478. In this paper, the term "European law" is used in a wide sense. It includes both member states' laws and European Union instruments such as CESL or DCFR.

915 Id, p. 477–478.

916 Article 164 CESL.

917 According to the empirical statistics by Lando & Rose in Denmark, Germany and France, specific performance has been rarely enforced in practice. Rather, cover purchase is more welcome in both civil and common law as a "way of economizing on enforcement costs". Lando & Rose 2004, p. 483.

procedures. Sometimes, it may require introducing measures such as periodic fines on the breaching party in order to force him to perform; or the plaintiff will incur additional costs if the breaching party delays in performance.[918] For this reason, specific performance is used very rarely in practice, even within the countries with a civil-law tradition.[919] In comparison, substitutive performance is generally granted in a less costly way but brings out effects similar to specific performance. Therefore, it is commonly recognized that specific performance will not be enforced if it is easier for the plaintiff to obtain substitutive performance. However, substitutive execution in China is assumed to fit into an administrative procedure in order to guarantee performance. In this sense, substitutive execution does not enjoy any priority over direct specific performance in China.[920]

2.3. Damages Rules

In addition to specific performance, the remedy of monetary damages is another important remedy provided in Chinese contract law. Article 112 in both the GPCL and the CCL establish the primary rules entitling the non-breaching party to monetary damages.

2.3.1. The Complementary Function of Monetary Damages

As explained above, one important goal of monetary damages in Chinese law is to fully compensate the aggrieved party.[921] This is implied in Article 112 of the GPCL:

> *The party that breaches a contract shall be liable for compensation equal to the losses consequently suffered by the other party.*

The compensatory function of contract damages is further embodied in Article 112 of the CCL. Article 112 of the CCL holds:

> *Where either party fails to perform its obligations under the contract or does not perform its obligations as contracted, and losses are still caused to the other party after the performance of obligations or the adoption of remedial measures, the party in fault shall compensate for the losses.*

918 Id, pp. 480–482.

919 Lando & Rose 2004, pp. 484–485.

920 To be noted, in the official draft of the CCL, the drafters included that performance cannot be demanded if it is easy to obtain the alternative objects from the market. However, this rule was cut out from the final version of the CCL. The official draft of the CCL was proposed in the 4th meeting of the Standing Committee of the NPC on 24 August 1998. Article 116(2) of the Official Draft of Contract Law; Han (韩世远) A 2011, p. 607.

921 In Chinese literature, "full compensation" is deemed as an important principle concerning the private law remedy of damages. Han (韩世远) A 2011, p. 631; Zhang 2006, p. 305.

According to this article, monetary damages could still be applied even if the aggrieved party has already obtained the remedy of specific performance or other remedial measures provided he still suffers other losses caused by the breach. In this sense, specific performance and damages can be accumulated as long as they don't conflict with each other. For instance, in the case where the seller is late in the delivery of the goods, the buyer may ask the seller to make the delivery as required by the contract as well as to compensate for his loss caused by the delay. Nevertheless, specific performance and damages cannot be accumulated when the monetary damage is supposed to be the alternative remedy of specific performance.[922] Therefore, the remedy of damages in Chinese contract law plays a supplementary and alternative function by filling the gaps left by other types of remedy. What also needs to be noted is that, as is observed by some empirical data, Chinese courts in practice are actually more willing to choose monetary damages which only involve monetary calculation.[923] In contrast, specific performance which heavily relies on state authority and enforcement, is awarded less frequently by the court. But the plaintiff's choice will still be respected if the plaintiff has chosen specific performance in his claim. Although the position of monetary damages is strengthened via the establishment of the CCL, Chinese contract law does not provide full compensation for all types of losses incurred by breach of a contract. This is implied in Chinese law's attitude towards non-pecuniary damages.

The topic regarding non-pecuniary damages in contract law cases has caused a lot of debate in China. Chinese scholars who suggest to extend non-pecuniary damages to contract cases, argue that the term "loss" contained in Article 112 of the CCL should also include the non-breaching party's mental losses.[924] According to them, non-monetary losses incurred by breach should be compensated in order to completely protect the aggrieved party's expectation and other interests.[925] Moreover, they argue that Article 122 of the CCL offers the legal basis for the claim of non-pecuniary damages in contract law.[926] Article 122 requires the courts to accept the plaintiff's claim if the plaintiff's personal right or property right has been infringed by the breach of contract. However, it seems Chinese law has not accepted the idea of applying non-pecuniary damages to contracts. In 2012, the Supreme Court in its Interpretation regarding disputes in tourist contracts has explicitly indicated that damages for mental losses will be awarded only if the plaintiff has made an action in tort. In judicial experience, moreover, most courts still take a traditionally conservative attitude toward non-pecuniary losses in contracts.

922 Cui (崔建远) 2010, p. 316.

923 Wang 1992, p. 23.

924 Han (韩世远) A 2011, p. 620; Cui (崔建远) 2012, p. 22–30; Lu (陆青) 2011, p. 151–154.

925 Han (韩世远) A 2011, p. 620; Cui (崔建远) 2010, p. 320.

926 See Article 122 CCL:

> *If the breach of contract by either party causes infringement on the personal or property rights and interests to the other party, the injured party has the right to choose whether to demand that the breaching party bear the liability for breach of contract pursuant to this Law or bear the liability for infringement of rights in accordance with other laws.*

As is shown, Article 122 allows an infringed party to bring either a lawsuit of contract breach or a lawsuit of tort. However, it doesn't inform the specific conditions for either a suit of breach or a suit of tort. Zhang 2006, p. 306.

They insist that a plaintiff who claims for compensation over his non-pecuniary losses should bring the lawsuit under tort law rather than under contract law.[927] Recently, although a few Chinese courts have granted non-pecuniary damages in cases regarding breaches of contracts,[928] the reason for this is that the promisors' breaches have also constituted torts. Moreover, most of those cases concern consumer contracts involving personal interests. With regard to pure commercial contracts, there is no evidence that the court will grant damages for the plaintiff's mental loss caused by breach.

2.3.2. Measurement of Damages: Expectation Damages

One of the most important issues concerning monetary damages is the measurement of damages. Article 113 of the CCL provides the principal rule of damage calculation:

> *If either party fails to perform its obligations under the contract or does not perform its obligations as contracted and thus causes losses to the other party, the amount of compensation for the loss shall be equivalent to* the loss actually caused by the breach of contract and shall include the profit obtainable after the performance of the contract...

As shown, the damages that the non-breaching party could obtain should be equal to the loss actually caused by the breach and should include the profit from the contract, had the contract been performed.[929] This provision frames the structure of expectation damages in Chinese contract law. In this sense, under the circumstances where a sales contract is broken, the non-breaching buyer is entitled to the amount of damages which will put him in as good a position as he could enjoy if the contract had been performed.

927 For instance, in 2010 the Supreme Court published the "Interpretation of Issues concerning the Trial of Cases of Disputes over Tourist Contracts". Article 21 states if the tourist brings a suit claiming non-pecuniary damages, the court should suggest the plaintiff brings a suit under the tort law. If the plaintiff insists on claiming for contract remedy, the court should reject his claim.

928 For instance, in 1997 the Lubei District Court (Heibei Province) granted damages for the plaintiff's mental loss in the case where the defendant (a photography studio) mistakenly destroyed the plaintiff's parents' photos. In this case, the plaintiff had collected two pieces of photo films of his parents who had passed away and sent it to the defendant in order to develop more photos. However, the defendant lost the films. The district court held that the plaintiff suffered from mental losses because of the studio's breach and this kind of loss is recoverable.

929 This article was influenced by Article 74 of the United Nation's Convention on Sales of Goods (CISG). In Article 74, it is stated:

> Damages for breach of contract by one party consist of a sum equal to the loss, including loss of profit, suffered by the other party as a consequence of the breach. Such damages may not exceed the loss which the party in breach foresaw or ought to have foreseen at the time of the conclusion of the contract, in the light of the facts and matters of which he then knew or ought to have known, as a possible consequence of the breach of contract.

Xing (刑建东) 2006, p. 357.

2.3.2.1. Market Price Rule

With regard to the specific rules of damage calculation, nevertheless, neither the GPCL nor the CCL provides any further statement. In the CCL, the aggrieved party's loss is denoted by some abstract expressions as the losses actually caused by breach as well as the loss of future opportunity. The question on the calculation of expectation loss in Chinese contract law still gives rise to a lot of academic debates. In the academic controversy, there are two approaches to calculate the plaintiff's losses, namely, the concrete assessment and the abstract assessment.[930] By adopting an abstract approach to assess the damages, the court only considers some general and objective criteria, such as the price of the product in the current market and the price stipulated by the parties in the contract. This approach is also analogous to the common-law rule of "market price rule".[931] In contrast, when taking a concrete approach, the court should take all the factors contributing to the loss into account in order to award the non-breaching party all the benefits and profits that he assumed to enjoy, had the contract been performed. For example, the court may consider whether the products are supposed to be re-sold by the buyer or are for his own use, whether the buyer has made a substitutive purchase or not after he finds out the fact of breach as well as the cost of producing the product, etc. The prevailing idea in academic studies suggests that a compromising approach should be taken. Accordingly, the rule of the "market price" should be elected as the basic method of calculating the buyer's expectation loss.[932] However, if the market price does not exist, the court should take other factors into account in order to provide the aggrieved party with full compensation and protection.[933]

One precondition for adopting the "market price" rule is that the price of the goods stipulated by the contract can be ascertained when the breach takes place. When applying the rule of "market price", the court has to take into account the concrete type of breach in specific cases.[934] If the seller fails to deliver the goods as agreed, the buyer is entitled to damages amounting to the difference between the contract price and the price of the goods in the current market. However, the price of a specific product might fluctuate in the market. Another question arising in the scenario of non-delivery is how to fix the base date for measuring the price of the goods. Chinese law offers the non-breaching party great flexibilities in choosing the date for evaluating the market price of the goods. The aggrieved buyer is able to choose from the date when the contract was formed, the date when the contract was broken, the date when the judicial decision was made as well as any date after breach happened and before the court made the judicial decision.[935] In

930 Han (韩世远) A 2011, p. 659; Cui (崔建远)2010, p. 339; Wang 1996, p. 432; Zeng (曾世雄) 2001, p. 184.

931 Han (韩世远) A 2011, p. 659.

932 Cui (崔建远) 2010, p. 340; Han (韩世远) A 2011, p. 654.

933 If an objective criterion is unavailable to a judge, the judge can resort to the subjective approach to assess the damages. As suggested, the judge's freedom of using his discretion in the assessment of the magnitude of damages should be restricted. However, it is difficult to draw restrictions to this kind of discretion. Han (韩世远) A 1999, p. 445.

934 Han (韩世远) A 2011, p. 654–656.

935 Id.

this sense, as long as the buyer is able to provide sufficient proof,[936] he is able to recover the difference between the contract price and the price of the product at the time when its market price is estimated as the highest one. For example, suppose that the market price is increasing after the breach occurred, then a rational buyer would always choose the time of the litigation as the basis for assessing his expectation loss. To some extent, there is a possibility that the non-breaching party might delay the litigation on purpose. In this way, the aggrieved buyer can maximize the shortfall between the contract price and the market price and get the highest amount of monetary compensation. As a result, the risk of the fluctuation of market price is shifted to the seller and it is more difficult for the seller to predict the magnitude of his liability in advance. In addition to non-delivery, breach may take the form of late-delivery or defective delivery. According to Chinese law, if the seller is late in delivering the goods, the other party's loss is manifested as the discrepancy between the market price of the goods at the due date of the delivery and the price at the actual date of delivery. In the circumstance where the goods delivered by the seller are inconsistent with the contract, then the seller should cover the price difference of the defective goods and the conforming goods.[937]

In general, the Chinese court only takes the "market price" as the primary rule for calculating the aggrieved party's expectation loss. The reason, as provided by one of the prevailing Chinese legal theories is that, whenever a seller fails to deliver the goods, the buyer only loses the extra amount of money that he has to afford when buying substitute goods in the market.[938] Even if the buyer expected to re-sell the goods at a higher price than the market price, what will be referred to by the court in damage assessment is still the market price. By the same token, it is proposed that if the aggrieved buyer has made a substitute purchase after he found out the fact of breach, the market price rather than the substitute price should be adopted for measuring his damages except in an urgent situation.[939] An urgent situation is usually described as the situation where the non-breaching party has to make substitute transactions immediately, for instance, because the subject of the sale might get spoiled quickly.[940] Moreover, both the actual price of the substitute purchase and the price in sub-sale are considered to be more relevant to the non-breaching party's capacity to bargain. They don't increase the non-breaching party's expectation loss as long as a definite price for the goods exists in the market.

In the absence of a certain price within the relevant market, however, other indicators will be considered by the court in order to measure the buyer's loss. An important factor influencing the damage calculation is the buyer's loss of profits caused by breach. This has been confirmed in Article 113 of the CCL: "the amount of compensation for the loss ... shall include the profit obtainable after the performance of the contract". In addition, the Supreme Court's Opinions on Contact Law 2009[941] provides further explanations on

936 For instance, the buyer could prove the causation relationship between the seller's breach and the buyer's loss, which will be discussed in the section 2.3.2.A.

937 Han (韩世远) A 2011, p. 654.

938 Id, p. 654.

939 Wang (王利明) 2003, p. 515.

940 Id.

941 合同指导意见 [Guiding Opinions].

how to measure the non-breaching party's loss of profit. As included in Article 9 of this Opinions, the non-breaching party's loss of profits is normally presented as different categories of losses when the features and the goals of transactions are taken into consideration.[942] For example, if the buyer's purpose of purchasing is to obtain facilities and raw materials for future production, the loss of profit is the buyer's expected profit from producing the assumed products. Or, if the buyer expects to use the goods provided by the contract for carrying out a specific business, his loss from the other party's breach is the potential profits yielded from operating this business, such as the profits from opening a shop in the business premises provided by the contract. Besides, the buyer's re-sale price is also considered to be a significant indicator for his loss if the seller has noticed or should have noticed the existence of the sub-sale.[943] However, what should be noticed is that those indicators only provide an important clue but not a decisive clue for assessing the buyer's expectation loss in the absence of a clear market price for the goods. The role of those indicators in damage assessment is subject to some restrictions.

2.3.2.2. Limits of Damages

Similar to other legal systems, Chinese contract law also has incorporated the limitation rules on damage calculation, including the foreseeability rule, the causation rule, the contributory fault rule,[944] as well as the mitigation rule.[945]

Above all, the seller is only liable for the amount of the loss that is caused by a breach and is within his anticipation at the time of contract formation. This is included in Article 113 of the CCL which states:

> *[T]he amount of compensation...but shall not exceed the sum of the loss that might be caused by a breach of contract and has been anticipated or ought to be anticipated by the breaching party in the making of the contract.*

To be noted, when assessing the causation relationship between the buyer's loss and the seller's breach as well as the seller's capacity to predict, the court is inclined to adopt an objective approach.[946] That is, the court would stand in the position of a neutral third party and ask: whether or not the causation relationship is reasonable; and whether or not the loss is within a general businessman's reasonable estimation.[947] Moreover,

942 合同指导意见 [Guiding Opinions], Article 9.

943 Han (韩世远) A 1999, p. 405.

944 In some literature, it may also be referred to as "contributory negligence".

945 To be noted, in some literature, Article 31of the Interpretation over Contract dispute by the SPC is also regarded as the rule limiting the breaching party's damage. Article 31 states:

> *[w]here a party to the sale and purchase contract gains benefits from the breach by the other party, and the breaching party claims a deduction of such benefits from the compensation for losses, the people's court shall uphold such claim."*
>
> *The rationale of Article 31, however, is the doctrine of "unfair enrichment". In the strict sense, the aim of Article 31 is to prevent the non-breaching party obtain additional gains from breach.*

946 Cui (崔建远) 2010, p. 327.

947 Id.

derived from the causational rule, the breaching party does not have to compensate the other party's losses which are caused by the non-breaching party's own fault instead of his breach. In European law, this is referred to the rule of "contributory fault". Article 131 of the GPCL provides the basic rule of "contributory fault". It holds that "If a victim is also at *fault* for causing the damage, the civil liability of the infringer may be *reduced.*" The rule of "contributory fault" has been re-confirmed by Article 30 of the Interpretation over sales dispute by the SPC in 2012,[948] which holds:

> *[w]here a party to the sale and purchase contract breaches the contract and causes loss to the other party, if the other party's own fault also* contributes to *his loss and the breaching party claims to* reduce *the amount of damages, the people's court shall uphold such a claim.*

Chinese contract law also mentions a situation where both contract parties have failed to perform the contract. This is included in Article 120 of the CCL as:[949]

> *"If both parties breach the contract, they shall bear their respective liabilities accordingly".*

Some might confuse this rule with the contributory fault rule. When the rule of contributory fault applies, the breaching seller is exempted from the liability for those losses contributed by the other party. In contrast, Article 120 applies to the case where both of the contractual parties fail to perform the contract, which may cause loss to each other. In some literature, Article 120 is referred to as "mutual breach" rule.[950] In a strict sense, the rule of "mutual breach" is not a damage limitation rule.[951]

In addition to the foreseeability rule and the contributory rule, the rule of "mitigation" will limit the amount of damages that are available to the non-breaching party as well by imposing a duty to mitigate the loss on this party. Both Article 119 of the CCL and Article 114 of the GPCL state this rule.

> Article 119 of the CCL holds
> *After either party breaches the contract, the other party shall take* appropriate *measures to prevent the increase of the loss; the party that fails to take appropriate preventive measures and thus aggravates the loss may not claim compensation for the* increased part of the loss.
> *The reasonable expenses incurred by the other party in preventing the aggravation of the loss shall be borne by the breaching party.*
> Article 114 GPCL also includes the rule of mitigation, which is indicated as
> *If one party is suffering losses owing to the other party's breach of contract, it shall take* prompt measures *to prevent the losses from increasing; if it does not promptly do so, it shall not have the right to claim compensation for the additional losses.*

948 买卖合同司法解释 [Interpretation over Sales Disputes].

949 A similar provision is Article 132 of the GPCL:
Article 132: If none of the parties are at fault in causing damage, they may share civil liability according to the actual circumstances.

950 Han (韩世远) A 2011, p. 641.

951 Id, p. 642.

As shown, when a breach of contract happens, the non-breaching party should take appropriate and prompt measures in order to mitigate his loss from breach, otherwise, the increased loss suffered by him cannot be compensated. Meanwhile, whether the measure taken by the aggrieved party is appropriate and prompt or not has a great impact on the magnitude of the damages. This refers to the reasonableness test of the mitigating behavior.[952] Since Chinese law hasn't established clear standards for assessing the mitigating behavior of the non-breaching party, the court has great freedom to make the assessment.[953] A buyer's mitigating behavior will be considered to be reasonable if, for instance, he stops further performance after learning the fact of the breach or arranges an alternative purchase in an appropriate way in order to decrease his loss. However, to some extent, the existence of a mitigation rule is inconsistent with the Chinese contract law's attitude towards substitutive performance. As shown in section 2.2.2, Chinese law only has stipulated the so-called "alternative execution" in the civil procedure law as a special measure for promoting the execution of a judgment. Authorization by the court is one pre-condition for the non-breaching party to arrange substitutive transaction and to claim for compensation over the extra cost of substitute purchase. Otherwise, the market rule will normally apply even when the buyer has made a substitutive purchase. According to the mitigation rule, the non-breaching buyer should take reasonable measures to decrease his loss from breach and is entitled to compensation over the additional cost of taking the mitigating measures. In this sense, an aggrieved buyer's substitutive purchase can be justified as proper mitigating behavior. A more preferable approach as proposed by some Chinese legal scholars is to establish the remedy of substitutive performance as the alternative of specific performance.[954]

2.3.3. The Case of Punitive Damages in Sales of Commodity Premises

Expectation damages are the basic damages adopted by the Chinese sales law. However, the Supreme Court's interpretation also elected punitive damages as a supplementary remedy available to the non-breaching party in certain circumstances. By definition, punitive damages refers to "the damages aimed only at punishing the party in breach, and the amount of such damages is usually much higher than the actual loss that has incurred to the aggrieved party."[955] Punitive damages in Chinese Law mostly apply to breaches of contracts which also constitute torts, particularly in the area of consumer

952 In theory, there are two basic ways of making a reasonableness test. On the one hand, it is suggested that the court should consider the external behaviour taken by the non-breaching party in an objective perspective. By this approach, the court should ask whether or not an ordinary business man would take similar measures as that of the aggrieved party. On the other hand, another approach refers to the "subjective approach" which suggests that the court should also consider the subjective intention of the aggrieved party. Accordingly, as long as the non-breaching party can prove that he has tried his best in good faith to mitigate the loss, then his mitigating behaviour is considered reasonable. Han 1999, p. 391.

953 Cui (崔建远) 2010, p. 334.

954 Sun (孙良国) 2009, p. 93–94.

955 Zhang 2006, p. 310. In theory, punitive damages can be stipulated either by the law or by the agreement of the contract parties. Punitive damages in this section only refer to the damages defined by the law. For discussion about party-agreed punitive damages, see section 2.3 of this chapter.

contracts. Article 113 of the CCL opens the window for extending punitive damages in consumer contracts.[956] Moreover, Article 49 of the consumer right protection law,[957] Article 96 of the Food Safety Law[958] as well as Article 47 of the tort liability law[959] have expressly imposed punitive damages on a business' behavior, which is considered to be opportunistic and outrageous, such as fraud, subreption, violation of good faith or other outrageous breaches which cause death or severe damage to others. As is suggested, in consumer contracts where one party always takes an advantageous position over the other party, punishment is necessary for deterring opportunistic and outrageous breach, protecting the rights of the vulnerable buyer as well as facilitating market operation. Accordingly, with regard to those types of outrageous breaches, Chinese law stipulates damages which are much higher than the actual cost born by the consumer buyer. The largest magnitude of damages defined by law amounts to ten times the value paid by the consumer. However, punitive damages in Chinese law are not restricted to consumer contracts, but also play a role in business contracts.

What is also commonly mentioned in relation to punitive damages in China is the damages rules provided by the "Interpretation of the Supreme People's Court on Certain

956 Article 113 (2) CCL:

A business operator who practices fraud in providing commodities or services to consumers shall undertake to compensate for the damage in accordance with the provisions of the Law of the People's Republic of China on the Protection of Consumers' Rights and Interests.

957 "中华人民共和国消费者权益保护法[Law of the People's Republic of China on the Protection of Consumer Rights and Interests]", which was adopted at the Fourth Meeting of the Standing Committee of the Eighth National People's Congress and promulgated by Order No.11 of the President of the People's Republic of China on October 31, 1993. Article 55 states:

Business operators engaged in fraudulent activities in supplying commodities or services shall, on the demand of the consumers, increase the compensations for victims' losses; the increased amount of the compensations shall be three times the price that the consumers should pay for the commodities purchased or services received. If the increased amount is less than 500 RMB, the court shall set the increased amount of the compensation as 500 RMB. Where other laws provide different rules, such rules shall apply.

If business operator knowingly sells defective products or services which cause death or severe harm to the consumer's health, a consumer is entitled to damages of his losses according to Article 49 and Article 51 of this law as well as other laws. In addition, the consumer is entitled to punitive damages up to twice the amount of the losses suffered.

958 中华人民共和国食品安全法 [Regulation on the Implementation of the Food Safety Law of the People's Republic of China] was adopted at the 73rd State Council executive meeting on July 8, 2009 and hereby promulgated, which will enter into effect as of the date of its promulgation. Article 96 states:

A violator of this Law who causes personal, property or other damages shall bear the compensation liability.

Besides claiming damages, a consumer may require the producer, who produces food which does not conform to the food safety standards, or the seller who knowingly sells food which does not conform to the food safety standards, to pay 10 times the money paid.

959 中华人民共和国侵权责任法[The Tort Law of the People's Republic of China], which was adopted at the 12th session of the Standing Committee of the Eleventh National People's Congress on December 26, 2009, is hereby promulgated and shall come into force on July 1, 2010. Article 47 states:

Where a manufacturer or seller knowing any defect of a product continues to manufacture or sell the product and the defect causes a death or any serious damage to the health of another person, the victim shall be entitled to require the corresponding punitive compensation.

Issues Concerning the Application of Law in Trial of Cases Involving Disputes over Contracts on Purchase and Sales of Commodity Premises" (hereinafter Interpretation on Sales of Commodity Premises).[960] As is defined in Article 1 of the Interpretation, it applies to contracts for the sale of real estate between a real-estate enterprise and a buyer.[961] But the interpretation does not specify the scope of the buyer. In legal practice, it is well-accepted that this Interpretation equally applies to the consumer buyer who intends to use the real-estate as his home as well as the business buyers who expect to take the real-estate for business use.[962]

2.3.3.1. The pre-conditions for Awarding Punitive Damages

As explained by the Supreme Court,[963] the goal of the punitive damages rules in real-estate contracts is to punish and deter frauds as well as other illicit breaches in order to completely protect the non-breaching party's expectation benefit and to re-establish credibility among traders in the Chinese real estate market. This is the starting idea of introducing punitive damages into contracts for sales of houses. Accordingly, punitive damages are imposed on six major types of breach that are considered to be outrageous and illicit.[964] Those six types of breach fall into two categories.

960 商品房买卖司法解释 [Interpretation on Sales of Commodity Premises] was adopted at the 1267th Meeting of the Judicial Committee of the Supreme People's Court on 24 March 2003; Effective as of 1 June 2003. The Chinese term of "commodity house or commodity premise (商品房)" originates from the revolution of the Chinese housing system. Before the 1980s, houses in China were allocated to people through distribution while they could not be traded in the market. Since the 1980s, China started to reform the old housing system by allowing individuals and enterprises to purchase houses within the market, just as purchasing other commodities. At the same time, China retained the distributive housing system in certain areas for public use, and houses belonging to those parts are not tradable. The concept of "commodity house" first appeared in an interim regulation about planning the construction of commodity houses (repealed in 2011), which was co-published by the State Development Planning Commission, the Ministry of City and Rural Construction and Environmental Protection as well as the National Bureau of Statistics in 1987. According to this regulation, the concept of commodity houses refers to residential houses, commercial premises as well as other buildings, which are developed and constructed by real estate enterprises and to be sold to other individuals or enterprises. Under the current premise, the concept was kept in use in order to be distinguished from privately built houses and other premises for public use. In this thesis, the terms of house and premises are used instead of commodity house in order to avoid confusion."

961 商品房买卖司法解释 [Interpretation on Sales of Commodity Premises], Article 1 indicates:

> *For the purposes of this Interpretation, "contract on purchase and sale of houses" shall mean the contracts by which a real estate enterprise (hereinafter, "Seller") publicly sells premises that are not yet completed or that are already completed and transfers the ownership of such premises to the buyer who pays for the premises.*

962 For instance, see Great Wall Company v. Ocean Plaza Company, 2004 Sup. People's Ct. Gaz. 10.

963 Guo (郭世辉) 2003.

964 According to Article 1 of the Interpretation, this Interpretation only applies to contracts for sales of houses between a real estate enterprise and a public buyer. In this sense, in the sales of a second-hand house, even if a seller's behaviour falls into the scope of Article 8, Article 9 or Article 14, punitive damages will not be induced.

Article 8 and Article 9 of the Interpretation on Sales of houses stipulate five types of breach that are based on fraud or bad faith ("E Yi Wei Yue").[965] According to Article 8:

> *If any of the following circumstances result in the* frustration *of the purposes of a contract on purchase and sale of commodity premises, the buyer who fails to obtain the premises may request the termination of the contract ...:(1) The Seller, after a contract on purchase and sale of houses is concluded,* mortgages the premises to a third party without informing the buyer *thereof; or (2) The Seller, after a contract on purchase and sale of houses is concluded,* sells *the houses to a third party.*

Article 9 of the Interpretation on Sales of Houses further stipulates three other types of behavior that are punishable:

> *Where any of the following circumstances occur when a Seller concludes a contract on purchase and sale of houses,* rendering the contract invalid, *revoked, or terminated...:(1) The Seller* deliberately conceals *the fact that he has not obtained a house pre-sale permit or provides a false house* pre-sale permit*; (2) The Seller* deliberately conceals *the fact that the houses being sold* have already been mortgaged*; or (3) The Seller* deliberately conceals *the fact that the houses being sold* have already been sold to a third party *or designated as premises for compensation and relocation.*

As shown, if a seller's breach belongs to any category of behavior defined in Article 8 and Article 9, the seller will have to pay damages that are higher than the buyer's actual loss. Article 8 stipulates two types of punishable behavior committed by the seller after the conclusion of the contract for sales of a house, including the behavior of reselling or mortgaging the house to a third party. But Article 8 does not mention the breaching seller's subjective intention. In Chinese literature, the seller's breaches stipulated by Article 8 are commonly referred to as illicit breaches or bad-faith breaches[966] which are not fraudulent or deceptive but have violated the principle of good faith.[967] In addition, according to Article 9, three types of fraudulent acts at the stage of contract formation will be punished as well if the behavior has rendered the sale contract invalid, rescinded or terminated. Punitive damages will be incurred in the circumstances where the seller deliberately hides the truth that he has not obtained a house pre-sale permit[968] or that he

965 Dong (董玉鹏) 2005, p. 58.

966 Li (李胜利) 2006, p. 59.

967 According to Article 68 in the Opinion of the Supreme People's Court on Questions concerning the Implementation of the General Principles of Civil Law of the People's Republic of China (hereinafter Opinion on the GPCL), an act is deemed an act of deceit if one party wilfully misrepresents to, or deliberately conceals from, another party facts and thereby induces the other party to make a mistaken expression of intention. For the English version of the Opinion on the GPCL, see Gray & Zheng 1989, p. 70.

968 Article 45 of the 城市房地产管理法[Urban Real Estate Administration Law of the People's Republic of China] which was adopted by the 8th meeting of the Standing Committee of the 8th National People's Congress on July 5, 1994 and amended in 2007, has provides the conditions for pre-sale of commodity houses.

has already sold or mortgaged the houses to a third party or that the houses are specially designed for compensating the victims of house demolition.[969] However, in the strict sense, the scenario defined in Article 9 refers to "*culpa in contrahendo*",[970] where one party's fraudulent conduct has contributed to the invalidity of a contract. To be noted, a crucial precondition for triggering punitive damages is the fact that the seller's illicit or fraudulent behavior has rendered the sales contract invalid, terminated or rescinded so that the buyer could not obtain the ownership of the houses. In this sense, as long as the buyer is able to obtain the premises ultimately, punitive damages will not be incurred even if the seller has re-sold or mortgaged the house to a third party.[971]

In addition, it is considered that a seller has fraudulently broken the contract if the size of the premises delivered by him is smaller than that agreed in the contract. Article 14 provides the rule to the circumstances where the size of the house delivered by the seller is inconsistent with what is required by the contracts. Article 14 states:

> In the event of inconsistency between the floor area or construction area *of the premises delivered for use by the Seller* and the area specified in the contract *on purchase and sale of*

> Article 45: *An advanced sale of houses must meet the following conditions: (1) All the lease fees of the right of land use have been paid and a land use certificate has been obtained; (2) A construction planning permit has been held; (3) Funds put for construction of the houses for advanced sale have exceeded 25 percent of the total budgetary investment for the project and the construction schedule and date of completion of the project have been set; and (4) An advance sales registration has been made with the real estate administration of the people's government above the county level and a permit of advance sales of house has been obtained...*

A Similar rule can be found in Article 23 of the Regulations on Urban Real Estate Development and Management Control which was promulgated by Decree No. 248 of the State Council of the People's Republic of China on July 20, 1998. The rules on the permit of advance sales of houses are mandatory. Moreover, Article 52 of the CCL provides that contracts that conflict with the mandatory rules in China will be invalid. Therefore, only if a seller has obtained a permit of advance sales according to those laws and regulations, will the sales contracts signed by him be valid. Xiao & Qi (肖丕国 &祁圣友) 2006, p. 44.

969 Demolition might occur if the government has to demolish a certain area of residential houses for the sake of public interest. In the event of demolition, the government will compensate the owner of the residential houses in accordance with the architectural area of the demolished houses and the stipulated standard amount of compensation. For instance, in some situations, a new house will be allocated to the victims as compensation for the demolished house. Those houses designed as premises for compensation or relocation should not be sold in the market.

970 The concept of "*culpa in contrahendo*" goes back to a famous article by Jhering. It describes a situation where a "careless promisor has only himself to blame when he has created for the other party the false appearance of a binding obligation." For instance, a party in the stage of contract formation mistakenly transmits an offer or an acceptance or provides wrong information about the subject of the contract. That behaviour might affect the validity of a contract. The "blameworthy" party should be held liable to "the innocent party who had suffered damages relying on the validity of the contract". Jhering suggested that the law "has to provide for the restoration of the status quo by giving the injured party his 'negative interest' or 'reliance damages'." As a result of the compensation, the innocent party should be restored to the position that he could enjoy as if the contract had not existed. See Kessler & Fine 1964, p. 401–403.

971 For instance, the seller has cancelled the mortgage before the agreed time for performance. Xiao & Qi (肖丕国 &祁圣友) 2006, p. 44.

> *premises, the matter, if agreed upon in the contract, shall be handled in accordance with the contract;* if there is no such agreement *or this agreement is unclear in the contract, the matter shall be handled in accordance with the following principles: ... (2) If the absolute value of the error ratio of the area exceeds* 3% *and the buyer requests the termination of the contract and the return of the purchase price already paid with interest thereon, such a request shall be upheld.* If the buyer agrees to continue the performance of the contract and ... if the actual area of the premises is less than that specified in the contract ...

According to Article 14, punitive damages only apply to the situation where the actual size of the premises delivered by the seller is smaller than that stipulated in the contract and the error ratio[972] has exceeded 3%. However, if the contracting parties have made an agreement on the solutions to the issue of error in area, this agreement prevails. Moreover, another pre-condition for triggering punitive damages according to Article 14 is that the buyer decides to stay in the contract. If the buyer decides to terminate the contractual relationship, what he may obtain is merely the refund of his payment and the interests.[973]

2.3.3.2. The Amount of Punitive Damages

If a seller's behavior is defined as either a fraudulent or illicit breach according to the SPC's Interpretation over sales of premises, the buyer may request compensation which is larger than his actual loss. An important question is the amount of compensation stipulated by Article 8, Article 9 and Article 14. The articles read as follows:

> Article 8: *[T]he buyer who fails to obtain the premises may request the termination of the contract and return of the purchase price already paid with interest thereon and the compensation for losses, and* may also request compensation *by the Seller in* an amount not exceeding one time the purchase payment that has been paid...
> Article 9: *[T]he buyer may request the return of the purchase price already paid with interest thereon and the compensation for losses, and* may also request compensation *by the seller in* an amount not exceeding one time the purchase payment that has been paid...
> Article 14: *[T]he Seller shall return the payment for the portion of the area within an error ratio of 3% or less with interest thereon to the buyer, and the* Seller shall return an amount of double the price for the portion exceeding 3% to the buyer.

In response to a seller's punishable breach, the Interpretation allows Chinese courts to determine the magnitude of damages. In general, punitive damages in the Chinese law of sales of houses are decided on the basis of the actual payment made by the buyer. The aggrieved buyer may request compensation in an amount "not exceeding" 100% of the

972 If the size of the premises according to a sale contract is $100m^2$ and the actual size of the premises delivered by the seller is $97m^2$, then the error ratio is calculated as 100 – 97/100. Liang (梁书文) 2006, p. 130.

973 In any case when the ratio of discrepancy between the delivered area and agreed area has exceeded 3%, the buyer may terminate the contract. However, if the ratio of discrepancy is smaller than 3%, the buyer's request of terminating the contract will not be held.

price that has already been paid by the buyer.[974] In the circumstances where the buyer accepts property that is smaller than what has been agreed by the contract, the amount of damages shall be equal to twice the value of the gap between the delivered house and the agreed one unless the contract parties have stipulated other solutions. However, the buyer's request of punitive damages is subject to the free discretion by the court. As shown in these three articles above, if a seller's behavior falls into the scope of these articles, the buyer may request punitive damages amounting to twice the price that has been paid. But the buyer's request may still be denied by the court or the amount of damages may be modified by the contract parties or the court. For instance, in the case of Great Wall Company v. Ocean Plaza Company which was dealt with by the People's Court of Xicheng District in Beijing in 2004, it was held that the parties' stipulation should prevail over Article 14 of the Interpretation.[975] The Xicheng District court considered that the parties had reached an agreement regarding the issue on area shortage within 5% of the error and this agreement should be respected. As a result, the portion of purchasing price within 5% of the error should be refunded at the unite price stipulated by both parties in the contract, while the portion of purchasing price in excess of 5% of the error should be doubled and refunded by the defendant.

Concerning the aspect of the magnitude of punitive damages, consumer law provides different rules.[976] On the one hand, Chinese consumer law adopts the term "should" rather than "may", which restricts the court's discretion. In the case where business operators engage in fraudulent activities in supplying commodities or services, the amount of damages paid by the business party should be increased and the increased amount will be three times the price that the consumer should pay. In specific cases, if the increased amount is less than 500 RMB, the court will set the increased amount of the compensation at 500 RMB. In this sense, the rules on punitive damages in consumer law are mandatory and hence cannot be modified or denied by the contractual parties or the court.[977] Moreover, the amount of damages is three times the price stipulated by the contract. So the baseline for measuring punitive damages in the light of Chinese consumer law is the contract price rather than the actual price paid by the buyer.

974 In this sense, if a buyer has not made any payment for the commodity premise, he may not ask for punitive damages. Xiao & Qi (肖丕国 &祁圣友) 2006, p. 43.

975 Great Wall Company (the plaintiff)] concluded a 'Contract for the Advance Sale of Foreign-Oriented Premises' with the defendant (Ocean Plaza Company) on 1 March 1999, according to which Great Wall Company purchased the Suite G01 of Ocean Plaza, with a floor area of 105.62 square meters, and the unit price of 2,800 USD per square meter, totalling 295,736 USD… On 22 April 2003, Great Wall Company came to know that the actually measured area of the purchased premise was 28.12 square meters smaller than that stipulated in the contract. The ratio of error in respect of area was 26.6% … Great Wall Company actually paid a total sum of RMB 653,508.8 RMB of excessive purchasing price… In this case, it is proved that the parties have come into an agreement on the error in area. As stipulated by the parties: when the error ratio was less than 5%, the purchase price should be settled according to the premises price stipulated in the contract; when the error ratio was more than 5%, Great Wall Company should have the right to rescind the contract within 15 days. See Great Wall Company v. Ocean Plaza Company, 2004 Sup. People's Ct. Gaz. 10.

976 消费者保护法 [consumer protection law], Article 55.

977 Li (李胜利) 2006, p. 59.

To summarize, punishable breaches according to the Chinese law of sales of houses fall into two categories: bad faith breach and deceits. After the conclusion of a contract, if the seller re-sells or mortgages the premises to a third party and thus frustrates the buyer's expectation, it is inferred that the seller has bad faith.[978] Besides, deceits describe situations when the premises delivered by a seller are inconsistent with that described in the contract, such as the cases in which the property has already been sold to a third party or the actual size of the property is different from that stipulated by the contract. Those two types of breaches are punishable and the baseline for damage calculation is the amount of payment that has been made by the buyer. As shown, the law on sales of commodity house tries to protect the performance interests of the buyer and thus increase the threshold of breach. After the conclusion of a contract, the seller is induced to breach only when the profit of doing so is higher than twice the amount of payment that has been made by the original buyer.

2.4. *Liquidated Damages*

Similar to other legal systems, Chinese Contract Law also allows contract parties to stipulate the damages for breach in advance. Article 112(2) of the GPCL provides that:

> *The parties may specify in a contract that if one party breaches the contract it shall pay the other party* a certain amount of damages; *they may also specify in the contract the* method of assessing the compensation *for any losses resulting from a breach of contract.*

In addition, Article 114(1) of the CCL also states:

> *The parties may stipulate that in case of breach of contract by either party a* certain amount of damages *shall be paid to the other party according to the seriousness of the breach, and may also stipulate the* method for calculating the sum of compensation *for losses caused by the breach of contract.*

These two articles provide the preliminary rules for liquidated damages in China. In these two articles, two types of damages calculation have been indicated. The contracting parties can agree on either a certain amount of damages that should be paid by one party or the method of damage calculation in light of breach. Once an agreement on contract damages exists, the court will enforce this agreement irrespective of the actual loss suffered by the non-breaching party.

In practice, it is inferred that liquidated damages reflect the party's pre-estimation of the potential loss caused by the contract.[979] Chinese law does not require that the amount of liquidated damages should be equal to the magnitude of the loss caused by a breach. Hence, the stipulated amount of damages might be either higher or lower than the actual loss suffered by a non-breaching party. However, the contractual parties' freedom of

978 Dong (董玉鹏) 2005, p. 58.
979 Han (韩世远) A 2011, p. 658.

stipulating contract damages is restricted to some extent. When the difference between the stipulated damages and the actual loss is great, the court or the arbitrator is authorized to revise the amount of damages upon the request of one of the contract parties. This is shown in the second clause of Article 114 in the CCL as:

> *If the stipulated damages for breach of contract are* lower *than* the loss caused by the breach, *the party concerned may apply to a people's court or an arbitration institution for an* increase. *If the stipulated penalty for breach of contract is* excessively higher *than the* loss caused by the breach, *the party concerned may apply to a people's court or an arbitration institution for* an appropriate reduction.

According to Article 114, if the stipulated amount turns out to be lower than the actual loss incurred by a breach, a party may ask the court or the relevant arbitration authority to increase the sum of compensation accordingly. Furthermore, Article 28 of the Supreme Court's Interpretation of the CCL II[980] sets a limit to the extent of increase. According to this article, if one party requests the court or the arbitration institute to increase the sum of damages, the amount of damages after increase should not exceed the actual loss caused by the breach.[981] After the increase, the aggrieved party cannot require any additional compensation for his loss.

Other circumstances where a contract party may ask for a revision of the damages is when the agreed amount of damages turns out to be excessively higher than the actual loss suffered by the non-breaching party. It points directly to the topic of penalty clauses in Chinese law. Article 114 of the CCL takes a cautious attitude towards the reduction of liquidated damages. Firstly, Article 114 sets strict conditions for damage reduction. Article 114 states that a reduction of the liquidated damages is only possible when the amount of stipulated damages is excessively higher than the actual loss caused by the breach and one party to the contract has made a request for a reduction. In other words, the court or the arbitration institute cannot decide to reduce the amount of liquidated damages automatically. Besides, damages that are slightly higher than the aggrieved party's actual loss are allowed in any type of contracts.[982] Then the following question concerns the border between a slightly high amount of damages and an excessively high amount of damages. Article 29(2) in the Supreme Court's Interpretation of the CCL II provides an answer by setting the actual loss caused by a breach as an important but not decisive indicator of the excess.[983] If the stipulated damages are higher than 30% of the actual loss caused by the breach, it is normally considered that this amount of damages

980 合同法司法解释二 [Interpretation over the CCL II].

981 合同法司法解释二 [Interpretation over the CCL II], Article 28.

982 The punitive damages discussed in the section 2.3.3 of this chapter only apply to contracts for sales of commodity premises.

983 合同法司法解释二 [Interpretation over the CCL II], Article 29(2) indicates:

> *Where the parties claim that the liquidated damages agreed upon are too high and require a moderate decrease, the people's court shall, according to the principle of fairness and good faith, based on the actual losses and in light with overall factors such as the performance of the contract, the extent of fault of the parties and anticipated profits thereof, etc., weigh and make a judgment.*

is excessively high. However, when making the assessment, the court should also take into account several other factors, such as to what extent the contract has been performed as well as the contractual parties' expectation.[984] Secondly, the reduction of the liquidated damages should be appropriate according to Article 114(2) of the CCL. With regard to the extent of the reduction, the CCL doesn't provide any further guidance. But in the Supreme Court's Opinions on Contract Cases 2009,[985] the Supreme Court proposed several factors influencing the extent of the reduction, including the loss caused by the breach, the extent to which the contract has been performed, the wrongdoing of the parties concerned, the expected benefits and the relative strength and weakness of the parties' positions when they make the contract, etc. According to the Chinese Supreme

In case the liquidated damages agreed upon exceeds 30% of the losses caused, it may generally be deemed as "excessively higher than the losses caused" as stipulated in Paragraph 2 of Article 114 of Contract Law.

984 Id.

985 合同指导意见 [Guiding Opinions],

Section 2 (5): At the present stage, owing to changes in the domestic macro-economic situation and their effect, quite a lot of breaches arise in the course of civil and commercial contract performance. Regarding any breach penalty which is excessively higher than the loss caused by the breach, or any breach penalty clause which is highly punitive in nature, agreed between the parties in their contracts in each case, the people's courts shall reasonably adjust the amount of breach penalty and fairly resolve the issue of liability for breach of contract in accordance with the content and spirit of the provisions of the second paragraph of Article 114 of the Contract Law and Article 29 of the Interpretation of Several Issues Concerning the Application of the Contract Law of the People's Republic of China (II) of the Supreme People's Court regarding adjustments to excessively high penalty.

(6):In the present business environment which is relatively difficult, where a breach penalty is excessively higher than the loss caused by a relevant breach of contract, pursuant to the principle of integrity and the principle of fairness stated in the Contract Law, [the people's court] shall uphold the principle that breach penalty shall be compensatory in the first place and punitive in the second, reasonably adjust the extent of discretion, and earnestly prevent the parties from agreeing on an excessively high breach penalty by reason of autonomy of will.

(7): In adjusting an excessively high breach penalty pursuant to the second paragraph of Article 114 of the Contract Law, the people's court shall, on the basis of the specific case facts and the loss caused by the breach, and on the principle of fairness and the principle of integrity, make a comprehensive assessment of the extent to which the contract has been performed, the wrongdoing of the parties concerned, the expected benefits, the relative strength and weakness of the parties' positions when they make the contract, and the application, if any, of any pro-forma contract or term, so as to avoid any indiscriminate approach and keep alert against any mechanical performance of judiciary work and the resultant gross injustice.

(8): In order to reduce the litigants' burden and properly resolve disputes over breach penalties, where the breaching party submits a request for adjusting a breach penalty and makes a disclaimer defence by claiming that no contract is formed, that the contract has not taken effect, that the contract is invalid or that no breach of contract has been constituted, the people's court may make an exposition on the issue whether the party concerned needs to make a claim for excessively high breach penalty. The people's court shall correctly determine the burden of proof. Where the breaching party claims the breach penalty to be excessively high, the burden of proof shall be on the breaching party. Where the non-breaching party claims the breach penalty provision to be reasonable, the non-breaching party shall provide corresponding proof. Where a contract is rescinded and the parties claim that the breach penalty clause survives the rescission, the people's court may handle the claim pursuant to the provision of Article 98 of the Contract Law.

Court, many enterprises were experiencing financial difficulties in the late 1990s when the CCL was enacted. In such circumstances, the enforcement of liquidated damages that are excessively high would create more difficulties for the development of Chinese enterprises. A reduction of the liquidated damages was necessary for creating a better economic environment in China at that period. This explains why Chinese Law allows the court to reduce the amount of liquidated damages that are excessively high.[986] In order to solve this problem, Chinese courts function as a regulator of liquidated damages clauses on basis of the principle of fairness and the principle of good faith. Hence in practice, the courts and the arbitration institutes have great freedom in deciding the amount of reduction of the liquidated damages, especially when it is difficult to assess the aggrieved party's actual loss.

Take the case of *Chengdu Bai Shun Shi Ye Co.Ltd. & China Building Technique Group Co., Ltd. (CBTGC)* for example.[987] On Sep 22nd 2008, Bai Shun Co. Ltd (plaintiff) agreed to sell 400 tons of steel to the CBTGC's Southwest branches based on the market price at the time of contract formation. In this contract the parties agreed on a liquidated damages clause that the defendant should pay 5% of the total payment per day if he delayed in making the payment. Until Dec 25th 2008, the total amount of debt owed by the defendant to the plaintiff amounted to 2,354,683.97 RMB with interest of 334,566.75 RMB. In this case, the High court of Si Chuan province considered that the way of damage calculation stipulated by the parties would impose a heavy burden on the defendant since the market price of the steel kept on increasing. It was held that the disparity between the stipulated amount of contract damages and the plaintiff's real loss was extremely great. In light of fairness, the court decided to reduce the amount of liquidated damages by setting it as 1% of the total payment. However, there is no further explanation over the reason why the court chose 1% as the baseline for damage calculation.

As shown, Chinese law in principle has accepted liquidated damages in contracts. But the actual loss caused by the breach is still a significant factor in assessing whether or not the damages stipulated by the contracting parties are appropriate. As long as the discrepancy between the liquidated damages and the aggrieved party's actual loss is considered to be excessively high, the court will have great discretion in modifying the amount of damages.

3. Applicati.on of the Efficient Breach Model in relation to an Unexpected Contingency

After the conclusion of a contract, the parties should perform the contract as has been agreed in their contract. Accordingly, the contract law system in China, which is formed by various general rules of civil law, contract law statutes, and Interpretations as well as other laws, provides various remedy regimes in order to encourage performance of

986 Grobowski & Li 2009.

987 Chengdu Bai Shun Shi Ye Co. Ltd. & China Building Technique Group Co., Ltd. (CBTGC)] (Sichuan High People's Ct. 13 August 2011.

contracts. However, for those contracts involving future performance, the unexpected contingency arising after the formation of the contracts might render performance of the contract non-profitable, costly or even impossible. In the law and economics theory, this refers to the scenario of efficient breach in relation to the increase of the performance cost. Thus it is suggested that contract law should avoid wasteful performance in order to reach an efficient result.

3.1. Unexpected Contingencies in Chinese Law

Similar to other legal systems, Chinese contract law has also incorporated the doctrines of *force majeure*, change of circumstances as well as impossibility and possibility to deal with the scenario of efficient breach concerning unexpected contingencies.

3.1.1. *Force Majeure*

Firstly, Article 153 of the GPCL and Article 117(2) of the CCL defines the term of *force majeure* as objective contingencies that are unforeseeable, unavoidable and insurmountable as following:

> *For the purpose of this Law, "force majeure" means* unforeseeable, unavoidable *and* insurmountable objective conditions. (*Article 153 of the GPCL*)
> *For purposes of this Law, force majeure means any* objective circumstances, *which is* unforeseeable, unavoidable *and* insurmountable. *[Article 117(2) of the CCL]*

In Chinese law, *force majeure* contains three typical categories: natural disasters, social events and government behavior.[988] For instance, if the products stipulated by a contract have been totally destroyed by an earthquake, flood, or volcanic eruption and so performing the original contract turns out to be impossible, the court might treat this type of events as natural disasters and apply the *force majeure* rules. With regard to social events, they usually refer to war, strike, stoppages or restraint of labor which set barriers to performance. The third type of *force majeure* is presented such as legislating behavior, quarantine restrictions or seizure under legal process. However, Chinese courts will not regard every kind of natural disaster or state behavior as *force majeure*, but will go through careful evaluations in specific cases.

In practice, the courts adopt strict criteria when determining whether or not a certain contingency amounts to a *force majeure* event. Firstly, the contingency must be an objective event, independent from the promisor's personal behavior. In this sense, self-

[988] For example, 中华人民共和国海商法[the Maritime Law of the People's Republic of China] which was adopted on November 7 1992, and took effect in 1992 lists some typical events which might be considered to be *force majeure* events in maritime transport. *Force majeure* according to Article 51 contains: 1) Fire, unless caused by the actual fault of the carrier; 2) *Force majeure* and perils, dangers and accidents of the sea or other navigable waters; 3) War or armed conflict; 4) Act of the government or competent authorities, quarantine restrictions or seizure under legal process; 5) Strikes, stoppages or restraint of labour… Han (韩世远) A 2011, p. 373–375.

induced events are precluded from the scope of *force majeure* rules.[989] Secondly, the contingency is unpredictable at the time of the contract conclusion. Usually, if the occurrence or the extent of a *force majeure* event cannot be predicted by an ordinary business man in the same case, this event will be considered to be unpredictable.[990] For example, in a case dealt with by the High Court of Tian Jing, it was held that the No. 9711 storm surge should be treated as a *force majeure* event although it had been forecast by the National Marine Environmental Forecasting Center. In this case, the weather report over the No. 9711 storm was made after the contract had been signed. Therefore, it is considered: although an expert could foresee the storm in advance, it doesn't necessarily mean the contractual party could expect the possibility of the storm at the time of contract formation.[991] In another case involving a flood, the defendant had foreseen the possibility of the flood at the time when he signed the contract. However, the flood was still treated as a *force majeure* event since there was sufficient evidence showing that the actual level of water turned out to be much higher than what had been expected.[992] Thirdly, the contractual parties cannot prevent a *force majeure* contingency or avoid its consequence. Normally, the appearance of this type of event will render the performance of the original contract impossible.

3.1.2. "Change of Circumstances"

Another situation closely relevant to the efficiency of performing a contract is the "change of circumstances". With regard to the concept of "change of circumstances", neither the GPCL nor the CCL has made any illustration.[993] Rather, this terminology was firstly raised by Article 26 of the Supreme Court's Interpretation of the CCL II in 2009 against the background of the global financial crisis in 2008.[994] This article states:

989 Tong (佟柔) 1990, p. 575.

990 Han (韩世远) A 2011, p. 373.

991 Zhhongjitongyong Import and Export Co. Ltd. vs. Tianjin No.2 Port Co. Ltd, 2000 Sup. People's Ct. Gaz. 5.

992 Han (韩世远) A 2011, p. 373.

993 The drafters of the CCL in the beginning did include an article dealing with the case where an unexpected event changed the circumstances of the contract. In the end, this article was considered to have a vague meaning and was deleted from the final version of the CCL. See Zhang & Huang, 2000, p. 439.

994 It was noticed that within a fluctuating market, various adverse changes took place. Accordingly, there is an increasing number of contractual parties seeking to renegotiate or terminate their contract. Faced with a wave of commercial disputes, the SPC considered it should take prompt measures dealing with those adverse changes and promulgated two pieces of interpretations concerning contract law during the year of 2009. These are the Interpretation of the CCL II as well as the Opinions on Contract Cases. Section 1(1) of the Opinions on Contract Case states:

> *At present, because of sharp fluctuations of raw material prices, changes of supply and demand relationships, and insufficiency of working capital, market subjects have a lot of disputes between them. Any requests made by litigation parties for application of the principle of change of circumstances or rescission of contracts shall be examined by the people's court in strict accordance with the principle of fairness and the principle of change of circumstances.*

See also Chan 2011, p. 4–5.

> *Where* material changes *which are* unforeseeable by the parties *at the time of concluding the contract and which are* not caused by force majeure and are not commercial risks *happen to objective conditions after the contract has been concluded, and* specific performance of the contract will be obviously unfair for one party or cannot realize the contractual purposes...

What needs to be specially mentioned is the explanation of "material changes". In Chinese legal theory, it is accepted that a change greatly impacting the market conditions on "a large scale" should be regarded as a material change. In contrast, if a change only affects "a limited number of persons", it is only a small change which will not influence the promisor's obligation to perform.[995] In terms of the consequences, a material change will fundamentally change the conditions for the contract and hence performance of the original contract will lead to an unfair result. In China, the concept of "change of circumstances" derives from the principle of fairness and the principle of good faith. Accordingly, contract parties should "treat each other in a fair manner" with good intention.[996] Once a change leads to a fundamental change in the equilibrium of the contract, the parties should take appropriate measures to deal with their contractual relationship. In legal theory, it is suggested that the international customs on "change of circumstances" should be incorporated into Chinese law in order to assess whether or not a change will alter the equilibrium of a contract.[997] For instance, the official comment to Article 6.2.2 of the UNIDROIT Principles of International Commercial Contracts 1994 (hereinafter UPICC 1994) mentions:[998]

> *"[I]f, however, the performances are capable of precise measurement in monetary terms, an alteration amounting to 50% or more of the cost or the value of the performance is likely to amount to a 'fundamental' alteration."*[999]

In terms of the criterion of "in-equilibrium", it is considered that Chinese judicial practice has followed the rule in the UPICC 1994 by treating 50% as the threshold of a material change.[1000]

A material change of circumstances in Chinese law is distinguished from a commercial risk. As is explained by the Supreme Court in its Opinion on Contract Case[1001], risks inherent to any commercial activity should be treated as normal commercial risks.[1002]

995 Ling 2002, p. 297.
996 Chan 2011, p. 13–14.
997 Chan 2011, p. 14.
998 The Principles of International Commercial Contracts (PICC) has three versions. The fist edition of was published in 1994, and the second, enlarged edition came out in 2004. The newest edition was published in 2010.
999 Article 6.2.2 UPICC 1994ed, p. 147.
1000 Ling 2002, p. 298.
1001 合同指导意见 [Guiding Opinions].
1002 合同指导意见 [Guiding Opinions], Section 1 (3).

Section 1(3):"Commercial risks are risks inherent in any engagement in commercial activities so far as they are not at a level of abnormality, such as changes in supply and demand relationships and the rise or fall of prices."

In the light of commercial risks, they will not render abnormal changes of market conditions, and actors in the market should foresee and assume this type of risk. For example, contracts which involve items such as oil, coking coal, and ferrous metals which are provided on a large scale, are always subject to substantial price fluctuations in the market. Hence price fluctuation of those products in the relevant market will only be considered as a normal commercial risk. Moreover, financial contracts, such as contracts for sales of equity, futures or real estate also belong to high-risk contracts.[1003] The Supreme Court further provides some indicators for material changes of circumstances.[1004] When deciding whether one type of risk amounts to a material change of circumstances, the court shall consider the nature of the transaction and disregard those contracts involving high risk but incurring high profit.[1005]

3.1.3. "Impossibility and Impracticability"

The third rule in relation to efficient breach is the rule of "impossibility and impracticability". Greatly influenced by the UPICC,[1006] the CCL also establishes the rule of "Impossibility and impracticability" in its Article 110. According to this article, where a party fails to perform, or rendered non-conforming performance of, a non-monetary obligation, the other party may require performance, except where: (i) Performance is impossible in law or in fact; (ii) The subject matter of the obligation does not lend itself to enforcement by specific performance or the cost of performance is excessive; (iii) The obligee does not require performance within a reasonable time.

1003 合同指导意见 [Guiding Opinions],Section 1 (2).

1004 Section 1(3) of合同指导意见 [Guiding Opinions] provides:

[I]n determining whether a substantial objective change shall be regarded as a change of circumstances, the people's court shall carefully determine whether the type of risk in question is unforeseeable in the sense of the general public, whether the degree of the risk is far beyond the reasonable expectation of a reasonable man, whether the risk can be guarded against or controlled, and whether the nature of the transaction falls within the general sense of "high risk and high return", and the people's court shall also make its decision in the light of market actualities, and shall distinguish in each case between changes of circumstances and commercial risks.

1005 In the general sense, this type of contract has been given a name of "high risk and high return contract".

1006 Article 7.2.2 of UPICC provides:

Performance of Non-Monetary Obligation: Where a party who owes an obligation other than one to pay money does not perform, the other party may require performance, unless

(a) performance is impossible in law or fact;
(b) performance or, where relevant, enforcement is unreasonably burdensome or expensive;
(c) the party entitled to performance may reasonably obtain performance from another source;
(d) performance is of an exclusively personal character; or
(e) the party entitled to performance does not require performance within a reasonable time after it has, or ought to have, become aware of the non-performance.

The concept of impossibility in Article 110 shares the same definition as that in other legal systems.[1007] Performance could not be required when it is physically impossible or unlawful. To be noted, the CCL directly refers to the "cost of performance" when defining the term of "impracticability". In judicial practice, if the cost of performance to the promisor is not balanced with the benefit of performance to the promisee, strict performance of the original contract will be considered to be excessively costly. In this sense, some scholars consider that Article 110 is partially in line with the doctrine of efficient breach by directly indicating the influence of performance cost on the contract.[1008]

3.2. *Rules within the Efficient Breach Zone*

According to Chinese law, a contract may fall into the zone when performance is rendered impossible (physically or legally) or excessively expensive because of *force majeure* or material change of circumstances or other intervening event. According to the efficient breach theory, a promisor to a contract should not be forced to perform if doing so is inefficient. When dealing with the contract within an efficient breach zone, Chinese law has provided different solutions to different types of intervening events.

As long as a *force majeure* event is recognized, the non-performing party will be discharged from the contract.[1009] This has two meanings. One of the most important meanings of discharging is that the non-breaching party will neither be held liable nor be required to bear any liabilities for breach. Article 107 of the GPCL as well as Article 117(1) of the CCL have confirmed such a result.[1010] Besides exempting a non-performing seller from any liability for breach, discharging also means that the promisor will be excused from any future obligation to perform the original contract in the case of *force majeure*. At this point, Chinese law is consistent with the rules adopted by international customs.[1011] Moreover, Article 94 of the CCL stipulates that: "The parties may terminate a contract if: (i) *force majeure* frustrated the purpose of the contract …" In this sense, *force majeure* constitutes a reason for the parties to terminate their

1007 Article 7.2.2 UPICC; Article 9:102 of the Principles of European Contract Law; Article III.–3:302 of the Draft Common Frame Reference; Article 110 of the Common European Sales Law.

1008 Liu (刘云生) 2000, p. 106.

1009 In Chinese law, *force majeure* is a significant reason for exempting a debtor's duty. Hence, it is also referred to as "Mian Ze Shi You".

1010 GPCL Article 107: Civil liability shall not be borne for failure to perform a contract or damage to a third party if it is caused by *force majeure*, except as otherwise provided by law.
CCL Article 117(1): A party who was unable to perform a contract due to force majeure is exempted from liability in part or in whole in light of the impact of the event of *force majeure*, except otherwise provided by law. Where an event of *force majeure* occurred after the party's delay in performance, it is not exempted from liability.

1011 For instance, Article 7.1.7 of the UPICC provides:
Non-performance by a party is excused if that party proves that the non-performance was due to an impediment beyond its control and that it could not reasonably be expected to have taken the impediment into account at the time of the conclusion of the contract or to have avoided or overcome it or its consequences.

contractual relationship as well. In a case of *force majeure*, each party may terminate the contractual relationship merely by informing the other party.

Force majeure is the only reason for discharging a contract according to Chinese law. Unless non-performance is excused by the rule of *force majeure*, a seller who fails to perform the contract should bear the liability for breach (or take remedial measures). In this sense, the doctrines of impossibility, and impracticability as well as a material change of circumstances will only lead to the result that specific performance might not be obtained by the promisee, but the party who failed to perform the contract should still take corresponding action according to the liability law. An important form of remedy in those cases will be the remedy of damages. As is accepted by the prevailing theory in China, the major goal of the contract remedy system is to fully compensate the aggrieved party's loss.[1012] Hence, in the situation when performance turns out to be impossible or impracticable after the contract formation, the non-performing party has to pay damages amounting to the value of the other's expectation according to Article 112 and Article 113. If the parties have stipulated a liquidated damages clause in their contract, the damage clause should be enforced.

What needs to be specially mentioned are the rules dealing with change of circumstances in Chinese contract law. In this respect, Chinese Law has placed an emphasis on a mechanism based on a third party's adaptation of contracts. In the event of change of circumstances, the court is required to reasonably adjust the allocation of benefits and duties between both parties or terminate the contract.[1013] However, Chinese law also has realized that any alteration of a contract by a third party has a danger of infringing party autonomy and thus has set out some restrictions on the court's power of adaptation. First of all, the Supreme Court's Interpretation of the CCL II requires that any modification or termination of a contract should be pre-conditioned by the contract parties' claim. In another words, the court may not decide to alter a contract merely based on its own discretion without any request from contract parties. In addition to restricting the court's power of starting adaptations of contracts in the case of material change of circumstances, Chinese law also creates three other requirements on the court in relation to the content of adaptations. These have been included in the SPC's Opinion on contract cases.[1014] The first requirement concerns protection of a promisee in the case

1012 There is a famous story stating:" [A debtor failing to perform should] cover [the obligor's] loss, unless [he is] exempted" ("Tian Bu Sun Hai, Mian Ze Chu Wai"). Peng 2005, p. 282.

1013 (合同法司法解释二) [Interpretation over the CCL II], Article 26:
"Where ... and a party files a request for the modification or rescission of the contract with the people's court, the people's court shall decide whether to modify or rescind the contract under the principle of fairness and in light of the actualities of the case.".

1014 合同指导意见 [Guiding Opinions], Section 1(4):
"Regarding the approach to be adopted for criteria adjustment, the people's court shall still follow the principle of giving the priority to abiding party protection as far as possible. In applying the principle of change of circumstances, instead of simply exempting the debtor of its obligations and making the creditor bear the adverse consequences, the people's court shall pay full attention to the balance of interests and adjust the interest relationship between both parties in a fair and reasonable manner... To prevent any disruption which may be caused to the market's normal transaction order by any abuse of the principle of change of circumstances, when applying the said principle to render a judgment, the

of non-performance. It is required that the court should adapt a contract from the perspective of a promisee by optimally protecting the promisee' interests. Secondly, an idea of sustaining the validity of contracts has been indicated in the Opinion. Accordingly, modifying a contract is prior to terminating it. The third requirement derives from a general idea of good faith. It is aware that a material change of contract circumstances may alter the balance of a contract and make it unfair for the promisor to continue performance. Hence the court should carefully re-allocate the benefit between contract parties and try to restore the contract balance in "a fair and reasonable manner". Termination of a contract is allowed only if the change of circumstances has led to a result that the purpose of a contract cannot be realized and the continued existence of the contract does not make any sense. Although the Chinese Supreme Court has indicated the aforementioned restrictions on adaptation of contracts through a series of Interpretations and guiding opinions, Chinese courts in judicial practice still play a patriarchal role in judging the relationship between the contractual parties. As is indicated in section 3.1.2, the rule of change of circumstances derives from the principles of fairness and good faith in Chinese law. In view of the abstract features of "fairness and good faith", the courts are provided with great freedom in giving explanations. Hence, personal bias and the subjective ideas of an individual judge will make a difference to the result of adaptation.[1015]

The Supreme Court in its Opinion on contract cases has also indicated the importance of re-negotiation and mediation.[1016] As is stated by the SPC, the court should first encourage contract parties to solve disputes through re-negotiation with a view to amending their contract when receiving a request by a party to a contract in the case of changes of circumstances. When re-negotiation is unavailable, the court shall take the initiative to mediate the dispute between the contractual parties. Such a statement is derived from the Chinese traditional concept of harmony. For a long time, China has been influenced by Confucianism, one significant idea of which is that harmony is precious and people should avoid conflicts. Moreover, re-negotiation and mediation are considered to be the optimal way of achieving fairness and harmony. Through re-negotiation and cooperation, contract parties will achieve a more preferable result by replacing the original contract with a more fair and reasonable contract. However, the Chinese Supreme court has only made it a suggestion that courts should encourage contract parties to re-negotiate instead of making re-negotiation as an obligation that contract parties should follow. Therefore, in legal practice, even if one party refuses to

people's court shall go through the procedures for examining and verifying changes of circumstances in strict accordance with the requirements under the Notice on Interpretation on Several Issues Concerning the Correct Application of the Contract Law of the People's Republic of China (II)."

1015 According to empirical studies, it is found that when deciding criminal cases, judges in imperial china would only follow formal laws and legal procedures in China. In contrast, judges are more willing to follow the "common sense feeling of justice and equity" to make judgement in civil and commercial cases. Shuzo 1998, p. 13.

1016 合同指导意见 [Guiding Opinions], Section 1 (4):
"[T]he people's court shall in the process of litigation proactively encourage the parties to commence renegotiation with a view to amending their contract. Where the dispute cannot be resolved through re-negotiation, the people's court shall seek to resolve the dispute through mediation."

re-negotiate or breaks off re-negotiation in bad faith, he will not bear any liability according to Chinese law.

The Chinese law's attitude of encouraging re-negotiation or mediation and alternation by the court in the light of change of circumstances, in another aspect seems to indicate the unavailability of specific performance. However, both the Interpretation of the CCL II and the Opinion on Contract Case have not explained whether the party influenced by a material change should keep on performing the contract or not. In judicial practice, some courts insist on the binding ability of the contract even when there is a change of circumstances. For instance, in the case of *Changchun Foreign Economic & Trade Co. Ltd. & Changchun Chaoyang Real Estate Development Co., Ltd,*[1017] it is held that a severe change in the market conditions will not influence the seller's obligation to perform. Hence, the defendant's suspension of performance was considered as a breach of the contract.

4. Economic Analysis

4.1. Will Chinese Law Encourage Efficient Performance and Deter Inefficient Breach?

According to economic theory, contracts that are based on voluntary transactions are efficient since they will bring out mutual benefits to the parties and create economic surplus for both the contractual parties and the society. This provides the preliminary economic justification for contract enforcement. Hence it is considered that contracts should be performed unless performance will decrease the welfare of both of the parties.[1018] The contract remedy system is therefore an important mechanism for encouraging performance and protecting the parties' expectations in transactions.

4.1.1. The Remedy System

After the conclusion of a contract, the direct motivation of performing the contract comes from the profits yielded by this contract. So, in normal cases, the parties have incentives to comply with their agreement voluntarily. In addition, the remedy rules will also change the parties' incentive to perform.

The most direct way of encouraging performance is the remedy of specific performance. The Chinese contract law gives a priority to this remedy. On the one hand, the non-performing party is able to request specific performance when the other party fails to perform. Thus specific performance in Chinese law is also considered to be the major mechanism for realizing the contractual parties' expectation.[1019] Accordingly,

1017 Han (韩世远) A 2011, p. 390.

1018 Barnes 1998, p. 399.

1019 In China, the aggrieved party is given the freedom to choose which types of remedy that he could resort to. As is stated by a vice president of the SPC: "specific performance should not be abandoned no matter under what kind of economic conditions, while whether it is prior to other remedies for breach of contract depends on the will of non-breaching party". Zhu 2005, p. 1149.

some special regimes have been established to ensure the enforcement of specific performance, such as fines and compulsory measures stipulated by the civil procedure law. The direct effect is that large administrative costs are incurred so as to facilitate the enforcement. In addition, substitute performance has been neglected in Chinese law. Hence, even when it is easier for a buyer to make substitute transactions, the buyer may still require specific performance unless the court has made a different decision. As a result, on the one hand, the absence of a substitute performance rule would lead to wasteful performance in the circumstances where an aggrieved party could obtain substitutes from a third party without significant efforts or expense. On the other hand, the risk of market price fluctuation is moved to the seller since the amount of damages paid by the seller is based on a market price no matter how much the aggrieved buyer has actually spent on the substitute. Moreover, the aggrieved buyer is allowed to choose the time for assessing the market price and he may always choose the timing point at which the market price of the goods reaches the highest amount in order to expand the amount of damages received by him. As a result, Chinese rules on damages may make it uncertain for a promisor to predict his liability for breach. In reverse, the aggrieved buyer will bear the risk that a reluctant seller might provide low-quality performance since he does not want to be blocked in an undesirable contract.

In addition to specific performance, monetary damages will also provide a seller with incentives to perform. In this aspect, Chinese law has followed what is commonly accepted in other legislations by selecting expectation damages as the basic damages rule for breach. Moreover, liquidated damages are permitted and widely used in China. Nevertheless, questions arise concerning the Chinese court's power of altering the amount of punitive damages. The court has the power to increase the amount of liquidated damages when they are lower than the non-breaching party's actual loss or decrease the amount when the stipulated damages are excessively higher than the actual loss. However, the court is not better than contract parties in assessing their own benefit and cost from the contract. Some may argue that the court should be given such a power because contract parties are sometimes irrational when drafting the liquidated clauses. Some studies, however, show that liquidated damages are always used in practice as a way of indicating contract parties' true valuations about risks and profits.[1020] For instance, if a liquidated clause defines an amount of damages lower than the expected loss, the difference between the stipulated amount of damages and the actual loss might be outweighed through a lower contract price or other benefits rewarded to a promisee. By the same token, in the cases where a promisor charges a higher price reflecting the risks assumed by him as well as the profit expected by him, a promisee might require higher compensation, or sometimes a penalty. However, rather than helping the contract parties to maximize their welfare, a court's free power to modify the amount of liquidated damages will deter the parties from making correct evaluations of their expected benefits and costs in a transaction. As a result, a promisor is faced with more difficulties in making rational decisions regarding whether or not he should perform the contract. Moreover, regulating the amount of liquidated damages brings a danger of increasing

[1020] Edlin & Schwartz, 2003, p. 36, 37.

the administrative costs since the courts are worse than the contract parties in searching for information and assessing damages. This also creates more possibilities for legal errors. Regarding the damages stipulated by contract parties, the real problem, nevertheless, is that one party might intend to use a liquidated damages clause in order to impose an unreasonable burden and conditions on the other one. For this problem, a better option is to regulate the process of damages stipulation instead of controlling the amount of liquidated damages.

4.1.2. The Mechanism of Punitive Damages in Chinese Law regarding Sales of Houses

In the traditional theory of contract law, the goal of contract damages is to compensate the non-breaching party and to realize his expectation benefit. Accordingly, expectation damages have been established as the common measurement of contract damages but punitive damages have not been available within the contract law.[1021] One important reason, as given by some law and economics literature in the early time, is that punitive damages which are much higher than the non-breaching party's loss will deter efficient breaches that lead to a higher welfare.

Since the middle of the 20th century, however, the evolution of punitive damages in American contract law has made law and economics scholars rethink about the possibility and purpose of imposing punitive damages on breach of contracts. In certain circumstances, it is pointed out that traditional compensatory damages are unable to create effective incentives for a promisor to prevent inefficient breach of the contract. Examples are breaches of fiduciary duties, breaches by public servicing companies, bad

[1021] Punitive damages in the traditional American private law theory are mainly imposed in relation to certain types of tort such as automobile accidents, intentional torts, slander or libel, which are based on the doctrines of deterrence, over-compensation and punishment. As suggested, punitive damages rather than compensatory damages should be awarded by private law only in those four scenarios: 1) there is a chance that an injurer would escape the liability for the harm he has caused (the injurer intentionally commits the injury); or 2) compensatory damages would systematically undercompensate the injured party, or 3) the cost or benefit of the behaviour is socially illicit; or 4) the transaction cost is low that the injurer should be induced to seek a voluntary transfer from the victim...In terms of a proper magnitude of punitive damages, two basic approaches are available for calculating the damages. The first approach refers to "loss internalization", which applies to those categories of misconduct, which might incur larger gains to the injurers than the losses to the victim. It is held that the amount of damages should be equal to "the harm the defendant has caused, multiplied by a factor reflecting the probability of his escaping liability". In this sense, the punitive damages could internalize the loss caused by the offender and generate an appropriate level of deterrence. The social welfare will ultimately increase in this way: If an offensive act incurs higher surplus to the actor than the loss to the victim, the act will not be deterred as long as the offender is willing to fully pay the social cost of his act. However, another approach of "gain elimination" should be taken to those misconducts when the injurer is certain to gain less than the victim's loss and it is easier to measure the victim's total losses. This type of offensive activities should at any time be punished and eliminated since "the society has no interest in permitting it". In this case, the court should adopt the approach of "gain elimination" by making the injurer pay damages amounting to the gain he has obtained, multiplied by the probability that he might take the liability. Polinsky & Shavell 1998, p. 734, p. 936.

faith breaches of insurance contracts or bad faith refusals to pay. Those types of breaches have been given the name of "opportunistic breaches" which do not "increase the size of economic pie" but are aimed to gain "simply by capturing a larger share of the pie at the expense of the non-breaching party". Imposing punitive damages on opportunistic breaches of contract is justified by three major reasons. The first and most important one arises from the under-compensation problem raised by the traditional expectation damages. When an opportunistic breach takes place, the breacher is very likely to have a bad intention to escape his liability of paying damages. Moreover, the possibility of making an opportunistic party fully compensate the other party decreases if he commits the breach intentionally by looking for loopholes in the contract or knowing that the other party will not sue.

In Chinese law, what has been debated a lot concerns the punitive damages incorporated in the law of sales of houses. As is explained in section 2.3.3, the primary goal of punitive damages in this area is to establish trust and commercial order in the real estate market. It seems that the rationale of incorporating punitive damages in Chinese law deviated from that in law and economics theory. The first question arises regarding the scope of punishable breaches according to Chinese law.

In Chinese sales law, it is summarized that the punishable breaches according to Chinese law of sales of commodity premises fall into two categories: bad faith breach and deceits. With regard to the bad faith breach, SPC's Interpretation on Sales of Commodity Premises indicates it contains two types, namely a seller's behavior of re-selling the premises as well as his behavior of mortgaging the premises to a third party after the conclusion of a contract. The amount of punitive damages that a "bad faith" seller should pay will amount to twice the payment made by the buyer. In this sense, the threshold for breaching a contract is increased for the seller. Moreover, In commercial premises, it is difficult to prove that a seller has bad faith when re-selling the premises to a third party for a higher price as long as he is willing to pay sufficient damages to the other party. For this reason, re-selling or mortgaging can hardly be treated as bad faith. In terms of deceits, Article 9 of the interpretation defines three types of behavior leading to the revocation of a contract as punishable deceits and Article 14 defines a size error as the indicator of deceits as well. In terms of the former behavior, they do not refer to breach in the strict sense since the contractual basis is destroyed. Moreover, when a problem of size error occurs, it is sufficient for the traditional compensatory measure to cover the buyer's loss. Especially in commercial cases, professional business buyer would check the quality and quantity of the products that he received and request damages as long as he finds any size error.

4.2. *Will Chinese Law Encourage Efficient Breach?*

In the case where performance of contract turns out to be costly and consumes all the profit yielded by the contract, it is suggested that performance of the contract should be avoided so as to prevent wasteful performance and breach is considered as one efficient approach to achieve this result. However, the Chinese contract remedy system plays a limited role in avoiding inefficient performance. As is indicated in section 2 of this chapter, the contract remedy system in China appears to be performance-orientated.

Although the new CCL has enabled an aggrieved promisee to choose between specific performance and monetary damages, specific performance is still considered to be the ordinary remedy derived from contractual obligations. In this sense, the Chinese contract remedy system is generally not in favour of the theory of efficient breach.

In order to deal with the case where performance is impossible or extremely costly, Chinese law provides special rules including *force majeure*, change of circumstances, impossibility and impracticability. The effect of adopting those rules in Chinese contract law is either to end a contractual relationship or to alter the contract content or merely to decline a promisee's request of specific performance. A basic idea held by Chinese courts is to strictly interpret the pre-conditions for adopting those rules and preserve the validity of a contract rather than simply discharge the non-performing party from the contract.[1022] Moreover, a more desirable approach for Chinese courts to deal with a contract falling into an efficient breach zone is to adapt the contract to the new circumstances or to encourage re-negotiations or mediations.

5. Conclusion

With the establishment of the new contract law system in China, the function of law in the society switched from implementing mandatory state goals into facilitating market activities. In terms of contract remedies, the role of the traditional remedy of specific performance has decreased. Alternatively, the acceptance of compensatory damages by Chinese law offers contract parties more flexibility in handling their on-going relationship. However, the whole system of remedy rules in contract law still works towards encouraging performance of contracts generally. According to the prevailing ideas, contracts have acquired moral values and breaches of contracts are immoral, condemnable and punishable. After the conclusion of a contract, if the conditions for the contract have been altered by unexpected contingencies, the contract parties are encouraged to engage in negotiation and assist each other in good faith. This is inconsistent with the idea of harmonization in Chinese culture. Moreover, courts are given great discretion in handling contractual relationships. Efficient breaches in general have not been accepted within Chinese sales contract law.

[1022] 合同指导意见 [Guiding Opinions], Section1(4).

Chapter 9

A COMPARATIVE LAW AND ECONOMICS ANALYSIS OF EFFICIENT BREACH IN ENGLISH LAW, EU LAW AND CHINESE LAW

In law and economics, the theory of efficient breach arises from a situation where non-performance of a contract, compared to its performance, might produce higher payoffs to the parties after the contract has been concluded. Under this situation, it is assumed that non-performance of the contract is economically more desirable than performance. Breach is one of the approaches to realizing non-performance. In order to achieve non-performance, the party who has to perform (promisor, obligor or seller) could either breach the contract or negotiate with the other party for a release from the contract. If the party contemplating breach is able to take the benefit and the cost of breach into account, he will breach only when the profit of doing so is higher than other choices. His choice of breach is considered to be efficient as long as he could still make profits after paying damages and the damages he pays could put the non-breaching party in as good a position as he could enjoy had the contract been performed.

The central question in this thesis is to what extent the sales law in different legal systems can promote efficient breach and efficiency. Efficiency is the central concept for evaluating remedy rules in different legal systems. In the real world, it is costly for contracting parties to draft perfect contracts ex-ante, which have considered all possible risks, as well as the other party's opportunistic behaviour that might occur after the conclusion of the contract. By the same token, achieving settlements ex-post might also be discouraged by the high negotiation costs. By providing various default rules as well as mandatory rules in relation to different risks, contract law may thus facilitate transactions for instance by filling the contract gap, disambiguating contract terms, motivating efficient behaviour as well as preventing opportunistic behaviour. According to the efficient breach theory, efficient contract rules should enable contracting parties to behave efficiently, for example to only breach a contract when it is efficient to do so but otherwise to take proper measures of performing their contract. This thesis focuses on how different contract law rules shape a seller's incentives to breach efficiently, or more broadly, to take efficient solutions in the situation when strictly performing a sales contract is less efficient than not performing it.

Chapters 5, 6 and 7 of this thesis have indicated the remedy rules of three legal systems as well as how those rules react to the sales contracts that have fallen into the efficient breach zone. Three legal systems are the targets for this comparative study, including English sales law, European Union contract law and Chinese sales law. Among these three legal systems, English law is considered to be a typical example of a common law system and a well-developed legal system under the impact of case law. In contrast, European Union contract law represents the recent achievement of Europeanization of contract law and many rules in it result from a compromise among the contract laws of the Member States. Chinese law, which is basically modern Chinese sales law, stands for a developing contract law system and its establishment has been influenced by other legal systems as well as the political and economic elements in China. This chapter will make a comparative analysis of those three legal systems in order to find out to what extent each law encourages efficient breach and to find out the difference among those legal systems in shaping a seller's incentives to perform, breach or to re-negotiate. A comparison of the remedy systems in the EU, England and China will be provided in section 1. In addition to contract remedies, contract laws may also provide contract parties with specific solutions to the situations where performance of the contract is considered to be inefficient, such as the *force majeure* rule, the hardship rule and the impracticability rule. Section 2 will provide an observation of how different legal systems react to the contracts that fall into the efficient breach zone. The explanations of the differences among the three sales law systems will be given in section 3, and Section 4 will conclude.

1. How does Contract Law Motivate Performance within the Efficient Performance Zone?

Contract remedy rules indicate on the one hand the possible solutions available to an aggrieved party at the time of breach[1023] and on the other hand the consequences that a promisor contemplating breach of contract should face. By indicating the consequences of the breach, remedy rules would shape the contract parties' incentives to perform the contract, which is concluded on the basis of voluntary agreement. A preliminary hypothesis in the traditional efficient breach theory is that contract law could align a promisor's incentive to breach with social welfare by making him provide compensation in the case of breach of contract. Ideally, the compensation should put the aggrieved party in as good a position as that he would enjoy had the contract been performed. In this way, the losses caused by breach to an aggrieved party will be shifted to the breaching party. A rational promisor is motivated to perform a contract, unless he can make a higher profit by breaching it without making the other party worse off. As a result, the total social welfare is increased.[1024] In this sense, the traditional efficient breach theory largely provides a justification for the common law remedy of expectation damages. However, the traditional expectation damage theory in recent times has been challenged more and more because of, for instance, its under-compensatory character or high costs involved in the damage calculation. Instead, the remedy of specific performance is assumed to be better in motivating a promisor to perform as well as protecting a

[1023] Treite 1988, p.2.

[1024] According to the classical theory of deterrence by private law, the optimal damages should be equal to the harm if a strict liability rule applies in order to motivate optimal compliance and precaution. *See* Polinsky & Shavell 1998, p. 878–879.

promisee's performance interest. In this section, rather than merely focusing on the relationship between the efficient breach theory and a simple rule of specific performance or expectation damages, the analysis of efficient breach is considered against a broader background by treating the contract rules of one legal system as an integrated one. The remedy rules in England, the EU as well as China will be compared in order to find out to what extent these three remedy systems are different and similar in motivating contract parties to perform a contract that has been concluded.

1.1. *The Role of Specific Performance*

One of the most obvious divergences among English, EU and Chinese contract law remedy systems is the extent to which each law forces a seller to comply with a contract. Forcing a breacher to perform the contract provides the promisor with a direct incentive to comply with the contract, while it enables the promisee to obtain the benefit related to performance of the contract. Thus specific performance is the most satisfactory form of compensation from the perspective of the promisee in the sense that it gives the promisee exactly what he expected at the time of contract formation.

The central element embodied in the remedy system of English sales law, however, is to compensate a non-breaching party's expectation interest and this indicates a basic difference between the remedy rules in English contract law on the one hand, and EU and Chinese contract law on the other hand. The goal of compensation shapes the remedy system of English sales law in a way that different types of remedy become available to an aggrieved party in order to eliminate the impacts of breach on him and monetary damages are considered as a natural right to the aggrieved party for the fact that he "has not received the performance he bargained for".[1025] Through the evolution of common law cases, England has fostered the rule of monetary damages as the primary contract remedy that "seeks to ensure that the promisee obtains the economic benefit for which he contracted".[1026] In most situations, damages equal to an aggrieved party's expectation from the contract will enable him to afford replacements from a third party in the marketplace and thus realize his expectation. Specific performance, however, has been selected as an equitable remedy, which will be granted merely when a court thinks it is just and necessary to do so. The most important rule setting obstacles to specific performance is the "inadequacy of damages", which means specific performance should be awarded only when the traditional compensatory damages are insufficient for the aggrieved party to obtain a substitute from a third party in the market. In judicial practice, sales of land, unique goods,[1027] negative obligations[1028] or consumer goods are commonly cited as examples where damages are considered to be inadequate.

1025 Kogelenberg 2013, p. 27.
1026 Rowan 2012, p. 52.
1027 Such as a contract for selling works of art.
1028 In England, the court makes a distinction between negative obligations and positive obligations. The concept of positive obligation refers to an obligation to take positive action, such as delivering goods or handing in a document. A mandatory injunction applies to such an obligation by requiring the debtor to take a positive act. In contrast, a prohibitive injunction applies to a negative obligation by prohibiting

In comparison, remedy systems in both EU law and Chinese law are structured on the basis that the performance of a contract is an inherent obligation that results from the contract. In this sense, damages are treated as the secondary remedy for ensuring the enforceability of a contract and as a complementary remedy for specific performance.[1029] Starting from this idea, both EU sales law and Chinese law put forth several categories of remedy measures, which are grounded on the dichotomy between specific performance and expectation damages. Moreover, deriving from the notion of written law,[1030] both EU law and Chinese law have adopted a general article[1031] indicating the application of different types of contract remedies in response to different cases of breach.[1032] The EU measures, including the PECL, the DCFR as well as the CESL, without exception, all indicate an aggrieved party's free choice among the remedies of specific performance, withholding performance, termination of contract, price reduction as well as monetary damages in response to different cases of breach.[1033] Similarly, Chinese contract law enables a non-breaching party to require either specific performance (continuing performance), reparation, replacement and return or monetary compensation. In this sense, both EU law and Chinese law provide fewer obstacles to specific performance than English law. An aggrieved buyer can freely choose the remedy of specific performance according to his preference as long as there is no contrary rule in law (such as the rule of impossibility or impracticability). Moreover, the importance of specific performance has been strengthened by EU contract law in the case where a seller delivers non-conforming goods.[1034] In such a case, a seller has been given the possibility to cure the defect before the buyer requests terminating the contract. The seller must do this before the due time for performance has lapsed unless the defect has rendered the contract fundamentally broken.[1035] Legal studies

the debtor from committing an action. What has been frequently cited as a negative obligation refers to an employee's obligation of non-competition. English courts always hold that monetary damages are insufficient in relation to a negative obligation. *See* Rowan 2012, p. 30; *See also* chapter 7, section 2.2.

1029 Id.

1030 EU contract law measures, such as the DCFR (Draft Common Frame of Reference) or the CESL (Common European Sales Law) are considered to be primary achievements of Europeanization of contract law within the European Union (chapter 6). Those EU contract law measures have been impacted by the tradition of written law, which commonly exists in continental Europe. Chinese contract law, as shown in chapter 8 of this thesis, appears as the result of modernization and implantation of law in china. Chinese legislators had followed the idea of written law by publishing the new code of CCL (Chinese contract law) in 1999.

1031 Article 8:101 PECL; Article III 3:101 DCFR; Article 106 CESL; Article 111 GPCL; Article 107 CCL.

1032 A breach of a contract might appear as a delay of performance, a refusal to perform, a defective performance, or other ways of non-performance. According to EU contract law and Chinese contract law, the application of a remedy measure is closely related to the type of breach in a specific case. Treite 1988, p. 130.

1033 To be noted, an aggrieved buyer's free choice of remedies is subject to some conditions. For example, a buyer cannot choose two or more types of remedies if those remedies conflict with each other. Moreover, a buyer's free choice of remedy is subject to the seller's cure when the contract is for commercial sales.

1034 As shown in chapter 5, a distinction has been made in European law between consumer contracts and commercial contracts. In a consumer contract, a buyer's free choice of remedy is not subject to a seller's right to cure. In this sense, if a seller delivers non-conforming products in consumer contracts, the buyer may either require replacement or repair or choose to terminate the contract immediately.

1035 Article 8:104 PECL; Article III -3:202 DCFR; Article 109 CESL.

even call this possibility a seller's right to cure, which is based on performance-orientation.[1036] If a seller has been given a second chance to perform the contract by curing the problem, this increases the chances of preserving the contract's validity and fully realizing the buyer's performance interest.[1037] Under the impact of European directives,[1038] English law also accepts repair or replacement as the remedy in the case of non-conforming performance. However, this is limited to consumer contracts. Only the consumer buyers may require the seller to "repair or replace" the goods that are not in conformity with the contract.[1039] With regard to commercial contracts, the "inadequacy of damages" rule still prevails. In a case concerning defective goods, the seller may have the opportunity of avoiding paying damages by curing the defect, but he will not be compelled to do so.[1040]

Chinese law carries the idea of performance-orientation even further. Although the new Chinese contract law allows an aggrieved promisee to choose either specific performance or monetary damages in the case of breach, specific performance in legal practice is considered to be the inherent obligation in a contract and the primary remedy for breach of contract.[1041] The reason, as given by Wang (2012) is that specific performance is the best way to realize the promisee's performance interests and enforcement of specific performance avoids the difficulty of damage calculation.[1042] In order to ensure the enforcement of specific performance, Chinese civil procedure law authorizes the courts to carry out specific measures on the breacher upon the request of a creditor, such as seizing his property, forcing him to leave his property or sometimes issuing a fine or criminal liability on him.[1043] In contrast, the English court will not directly take executive measures, but only issue an order of performance at the request of the claimant, such as an order vesting the property in the claimant.[1044] The cost of executing performance will be allocated to the breaching party. Moreover, if continuous supervision by the court is required for executing the specific performance, the English court will reject the claim of specific performance as well.

The possibility of awarding specific performance provides contract parties with a direct incentive to perform the contract that has been concluded. However, in the traditional efficient breach theory, there is always a tension between efficient breach and a court's enforcement of specific performance by "issuing mandatory injunctions or restraining orders".[1045] It is argued that frequently issuing the remedy of specific performance would increase obstacles to breach and incur high enforcement costs. Within the three

1036 Mak 2009, P. 150, 207, 208.

1037 Id, P. 150.

1038 On the implementation of Directive 1999/44/EC of the European Parliament and of the Council of 25 May 1999 on certain aspects of the sale of consumer goods and associated guarantees.

1039 The Sale and Supply of Goods to Consumers Regulations 2002.

1040 Treitel 2012, P. 45.

1041 Wang (王洪亮) 2012 considers that specific performance belongs to the category of contract obligations. An obligation has two meanings. Firstly, the creditor may require the debtor to carry out his obligation. Secondly, if the debtor fails to perform the obligation, the creditor has the right to sue and require the debtor to perform under the threat of state authority. Wang (王洪亮) 2012, p. 105, 107.

1042 Id, p. 107.

1043 民事诉讼法 [CPL], Article 114, Article 224, Article 241, Article 250, Article251, Article 253.

1044 Supreme Court act 1981", section 39.

1045 Perillo 2000, p. 1102.

legal systems, English law provides contract parties with the lowest requirement of specifically performing the contracts. Generally speaking, specific performance in English law is an exceptional remedy, subject to the rule of inadequacy of damages. On the contrary, specific performance in EU law as well as in Chinese law is established as the primary remedy available to the aggrieved party unless the pre-conditions for specific performance are not satisfied. Chinese law particularly emphasizes the importance of specific performance as a vehicle for enforcing the content of the contract that has been concluded.

1.2. The Price for Breach: the Damage Rule

In law and economics theory, specific performance is presented as mandatory injunctions that allocate the contract entitlement to the promisee. In this sense, non-performance can be achieved only if the promisor can obtain permission from the promisee. In contrast, monetary damages denote the price that a breacher should pay for his behavior. Under the remedy of monetary compensation, a promisor is allowed to breach the contract as long as he can compensate the non-breaching party's loss from non-performance.

In English law, damages are generally awarded in the case of breach of contract unless damages are insufficient for compensating the non-breaching party. Therefore, in most cases where the promisee can find substitutes in the market such as for general goods, damages are considered as adequate and always available to the non-breaching party according to English law. However, in EU law as well as in Chinese law, monetary damages are considered to be optional. In theory, the victims can either resort to specific performance or monetary damages in the case of breach of a contract (except for the case of defective delivery). Moreover, damages in both EU law and Chinese law share a characteristic of complementing the function of specific performance. It is stated that damages can still be claimed after the enforcement of specific performance provided that the promisee suffers other losses.[1046] This derives from the idea of performance-orientation, according to which damages and other types of remedies can be accumulated so as to realize the effect as if the contract has been performed. The goal of fully protecting the promisee's performance interest, however, does not mean that all breach-related losses are recoverable. What has been heavily debated is whether non-pecuniary losses should be compensated within the context of contract law. EU law generally allows a non-breaching party to claim for damages covering their non-pecuniary losses caused by the other party's breach.[1047] But the CESL limits non-pecuniary damages in contract to the scope of physical pain and suffering, and excludes other types of non-pecuniary losses such as impairment of the quality of life and loss of joy.[1048] In English law, there are conflicting decisions on this point, although the traditional opinion is that non-pecuniary damages are in principle not available in contracts. In some cases, English judges explicitly held that loss of reputation or loss of

1046 For instance, see Article III.–3:102 DCFR; Article 112 CCL.
1047 See Article 9:501 PECL; Article III.–3:701 (3) DCFR; Article 122 CCL.
1048 Article 2 (c) Prop. CESL.

enjoyment because of breach of a contract is recoverable.[1049] Compared to EU law and English law, Chinese law shows a relatively conservative attitude towards non-pecuniary damages in contract law. In China, a victim who incurs non-pecuniary losses because of the other party's breach of contract can only get compensation via an action in tort.[1050]

In terms of damages measurement, a general rule that has been adopted in all the three contract law systems for measuring contract damages is the rule of expectation damages. The damages paid by the breacher should be able to put the other party to as good a financial status as that he could enjoy had the contract been performed.[1051] More specifically, the rule of market price has been generally accepted without exception by all three legal systems. A buyer's expected loss from the breach is calculated as the difference between the contract price and the current market price of the goods. However, in terms of current market price, English law, EU law and Chinese law choose different time points for making the assessment. This difference is shown in the table 39 as follows:

Table 39. Time for Assessing the Market Price From a Comparative Perspective

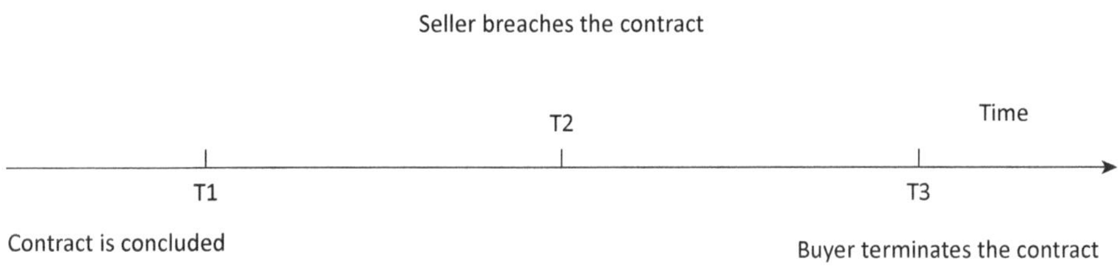

English law generally adopts the breach date (T2) rule[1052] while EU contract law chooses the time when the aggrieved buyer terminates the contract (T3)[1053] for assessing the

1049 E.g. *Wilson v. United Counties Bank Ltd.* [1920] A.C. 102; *Jarvis v Swans Tours Ltd* [1972] EWCA Civ 8; see also Beale 2012, p. 106.

1050 Han (韩世远) A 2011, p. 620; Lu (陆青) 2011, p. 151–154. For more discussion about contract damages in Chinese law, see chapter 8, section 2.3.1.

1051 Article 9: 502 PECL; Article III.–3:702 DCFR; Article 160 CESL; Article 113 CCL.

1052 It is stipulated in section 51(3) of the SGA 1979 that the aggrieved buyer's expected loss is measured as the difference between the contract price and the market price of the goods at the time when they ought to have been delivered or (if no time was fixed) at the time of the refusal to deliver. In the case of non-delivery, the breach date is deemed as the date when the goods ought to be delivered or when the seller refuses to deliver. In the case of delayed performance, the buyer's loss is calculated as the discrepancy between the contract price and the market price of the goods at the time when the goods are actually delivered. However, what needs to be noted is that the breach date rule does not apply to all kinds of breach cases. In practice, the breach date rule is applied quite flexibly and there are exceptions to this rule. For instance, in the case of anticipatory breach, the promisee's losses might be based on the market price of the goods on the date when the good should be delivered. The breach date rule is discussed in more detail in section 2.3.1 of chapter 7.

1053 Article 9:507 PECL; Article III.–3:707 DCFR; Article 165 CESL. The pre-condition for application of the termination rule is that there is a current price for the goods and the buyer hasn't made an alternative purchase after the breach. According to the EU law, the alternative price will make a difference if the buyer has made an alternative contract after the breach. This will be discussed in section 1.3.

current market price. This makes a difference in influencing the parties' acts of breaching or terminating the contract. Making the breach date as the time (T2) for assessing the market price of the goods requires the seller to evaluate the buyer's potential loss from breach at the time of T2. Whether the buyer terminates the contract earlier or later doesn't make any difference in the amount of damages that he can obtain.[1054] In contrast, under the EU rule, the fluctuation of market price will influence the buyer's incentive to terminate the contract earlier or later. If an aggrieved buyer expects that the price of the goods will decrease in the market, then he has an incentive to terminate the contract immediately after the breach (nearly T2) in order to obtain a higher amount of damages. But the buyer will delay the termination (for example, until T3) if he expects that the price of the goods will increase in the market. In this sense, the England's breach date rule helps the seller to take into account the buyer's expected loss when deciding to breach or not; while the termination rule enables the non-breaching buyer to choose the termination time which is most favorable to him. In contrast, Chinese law offers the non-breaching party the greatest flexibility to choose the time for assessing the market price.[1055] In Chinese legal practice, an aggrieved buyer's damages are assessed at the date either when the contract is concluded (T1) or when the seller breaches (T2) or when the contract is terminated or when the buyer makes his damage claim. Thus the buyer is able to choose the day when the market price reaches the climax as the time for damage assessment.

Where there is no current market for assessing the non-breaching's expectation loss or the non-breaching party suffers other consequential losses, the English courts and Chinese courts may take other factors, such as the sub-sale price[1056] or the profits from using the goods, into account as indicators for damage calculation. However, estimation of the aggrieved buyer's damages is subject to several damage limitation rules. For example, in the case where the aggrieved buyer intended to sub-sell the goods to a sub-buyer, the sub-sale price will be considered only when the seller could reasonably expect the existence of the sub-sale price. This refers to the "Hadley rule" or "Foreseeability rule" which has been accepted by all the three legal systems.[1057] That is the breaching party is only liable for the losses that he could foresee at the time of contract formation. As a result, the promisee is motivated to disclose as much information as possible concerning his expected benefit at the stage when the contract is concluded.[1058] Furthermore, England, EU and China all exclude damages for the losses to the extent that the promisee contributed to the non-performance or its effects (the "Contributory loss rule"),[1059] or the

1054 Mackay 2005, p. 216.

1055 The reason for this, as is stated by Chinese scholars, is to offer the non-breaching party the greatest protection. See Han (韩世远) A 2011, p. 655, 656.

1056 A similar indicator is the price for rent. For instance, in the case where the buyer intends to use the goods for rent, the payment for rent from the tenant may also be considered for calculating the buyer's damages.

1057 English law uses the term of "Hadley rule", which was established in the case of Hadley v Baxendale [1854] 9 EX 341. EU law and Chinese law, however, adopt the concept of "Foreseeability rule". See Article 9:503 PECL; Article III.–3:703 DCFR; Article 161 CESL; Article 113 CCL.

1058 Posner 2000, p. 164–169.

1059 Article 9:504 PECL; Article III.–3:704 DCFR; Article 162 CESL; Article 131 GPCL; Article 30 of the Interpretation of Issues Relating to the Interpretation of Law Arising from the Adjudication of Sales

promisee omitted reasonable steps to reduce the loss (the "Mitigation rule"). Through those damages limitation rules, a breacher is only liable for the loss that is foreseen by him and the amount of damages that he has to pay will be limited to the scope of loss that is contributed by his breach. In return, this assists the potential breacher to gather information concerning his expected liability and benefit from breach.

Contract damages denote the price for breach.[1060] According to the efficient breach theory, the desirable damage rules should shape the potential breacher's incentive to behave efficiently. It is required that the damage rules should enable the potential breacher to predict the benefit and the cost of a decision. In theory, by establishing the expectation damages as the damage measures, English, EU, as well as Chinese sales law, all make the breacher internalize the loss caused by the breach. Thus, the party who is contemplating a breach of contract is forced to consider the harm suffered by the other party in the event of breach. Moreover, the damage limitation rules such as the "Foreseeability rule" or the "Mitigation rule" facilitate the potential breacher to predict his potential liability by restricting the compensable losses to those that are certain and foreseeable. On the other hand, the promisee is motivated to disclose relevant information regarding a potential type of loss incurred by non-performance or otherwise to take precautions against such a loss if he prefers non-disclosure.[1061] However, the damages systems in England, the EU and China differ from each other in several aspects. Basically, the remedy of monetary damages plays a different role in different contract law systems. English law holds compensatory damages as the primary remedy available to a non-breaching party, while both EU law and Chinese law treat damages as a complement to specific performance. Moreover, the idea of completely realizing the non-breaching party's performance interest has been absorbed in the detailed rules of EU law and Chinese law, such as the victim-favored rule concerning damage assessment. China in this regard attempts to provide the greatest protection to an aggrieved buyer in a way that it allows the buyer to choose his desirable time point for damage assessment. In contrast, the English damage system in theory offers the potential breacher more certainties in predicting his liability for breach.

1.3. *Substitutive Performance*

Ideally, both specific performance and expectation damages work for the goal of restoring the disappointed promisee to as good a position as he could have enjoyed had the contract been performed.[1062] At first glance, specific performance seems to provide the most satisfactory approach to achieving this goal from the perspective of the promisee because it directly compels the promisor to perform the contract. However, the additional costs

Contracts Disputes 2012 (hereinafter referred to as Interpretation over Sales Disputes).

1060 Cooter 1984, p. 1545. There has been a controversy about whether contract damages are a sanction for wrongdoing or a price of breach. According to Cooter 1984, in most cases, it is a victim's loss rather than a promise breacher's state of mind that influences the court's assessment of expectation damages. In this sense, damages for breach are a price, not a sanction.

1061 Posner 2007, p. 126.

1062 Depoorter & Tontrup 2012, p. 680.

entailed by specific performance render this remedy less welcome by some courts.[1063] On the one hand, frequently imposing specific performance is accused of leading to excessive performance costs or re-negotiation costs. The reason is that the promisor has to perform unless he can obtain the other party's permission through re-negotiation under the default remedy of specific performance.[1064] On the other hand, the costs for executing specific performance are high and a promisor's reluctance to perform in some cases might dilute the quality of performance.[1065] In comparison to specific performance, damages shape the promisor's incentive to perform or breach by setting the price for breach. Thus, the promisor will breach the contract when he earns more than he pays for the breach, but he will stick to the contract if he pays more than he earns. Nevertheless, monetary damages have also been challenged. For example, expectation damages are criticised for incurring additional litigation costs as well as damage-assessment costs. Moreover, it is also argued that systematic under-compensation is created because damages are generally insufficient for fully recovering the aggrieved party's performance interest.[1066]

Realizing both the merits and shortcomings in specific performance and monetary damages, the PECL, the DCFR as well as the CESL which are established as the achievement of the Europeanization of contract law all include substitutive performance as another approach to realizing performance interest.[1067] Accordingly, where an aggrieved party has arranged a substitutive transaction after the breach of the contract, then he is entitled to damages for the difference between the contract price and the price of the substitutive transactions.[1068] If an aggrieved buyer has purchased the goods from an alternative seller for a higher price, estimation of damages can be based on the higher substitutive price instead of the market price. As a result, the promisee is able to enjoy the same efficiency brought out by specific performance without causing high enforcement costs.[1069] It is assumed that substitutive performance shares the merits that specific performance and monetary damages have, but avoids the disadvantages of each remedy.[1070]In order to increase the promisee's incentive to conduct substitutive transactions, DCFR and PECL further indicate that substitutive performance comes before specific performance. The promisee's right of specific performance will be excluded if he could obtain reasonable substitutes from an alternative transaction

1063 Lando & Rose 2004, p. 481–484.

1064 Yorio 1982, p. 1405–08.

1065 Schwartz 1979, p. 277.

1066 For more criticism on expectation damages, see chapter 3 of this thesis.

1067 Article 9:506 PECL; Article III.–3:706 DCFR; Article 164 CESL.

1068 To be noted, in the PECL, the DCFR as well as the CESL, one condition for adopting substitutive price is that the aggrieved promisee has terminated the contract. Moreover, it is required that the substitutive transaction is made in a reasonable time and by a reasonable manner.

1069 Webb 2006, p. 58.

1070 Treitel 1988, P. 47.

"[A] substitute may be brought at the expense of the debtor... In these cases no order to perform is directed to the debtor, but the result from the creditor's point of view is similar. He does not get precisely what he bargained for, but that may be true as well where a decree of specific performance is issued."

without making significant efforts.[1071] The DCFR provides the consequences for the promisee's unreasonably insistence on specific performance when he could obtain substitutes from another resource. Accordingly, the promisor in such a case will lose the right to claim damages for the loss caused by his insistence.

Similar to the concept of substitutive transaction, alternative execution ("Ti Dai Lv Xing") in Chinese civil procedure law (hereinafter CPL) denotes a case where the defendant is required to bear the cost of enforcing the performance by the court or a third party or the plaintiff.[1072] If a promisor fails to perform the acts specified in a judgment and such acts can be accomplished by a third party, the people's court may carry out compulsory execution or authorize a third party to do so and make the promisor bear the cost of performance. But the essential difference between alternative execution in Chinese law and substitutive performance in EU law is the interference of the alternative transaction by courts. In China, the recovery of the price difference between the original contract and alternative transaction is based on the permission for the substitutive execution by the court in the execution procedure.[1073] If an aggrieved party conducts an alternative purchase without the permission of the court before the execution procedure, such an act is subject to the duty to mitigate.[1074] In the case of breach, the non-breaching buyer is required to mitigate his loss by conducting a substitutive purchase consistent with his demands and the fluctuation of the market price.[1075] In legal practice, it is commonly accepted that the substitutive price should be recovered if it does not exceed the market price of the goods.[1076]

The idea of substitutive performance, however, has not been completely accepted by English contract law. In the ordinary course of business, damages based on the "market price" rule are considered to be sufficient for the aggrieved buyer to purchase substitutive goods in the market. In the case of a substitutive transaction, the difference between the substitutive price and the contract price should be deemed to result from the bargaining capacity of the aggrieved promisee rather than directly and naturally from the breach.[1077] Therefore, expectation damages are generally considered to be sufficient for fulfilling an aggrieved party's expectations and the English court might refuse to take the substitutive price as the basis of damage assessment.[1078] However, the exception is the case when there is no current market price for the goods, in which the court might take the substitutive

1071 Article 9:102 (2) d PECL; Article III.-3:302 (5) DCFR.

1072 民事诉讼法 [CPL],Article 252 CPL.

1073 In Chinese legal practice, the plaintiff may request the court to authorize a third party to enforce the judgement or the court in some cases may decide the authorization by itself. Qiao (乔宇) 2011, p. 39.

1074 Zhao (赵刚) 2010, p. 113.

1075 For instance, in the case when the market price of the goods is increasing, the buyer should conduct the substitutive purchase as soon as possible in order to diminish his losses. Zhao 2010, p. 173.

1076 For instance, in the case of Zhong Jian SanJu construction ltd. v. Anhui Province Youbang concrete ltd, the court held that the price of the substitutive transaction between the Zhong Jiang Co. and the third party is recoverable since it is reasonable. The substitutive price in this case is not higher than the current price in the market. See *China Construction Third Engineering Bureau Co. Ltd. vs. Anhui concrete Co. Ltd.*, Hefei High People's Ct. 2007.

1077 SGA 1979, s. 51.

1078 Brown 2001, p. 693; Adams & Macqueen 2010, p. 535. Treitel 2003, p. 928.

price into consideration. Moreover, the issue of substitutive transaction is frequently discussed in relation to the common law rule of mitigation. If an aggrieved buyer has arranged a substitutive transaction, the court might apply the mitigation rule in order to examine whether the substitutive purchase is reasonable or not. If the substitutive transactions are in accordance with the aggrieved party's mitigation duty, the substitutive price might be cited as the basis for damages assessment.[1079]

As indicated in the beginning of this section, substitutive performance enables the aggrieved party to realize his expectation in a cost efficient way by avoiding assessment of damages and enforcement of specific performance. Moreover, since the price difference in the original contract and the alternative contract is recoverable, the risk of price fluctuation in the market is shifted to the potential breacher (the seller). However, in English law where the market price works as the prime facie rule, the aggrieved party (the buyer) has to conduct substitutive transactions according to the market conditions as well as his own demand in order to decrease his loss. In contrast, Chinese law makes the permission by the Chinese court as the pre-condition for awarding the difference between the contract price and substitutive price. This renders it more uncertain for the potential breacher to predict his liability. However, the mitigation rules in English law and Chinese law decrease the practical difference among the three legal systems. If the aggrieved party has made a substitutive transaction in a reasonable way and such a substitutive transaction is necessary for mitigating his loss from the breach, the cost of the substitutive transaction is basically recoverable.

1.4. Party-agreed Remedy

A Party-agreed remedy in legal practice is always presented as a certain amount of damages stipulated by contract parties for breach of the contract. If the party-agreed damages reflect the parties' estimation of the expected loss from the breach, they are referred to as liquidated damages. But on some occasions, the parties will stipulate damages that are much higher than the actual loss from breach through so called penalty clauses.

Without exception, all the three legal systems allow contract parties to stipulate liquidated damages that truly reflect their pre-estimation of the probable loss resulting from the breach at the stage when the contract is concluded.[1080] If a contract contains a liquated damages clause, it in fact permits breach as long as the potential breacher is able to pay the agreed amount of damages. In this sense, liquidated damage clauses prescriptively avoid the uncertainty in the liability for breach and directly indicate the extent to which contract parties' want to make the contract binding. Such clauses are basically enforceable in commercial contract.

1079 An example is the case of *Bacon v Cooper (Metals) Ltd*, where the buyer has no chance but to buy a new rotor for a higher price through a hire purchase contract, otherwise he will suffer larger losses because of the defendant's breach. In this case, the cost of acquiring a new rotor was held recoverable. [1982] 1 All ER 397.

1080 Article 9:509(1) PECL; Article III.–3:712(1) DCFR; Article 112(2) GPCL; Article 114(1) CCL.

England, the EU and China, however, differ from each other in detail when dealing with the case where the estimated damages are higher or lower than the actual loss from the breach. The first issue concerns the laws' attitude towards so-called penalty clauses. In England, the court holds a basic rule that penalty clauses are unenforceable. According to the English courts, a penalty denotes a payment of money stipulated as "in terrorem" of the promisor in order to terrify him to perform the contract. This distinguishes a penalty clause from a normal liquidated damages clause.[1081] In effect, a penalty leads to over-compensation and would leave the promisor exposed to the risk of the promisee's extortionate demands. Hence, it is commonly accepted by the courts that pre-estimated damages are enforceable only when they represent a "genuine" *bona fide* attempt of the parties to estimate the loss caused by the breach in question.[1082] Realizing that a precise estimation is almost impossible, some English courts state that an honest and bona fide estimation is required.[1083] Typically, the stipulated sum will be otherwise considered to be a penalty if for instance it arbitrarily defines a single amount of damages for a number cases of breaches;[1084] or it is "extravagant and unconscionably" disproportionate to the "greatest loss that could conceivably be proved to have followed from the breach";[1085] or it is under a disguised penal bond, etc.[1086] In contrast to English law, Chinese sales law and EU soft law measures only refuse the enforceability of the estimated damages when they appear to be excessively high. A mere disproportion between an agreed sum and the actual loss will not necessarily render the agreed damages un-enforceable unless the disproportion is manifestly excessive. However, disproportion in English law might convey the information of "oppressiveness and procedural unfairness, such as inequality of bargaining power between contract parties".[1087] In respect of "excessive", China has established a objective criterion for this. In Chinese law, the stipulated damage clauses are normally treated as grossly excessive if the sum exceeds 30% of the actual loss suffered by the aggrieved party from the breach.[1088] Such a concrete criterion has not been established in EU law, although EU law also considers the aggrieved party's actual loss as an important factor for deciding whether the agreed damages are excessively high or not. Both the PECL and the DCFR have specially stressed the rules in respect of excessively high damages.[1089] According to them, a damage clause is not enforceable only if it has stipulated an amount of damages that is clearly higher than the actual loss.[1090] But there is no concrete explanation for the "excessiveness". A court has to take some other conditions

1081 Harris, Campbell & Halson 2005, p. 134.

1082 The concept of "genuineness", as established in the case of *Dunlop Pneumatic Tyre Co Ltd v New Garage and Motor Co*, is based on the parties' honest estimation of the potential losses. see [1915] AC 79.

1083 *Dunlop Pneumatic Tyre Co Ltd v New Garage and Motor Co,* [1915] AC 79.

1084 Rowan 2012, p. 185.

1085 [1915] AC 79.

1086 Hatzis 2003, p. 388.

1087 Lord Woolf's speech in the case of Philips Hong Kong Ltd v The AG of Hong Kong, (1993) 61 BLR 41.

1088 合同法司法解释二 [Interpretation over the CCL II], Article 29(2).

1089 Article 9:509(2) PECL; Article III.–3:712(2) DCFR.

1090 As is stated in the comment under Article III.–3:712(2) of the DCFR, the purpose of regulating party-agreed damages is to "control only those stipulations which are abusive in their effect". Comment of the DCFR, p. 978.

into account than the non-breaching party's actual loss from the breach when evaluating a party-agreed damage clause, such as the fact of abusive stipulation in the process of damage negotiation or the element of the loss which has been caused by the promisee's failure to take reasonable steps in mitigation of the loss.[1091]

Another issue that illustrates the divergences among these three legal systems is the role of a court in dealing with the case where the stipulated damages are identified as punitive or excessively large. If the English courts find that a damage clause actually constitutes a penalty clause, the result is that such a clause will be void without affecting the validity of the other parts of the contract. Hence the aggrieved party can only claim for non-liquidated damages directly resulting from the breach. In contrast, both the EU soft law measures and Chinese law empower the courts to reduce the sum of damages in the case where the agreed damages are considered to be grossly excessive. In terms of the extent of the reduction, Chinese law particularly emphasizes that reductions should be adopted by the court upon the request of the parties, in consideration of the promisee's actual loss, the principles of fairness and good faith, the status of the parties, as well as the parties' fault, etc.[1092] However, the EU instruments only use the term of "a reasonable amount" as the guideline for reduction without indicating the meaning of "reasonableness". A third, but not the last element that differs among the three legal systems, is the law's attitude towards the clauses stipulating a sum that is smaller than the non-breaching party's actual loss. In this aspect, both English law and the EU soft law measures have not established particular rules about the validity of the damage clauses. Such kinds of clauses are considered as enforceable, subject to the laws on unfair contract terms. In China, however, the aggrieved party is able to request the court to increase the amount of damages if the stipulated amount turns out to be lower than the actual loss incurred by a breach.

By specifying the damages to be paid in the case of breach, party-agreed damage clauses have the advantages of eliminating the uncertainty of the damages, reducing post-breach transaction costs, avoiding the risk of under-compensation as well as simplifying efficient breach. Such clauses, however, are subject to some legal rules. In general, it seems that EU law and Chinese law are more likely to give contracting parties freedom of stipulating damages for breach by allowing the existence of penalty clauses. Party agreed damages will be unenforceable only when they are substantially excessive and in such a case they are subject to a reduction by the court. The English courts basically hold penalty clauses un-enforceable and will enforce ordinary compensatory damages in disrespect of the damages clauses. However, the extent to which each legal system interferes with damage stipulation is narrowed down by some practical elements. On the one hand, the genuineness test applied in the English courts reduces the chance of applying the laws on penalty. Damages representing the parties' genuine assessment of the probable loss resulting from the breach will be enforced even though the agreed sum might be larger than the actual loss suffered by the non-breaching party. On the other

1091 Id.

1092 In addition to the GPCL and the CCL, the合同指导意见 [Guiding Opinions] has listed the elements to be considered when the courts are decreasing the stipulated amount of damages.

hand, damage stipulation in EU law and Chinese law is restricted through the rules on damages that are excessively high and the court's power to modify such kinds of damages. The court is able to modify the amount of damages if there is a great disparity between the agreed sum of damages and the actual loss from the breach even if the damage stipulation at the time of contract formation seems to be reasonable. In this aspect, Chinese law sets out more restrictions on damage-stipulation than EU law by holding concrete standards for damage assessment by the contracting parties.[1093] It should be noted that damage reduction in Chinese law in practice is largely based on the non-breaching party's actual loss. This actually produces an effect that the liquidated damages would be disregarded and the ordinary compensatory damages would be applied. In addition, the English law's restrictions on the stipulated damages have been eased through the court's recent inclination to uphold the clauses based on commercial negotiation.[1094] In practice, if there is no clear evidence showing the oppressiveness and procedural unfairness, courts are more willing to respect the wishes of the parties.

2. How Does the Law Discourage Wasteful Performance in the Efficient Breach Zone?

A starting point for the story of efficient breach is: what kind of approach should be chosen when some unexpected contingencies have rendered the contract "inefficient". According to economic theory, the law in such circumstances should discourage performance and encourage people to make efficient acts in response to the new conditions on which the contract is based. One type of contingency that has attracted the attention of all the three legal systems arises from the performance cost concern which might alter the equilibrium of a contract. The Contract laws have provided contract parties with specific solutions to the situations where performance of the contract is considered to be inefficient, such as the *force majeure* rule, the hardship rule and the impracticability rule, etc.

2.1. Where is the Boundary?

In economic theory, a contract falls into the efficient breach zone when the net profit from the performance is disproportionate to the profit from the non-performance. The elements that might alter the equilibrium of a contract include a good contingency that

1093 The parties should not stipulate damages that are 30% higher than the actual loss caused by the breach.

1094 In the Philips Hong Kong case, the Privy Council stressed that:

> *"Except possibly in the case of situations where one of the parties to the contract is able to dominate the other as to the choice of the terms of a contract, it will normally be insufficient to establish that a provision is objectionably penal to identify situations where the application of the provision could result in a larger sum being recovered by the injured party than his actual loss... Likewise, the fact that two parties who should be well capable of protecting their commercial interests agreed the allegedly penal provisions suggests that the formula for calculating liquidated damages is unlikely to be oppressive."*

See (1993) 61 BLR 58–9.

increases the net profit from breach as well as a bad contingency that decreases the profit from performance. However, contract parties in real life are unable to explicitly include all the possible changes in the relevant circumstances which may make the contract inefficient. The question left to the law therefore is how to avoid strict performance of the original contract in such circumstances.

In English law, the primary remedy available to an aggrieved party is monetary damages, which sets out a "liability-like" exit rule.[1095] In such a case, the promisor is entitled to the option of buying his way out of the contract for a price defined by an explicit or implicit mutual agreement.[1096] As a result, non-performance of the "inefficient" contract is achieved through the promisor's breach. Although the English jurisdiction has never expressly indicated the story of efficient breach, some cases seem to have implied this idea. For instance, Lord Hoffmann, in the case of Co-operative v Argyll, gave a speech, indicating that contracting parties may breach the contract in the situation when they do not have a "continuing financial interest in performance" any more.[1097] In contrast to English law, both EU law and Chinese allow the aggrieved party to claim for specific performance of the contract at a regular basis. Such a claim in effect sustains the contractual relationship between the parties and provides a safeguard for implementing the given content of a contract. Such an effect is extended to the case where strict performance of the original contract is inefficient unless there are special doctrines limiting the application of specific performance.

The primary doctrines that draw the boundary for the efficient breach zone refer to the rules concerning an "unexpected contingency". Unlike the CISG, both the EU soft law measures and Chinese law use two separate articles depicting this doctrine, including the rule of *force majeure* as well as the rule of change of circumstances. *Force majeure* usually denotes the case where non-performance of the contract will be excused because it has been caused by an impediment beyond the debtor's control and the debtor could not reasonably be expected to have avoided or overcome the impediment or its consequences.[1098] There is a large extent of convergence between EU soft law measures and Chinese law in defining the term *force majeure*. The term *force majeure* in these two legal systems is shaped by three distinctive pre-requisites: the impediment is out of the promisor's risk and control; it must have been unexpected by the promisor when the contract was concluded; the impediment or its consequence is un-avoidable. Typical cases of *force majeure* events are for example an earthquake, war, strike or change of laws. Besides the term *force majeure*, an exceptional or material "change of circumstances" denotes the case where performance of a contract becomes excessively onerous because of an exceptional change of circumstances. Both EU soft law measures and Chinese law have used a separate provision to distinguish this concept from the term of *force*

1095 Medina 2005, p. 58–59.

1096 The price for breach might be stipulated by liquidated clauses, which are based on contract parties' explicit contract. Or the law may also fix the price for breach as for example the expectation damages. In the latter case, such a price is included by a missing term in the contract. Kornhauser 1986, p. 697.

1097 Rowan 2012, p. 53.

1098 Article 8:108 PECL; Article III.–3:104(1) DCFR; Article 88 CESL; Article 153 GPCL; Article 117(2) CCL.

majeure.[1099] Although both *force majeure* and "exceptional change of circumstances" deal with unexpected events arising after the conclusion of the contract and neither of the parties is at fault in causing them but such events have influenced the performance of the contract, differences exist at the extent of the influence. In the case covered by the term of *force majeure*, performance is prevented by "a factual or legal impediment that the debtor cannot overcome by any specific means or efforts".[1100] In contrast, the impediments causing change of circumstances of contracts usually are not insurmountable but merely lead to an effect that performance of a contract becomes onerous.[1101] In addition, attention have been placed on a grey zone where performance merely becomes more onerous but not excessively onerous. According to EU law, the fact that performance becomes onerous because of a mere increase of the performance cost or decrease of the value to be obtained will not affect the promisor's obligation to perform the contract. The rule of "exceptional change of circumstances" applies only when the degree of decrease in the utility of the contract is "excessive"; and as a result performance becomes so burdensome and it would be manifestly unjust to hold the debtor to the obligation.[1102] In this aspect, Chinese law has not addressed any specific pre-requisites for such "a material change of circumstances" in neither the CCL nor the Interpretation over the CCL II.[1103] However, Chinese courts in judicial practice choose to follow the rules in the UNIDROIT Principles of International Commercial Contracts 1994 (hereinafter UPICC) by setting a threshold for distinguishing a "material change".[1104] Accordingly, any alteration amounting to 50% or more of the cost or the value of the performance is commonly treated as a material change of circumstances of the contract. As a result of a material change, it would be unfair to hold the promisor to the contract or the purpose of the contract would have been frustrated so that performance of the contract is meaningless for both of the parties.[1105] In contrast, any less severe alteration will not make any difference in the promisor's obligation to perform the contract. Besides non-material changes, the Chinese Supreme Court stressed that commercial risks born by the promisor, particularly the risk of price fluctuation, should not affect the binding nature of the contractual obligation.[1106]

1099 In EU soft law measures, Article 6:111(2) PECL, Article III.–1:110(2) DCFR as well Article 89(1) CESL define the rule of "change of circumstance". What has been cited in those articles is the term of "exceptional changes of circumstance". In Chinese law, definition of "change of circumstance" has been done by the SPC's 合同法司法解释二 [Interpretation over the CCL II]. Article 26 includes the term of "a material change of circumstance".

1100 Uribe 2011, p. 10.

1101 In practice, drawing a clear line between these concepts is not always easy.

1102 Article III.–1:110(2) DCFR.

1103 合同法司法解释二 [Interpretation over the CCL II], Article 26 only states:

> *"[W]here material changes which are unforeseeable by the parties at the time of concluding the contract and which are not caused by force majeure and are not commercial risks happen to objective conditions after the contract has been concluded, and specific performance of the contract will be obviously unfair for one party or cannot realize the contractual purposes..."*

1104 Article 6.2.2 UPICC.

1105 *See* Han (韩世远) 2014, p. 668–670; *See also* Han (韩强) 2010, p. 61–3. In Chinese law, the fact that performance is unfair and that performance is meaningless will lead to different results. More discussion will be given in Section 2.2.1.

1106 合同法司法解释二 [Interpretation over the CCL II], Article 26.

Besides the doctrines of *force majeure* and "change of circumstances", EU law as well as Chinese law also recognize some occasions where specific performance cannot be required. Firstly, EU law and Chinese law both stipulate that performance cannot be requested if: 1) performance is impossible or has become unlawful; 2) performance would be unreasonably burdensome or expensive. Such cases are frequently referred to as the legal doctrines of "impossibility" and "impracticability". In terms of "unreasonably expensive", CESL further defines it as an unreasonable disproportionality between the burden or expense of performance and the benefit that the buyer would obtain.

English courts, in contrast, seem to avoid using the terms *force majeure* or change of circumstances or impossibility although contract parties in practice frequently use the term *force-majeure* in their contracts for a certain category of contingencies. But English courts do distinguish some occasions where unexpected events arising after the conclusion of the contract may alter the efficiency of contracts. What is commonly cited in English legal practice is the term frustration, which in fact solves the problem that would be dealt with by the doctrine of *force majeure* in a way that it discharges the promisor from his non-performance.[1107] The English law concept of "frustration" depicts the case where the supervening contingency has rendered a contract "radically" different from what has been contemplated by the parties.[1108] The contract in fact was physically or legally impossible to perform or performance of the contract is actually pointless.[1109] In this sense, the concept of frustration has exceeded the usual meaning of "excessive onerosity", "changed circumstances", "impracticability" or other similar expressions used in EU soft law measures or in Chinese law. In practice, frustration of contract takes place for example when the specific goods agreed in the contract have expired and such a risk is not assumed by the seller[1110] or when a change of the law has rendered performance of the contract illegal.[1111] When applying the doctrine of frustration, the courts have to ask whether the foundation of the contract has been altered or the impediment merely amounts to general hardship in performance.[1112] The border between a "frustrated" contract and general hardship in performance of the contract is whether or not the existence of the contract could achieve the expected goal of the contracting parties. If the performance of a contract has been rendered pointless for achieving the purpose of the contract, the doctrine of "frustration" might be adopted and the parties will be discharged from the contract.[1113] Typical contingencies that frustrate contracts are perishing of specific goods beyond both parties' control and changes of law which turn a contract into

1107 McKendrick 2013, p. 7.

1108 The classical definition of "frustration of contracts" was made in the case of Davis Contractors Ltd v Fareham U.D.C. [1956] AC 696, 728–729. For the full statement, please see section 3.1.1 in chapter 7.

1109 Hondius & Grigoleit 2011, p. 7.

1110 See SGA 1979, S7.

1111 See Uribe 2011, p. 140–142; See also Whincup 1992, p. 235. (In the early stage, English court only accepted the rule of "frustration of contracts" in the case where the intervening event had rendered performance impossible, such as the expiration of the goods. But since the end of the 18th century, this rule was also applied to the cases where performance was rendered illegal by the change of law. The classical case concerning the illegality of performance is Hadley v Clarke [1799] 101 E.R. 1377.).

1112 Uribe 2011, p. 139.

1113 Goode 2004, p. 135–136.

an illegal one. However, the courts will refuse to discharge the contract merely because performance is excessively onerous or impossible.[1114] An event rendering the performance more onerous or impossible is typically referred to as "hardship", which merely constitutes a good reason for the court to reject the plaintiff's request of specific performance. However, the degree of hardship necessary for such a rejection is high although the English courts have never articulated a specific and general definition for such a hardship.[1115] When deciding whether specific performance should be rejected or not, the courts usually take into account the elements that will alter the balance in the parties' respective obligation, such as the financial burden that performance will impose on the breacher as well as the benefit that performance will confer on the non-breaching party. If the burden of specific performance is wholly out of proportion to the benefit that performance will grant to the promisee, the courts are very likely to reject the enforcement of the specific performance.[1116] Sometimes, the court may also consider the adverse effect that performance creates on the defaulting party or on the third party. For instance, if the promisor is bankrupt, the promisee's request of specific performance (transfer of a real property) might be declined so as to avoid undermining other creditors' rights to the promisor's liquidated property.[1117] But a mere financial difficulty suffered by the defaulting party will not create obstacles to the awarding of specific performance.[1118]

In brief, there is some extent of convergence between English law, EU law and Chinese law, particularly concerning the awareness that unexpected contingencies arising after the conclusion of the contract may alter the efficiency of contracts. Thus, these three legal systems to some extent all establish the rules discharging the promisor from the obligation to perform. Moreover, with regard to the content of specific rules concerning unexpected events, there is some degree of overlap among these legal systems as well. For instance, the content of the rules about change of circumstances in Chinese law results from mixing the EU rules concerning change of circumstances and the English rules of frustration. However, differences exist among these three legal systems as to how to draw the border between the zone in which performance is encouraged and the zone in which non-performance is permitted. In English law, non-performance is achieved through two types of mechanisms. On the one hand, the remedy system primarily functions as exit rules for the promisor who is willing to pay damages for the breach.[1119] On the other hand, the doctrines of contract frustration as well as hardship set out special rules restricting the application of specific performance. In contrast, the remedy systems in both EU soft law measures and Chinese law function as the safeguard for performance.

1114 Denny, Mott & Dickson Ltd. v. James B. Fraser & Co. Ltd. [1944] A.C 265, at 274–275. (Lord Radcliffe emphasized that

> *"[I]t is not hardship or inconvenience or material loss itself which calls the principle of frustration into play. There must be as well such a change in the significance of the obligation that the thing undertaken would, if performed, be a different thing from that contracted for".).*

1115 Rowan 2012, p. 29–30.

1116 Wedgwood v Adams (1843) 49 E.R. 958; *see also* Harris, Campbell & Halson 2006, p. 222.

1117 There are some exceptions as well. For instance, if the promisor has mortgaged the property to the promisee, the promisee has a priority to obtain the property.

1118 See Francis v. Cowcliffe (1976) 33 P & CR 368 (ch).

1119 Medina 2005, p. 57.

In such cases, special doctrines including *force majeure*, change of circumstances as well as impossibility and impracticability shape the zone in which non-performance is allowed. It should be noted that, although EU law still includes the traditional principle of fairness as an important criterion for triggering those doctrines, it introduces criteria on the basis of economic doctrines as well. When addressing those doctrines, EU soft law particularly takes into account the elements that are essential to the equilibrium of the contract, including the cost of performance, the expected value of the counter-performance as well as the risk allocation between the contract parties. Unexpected contingencies that have changed the equilibrium of the contract will render the contract inefficient. However, Chinese law includes more opaqueness and uncertainties when addressing those doctrines.

2.2. *Ways to Achieve Non-Performance*

After the contract falls into an efficient breach zone, England, EU and China to some extent all provide specific approaches for the parties to achieve non-performance of a contract, although there are several divergences existing in the specific ways adopted by each system. The first approach refers to directly declining the promisee's request of specific performance of the contract (section 2.2.1). This particularly results from the cases of *force majeure* and the English principle of frustration where the contracting parties will be discharged from the contract. Moreover, both EU soft law measures and Chinese law have addressed two other approaches to achieving non-performance of the original contract, in relation to the negotiation rule and modification of the contract by a third party (section 2.2.2 and section 2.2.3).

2.2.1. Refusal of Granting Specific Performance & Award of Damages

The most direct way to achieve non-performance of an inefficient contract is to decline the promisee's performance claim if performance of the contract would be less efficient than it was at the time of contracting.

First of all, English law usually directly refuses to implement specific performance in the case where compensatory damages are sufficient for the promisee to obtain an equivalent from the market, particularly when the subject of the contract is general goods.[1120] In contrast, where damages are insufficient to fully compensate the non-

[1120] To be noted, "sufficiency of damages" does not definitely lead to a result that specific performance will be rejected by English courts. As is noted in section 2.2 in chapter 7, specific performance in English law is a discretionary remedy and courts have a wide discretion to determine whether such a remedy should be granted. In the process of decision-making, the court will also consider other factors such as the insolvency of the breacher in addition to the "sufficiency test". Moreover, the distinction between a unique good and a general good does not lead to an absolute difference in the court's deciding about whether or not specific performance should be awarded as well. For instance, sometimes even when the aggrieved buyer has to take enormous efforts to obtain a substitute, the court may still refuse to award specific performance. By the same token, the court will award specific performance even if the subject of the contract is general goods, as long as she thinks that the compensatory damages are inadequate

breaching party such as in the cases concerning sales of lands or specific goods, specific performance will be awarded. Interestingly, the PECL and the DCFR both exclude the promisee's request for specific performance of the contract in the case where he could obtain substitutes from a third party without significant effort or expense.[1121] The goal of excluding specific performance in such a situation is to discourage the aggrieved promisee from abusing remedy, encourage him to conduct substitutive transactions and diminish the loss caused by the breach in a less costly way.[1122] The result of stipulating such a rule is consistent with the policy of mitigation as well. Whereas, if the aggrieved party is able to expect the remedy of specific performance in any case, he will not take any steps to conduct cover purchase and mitigate his loss, even when finding substitutes is possible.[1123] In this sense, the rule of restricting specific performance when substitutes are available to the aggrieved party has challenged the distinctive rule of equitable remedy in the English law that specific performance is treated as an exceptional remedy.

What has been accepted in all the three legal systems is that declining a promisee's claim for specific performance is an effect naturally resulting from applying either the rule of *force majeure* or frustration since in such cases the contract will be brought to an end and the contracting parties will be discharged from future performance.[1124] In most cases where *force majeure* or frustration applies, performance has been rendered impossible or illegal by supervening events that occur without the fault of the contract parties. As a result, the contract is brought to an end forthwith and automatically.[1125] This is different from the cases when the rule of excessive change of circumstances applies in EU law or Chinese law where the parties are encouraged to enter re-negotiations to seek a termination or modification of the contract.[1126] In terms of whether specific performance is available or not under an exceptional change of circumstances, neither EU law nor Chinese law provides an explicit answer. However, the negotiation rules adopted by EU soft law measures indirectly imply that the aggrieved party is discouraged from directly claiming for specific performance of the contract if the circumstance has changed excessively.[1127] Moreover, it is inferred from a general principle of good faith in EU law that a promisee should not unreasonably require performance of the contract from the promisor who is placed in an advantageous position by the exceptional change of the

and specific performance is necessary. For instance see *Société des Industries Métallurgiques SA v Bronx Engineering Co Ltd* [1975] 1 Lloyd's Rep 465 (CA), where the seller failed to supply a large machine which is considered to be specific and finding a substitute is extremely costly; see also Bridge 2010, p. 1115.

1121 Article 9:102(2) d PECL; Article III.-3:302 DCFR.

1122 DCFR, p. 854. If the aggrieved party insists on specific performance when he could obtain substitutes without excessive expense, there is a danger that his loss from breach will increase. DCFR also exclude the aggrieved party's right to damages for the increased loss caused by his unreasonable insistence of specific performance.

1123 Harris, Campbell & Halson 2006, p. 223.

1124 Whincup 1992, p. 235.

1125 *See* Firoozmand 2007, p. 177; *See also* Kessedjian 2005, p. 427; *see also* Han (韩世远) 2014, p. 660.

1126 More comparisons will be made in section 2.2.2.

1127 Article 6:111(2) (3) PECL; Article III.-1:110(2) DCFR; Article 89(2) CESL.

circumstances.[1128] To this question, Chinese courts provide a different answer through some judicial decisions. As shown in those decisions, the promisor's refusal of specific performance is treated as a breach of the contract even if the circumstances of contract have been materially changed.[1129] In this sense, Chinese law actually still insists on the binding ability of the contract and allows the promisee to request specific performance of the contract.[1130] In English law, the performance of a contract basically will not be excused by an adverse change of circumstances. Nevertheless, English courts do recognize a situation where compensatory damages are inadequate but specific performance of the contract will cause undue hardship to the defaulting promisor. In such a case, it is very likely that specific performance will be refused.[1131]

The logic that specific performance will be blocked when it is more costly than non-performance, is also plausible in cases, where continued supervision or personal work is involved as well as in the case where performance is impracticable. Refusal of specific performance in contracts involving continued supervision is generally accepted in English courts. This usually points to the cases where there is a requirement of continuous or regular acts from the promisor by the courts, such as relational contracts.[1132] In contrast, refusal of specific performance in personal work contracts (sale of goods to be produced) as well as in contracts where performance is impracticable has been confirmed in all the three legal systems.[1133] In those cases, the costs of engaging in supervising the

1128 *See* Article III.-1:103 DCFR; Article 1:201 PECL; Article 2 CESL. Only the DCFR has stated the consequences of breaching the obligation of good faith. In contrast, the PECL and the CESL only express the existence of a general principle of good faith, but do not explicitly indicate the result from a party's violation of good faith.

1129 *Changchun Foreign Economic and Trade Co. Ltd. Vs. Chaoyang Real Estate Development Co. Ltd*; See also Han (韩世远) A 2011, p. 390.

1130 In Chinese theory, however, some scholars suggest providing the promisor with a right to defend against specific performance if the circumstances of a contract have materially changed. *See e.g.* Han (韩世远) 2014, p. 661.

1131 Rowan 2012, p. 29.

1132 In English law, another typical example of contracts for which continuous acts are necessary is a construction contract. In terms of a sales contract, a requirement of continuous or regular acts might exist for instance if the contract stipulates that the seller has to make continuous delivery of goods.

1133 *See* Harris, Campbell & Halson 2006, p. 182, 222; *See also* Article 9:102(2) PECL, which provides:
(2) Specific performance cannot, however, be obtained where: (a) performance would be unlawful or impossible; or (b) performance would cause the debtor unreasonable effort or expense; or (c) the performance consists of the provision of services or work of a personal character or depends upon a personal relationship, or (d) the aggrieved party may reasonably obtain performance from another source.
(3) The aggrieved party will lose the right to specific performance if it fails to seek it within a reasonable time after it has or ought to have become aware of the non-performance.
See also Article III.-3:302 DCFR, which provides:
(3) Specific performance cannot, however, be enforced where: (a) performance would be unlawful or impossible; (b) performance would be unreasonably burdensome or expensive; or (c) performance would be of such a personal character that it would be unreasonable to enforce it.
(4) The creditor loses the right to enforce specific performance if performance is not requested within a reasonable time after the creditor has become, or could reasonably be expected to have become, aware of the non-performance.
(5) The creditor cannot recover damages for loss or a stipulated payment for non- performance to the extent that the creditor has increased the loss or the amount of the payment by insisting unreasonably

promisor's performance or in forcing an unwilling promisor to maintain the contractual relationship and to carry out the performing act have outweighed the benefit to be obtained from specific performance of the contract.[1134] In addition, a claim for specific performance will be rejected if there is any unreasonable delay in making the claims. The PECL, the DCFR as well as the CCL all stipulate that an aggrieved party will lose the right to specific performance if he fails to seek it within a reasonable time after he has, or ought to have, become aware of the non-performance.[1135] Table 40 summarizes the cases where specific performance will or will not be awarded.

Table 40. Award of Specific Performance from a Comparative Perspective

	England		**EU**		**China**
1. Land	Inadequacy of compensation	*Yes*	*Yes*		*Yes*
2. Specific & Certain goods		*Yes*	*Yes*		*Yes*
3. Adequacy of compensation (General goods)	*No* (except when damages are insufficient)		**DCFR/PECL**	*No*	*Yes*
			CESL	*Yes*	
4. *Force majeure*	*?*[114]		*No (discharge)*		*No*
5. Frustration	*No (discharge)*		*?*		*No*
6. Excessive change of circumstances	*No*		*No*		*Maybe*
7. Hardship	*No*		*No*		*Yes*
8. Impossibility	*No*		*No*		*No*
9. Impracticability	*No*		*No*		*No*
10. Personal work (Goods to be produced)	*No*		*No*		*No*
11. Continuous supervision by courts	*No*		*Yes* (*Service: NO*)		*Yes*
12. Fail to request on time	*No*		*No*		*No*

As shown in the table, the differences between English law, EU law and Chinese law in restricting specific performance are more of theoretical than practical significance. In

on specific performance in circumstances where the creditor could have made a reasonable substitute transaction without significant effort or expense.
See also Article 110(2) CCL, which provides:
[T]he other party may request to perform it except under any of the following circumstances:
(1) it is unable to be performed in law or in fact;
(2)the subject matter of the obligation is unfit for compulsory performance or the performance expenses are excessively high;(3) the obligee does not require performance within a reasonable time.

1134 Refusing specific performance in contracts involving personal service derives traditionally from the concern of personal liberty and public policy.

1135 Article 110 CCL.

1136 The eroteme "?" represents the fact that the English courts do not use the concept of "force majeure" directly in judicial trails. Similar inference can be made in row 5 of table 40 and in table 41.

general, the courts in all the three legal systems will reject to award specific performance if performance of a contract becomes impossible or extremely costly because of a great disproportion between the cost and the benefit of the performance. To be more specific, the refusal of specific performance of contracts by English law is largely based on a comparison between the cost of performance to the promisor and the value of performance to the counterparty. Non-strict-performance of an inefficient contract is allowed to the extent that the promisor is able to pay monetary equivalence to the value of performance or the contract itself has been frustrated because of being unbalanced. A similar result of excluding specific performance from sales contracts involving replaceable goods is achievable in EU law (except CESL). By comparison, it is found that Chinese law sets the least restrictions to specific performance of contracts and imposes the highest degree of demand for performance of a contract on a promisor. Performance might be required even when there is a material change of circumstances and an excessive burden in performance. However, in some recent cases, Chinese courts show more willingness to reject specific performance in such cases by resorting to the rule of "impracticability".[1137]

After a contract falls into the inefficient performance zone (or efficient breach zone), efficiency is achieved on the one hand by rejecting the promisee's claim for specific performance of the contract; and on the other hand, by restoring the imbalance of benefit and burden between the contract parties. In all the three legal systems, damages are available to an aggrieved party who is unable to claim specific performance unless the contract has been discharged because of frustration[1138] or *force majeure*. In addition, sometimes an aggrieved person may also be entitled to other types of payment that offset his loss caused by non-performance, such as a price reduction or damages for his reliance loss. Hence, the aggrieved party will be restored to the position that he would enjoy as if the contract had been performed. A comparison of whether damages are available to an aggrieved party in an inefficient contract is shown in table 41.

Table 41. Award of Damages in Comparative Law

	England	EU	China
Frustration	*No*	*?*	*Maybe*
Force majeure	*?*	*No*	*No*
Hardship/ Change of circumstances	*Yes*	*Yes (Conditional)*	*Maybe*
Impossibility/Impracticability/Others (not amounting to *force majeure*)	*Yes*	*Yes*	*Yes*

1137 Xinyu Gongsi Su Feng Yumei Shangpu Maimai Hetong Jiufen An, (新宇公司诉冯玉梅商铺买卖合同纠纷案) [Xinyu Company v. Feng Yumei], 2006 Sup. People's Ct. Gaz. 6, (Nanjing Interm. People's Ct. 9 June 2004) (China). In this case, Feng bought one suite on the 2nd floor of a building owned by Xinyu company as her business premises. Before the contract was finished, the company decided to close the building and re-construct the whole building. The company proposed to terminate the sales contract with Feng and pay monetary damages. However, Feng insisted on specific performance of the contract and refused to return the suite. In the end, the courts resorted to Article 110 of the CCL by holding specific performance of the sales contract impracticable. Feng's request was declined.

1138 The Law Reform (Frustrated Contract) Act 1943, s.1(2), (3).

As shown in table 3, an interesting distinction in Chinese law is the possibility of damages in the case where the purpose of a contract has been frustrated. In Chinese law, frustration of contract purpose is treated as one prerequisite for triggering the rule of material change of circumstances. According to Article 26 of the Interpretation over the CCL II, if a material change of circumstances arises after the conclusion of the contract and leads to a result that the contract purpose cannot be realized through performance, the parties may request termination of the contract.[1139] In such a case, the performance of the contract is actually pointless and the continued existence of the contract does not have any practical meaning.[1140] However, the concept of frustration in English law exceeds the degree of frustration in the context of Chinese doctrine of change of circumstance. It is held by English courts that the doctrine of frustration should be strictly interpreted, kept within a very narrow scope and ought not to be extended because the effect of this doctrine is to "kill the contract and discharge the parties from any further liability".[1141] On the one hand, frustration in English law follows a strict interpretation which requires that the frustrating event which is beyond both the parties' foresight and control has completely reduced the value of the contract.[1142] Although there is no unified standard for defining frustration, it has been established in some English cases that an excessive burden in performance would not frustrate a contract.[1143] In contrast, although different Chinese courts have conflicting ideas when deciding whether or not contracts have been frustrated,[1144] it is generally accepted that an excessive burden may render a contract frustrated as long as the performance has been rendered pointless.[1145] On the other hand, frustration in China only leads to the result that the parties may require the court to terminate the contract, while frustration in English law leads to a result that the contract will be discharged automatically. Another difference among these three systems is the possibility of monetary damages within the efficient breach zone when there is a significant change of circumstances. In EU law, damages will be awarded conditionally, depending on the result of a renegotiation between the contract parties or a decision of terminating or modifying the contract by the court.

1139 合同法司法解释II [Interpretation over the CCL II], Article 26.

1140 Li Mou v. Huang Xiaoling, Zhejiang Ningbo Dist. People's Ct. 22 December 2011. In this case, the government of Ningbo issued a policy of restricting the quantity of houses to be purchased and such a policy was considered to have completely changed the circumstances of the sales between Li and Huang. In such a case, the plaintiff who had already owned two suites of a house could not purchase another suite from the defendant and the court thought that the existence of the sales contract does not make any sense. In the end, the contract was terminated and restored to the status that it would be had the contract never been concluded.

1141 *See* Bingham LJ's speech in *J Lauritzen AS v Wijsmuller BV* (The "Super Servant Two") [1990] 1 Lloyd's Rep. 1, p. 8.

1142 Uribe 2011, p. 147–150.

1143 This is indicated in the famous Suez case. Moreover, in some cases where contracts have been severely affected by the 1st world war, the English court also showed its rigid attitude toward the rule of frustration. English courts refused to apply this rule because of an excessive difficulty in performance of contracts. *See Ocean Tramp Tankers Corporation v V/O Sovfracht (The Eugenia)* [1964] 2 Q.B. 226 (C.A. 1963); *See also Blackburn Bobbin Co v TW Allen &Sons* [1918] 2 K.B. 467.

1144 Han (韩强) 2010, p. 66.

1145 Chinese law also shows a confused attitude in distinguishing frustration of contract purpose and *force majeure*. The courts sometimes might resort to the rule of material change of circumstances to solve the case where there is in fact a *force majeure*. Han (韩世远) 2014, p. 660.

2.2.2. Encouragement of Renegotiation

An obvious feature of an inefficient contract is the imbalance between the cost and benefit from performance. Through re-negotiation, the parties will alter the content of the contract and re-adjust the equilibrium of the contract. As a result, non-performance of an inefficient contract will be achieved.

Within EU instruments, both the PECL and CESL explicitly express that contract parties are bound to enter renegotiations if there is an exceptional change of circumstances.[1146] It is required that contract parties should attempt to renegotiate with each other in good faith, with a view to terminating or modifying an inefficient contract. However, only the PECL specifies the actual content of such an obligation. The obligation to negotiate in good faith under the context of the PECL includes the duty of proposing good faith negotiations as well as the duty to accept the counterparty's proposal if it is fair and reasonable. PECL further stipulates the consequences of a contract party's violation of the duty to negotiate in good faith.[1147] The party who refuses to negotiate or breaks off negotiations contrary to good faith and fair dealing has to pay damages for any loss caused by this. In this sense, the PECL makes the duty to re-negotiate, as well as the liability for breach of this duty, independent from the duties and liabilities included by a contract. In contrast, the DCFR expressly refuses to impose any obligation to re-negotiate on contract parties. As the official comment on the DCFR states, "there is no question of anyone being forced to negotiate or being held liable in damages for failing to negotiate" and a duty of negotiation imposed by the PECL is criticised as being "undesirably complicated and heavy".[1148] Instead, DCFR makes it a requirement for invoking the doctrine of change of circumstances that the affected party should have attempted in good faith to achieve a reasonable and equitable adjustment by negotiation. In other words, if the party affected by the change of circumstances maliciously refuses to negotiate or breaks off negotiation, he will be unable to rely on the rights and remedies provided by the rule of change of circumstances. Moreover, the DCFR imposes a general duty of good faith on both of the contract parties and indicates the result of breaching the obligation of good faith. Any party in breach of good faith will be precluded from "exercising or relying on a right, remedy or defense which that person would otherwise have".[1149] This implies that, if a promisee unreasonably refuses to re-negotiate in good faith, he might lose the rights or remedies that he would have, such as the right to specific performance or damages.[1150]

1146 Article 6:111(2) PECL; Article 89(1) CESL.

1147 Article 6:111(3) PECL; Uribe 2011, p. 212.

1148 DCFR, p. 738. (DCFR gives an example where the party affected by the change of circumstances is placed in an adverse position. As is mentioned, "for example, that a creditor in an obligation might be acting in a fiduciary capacity and might be placed in a difficult situation of conflict of interests if obliged to negotiate away an advantage.").

1149 Article III.–1:103 DCFR.

1150 See DCFR, p. 705–6. As is indicated by the official comment of the DCFR, imposition of the duty of obligation is not intended to correct or improve the contract by making it fairer than the parties did. Rather, the purpose of introducing the duty of good faith is to assist the court to fill contract gaps where necessary. Hence, a breach of good faith will not lead to an independent liability but only restricts the person in breach from exercising the rights or remedies that he would otherwise enjoy.

Rather than creating an independent obligation to re-negotiate, Chinese law only proposes a suggestion that, when there is a material change of circumstances, contract parties may enter a re-negotiation in order to modify or terminate the contract. Currently, neither the CCL nor the Interpretation of the CCL makes any reference to re-negotiations in the case of change of circumstances. Instead, in a document concerning some guiding rules for courts, the Chinese Supreme Court treats it as a suggestion that courts should encourage re-negotiations.[1151] In addition, the Supreme Court places an emphasis on the role of mediation after a dispute enters the court. Where the dispute cannot be resolved through re-negotiation, the court should try to resolve the dispute through mediation.[1152] It is generally held that re-negotiation of contract terms with the aim of adapting the contract to the new circumstances are greatly in accordance with the principle of good faith which is considered to be one of the fundamental principles in Chinese contract law.[1153] Moreover, a prevailing idea among academic scholars in China is that contract parties should be encouraged to re-negotiate, in order to better adapt the contract relationship to the new circumstances in a stable way.[1154] However, the idea of encouraging re-negotiation in Chinese law is more of theoretical importance and lacks legal effect. Chinese law does not impose any obligation to re-negotiate on contract parties and the parties are able to bring litigation immediately after the contract circumstances have been changed. Interestingly, the idea of encouraging re-negotiation has been well implemented in judicial practice in the absence of a legal obligation. In many cases, the disputes over change of contract circumstances have been solved through re-negotiations or mediations.[1155]

English law, in contrast to EU law and Chinese law, does not create any duty to re-negotiate. As a general rule, English courts refuse to admit the existence of any implied duty of good faith, loyalty or cooperation between contract parties.[1156] The concept of a duty to negotiate, according to English courts, is opaque, uncertain and not consistent with the existing theory of obligation.[1157] As a result, neither the contracting parties nor the court is able to clearly interpret and understand the content of such an obligation.[1158]

1151 合同指导意见 [Guiding Opinions].

1152 合同指导意见 [Guiding Opinions], S.1 (4).

1153 Cao (曹守晔) 2009, p. 46.

1154 Wang (王利明) 2011, p. 340.

1155 See e.g. the classical case of "Wu Mei An" (武煤案)[Wuhan Gas Co.] which took place in 1993. This case was considered as the first case where a Chinese court resorted to the doctrine of change of circumstances. In the end, the parties accepted to enter into mediation and to revise the contract. Wuhan Municipal Coal Gas Corp. v. Chongqing Measuring Instrument Factory, 1996 Sup. People's Ct. Gaz2; Han (韩世远) A 2011, p. 382.

1156 Uribe 2011, p. 155–6.

1157 It is held that any type of obligation is closely relevant to a liability which is based on a certain type of relationship, such as contract parties or injurers and victims. However, negotiations are not the type of relations that give rise to obligations and liabilities. Moreover, it is difficult to assess the loss generated by violating good faith negotiations. Poole 2014, p. 71.

1158 See Lord Ackner's speech in the case of *Walford v Miles* [1992] 2 AC 128:
"[C]an there ever be a duty to negotiate in good faith?...A duty to negotiate is as unworkable in practice as it is inherently inconsistent with the position of a negotiating party. It is here that the uncertainty lies. In my judgement, while negotiations are in existence either party is entitled to withdraw from

In addition, any insistence on the obligation to negotiate is considered to be disadvantageous to the party who takes an adversarial position in the negotiation.[1159] According to some judicial practices, even if the parties have included an expressed negotiation provision, such a provision will be held unenforceable for its lack of certainty.[1160] In this sense, if one party maliciously refuses to negotiate or breaks off the on-going re-negotiation process, such acts will not constitute a wrong or incur additional liability. However, English law does realize the advantages of re-negotiations and creates incentives for re-negotiation in at least three ways. First of all, the duty of mitigation requires that the promisee should enter a re-negotiation with the breacher if doing so is necessary for mitigating the loss from the breach. Although English law rejects any implied duty of good faith in re-negotiation, this does not mean that a malicious refusal or break off of re-negotiation will not lead to any disadvantageous consequences. Where a promisor refuses to cooperate unreasonably, he might encounter a risk that the damages to be obtained by him will be reduced in the light of his failure to mitigate the loss. Secondly, re-negotiations are encouraged by English law in such a way that many obstacles to re-negotiations will be removed. A significant effort is to lower the requirement by the traditional theory of consideration for an effective re-negotiation.[1161] This is achieved by giving the concept of consideration a wider interpretation.[1162] Modern English law is more likely to recognize that there is consideration if an adaptation of a contract resulting from re-negotiation is to diminish the undue costs incurred by an unexpected burden from the promisor.[1163] As a result, such an adaptation is enforceable and the original contract will be replaced by a new contract. Besides this point, removal of obstacles to re-negotiation is indicated in the English law's control of the negotiating process. An adaptation of the contract will be unenforceable if there is evidence of duress or opportunistic advantage-taking.[1164] Thirdly, although an implied duty to re-negotiate in good faith does not exist in English law, English courts in some recent cases seem to show a more lenient attitude toward party stipulated negotiation clauses, particularly in the context of commercial contracts.[1165] If the request of re-negotiation by one party does

those negotiations, at any time for any reason. There can be thus no obligation to continue to negotiate until there is a 'proper reason' to withdraw. Accordingly a bare agreement to negotiate has no legal content."

1159 Poole 2014, p. 71.

1160 As Lord Ackner mentioned in the Walford case. An agreement providing for negotiation is unenforceable because it does not have any legal content. *See* [1992] 2 AC 128.

1161 *See Stilk v. Myrick*, 2 Camp 317, 6 Esp 29 (1809). Traditionally, an adaptation of the contract resulting from renegotiation sometimes would be held invalid for lack of "consideration". In the Stilk case, the court held that by renegotiation, the promisor merely made another promise to perform what had already been promised in the original contract. In such a case, adaptations of the contract resulting from re-negotiation were held invalid.

1162 Williams v. Roffey Bros. & Nicholls (Contractors) Ltd., 1 QB 1 (Eng. C.A. 1991).

1163 Treitel 2002, P. 22–23. ("Performance of a contractual duty owed by the promisee to the promisor can constitute consideration for the new promise if that performance in fact confers a benefit on the promisor.").

1164 Collins 2003, p. 355.

1165 *See Petromec Inc v. Petroleo Brasileiro SA Petrobas* [2005] EWCA Civ 891, [2006] 1 Lloyd's Rep. 121. Longmore LJ in this case questioned Lord Ackner's speech in a previous case. According to Lord

not appear to be oppressive, an express provision giving rise to an obligation to negotiate in good faith is unlikely to be held invalid. But the agreement to negotiate the contract term must contain objective criteria[1166] enabling the court to determine the specific content of the obligation, particularly concerning what is to be negotiated according to the expectations of the parties.[1167] For instance, if there is an exceptional rise in the price of the goods, the parties may clearly include in the contract that the contract price is open to discussion.[1168]

By re-negotiating the contract terms, contract parties are able to adapt the contract to the new circumstances in a flexible way. At the same time, strict performance of an inefficient contract will be realized without triggering legal costs.[1169] Moreover, since contract parties are the best judges of their own benefits, the result achieved by re-negotiation will best reflect the contract parties' true expectations. In this sense, in the absence of a re-negotiation cost, re-negotiation will always be the best way to solve unexpected problems arising after the conclusion of the contract. However, owing to the involvement of negotiation costs and the parties' conflicting interests, negotiation is not always achievable. This opens a need that the law should try to remove obstacles to successful re-negotiations or provide alternative solutions to avoiding strict performance of an inefficient contract. Within the three legal systems, English law refuses to impose any implied obligation to negotiate on contract parties but accepts that the parties may agree on a duty to re-negotiate as long as such an agreement is clear and specific. In order to encourage re-negotiation, English law is more likely to respect the parties' freedom of re-negotiation, to remove the obstacles to re-negotiation as well as to control the form and the process of negotiation, instead of directly imposing obligations of re-negotiation.[1170] It is required that the negotiating process should be free from any oppression, duress or opportunism. Adaptations of the contract will be held enforceable only if they are resulting from voluntary agreements. In this sense, the contract parties have great freedom to decide whether or not to re-negotiate and what is to be re-negotiated under English law. European soft law shows conflicting attitudes toward how to encourage contract parties to re-negotiate in the case of hardship. But all the three EU soft law codifications share a common feature in relation to encouragement of re-negotiation by referring to a general duty of good faith. Within these three codifications, the PECL creates the highest requirements of re-negotiations by imposing a duty to re-negotiate in good faith on contract parties. What is to be negotiated concerns the existence as well as the content of the contract under new circumstances where strictly performing the

Longmore LJ, to decide that an express negotiation provision has "no legal content" will actually deliberately defeat the reasonable expectations of honest men. See also Poole 2014, p. 72.

1166 *See Shaker v Vistajet Groups Holdings SA* [2012] EWHC 1329 (Comm), [2012] 2 All ER (Comm) 1010, 2 Lloyd's Rep 93. Lord Teare J states that an agreement to negotiate will be enforced only if it includes objective criteria for assessing its content. If a provision only states that the parties have to negotiate, such a provision will be unenforceable.

1167 Uribe 2011, p. 156.

1168 *Staffordshire Area Health Authority v South Staffordshire Waterworks Co,* [1978] 3 All ER 769, Court of Appeal (1978), [1978] 1 W.L.R. 1387.

1169 Gotanda 2003, p. 1469.

1170 Collins 2003, p. 355.

original contract is inefficient. The CESL also includes an obligation of re-negotiation but has not further explained the content of such an obligation. In contrast to the PECL and CESL, the DCFR merely makes the attempt to re-negotiate a pre-condition for the contract parties to request remedies from the courts instead of directly using the term of "an obligation to re-negotiate". However, one may think twice about this technique. Within the relationship between the contract parties, each party seeks to maximize his own welfare and one party's interest sometimes might conflict with the other party's to a great extent.[1171] Hence, on those occasions where a change of circumstances leads to fundamental conflicts between the interests of the parties or the re-negotiation cost is extremely high, the contract parties might prefer to bring their dispute before the court straightaway. Such a possibility, however, is barred by the DCFR. Unlike English law which explicitly rejects an obligation to re-negotiate or EU law which sets a high requirement of re-negotiation, Chinese law only articulates a slogan that re-negotiation should be encouraged. However, there is no substantive legal rule binding contract parties to enter into re-negotiation. An interesting fact is that Chinese judicial practice shows an inclination to re-negotiate in the case of hardship or *force majeure* even if contract parties do not have any legal obligations to re-negotiate. If a dispute over a change of circumstances cannot be solved by re-negotiation, contract parties are willing to accept a suggestion of mediation by the court.

2.2.3. Modification by a Third Party

Both EU law and Chinese law have introduced a third approach to avoiding performance of an inefficient contract by granting a third party the power to modify or terminate the contract. Such an approach is aimed at adapting the contract to the new circumstances but its feature of giving a third party a more active role in adapting the contract makes this approach different from re-negotiation.

It seems that the idea of revising the content of a contract by a third party is rejected by English law. Generally, English law only accepts an excusing rule for a contract of which the purpose has been frustrated. For such a contract, performance is pointless and the result is to bring the contract to an end rather than to permit modification or termination by a court. However, there is a possibility that English courts are able to interfere with the content of a contract by inserting implied terms into it.[1172] If a term has not been expressly set out in a contract, but the court presumes that the parties must

1171 *See* [1992] 2 AC 128. As Lord Ackner in Wolford cases used the fact that parties to negotiation have conflicting interests as the argument against the possibility of a duty to negotiate in good faith. As he indicates:

> *"[E]ach party to the negotiations is entitled to pursue his own interest, so long as he avoids making misrepresentations. To advance that interest he must be entitled, if he thinks it appropriate, to threaten to withdraw from further negotiations or to withdraw in fact in the hope that the opposite party may seek to re-open the negotiations by offering him improved terms..."*

An example of the contract parties' conflicting interests is the case where a seller might pursue a higher price for the goods to be sold and an extended period for performance while a buyer might want to obtain the goods with a lower price and in a shorter time.

1172 Treitel 2003, p. 206.

have intended to include it since it is consistent with "reasonableness" or "business efficacy", then the court might make such a term part of the contract. Besides, another two sources of implied terms are business usage and rules of law, such as the rules in the Sale of Good Acts 1979 or statutes into contracts for the supply of goods.[1173] But the possibility of inserting implied terms into contracts does not give English courts great power to modify the content of contracts. When deciding whether or not to imply a term, the courts must consider the type of contract in question and the values of reasonableness and fairness. More importantly, a term cannot be implied if it is shown that one party would have not agreed to it.[1174]

In EU law, a modification by a third party is conditional. It is realized that any mechanism for adjusting obligations by an external court on the basis of hardship might, "if not strictly controlled, undermine fundamental principles of the law of contract and the stability of contractual relations."[1175] Based on this knowledge, several limitations have been set out in order to restrict a court's power of modification. First of all, EU contract law instruments all require that any involvement of a court in modifying or terminating the contract is possible only when there is an exceptional change of circumstances that is not expected and assumed by the promisor.[1176] The DCFR further makes it a pre-condition for the involvement of a court that the contract parties have already approached each other for negotiations. In such a case, either of the parties may bring the dispute to the courts and request the court to adapt the contract. Moreover, since the purpose of modification is to reallocate the risks instead of leaving the risks where they were, the court has to readjust the obligations between the contract parties according to the new circumstances.[1177] For instance, a court may increase or decrease the contract price or extend the period for performance so as to make the obligations more reasonable and fair in the new circumstances. A parameter for the court's power of modification is established that a court should redistribute the extra costs incurred by the unforeseen circumstances to both parties in a fair and just way. It can be noted that, what are to be redistributed are just the extra costs that have rendered performance excessively onerous rather than any additional cost incurred by the intervening event in order to merely eliminate the excessive burden.[1178] Hence, a modification should not push all the extra risks caused by the unexpected event onto only one party or render the equilibrium of the contract totally different from that when the contract was concluded. Besides, with the awareness that modification should not completely change the nature

1173 Id.

1174 Id, p. 211–213.

1175 DCFR, p. 739.

1176 Article 6:111 PECL; Article III.–1:110 DCFR; Article 89 CESL. Although the PECL only uses the term of "a change of circumstances" instead of "an exceptional change of circumstances" when introducing the court's power to revise a contract, the other conditions included in the provision indicate that such a power arises only in the case where the change is exceptional and severe.

1177 Hesselink 2008, p. 81.

1178 Uribe 2011, p. 213. The PECL, DCFR and CESL all define the concept of "exceptional change of circumstances" as the changes that have rendered performance excessively onerous. In this sense, in the ordinary course of performance, a party affected by the intervening event has to bear the extra costs incurred by the event to the extent that those costs are not excessively large.

as well as the content of the original contract, EU law requires that a moderate approach should be taken by the court in order to avoid alterations in the vital stability of the contract relationship.[1179]

Chinese law, in contrast, carries the idea of authorising the court to revise or terminate the contract even further. Instead of making contract parties' attempts to re-negotiate a pre-requisite for involvement of the court, Chinese law allows parties to bring their disputes before a court straight away if the circumstances change. To be noted, it is the fear of any infringement of contract freedom as well as contract stability that leads to a decision of excluding the rules concerning the court's power to adapt contracts from the CCL and restricting such a power.[1180] In order to restrict the court's power of adapting the contract, the Interpretation over the CCL II requires that the court's modification or termination of the contract should be based on a contract party's request while a court cannot make such a decision in the absence of any such request.[1181] In terms of the content of the adaptation, the court is required to make a distinction between the cases where the changes have rendered the performance unfair and where the purpose of the contract has been frustrated. In the former situation, the contract might be modified in order to fit into the new circumstances in a better way or be terminated if necessary. Where the court decides to modify the contract, the contract relationship will not expire but be brought to another stage. In the other situation where the purpose of the contract has been frustrated, the court will terminate the contract since there is no space for modification. In such a situation, the continued existence of the original contract does not make any sense and hence the court will put the contract relationship to the end.[1182] However, Chinese law sets a high threshold for terminating a contract by the court. The court is required to put a priority on the technique of modifying a contract instead of terminating it in order to keep the stability of a contract relationship to the greatest extent.[1183] Only when the existence of the contract relationship is considered to be pointless and it is useless to modify the contract terms, should terminating the contract be adopted by the court.

To summarize, by granting courts the power to modify contract terms, the law enables courts to engage in reforming the contractual relationship. Both EU law and Chinese law have included such a technique to deal with exceptional change of contract circumstances. It is realized that contract parties in real practice cannot always reach a complete contract ex-ante or a successful re-negotiation ex-post.[1184] On this point, English law does not directly give the courts the power to modify the content of a contract in the

1179 DCFR, p. 741.

1180 In the 4th version of the draft of the CCL, Chinese legislators had stipulated the doctrine of changes of circumstance by Article 76. However, this article was deleted from the final version of the CCL. One important reason for the deletion is the fear that the courts might have great freedom in deciding modification or termination of contracts. See Cao (曹守晔) 2009, p. 46.

1181 *See*合同法司法解释II [Interpretation over the CCL II], Article 26.

1182 Han (韩强) 2010, p. 66.

1183 Cao (曹守晔) 2009, p. 47.

1184 There are many reasons explaining why contract parties may fail to reach an ex-ante complete contract or a successful re-negotiation. For instance, such failures might be caused because of the parties' lack of foresight or of the high transaction costs.

circumstances of frustration. Instead, it takes an approach of either completely discharging a frustrated contract or making the affected party bear the risk of an intervening event. Nevertheless, inference with the content of contracts by English courts is possible if the courts decide to insert implied terms into contract. Empowering a court to modify inefficient contracts will therefore supplement contract parties' capacity to adapt the contract to new circumstances that are unexpected and exceptional. However, such a technique is a double-edged sword. Unduly widening the court's power and allowing excessive modifications will challenge the stability of contracts and create more uncertainties in transactions.[1185] For this concern, both Chinese law and EU law have set out several restrictions to the court's power. For instance, both of them require that the court's modification of a contract be subject to the pre-condition that one party has made a request and such a modification be fair to both of the parties. However, Chinese law differs from EU law in the aspect that it lacks concrete criteria for modification. Although Chinese law has established a general principle of fairness for guiding the court to make modifications, it is shown in judicial practice that the court still exercises wide freedom in deciding whether or not to modify a contract as well as how to modify it.[1186] For instance, the Chinese court sometimes may decide to modify the content of a contract even if the changed circumstances only amount to a normal commercial risk that should have been assumed by the promisor.[1187] Or in some other cases, the court may freely decide whether or not to increase the contract price and to what extent the price will be increased without giving reasonable explanation.[1188]

3. Explanations for the Differences

From the aforementioned comparisons, it is found that some extent of convergence exists among English law, EU law and Chinese law in shaping people's incentives to breach efficiently, particularly in relation to general concerns of party autonomy, performance costs, contract imbalance as well as contract expectation. To a certain extent, this is achieved by legal transplantation under a background of globalization and Europeanization. However, there are great differences among these systems with regard to the concrete rules affecting people's incentives to perform, breach and renegotiate. In this section, two explanations will be given indicating those differences and their causes in order to avoid the mere descriptive approach to comparison.[1189]

1185 Uribe 2011, p. 243–4.

1186 Han (韩强) 2010, p. 68.

1187 Ding & Guo (丁义军& 郭华) 2005, p.369; See also *Guangdong Changhong Highway Engineering Co. Ltd. Vs. Fujian Rongyuan Construction Co.Ltd.*, Shangluo Interm. People's Ct, May 12 2014.

1188 *Hainan Yuya saltworks vs. Taikun Real Estate Development Co. Ltd.*, Hainan High People's Ct., 21 December 2007.

1189 Rogers 1998–1999, p. 152. The traditional approach to comparative study focuses on the similarities and differences among different legal systems. As a result, the process of comparing laws is merely the scientific technique of description and analysis. Many comparativists fail to understand the limitations inherent in the task of comparing as well as the purpose of comparison. Unlike some hard sciences, "which are predicated on observable data and testable hypotheses, there exists no objective basis upon which to found the comparison of laws and different legal systems".

3.1. The Role of Contract

The role of contracts in society and polity reflects the values attached to contracts as well as the goal to be achieved by contracts. Modern English contract law gains its impetus of development from the demand of a dynamic commercial society.[1190] The understanding of the function of contract in English law is primarily derived from its dealing with its capitalist economy in which free transaction is the principal mechanism for the allocation of economic goods.[1191] Contracts in such a setting primarily serve for facilitating voluntary transactions and eliminating obstacles to those transactions. Such an idea, for instance, is indicated in the English law's attitude toward a free re-negotiation model. Besides, to a certain degree, the idea of facilitating the development of commercial society is also present in the English law's incorporation of more commerce friendly contract rules, e.g. a wider interpretation of consideration in the contracts resulting from re-negotiation. In terms of the remedy model, the rules of Contract remedies within the English contract law system, which receives implications from Fuller & Perdue's theory on contract interest, are shaped in such a way as to fully protect the promisee's expectation interest.[1192] Damages are granted to the non-breaching party not because he is worse off than was before the contract was made, but because the breaching party has failed to make him better off.[1193] The idea of compensation is thus to offset the profit to be obtained at the completion of performance. As a result, the aggrieved party may purchase substitutes to the performance from a third party. Naturally resulting from a compensation-based remedy system, non-performance of an inefficient contract is allowed as long as the promisor is able to fully compensate for the other party's expectation interest. Chinese sales law, staying at the other side, evolves from a moral centred conception that "Qique Bixu Yange Zunshoud" (agreement should be strictly complied with).[1194] In traditional culture, a contract created by a certain form[1195] represents a binding law between contract parties and any breach of a valid contract would lead to criminal liability.[1196] After the birth of the new People's Republic of China, the role of contracts was changed. Basically, contracts are considered to be a tool of implementing the orders of the state.[1197] It was recognized that only legal entities or economic

1190 *See* Brown 2001, p. 243–44.

1191 Harris, Campbell & Halson 2006, p. 5.

1192 Id, p. 6.

1193 Treitel 2002, p. 7.

1194 契约必须严格遵守.

1195 The form of contracting changed a lot from one dynasty to another. For instance, in the Zhou dynasty, a contract should be made of bamboo. A piece of bamboo would be split into two smaller pieces and each party took one to indicate his role in the contractual relationship. He 1992, p. 95.

1196 For instance, in the Tang dynasty, a seller would be beaten with a rod if he delivered a defective product. Zhang 1999, p. 7–8; Han 2011, p. 23–24.

1197 In 1981, the 经济合同法[ECL] was enacted as the first piece of Chinese contract law. Article 2 of ECL stipulates that:

> *"The economic contract is an agreement between legal persons specifying their mutual relations, rights and obligations in order to realize certain economic aims."*

organizations could enter into contracts in order to carry out specific economic plans.[1198] A breach of contract at this time was supplemented by criminal liabilities as well as administrative liabilities.[1199] Although the establishment of the new Chinese contract law (CCL) as well as several pieces of statutes and interpretations in relation to contracts[1200] has opened the time for modern Chinese contract law, the traditional moral and political elements still have an impact upon the function of contract and contract law to a great extent. The idea that contract parties should strictly perform what has been agreed is accepted as a fundamental principle in contract law. This creates the effect that the contract remedy system in Chinese law is performance-oriented. For instance, the court is likely to grant specific performance to an aggrieved promisee even if he is able to obtain substitutes from a third party or if the contract has been rendered inefficient because of a material change of circumstances. Another effect caused by the insistence on performance is that the law attaches a great emphasis to the subjective intention of the breaching party. For instance, in double sale, if a seller and a third party maliciously create a contract that leads to the buyer's failure to obtain the goods such a contract will be held invalid upon the request of the buyer.[1201]

EU soft law measures on sales contracts denote a harmonized contract law at the European Union level that is aimed at diminishing contract-law-related barriers and further facilitate cross-border transactions.[1202] A contract defined by EU law is a technique of certificating and validating the consensus of parties' free will.[1203] As a system providing model rules to member states, EU law presents a compromise of different legal systems as well as of contract theories from different perspectives. Under the influence of European civil law tradition, EU contract law instruments set specific performance as an ordinary remedy available to an aggrieved party. The scope of specific performance to be applied in specific cases, however, is narrowed down by the rule of substitutive performance that is included in all the three major EU soft law codifications. Such a rule is established with the awareness that on the one hand the possibility of substitutive performance is an important reason for rejecting specific performance in some national laws; and on the other hand, there is a need to motivate the promisee to mitigate his loss and lower transaction costs.[1204] However, such a system has several policy choices attached as well, e.g. in relation to the undertakings by the CESL of protecting small-

1198 Article 2 ECL.

1199 Article 29 ECL.

1200 The new Chinese contract law system consists of the CCL, contract rules in other statutes, the interpretations by the Supreme Court in relation to Contract. Examples of other statutes are 中华人民共和国民法通则[GPCL], 消费者保护法[Consumer protection law], 保险法[insurance law], 海商法[maritime law], etc.

1201 买卖合同司法解释[Interpretation over Sales Disputes], Article 10 provides:

> *"Where a buyer fails to obtain the premises as a result of malicious collusion between the Seller and a third party in the conclusion of a separate contract on the purchase and sale of commodity premises and the delivery of the premises to such third party for use, and files a request to invalidate such a contract, the request shall be upheld."*

1202 For instance in the prg. CESL, p. 14–21.

1203 Article II.–1:101 DCFR; Article 2 prg. CESL.

1204 DCFR, p. 854, 861.

medium sized entrepreneurs (also consumers), preserving a valid contract, reducing transaction costs as well as establishing an internal market.[1205]

3.2. *Legal Culture*

The concept of legal culture denotes a number of "relative stable patterns of legally oriented social behaviour and attitudes".[1206] In a wide sense, identifying legal culture is derived from a number of elements, such as a set of deeply rooted ideas and values about law, the ways judges make decisions, the ways that "law is made, applied, studied, perfected and taught."[1207] Those elements may affect the specific ways accepted by different legal systems to avoid strict performance of an inefficient contract.

The first element to be mentioned is the culture with regard to litigation, particularly concerning the people's attitude toward litigation. In China, people generally show an aversion to litigation.[1208] Under the impact of Confucianism, litigation is considered to be undesirable and bad for both the whole country and individuals. From the traditional Chinese political perspective, a large number of litigations denotes a bad government and should be avoided. Instead, Chinese culture over a long period favours the model that disputes should be solved in a harmonious way, such as by re-negotiation or mediation. This explains the fact that contract parties in China are willing to re-negotiate or accept the court or arbitrator's suggestion of mediation even if they do not have any obligation to re-negotiate.

Another element is how judicial systems work in practice, which may for instance affect the law's attitude toward judicial adaptation of contracts. As a typical common law system, English law is largely based on common cases law. The law of contract, to a great degree, is shaped by the way judges apply, interpret or even create law.[1209] In the context of English law, the courts are able to interfere with contracts via interpreting contract terms and inserting implied terms into contracts. EU law, in contrast, presents as a hurdle of written rules, serving as the organizing sign-posts at the policy level. It mostly presents as a type of soft law rules and guiding principles and there is a lack of evidence concerning how it is applied in practice. However, at the theoretical level, EU law is able to establish the technique of judicial adaptation of contracts, particularly by indicating specific criteria for judicial modification as well as imposing a general obligation of good faith. Different from English law, Chinese law is primarily based on written law under

[1205] Article 1. Prop. CESL. For more discussion, see chapter 6, section 1.6.

[1206] Nelken 2004, p. 1.

[1207] Merryman 1985, p. 2. Legal tradition is defined as:

> *"a set of deeply rooted, historically conditioned attitudes about the nature of law, about the role of law in the society and the polity, about the proper organization and operation of a legal system, and about the way law is or should be made, applied, studied, perfected, and taught."*

[1208] Zhang (张晋藩) 2009.

[1209] Holmes 1881, p. 1–2. As is stated by Holms:

> *"[t]he life of the law (common law) has not been logic; it has been experience. The felt necessities of the time, the prevalent moral and political theories, institutions of public policy, avowed or un conscious, even the prejudices which judges share with their fellowmen, have had a good deal more to do than the syllogism in determining the rules by which men should be governed."*

the influence of civil law tradition, such as German law.[1210] Besides, International instruments such as the CISG and the PICC has also influenced Chinese contract law a lot. However, the incomplete nature of written law,[1211] the idea of paternalism as well the preference of judicial flexibility, all create a large area for discretion in China.[1212] According to a famous Chinese proverb, "particular matters should be treated particularly".[1213] Such a story is indicated in Chinese judicial trials where courts prefer to deal with specific cases under the consideration of specific facts and the assessment of correct outcomes rather than to follow the technicality of law.[1214] For instance, the court is authorized with a power to modify the amount of party-stipulated damages, if it considers that the disparity between the stipulated amount and the actual loss from breach is great. Such a power to modify contracts will also arise if there is a material change of contract circumstances. As a result, there is an increasing danger that people might become more averse to litigation and lose their trust in the judicial system.

3.3. *Is One Legal System more Efficient than Others?*

In the traditional law and economics literature, there is an idea that the common law is, by and large, economically efficient because of its characteristic of openness. Compared to the common law, the statute law is claimed to be less efficient, but is more concerned with redistribution of special interests.[1215] Following this logic, we might feel that English sales law – a representative of common law – should be more efficient than EU law and Chinese law which are more based on written statutes.

The above statement is arbitrary, however. From the comparison, we can conclude that the three legal systems are different when coming to different issues, because of different preferences and cultural elements within each system. English law places more emphasis on compensatory damages and parties' autonomy while both EU instruments and Chinese law pay great attention to protecting an aggrieved buyer. However, such a difference is narrowed down by some particular designs of remedy rules included in each system as well as the environment in which each sale law system functions. For instance, the role of specific performance in EU law is limited when it comes to replaceable goods or personal work. This in effect creates a result similar to the English remedy of compensatory damages. In the end, a potential breacher is able to base his decision of breaching a contract on the respective benefit and the cost of breach as long as the compensation will restore the other party to a position that he would enjoy had the contract been performed. Furthermore, in terms of unexpected events arising after the conclusion of the contract, different solutions are provided by different legal systems. When dealing with contracts falling into the efficient breach zone, EU law prefers a

1210 Han (韩世远) A 2011, p. 600–613.

1211 Woo 1999, p. 584; Zhu 2005, p.1159. The incompleteness of written law is not particular to China. In many countries, there is a conflict between substantive justice and formal rules.

1212 Zhu 2005, p. 1158–1164.

1213 Id, p.1160.

1214 Woo 1999, p. 586–87.

1215 Rubin 1982, p. 205.

solution that contract parties should make efforts to reach re-negotiations and cooperation while Chinese law assigns courts an active role in modifying contract terms or terminating it. In contrast, English law prefers a free re-negotiation regime, which enables contract parties to freely decide whether to re-negotiate the contract or to terminate it in order to adapt their relationship to the new circumstances. However, the practical effects of those approaches point in the same direction, being that in the end strict performance of an inefficient contract will be avoided. In this sense, different legal rules actually share functional similarities at the operational level. It is difficult to conclude that one legal system works more efficiently than the others. Among the three systems, it is likely that Chinese sales law can be considered as the least efficient system, given the fact that it imposes the highest requirement of performance on contract parties and allows courts to freely interfere with contracts. However, it would be too quick to reach such a conclusion, as this would ignore the lack of consideration of other economic or cultural elements that constitute the legal environment in which contract law operates. It may be true that efficient breaches are incompatible with the performance-orientated remedy system in China, but this does not necessarily indicate that Chinese law leads to inefficient results when responding to a contract that turns out to be inefficient after its conclusion. As is indicated in section 3.2, Confucianism and its doctrines concerning harmony and peace have greatly influenced the ways in which Chinese people react to unexpected events arising in their on-going relationships. As a result, in the case where there is a change of contract circumstances, contract parties in China are very likely to enter re-negotiations or accept the result of meditations, even if Chinese law does not impose any mandatory obligation on the parties.

4. Conclusion

Instead of merely focusing on the relationship between the remedy of expectation damages and people's decisions to breach or perform contracts, this chapter places the discussion of efficient breach in a broader setting by considering the whole contract law system. This chapter makes some comparisons between English sales law, EU soft law measures and Chinese law. The emphases are placed on how a contract remedy system shapes people's incentives to perform or breach contracts as well as how the law promotes an efficient solution to the unexpected contingencies that make strict performance of the original contract inefficient.

In respect of the contract remedies, a desirable model for motivating efficient decisions of breach or performance should be able to help the promisor to estimate the prospective consequences of his decision and to fully protect the performance interest in a less costly way. After comparison, it is found that convergence is achieved among English law, EU law and Chinese law in certain aspects, such as specific performance, expectation damages, and damage limitation rules. However, differences exist between these three systems in the way that the law motivates people to perform or breach a contract. The Chinese contract remedy system, among the three legal systems, imposes the highest requirement of performance on the promisor. This is greatly impacted by the understanding of contracts as a mechanism of performing promises. In contrast, the remedy system in England is largely grounded on compensatory damages. On the one hand, it focuses on recovering the expected profit to be obtained by the promisee at the completion of performance; and on the other hand, it limits the amount of damages to be paid by a breacher to a scope that is foreseeable by the breacher at the time when the contract was made as well as when the breach is made. Although EU law makes specific performance as a primary remedy available to a non-breaching party as well, the rule of rejecting specific performance for the possibility of alternative transactions has narrowed down the difference between EU law and English law in the scope of specific performance.

When a contract falls into the zone where strict performance is inefficient, three major approaches are available to contract parties for avoiding strict performance. English law, and EU law as well as Chinese law forbid the promisee to request performance by discharging the contract in situations where the contract purpose has been frustrated or there is *force majeure*. However, the above legal systems differ as to the approaches to avoiding performance with regard to change of circumstances not amounting to impossibility. In this aspect, English law chooses an approach on the basis of complete discharge or no discharge. Change of circumstances not amounting to impossibility in English law will not lead to the parties' additional obligations to re-negotiate with each other nor the court's power to adapt the inefficient contract. However, English law does realize the efficiency of re-negotiations and hence motivates re-negotiations by way of removing the obstacles to modifications, including the acts of "unilateral imposed alteration" or "opportunistic advantage taking".[1216] In contrast, European law creates a high requirement on re-negotiation by imposing an obligation on contract parties to re-negotiate in good faith or setting an attempt to re-negotiate as the pre-condition for invoking the court's interference. If the parties cannot reach a settlement, the court will have the power to modify or terminate an inefficient contract. Chinese law treats the encouragement of re-negotiation as a policy preference in judicial trials but lacks operative rules. In practice, it is shown that disputes over inefficient contracts are mostly dealt with through judicial mediations or judicial adaptations.

1216 Collins 2003, p. 355.

Chapter 10

CONCLUDING REMARKS AND POLICY RECOMMENDATIONS

In the beginning of this chapter, a brief summary of the entire thesis is provided. After restating the subject question as well as the basic presumptions (section 1.1), this chapter summarizes what has been discussed and found by each chapter. Implications and policy recommendations will be formulated next (section 2). It is recognized that this thesis has many limitations as well, such as its lack of empirical statistics, ignorance of other types of contracts, and an insufficient consideration of legal rules beyond contract law (section 3).

1. Summary

1.1. Summary of Research Questions

The doctrine of efficient breach is grounded on an assumption that actors are economically rational and their acts are motivated primarily by economic profit.[1217] This is particularly the case in commercial sales where both of the parties are businessmen whose acts are to a large degree driven by economic concerns. As a result, they will perform the contract only when the economic surplus of performance is larger than that of breach.[1218] Economists have also been aware that every actor has limited rationality and foresight. Within a context where transaction costs are unavoidable, it is either impossible or too costly for people to consider every potential contingency that might arise within their on-going transactions.[1219] In the absence of perfect and complete contracts in addition to a well operating market mechanism, there is a possibility that people may choose non-cooperation such as opportunism which may decrease social welfare. This creates a demand for contract law. It is assumed that the introduction of contract law may alter people's incentives by switching a non-cooperating relationship into a cooperating relationship. Against this background, law and economic scholars have come up with their theory of efficient breach. According to this theory, legal rules should align trading parties' incentives with the social welfare and more particularly shape people's incentives

1217 Posner 1979.

1218 Shavell 1980, p.

1219 Chapter 2, Section 2.

to breach only when it is efficient to do so. An important mechanism for adjusting people's incentives to perform and breach a contract refers to remedy rules which may increase the cost of breach. The remedy of expectation damages is considered to be able to accomplish this goal best since it prices a breach at a reasonable level. The damages paid by a breacher will put the non-breaching party in the position that he would enjoy as if the contract had been performed. As a result, a promisor to a contract will breach only if he earns more by breaching and paying damages than by performing the contract and the total social welfare will increase since no one becomes worse off from the breach.[1220] In this sense, it is hypothesized that an efficient breach is consistent with Kaldor-Hicks efficiency.[1221] Moreover, any remedy that reaches a higher level or lower level than expectation damages will lead to either excessive performances or too many breaches.[1222]

The above description is often referred to as the simple model of efficient breach theory and there have been a number of critiques of this theory.[1223] Moralists consider that breaches in nature are immoral,[1224] while economists start to raise doubts concerning the economic justifications for efficient breach. For example, some scholars question the capacity of expectation damages to fully compensate the non-breaching party. It has been found that a general under-compensation problem is created when the traditional expectation damages are applied.[1225] A result caused by the under-compensation problem is that people in real cases actually have insufficient incentives to perform the contract.[1226] Moreover, there is a number of researches based on either sociological or psychological studies raising an argument that people's decisions (such as whether to perform or breach a contract) will not always be driven by economic profits.[1227] Facing critiques from different perspectives, the doctrine of efficient breach seems to be losing its attraction to law and economics scholars.[1228]

1220 Barton 1972, p. 277; Birmingham 1970, p. 273.

1221 *See* Cooter &Ulen 2011, p. 42. Kaldor-Hicks efficiency is considered as a modified version of Pareto efficiency. Pareto efficiency takes place in the case where a movement makes every member in a group better off without making anyone worse off. A movement is in accordance with Kaldor-Hicks efficiency if it creates a winner and a loser, but the winner gains more than the loser's loss and the loser is able to get compensation for his loss. In such a case, the total social welfare is increased because the winner still earns after compensating the loser.

1222 *See* Scott and Goetz 1977, p. 555; Shiffrin 2007, p. 730. Penalty clauses are criticised for deterring efficient breach since they threaten people to perform contracts through a high amount of damages. Similarly, disgorgement is also considered to be motivating excessive performance because this kind of remedy tries to eliminate all the profits to be obtained by the breach. See Scott and Goetz 1977, p. 555; Shiffrin 2007, p. 730.

1223 *See e.g.* Macneil 1982, p. 949; Adler 2008, p. 1681.

1224 *See e.g.* Perillo 2000, p. 1106; Katz 2012, p. 787.

1225 For instance Eisenberg 2005 argues that "*The compensation goal implies that specific performance should be routinely available. This is because damage awards actually under-compensate in more cases than is commonly supposed.*" *See* Eisenberg 2005, p. 989–97.

1226 Farber 1980, p. 1444–5; p. 1478.

1227 Wakol 1999, p. 344.

1228 For more arguments against the efficient breach theory, see e.g. Adler 2008, p. 1681; Bernstein 2001; Katz 2012; Macneil 1982; Menetrez 2000; Perillo 2000; Sidhu 2011.

This thesis reconstructs the problem to be answered by efficient breach theory. As is inferred, discussion of efficient breach theory derives from the idea that a contract which seems to be efficient at the time when it was concluded might turn out to be not valuable for the promisor any more after its conclusion. Starting from this cognition, breaching and paying damages is only one solution for the promisor to avoid performance.[1229] Even under the remedy of specific performance or other kinds of damage rule, performance can still be avoided if contract parties could enter re-negotiations in order to adapt the original contract to the new circumstances. Moreover, the focus of this thesis is placed on one type of contracts, namely, sales contracts, which include contracts to produce goods and contracts to convey goods. Two scenarios are analyzed. The first scenario refers to the case where the production cost is increased after a seller and a buyer conclude a contract to produce goods; and the second one is the situation when a seller gets a more profitable opportunity from an alternative buyer after he signs a contract to convey goods. It is found that efficient breach theory is better applied to the first scenario than to the second one when the standards concerning economic surplus, transaction costs, full compensation as well as risk allocation are taken into account. Such a result is explained by the unexpected cost of performance involved in a contract to produce goods. Performance of a contract is assumed to be inefficient and wasteful if the cost of it has increased to an extent that all the profits to be created by performance are consumed. In such a case, strict performance of the contract will impose a high risk on the seller and decrease the total welfare shared by the two parties. The question about how to promote efficient breach in this thesis is thus switched into how to motivate efficient performance as well as to avoid wasteful performance. In order to answer this question, this thesis brings the discussion beyond a simple comparison of specific performance and expectation damages by placing them into a broader context. From a theoretical perspective, this thesis treats different remedy rules as well as other contract law rules as a whole that may have an impact upon people's decisions to enter a contract, to perform the contract, to breach, to re-negotiate and so on. Moreover, this thesis brings the questions beyond mere theoretical discussions by fitting them into different sales law systems in order to find out to what extent each system will motivate parties to perform, and to breach as well as to avoid inefficient performance.

1.2. Summary of Each Chapter

The thesis is divided into two parts. Part I deals with the theory of efficient breach; Part II deals with the application of the efficient breach theory in specific legal systems.

1.2.1. Part I. Theoretical Framework

The first part of this thesis provides the theoretical framework of efficient breach theory, its limitations as well as its implications for contract law rules.

[1229] Posner 2003, p. 835.

Chapter 2 provides a basic introduction to the law and economic theories of contract and contract law in order to find the economic justifications for making contracts as well as introducing contract law and contract remedies. A basic idea is established that contract law rules should be able to facilitate people's capacities to maximize their welfare in transactions by aligning people's economic motivations with social welfare, filling contract gaps, disambiguating contract vagueness as well as regulating contracts if necessary.[1230] A bridge is built between contract law rules and people's decisions, such as to enter a contract, to invest in reliance cost, to disclose information and particularly to perform or breach a contract efficiently.

The doctrine of efficient breach is provided in Chapter 3, explaining under which circumstances a breach of a contract should be considered to be efficient. An efficient breach denotes the case where a breacher can profit from his breach after putting the other party in a position as good as he could enjoy had the contract been performed.[1231] In such a case, the result created by the breach will be consistent with Kaldor-Hicks efficiency that the total profit from the breach is increased and the loss suffered by a loser will be offset by the winner. Under the context of a sales contract, an efficient breach might take place if, after the conclusion of a contract, an unfortunate contingency occurs, making it extremely costly for the seller to perform the original contract or a fortunate contingency arises making it more profitable for the seller to allocate the goods to an alternative user (a third party or the seller himself).[1232] In order to encourage efficient breaches while discouraging inefficient ones, contract remedies should be set at a reasonable level where a breacher will internalize the losses suffered by the non-breaching party from the breach. In this sense, the efficient breach theory favors the common law remedy of expectation damages which makes a breacher compensate the other party's expected loss from the breach.

Chapter 4 brings the story of efficient breach into re-evaluation. On the one hand, it summarizes the arguments against the efficient breach theory from economic and ethical perspectives.[1233] In addition, Chapter 4 also re-considers the traditional efficient breach theory by taking into account several elements that might influence the efficiency of an act. A breach might be efficient if: 1) the total economic surplus from it was higher than that from performance; 2) the non-breaching party was indifferent between breach and performance; 3) the social costs of the breach and paying expectation damages were low; 4) the expectation damages would optimistically allocate risks between contract parties, for instance move the risk of non-performance from a risk averse promisee to the promisor who is indifferent to the risk. However, the efficient breach theory presented in its simple version is considered to be theoretically ideal but is lacking support from contract practice. On the one hand, the simple version of the efficient breach theory is

1230 *See* Chapter 2, Section 2.

1231 Birmingham 1970, p. 284.

1232 The reasons why people commit breaches are complicated. People may breach opportunistically, merely seeking a higher share of the economic pie at the expense of the other party. But in many occasions, a person chooses to breach a contract because he does not value the performance of contracts any more if the utility of the contract has been altered by some unexpected contingencies. Miceli 1997, p. 71.

1233 *See* Chapter 4, Section 4.1, Section 4.2.

only focused on the surplus gained by a breaching party, irrespective of transaction costs incurred by the approach of expectation damages, the weakness of the compensatory damages as well as contract parties' risk preferences. On the other hand, legal scholars who disagree with the traditional theory of efficient breach point out that such a theory is simply based on the assumption of a positive relationship between expectation damages and the efficiency of people's breach or performance decision; while it ignores that there are multiple elements affecting the actions of the parties to a contract.[1234]

Realizing the limits of a simple efficient breach theory, chapter 5 re-examines the relationship between people's acts and different types of contract remedies. A starting point for discussing the efficient breach theory is that performance of a contract might turn out to be inefficient because of an unfortunate contingency increasing the performance cost or a fortunate contingency that creates a more profitable alternative to the performance. These two scenarios of contingency in chapter 5 fit into the contexts of contracts to produce goods and contracts to convey goods. Breach of a contract is merely one of the approaches to avoid wasteful performances in the context of contracts to produce goods or to reallocate the goods to the optimal user in the contracts to convey goods. Based on this hypothesis, this chapter is aimed at finding out how different contract remedy rules may affect a seller's decision regarding breach as well as the possibility of reaching efficient solutions within the above two contract contexts. Firstly, between the remedy of specific performance and monetary damages, it is found that both of them may induce efficient solutions to avoid wasteful performance or to reallocate the goods to the best user. However, expectation damages are more efficient for avoiding wasteful performance and inducing efficient breaches of contracts to product goods. In contrast, specific performance works better on inducing efficient allocation of goods, but does not favor efficient breach by requiring a potential breacher to re-negotiate for an efficient solution. Secondly, among different damage measures defined by law, only the measure of expectation damages has set a reasonable price for breach and would create an optimal level of incentives to perform or breach contracts.[1235] Thirdly, between the damages stipulated by contract parties as well as that by law, agreed damages will better reflect the parties' expectations from contracts and induce an optimal level of breach and performance of contracts.[1236] Based on the above findings, the doctrine of efficient breach theory opens a new perspective to assess a specific legal system's capacities to encourage performance of an efficient contract as well as to avoid performance of an inefficient one.

1.2.2. Part II. Comparative Study

Part II brings the discussion of efficient breach theory into the specific contract law systems, consisting of EU law, English sales law as well as Chinese sales law which respectively represent the current achievement of Europeanization of contract law, a

1234 *See* Chapter 4, Section 4.1.1; *see also* Wakol 1999, p. 344. Klass 2013, p. 8.
1235 *See* Chapter 5, Section 2.2.
1236 *See* Chapter 5, Section 3.2.

common law tradition and a developing contract law system. The following questions have been addressed within each legal system:

1. How does the law shape people's incentives to perform a contract?
2. How does the law deal with remedies created by the contract parties themselves, especially with regard to liquidated damages clauses and penalty clauses?
3. How does the law draw the boundary for the Zone in which non-performance of a contract is encouraged and whether or not such a zone is consistent with the efficient breach zone?
4. How does the law deal with a contract falling into the efficient breach zone?

In chapter 6, the theory of efficient breach is discussed within EU law, which refers to sales law measures resulting from the Europeanization of contract law at the EU level, particularly in relation to the Principles of European Contract Law (hereinafter the PECL) which were published by the Lando Commission,[1237] the 2009 Draft Common Framework Reference (hereinafter the DCFR)[1238] as well as the Common European Sales Law (hereinafter the CESL).[1239] After a brief introduction of the process of Europeanization of contract law as well as the content of EU sales law, this chapter describes the system of a buyer's remedies in order to find out whether or not it can adjust a seller's incentives to perform or breach a contract in an efficient way (section 2). According to economic theory, a seller should be encouraged to perform the contract within the efficient performance zone. A direct way of motivating performance provided by EU law measures is to allow a request of specific performance of the contract. Moreover, the enforceability of party-agreed damages as well as expectation damages creates a result that the cost of breach is increased so that the party contemplating a breach should take this into consideration. He will perform the contract if the cost of a breach is higher than the benefit of performance. In terms of the cases where performance is less efficient than breach, EU law established the doctrines of *force majeure*, change of circumstances (also referred to as hardship) as well as impossibility and impracticability. When determining the application of those doctrines, EU law treats it as one of the most important pre-conditions that the performance costs have increased to an excessive extent although each doctrine is pre-conditioned upon some other requisites as well.[1240] Non-performance of a contract within the efficient breach zone is achieved primarily through three approaches, including the approaches of directly rejecting specific performance,

1237 *See* Van Zelst 2008, P. 4; *see also* section 1 of chapter 6.

1238 Similar to the PECL, the DCFR also represents scholars' endeavor of creating a common European private law. For more explanations of the DXFR, *see* section 1 of Chapter 6.

1239 Rather than be a soft law, the CESL is intended to be an optional instrument for cross-border transactions that could be chosen by the parties as the law regulating their contracts and thus works as an alternative to national law. For more discussion, see section 1 of chapter 6.

1240 Although there are some debates over the differences between *force majeure* and hardship. Some literature considers that the two doctrines belong to the same category in relation to unexpected contingencies. For instance, within the 1980 Vienna Convention (Convention on International Sales of Goods), the doctrines of *force majeure* and hardship are stipulated in one article. *See* Article 79 CISG.

imposing an obligation of re-negotiation as well as allowing a court to adapt the contract. However, application of efficient breach theory to the current EU law measures meets some practical difficulties in relation to the features of transactions within the EU and this is discussed at the end of this chapter.

Chapter 7 applies the theory of efficient breach to English sales law, which is primarily based on common law, parliament acts (e.g. Sales of Good Act 1979, Sales of Good Act 1994 and Sales of Good Act 1995) as well as European Directives and a number of other statutory provisions promoting the interpretation and development of the Sales of Good Act.[1241] Discussion of the remedy system in England is mainly grounded on the remedy of expectation damages which aims to put the non-breaching party in a position that he would expect had the contract been performed. In contrast, specific performance in English law is applied to a limited scope that it is works as an equitable remedy pre-conditioned on the inadequacy of monetary damages. In this sense, the approach of breach can be chosen by a seller directly who considers that performance is inefficient. Moreover, the breach date rule, the foreseeability rule as well as some other damage limitation rules increase the certainty for a potential breacher to foretell the cost of breach. English law, however, puts more limits on party-agreed damage clauses, particularly by refusing the enforceability of damage clauses which are considered to be punitive. English law also sets out particular doctrines restricting the availability of performance of a contract that falls into an efficient breach zone. On the one hand, a contract is discharged if the purpose of it has been frustrated by an intervening contingency that is unexpected and unavoidable by contract parties. In such a case, the party who does not bear the risk of the frustrating event will be exempted from his non-performance as well as any liability for damages. On the other hand, English law refuses the enforceability of specific performance of a contract if performance may lead to great hardship.

The relationship between Chinese sales law and the application of the efficient breach doctrine is explained by Chapter 8. The beginning of this chapter also gives the basic framework of Chinese sales law which evolves from the Chinese ancient term of "Qi Yue" (agreement)[1242] and the traditional idea that "Min you Siyue Ru Lv Ling" (agreements constitute laws and orders).[1243] The modern Chinese sales law is largely created upon the

1241 The Sales of Goods Act 1979 (hereinafter SGA 1979) was largely based on the Sales of Goods Act 1893 which was the result of a process of codifying sales law since 1889. This act provides important resources for English commercial sales until now. Afterwards, codification and re-statement of sales law was continued by the publication of other Acts in relation to commercial transactions as well as the amendments of the SGA 1979, such as the Insolvency Act 1985, the Sale of Goods (Amendment) Act 1994, the Sales and Supply of Goods Act 1994, the Sale of Goods (Amendment) Act 1995 and so on. *See* Rodger 1992, p. 581; *see also* McKendrick 2010, p. 205–06; *see also* Mackay 2005, p. 17.

1242 Qi Yue (契约) in ancient times has two meanings. It depicts on the one hand the way that people made agreements and on the other hand the agreement itself. This concept can be derived to the West Zhou dynasty at which time people used "Qi (契)" to sell land, houses or other real estate. In modern China, "Qi Yue" is still frequently used by Chinese people as an alternative to contract. See Xu Shen (许慎) 2001, p. 592; see also Zheng (郑显文) 2003, p. 52–52.

1243 "Min you Siyue Ru Lv Ling (民有私约如律令)" has been established as an important rule of transactions since Zhou Dynasty. As was shown in many studies about Chinese ancient contracts, contract parties

1986 General Principles of Civil Law (hereinafter the GPCL), the 1999 Chinese contract Law (hereinafter the CCL) as well as other statutes and the Supreme People's Court's Interpretations giving interpretations and complements to the CCL. Within the Chinese contract remedy system, specific performance still plays an important role in realizing the content of a contract since it is considered as the inherent requirement deriving from a contract,[1244] although the modern Chinese sales law places less emphasis on specific performance by setting it as an optional remedy based on a promisee's choice.[1245] In addition, it is considered that the Chinese modern contract remedy system is also in a gradual transit into a compensatory system, which is indicated by the establishment of expectation damages in China.[1246] However, the damage rules defined by Chinese law basically function as a complement to specific performance and lack practical content about how to calculate expectation damages in specific sales cases. In judicial practice, it is common for Chinese courts to adopt the market price rule to calculate an aggrieved buyer's expectation loss which is subject to damage limitation rules (the foreseeability rule, the contributory fault rule as well as the mitigation rule). Even if the aggrieved party has arranged a substitutive transaction in replacement of the original one after he found out the fact of breach, the extra costs of the substitutive transaction will not be recovered unless this is in accordance with the mitigation rule or the court has permitted the substitutive transaction in advance. In terms of party-agreed damage clauses, Chinese law gives the court the power to modify the amount of damages if there is an inconsistency between the stipulated amount and the actual amount of loss resulting from a breach. But Chinese law will not directly refuse to enforce a damage clause merely because it is punitive. To summarize, instead of setting a specific price for breaches ex-ante, Chinese law is more willing to offer the court free discretion over the calculation of damages in specific cases. The analysis of the efficient breach model in relation to performance cost in Chinese law focuses on the rules of *force majeure*, material changes of circumstance, impossibility as well as impracticability which are similar to those in EU law. Nevertheless, the way of dealing with contracts falling into the efficient breach zone according to Chinese law is different from that by EU law. If a promisor refuses to perform a contract within the efficient breach zone, Chinese courts in some cases may still grant an order of specific performance unless the contract has been discharged.[1247] After a contract falls into the efficient breach zone, it is up to contract parties whether or not to enter re-negotiations, but Chinese courts in practice show a willingness to encourage re-negotiations or mediation. Moreover, upon the request of any party, a court may

at that time always wrote "Ru Lv Ling " or "Ru zhaoshu (如诏书)"(agreements are laws) in the contract emphasizing that this contract should be enforced. In Tang dynasty, what was favoured is the proverb that "Guan You Zheng Fa, Ren Cong Si Qi (官有政法, 人从私契)", namely, officers should follow laws and public orders and individuals in civil society should comply with the agreement that is promised by him. On some occasions, a private agreement even has priority over laws issued by the state. Huo (霍存福) 2008, p. 58–9.

1244 It is also considered that specific performance can provide full protection of a promisee' expectation interests from the contract. *See* Cui (崔建远) 2010, p. 601.

1245 Article 107 CCL.

1246 Article 112 CCL, Article 113 CCL; *see also* Zhang 2006, p. 296–297.

1247 Han (韩世远) A 2014, p. 661.

decide to modify the contract or terminate it in order to adapt the contract relationship to the new circumstances.

After presenting the application of efficient breach theory in EU contract law, English sales law and Chinese sales law separately, chapter 9 of this thesis offers a comparative law and economics study. The purpose of the comparison is to find out the similarities and the difficulties among these three sale law systems in shaping a seller's incentives to perform, to breach as well as to avoid inefficient performance. In order to develop this question, Chapter 10 first compares the remedy systems of these three systems, in respect of the rules of specific performance, monetary damages, substitutive performance as well as party-agreed damage clauses.[1248] It is found that the Chinese contract remedy system imposes the highest requirements of performing a contract on a seller and provides the court with great freedom in deciding how to implement specific performance, to assess the amount of damages and to revise the amount of stipulated damages as well as whether or not to allow the recovery of the additional cost of a substitutive transaction. As a result, a seller to a contract may fail to precisely predict the legal consequences of breach or performance. In contrast, English law sets specific performance as a discretionary remedy, but focuses more on compensatory damages. In terms of how to shape contract parties' incentives to perform or to breach a contract, English law provides a higher extent of certainties for a potential breacher to predict his liability to perform through the mechanism of the breach date rule, the damage limitation rule as well as the market price rule. EU law differs from English law with regard to the specific content of remedy rules, such as the availability of specific performance, the recoverability of substitutive price as well as the validity of penalty clauses. However, the difference between EU law and English law in shaping people's incentive to perform or to breach has been narrowed down by the same rules established in EU law as well,[1249] particularly by the rule of substitutive performance established in EU law that specific performance is excluded if alternatives are available to an aggrieved promisee. In addition to the comparison of remedy systems, chapter 9 also develops a further comparison upon the question of how the three legal systems deal with contracts falling into the efficient breach zone. In this aspect, English law develops an approach to avoiding specific performance of the contract based on either complete discharge or no discharge. Moreover, prevention against performance is possible because of the general non-availability of specific performance in English law. In addition to directly refusing specific performance, both EU law and Chinese law have established two other approaches to avoiding performance, including of encouraging contract parties to re-negotiate and allowing a court to adapt the contract. The approach of encouraging re-negotiation is carried out by EU law in a way that it imposes an obligation to re-negotiate on contract parties and setting re-negotiation as the pre-requisite for contract parties to bring a

[1248] Section 1 of Chapter 10.

[1249] For instance, the damage limitation rules of foreseeability and of mitigation have been incorporated into both EU law measures and English law. In addition, a certain degree of convergence also exists between these two legal systems at the case where specific performance is unavailable, such as the contracts involving personal service or the contracts concerning replaceable goods. See Chapter 9, Section 1.

lawsuit. In contrast, China shows more cases involving the courts' free adaption of contracts. The reasons for the differences among English law, EU law and Chinese law in motivating performance, breach as well as non-performance of inefficient contracts are presented at the end of chapter 9.

2. Suggestions for Developing An Efficiency-enhancing Contract Law System

The theory of efficient breach in this thesis provides a view point for analysing a remedy system as well as strategies for avoiding an inefficient performance. Suggestions for developing an efficiency-enhancing contract law system fall into at least three categories.

2.1. Remedy Rules

It is established that the introduction of contract rules shall be aimed at facilitating the capacities of the contract parties to maximize welfare in transactions. The difficulty that exists is how the remedy rules could align contract parties' economic motivations with social welfare.

A traditional idea is that the establishment of expectation damages makes the potential breacher take into account the non-breaching party's expected benefit from performance of the contract. Such an idea refers to the so called "simple model of efficient breach" and it favours the common law remedy of expectation damages. An opposite idea focuses on the merits of specific performance.[1250] Compared to the remedy of expectation damages, specific performance is assumed to be more efficient for protecting a non-breaching party's expectation interest[1251] and avoiding damage assessment by a third party.[1252] The controversy about the respective merits of expectation damages (also referred to as a liability rule remedy) and specific performance (also referred to as a property rule remedy) has existed for a long period.[1253] Another similar debate was developed with regard to the question whether the common law remedy system or the civil law remedy system is more efficient.[1254] It has been observed that the common law generally favors the remedy of expectation damages while the civil law takes an opposite approach by taking the specific performance as the default remedy. However, several practical elements actually reduce the differences between a remedy system that favors

1250 Polinsky, 1983; Shavell, 1984; Ulen, 1984; Kornhauser, 1986.

1251 According to this idea, contract parties are rational and will design an optimal contract. In most cases, contract parties want actual performance of a contract instead of a mere promise plus the right to win a lawsuit. See e.g. Depoorter & Tontrup 2012, p. 686.

1252 Id, p. 687.

1253 See e.g. Shavell 2006; Yorio 1982. For more discussions concerning debates between expectation damages and specific performance, see Chapter 5, Section 1.

1254 The default contract remedy accepted by typical common law countries refers to expectation damages. For instance, under English law and Anglo-American law, expectation damages are regularly applied and specific performance is treated as an exceptional remedy. In contrast, civil law tradition countries are more likely to favor specific performance.

monetary damages and one that takes specific performance as the default contact remedy. For instance, specific performance is generally unavailable in the cases involving high administrative costs, such as a contract providing personal work. Such a rule has been incorporated into all the three legal systems studied by this research. In addition, evidence shows an increasing willingness of courts in civil law tradition countries to carry out substitutive performance instead of specific performance when it comes to general goods.[1255] By the same token, common law courts are more likely to grant specific performance when it comes to irreplaceable goods.[1256] Instead of focusing on the respective merits of specific performance and expectation damages, this thesis favors a model in which the remedy rules are treated as an integrated system. The question to be answered is changed from whether specific performance or expectation damages is more efficient into a bundle of detailed questions. We may ask whether or not a remedy system as an integrated one will enable people to optimally predict the respective benefits and costs of their action; whether or not the remedy system is cost-efficient so that it saves the social costs of breach as well as; whether or not any interruption of a remedy agreement by a court is necessary. Starting from these questions, we identify several features that an efficient remedy system at least shares:

1) It provides contract parties with clear information about the form of remedy to be applied to a certain case, such as the information about when performance is required as well as when damages will be imposed.
2) It has incorporated damage limitation rules, such as the foreseeability rule, the mitigation rule, as well as the contributory damages rule, which makes the damages to be paid by a breacher more predictable and facilitates exchanges of information crucial for damage assessment.
3) It has restrained the court's discretion to a reasonable extent. For instance, instead of regulating the amount of damages stipulated by contract parties, the law should focus more on regulating the process of damage stipulation by eliminating obstacles to damage stipulation, such as duress or oppression.
4) It has taken into account the social cost of each remedy rule. What is favoured by this thesis is substitutive performance that shares the common merits of specific performance and expectation damages.
5) It has considered the specific breach type, showing different attitudes toward efficient breaches and inefficient ones.[1257]

1255 Zweigert & Kotz 1998, p. 472; Lando & Caspar Rose 2004, p. 476.

1256 Laycock 1990.

1257 Inefficient breaches are also referred to as opportunistic breaches. Some literature suggests a disgorgement approach to deterring opportunistic breaches. However, current theories on opportunistic breaches have not reached a unified solution to deterring such breaches.

2.2. *Efficient Breach Zone*

Another implication derived from the efficient breach theory is that contract law should draw the line between an efficient performance zone and an efficient breach zone, on the basis of cost-benefit analysis. When drawing the border for the efficient breach zone, the law should incorporate strict criteria by respecting performance of a contract that has been concluded upon voluntary agreement unless those criteria are satisfied. One significant pre-condition is that a contract may fall into the efficient breach zone only if the unexpected performance cost has increased to an extent that it consumes all the potential profits to be created by performance.[1258] Besides, attention should be paid to the approaches of avoiding performance of a contract that falls into the efficient breach zone.

No matter whether the law takes a model based on no discharge or complete discharge (English law model) or a model differentiating impossibility and excessively burdensome, a necessary way of minimizing the economic cost of unexpected contingencies is to reject specific performance of the original contract since the social cost of it will in the end exceed the profit from it. English law, and EU law as well as Chinese law have all accepted this if an intervening risk leads to the result that the contract has been discharged.[1259] What needs to be especially mentioned are the approaches of re-negotiation and adaptation by a third party in relation to the cases of exceptional changes of circumstances (or hardship, or material changes of circumstances in Chinese law). In economic theory, re-negotiation will be the optimal approach to dealing with unexpected contingencies. On the one hand, contract parties are the best judges of their own expectations and the result from re-negotiation will better reflect their preference than that from a third party's decision. On the other hand, re-negotiations avoid the cost of litigation as well as the problem of legal error in the judicial process. However, a successful re-negotiation might be deterred by several obstacles, such as high re-negotiation costs,[1260] fundamental conflicts between the interests of contract parties as well as one party's fraudulent acts or oppression. For example, in the cases where there is duress or fraud in the process of re-negotiation, the parties might have entered a settlement in the end, but the content of settlement might be oppressing so that it causes an effect that one party would maliciously reap the benefits from the other party. A preferable way of encouraging re-negotiations will be to diminish the obstacles to re-negotiations rather than to create a general obligation to re-negotiate in good faith. Encouragement of re-negotiations may be achieved for instance by invalidating the consequences of renegotiation (settlement

1258 Chapter 5, Section 4.

1259 In both EU law and Chinese law, what constitutes an excuse for non-performance and brings a contract to an end is *force majeure*. English law uses the term of frustration of contract purpose to deal with similar cases.

1260 According to the Coase theorem, negotiation and free transaction are always the optimal way of resource distribution in the absence of transaction costs. If there is no transaction cost or the cost is low, contract parties may always enter re-negotiations where there are unexpected events arising after the conclusion of the contract.

agreements)[1261] or by excluding the validity of agreements resulting from an unreasonable process of re-negotiation. In addition to encouraging re-negotiations, another approach taken by both Chinese law and EU law is to grant courts the power to adapt a contract to the new circumstances. Awarding a third party an active role in adapting the contract, however, should be made in a careful way because any incorrect adaptation is at the expense of party autonomy.[1262] Therefore, it is suggested that more limitations as well as criteria should be established in order to control the court's power of adaption within a reasonable scope. The law should set out on the one hand strict preconditions for triggering such a power and on the other hand explicit standards on how to exercise the power of adaption.

3. Limitations and future Research

3.1. Limitations of This Research

This research is developed from those cases where performance of a contract turns out to be inefficient because of unexpected performance cost. It bases the study of efficient breach theory in specific legal systems on the assumption that breach belongs to approaches to avoid inefficient performance caused by unexpected contingencies. However, there is a lack of empirical statistics showing the relationship between real case breach and contract rules although some existing empirical data have been considered by the research.[1263] As a result, there are still many unresolved fundamental questions concerning how to motivate people to act efficiently in transactions. The following questions are open to future research:

1. Whether a property rule remedy or a liability may decrease the role of moral concerns in people's breach decision making?
2. To what extent people will take into consideration contract remedies and precisely predict their potential liability of breaches?
3. Does de-regulating liquidated damages bring out or prevent more efficient breaches?
4. Will imposition of an obligation to re-negotiate bring out a positive result in encouraging re-negotiations?

   ...

In addition to lack of empirical data, another limitation of this research relates to the fact that it cannot fully consider the complexity of contract cases in modern society. This thesis is set within the framework of commercial sales and developed from the breach of

[1261] In present Chinese law, a settlement might be identified as invalid if one party regrets re-negotiating and brings a request to the court again. See Chinese Civil Procedure Law (民事诉讼法), Article 99.

[1262] Both EU legislators as well as Chinese scholars have realized that a court's adaptation has a danger of infringing the fundamental doctrine of contract freedom. *See e.g.* DCFR, p. 739; Cao (曹守晔) 2009, p. 46.

[1263] For instance, it has been aware that some existing empirical studies indicating businessmen's general aversion to breaches in a long-term relationship contract. See e.g. Bernstein 2001.

a sale contract by a seller. But the problem is that transactions in the present setting take more complicated forms where the content of a seller's performance is more than merely delivering goods as required. For instance, it is common that a sales contract might be mixed with a loan or involving a third party's interest, such as mortgages or financial leases which have become increasingly important in modern commercial sales. In those cases, it is more difficult to evaluate a party's breach when a third party's interests are involved. Such kinds of sales have been neglected in this research. Moreover, the thesis focuses on the efficient breach model in relation to performance costs while it neglects to incorporate another important category of efficient breach, involving a more profitable contract with a third party. A typical case regarding this type of efficient breach is what is called a double sales case. Accordingly, the research overlooks a large part of rules in relation to double sales, such as the rules of "tortious interference" and the rules concerning transfer of property rights. Furthermore, the economic explanations for the rules of unexpected contingencies (frustration or *force majeure*) in this research are largely based on a cost-benefit approach and other theories such as risk-sharing theories are ignored.

3.2. *Efficient Breach Theory: A Developing Topic*

Based on the traditional finding that a breach of a contract might in certain cases, bring out a higher economic surplus than performance, the theory of efficient breach opens a window for developing wider topics of law and economic analysis of contracts as well as introducing new approaches to studying people's acts of breach, performance, bargaining, re-negotiation and so on. For example, an interesting topic deserving more research is what is called opportunistic breaches which stand on the other side of efficient breaches. The story of opportunistic breach has been described in a famous statement from Posner:

> *"If a promisor breaks his promise merely to take advantage of the vulnerability of the promisee in a setting (the normal contract setting) where performance is sequential rather than simultaneous, we might as well throw the book at the promisor. An example would be where A pays B in advance for goods and instead of delivering them B uses the money in another venture".*[1264]

Under the current premise, it has been largely agreed that opportunistic breaches have a danger of decreasing social welfare. On the one hand, an opportunist merely attempts to obtain a larger share of the economic pie at the expense of the other party and thus creates a result that one party is worse off without getting fair compensation.[1265] On the other hand, more economic expenses might be invested by potential victims in order to avoid opportunist problems or obtain fair compensations and hence this creates additional social costs.[1266] Opportunism might take place when it is easy for a party to take

1264 Posner 2007, p. 130–131.
1265 Dodge 1999, p. 632.
1266 Muris 1981, p. 524.

advantage of the other party's vulnerability, such as in consumer contract cases;[1267] or when there is high possibility that a breacher might escape from his liability for breach, such as in the case where he deliberately commits fraud or appropriations;[1268] or when a breacher intentionally refuses to bear any kind of liabilities. In response to this kind of breaches, there are already some scholarly efforts to find out solutions to deterring such kind of breaches or minimizing their negative impact on social welfare.[1269]

Besides developing new law and economics topics, future studies could also adopt new mythologies and approaches to understand or solve legal problems. In recent law and economics research, the behavioral approach and empirical studies have gained more and more significance among scholars. For instance, in Wilkinson-Ryan 2014, a behavioral law and economics analysis was conducted in order to explain why some types of breach are more acceptable than others.[1270] This question is somehow related to one of the findings derived from this research, namely, that efficient breach theory is better presented in the model for saving money than in the model for obtaining an extra financial surplus from an economic perspective. However, economic analysis has been criticized for basing people's decision-making completely on financial incentives.[1271] It has been pointed out by many scholars that an individual's decision-making in real life is influenced by more factors than just financial benefits, such as the elements of a long-term relationship or moral intuition. Regarding those arguments and critiques, this research has not provided any explanations other than economic ones in order to better indicate why some breaches should be more encouraged than others. In this regard, Wilkinson-Ryan 2014 assumes that contract parties are self-interested but also concerned with moral norms and intuitions. It investigates how people incorporate moral incentives into their decision-making in different scenarios by creating an experimental game as well as a hypothetical questionnaire. As shown, people hold different attitudes towards prevention of loss and obtaining economic gains.[1272] Within a sale contract, it is accepted that a buyer is sitting in a loss frame since he will pay money for some goods; while a seller is in a gain frame for the fact that he obtains money for some goods.[1273] It is found that many people share a more sensitive feeling to losses than towards gains. When it comes to a seller's breach, people show a sensitive attitude toward whether he is trying to

1267 The US courts identified that there is a possibility of abusive breaches in some cases involving special relationships between contract parties, such as the relationships between retailers and consumers, innkeepers and guests, employers and employees, etc. In such cases, the plaintiff's breach tended to abuse the trust of the other party and "undermine the stability of expectations essential to the contractual relationship". Dodge 1999, p. 641.

1268 In the literature about opportunistic breaches in US law, it is found that courts are willing to impose an amount of damages higher than compensatory ones when there is evidence pointing out a breacher's fraudulent or malicious acts. For instance, see U.S. Department of Justice 1992, p. 6–9; U.S. Department of Justice 2001, p. 6; U.S. Department of Justice 2005.

1269 Such as Craswell 2009;Light 1968; Mattei 1995; Muris 1981.

1270 Wilkinson-Ryan 2014.

1271 Wilkinson-Ryan 2014, p. 30–36.

1272 Bigoni & Bortolotti & Parisi & Porat 2014; Kahneman &Tversky 1979; Wilkinson-Ryan 2014.

1273 Wilkinson-Ryan 2014, p. 32.

save money or to pursue more money.[1274] This explains why a loss-avoiding efficient breach is more acceptable than a gain-seeking efficient breach when the breaching party is the seller. This is merely one case showing the importance of a behavioral approach for supporting or challenging the traditional law and economic models. In addition, there are also some empirical studies showing that in some real-world cases parties who could profit by breaching but choose to comply with the contracts anyway, do so because an obligation plays a more important role in driving their acts.

To summarize, the law and economic theory of efficient breach in this thesis provides the criteria for an evaluation of existing contract law systems and sheds some light on how to design contract law. However, how contract law should be understood and designed is an open question, which opens to new perspectives and methodologies. An important point of view is to investigate the norms and rules operated in real-world trades. In future studies, behavioral analyses and empirical studies might be a good choice, as that may provide inspiration to better understand the role of laws in influencing people's choices and hence to make recommendations for possible areas of improvement and effective implementation.

[1274] Id.

REFERENCES

Adams & Macqueen 2010
Adams, J. N. & Macqueen, H., Atiyah's Sale of Goods (12th ed. Essex: Pearson 2010).

Adler 2008
Adler, B.E., 'Efficient Breach Theory through the Looking Glass', *New York University Law Review*, 2008, p. 1679–1725.

Aghion & Hermalin 1990
Aghion, P. & Hermalin, B., Legal Restrictions on Private Contracts Can Enhance Efficiency, Journal of Law, Economics, & Organization, (6) 1990, p. 381–409.

Allen 2000
Allen, D.W., 'Transaction Costs' in: B. Bouckaert & D.G. Geest (eds.), *Encyclopedia of Law and Economics, Volume I. The History and Methodology of Law and Economics*, Cheltenham, UK: Edward Elgar, 2000, p.893–926.

Atiyah 1981
Atiyah, P. S., *Promises, Morals and Law*, New York: Clarendon Press, Oxford Uni. Press, 1981.

Ayres & Gertner 1992
Ayres, I & Gertner, R., 'Strategic Contractual Inefficiency and the Optimal Choice of Legal Rights', *The Yale Law Journal*, 1992, p. 729–773.

Baker 1980
Baker, C. E., Starting Points in the Economic Analysis of Law, *Hofstra Law Review*, (8) 1980, p. 939–972.

Barnett 2011
Barnett, R.E., 'Contract is Not Promise; Contract is Consent', *Georgetown Law Faculty Publications and Other Works*, Paper 615, 2011, Available at <http://scholarship.law.georgetown.edu/facpub/615>.

Barnes 1996
Barnes, D.W., 'The Meaning of Value in Contract Damages and Contract Theory', *American University Law Review*, 1996, p. 1–37, Seton Hall Public Law Research Paper No. 899797, Available at SSRN: <http://ssrn.com/abstract=899797>.

Barnes 1998
Barnes, D.W., 'The Anatomy of Contract Damages and Efficient Breach Theory', *Southern California Interdisciplinary Law Journal*, 1997–1998, P. 397–490.

Barton 1972
Barton, J.H., 'The Economic Basis of Damages for Breach of Contract', *Journal of Legal Studies*, 1972, p. 277–304.

Bayern 2011
Bayern, S.J., False Efficiency and Missed Opportunities in Law and Economics, *Tulane Law Review*, (86) 2011, p.135–181.

Bayles 1983
Bayles, M.D., Introduction: The Purposes of Contract Law, *Valparaiso University Law Review*, (17) 1983, p.613–626.

Beale & Dugdale 1984
Beale, H. & Dugdale, T., 'Contracts between Businessmen: Planning and the Use of Contractual Remedies', *British Journal of Law and Society*, 1984.

Beale, Fauvarque-Cosson, Rutgers, Tallon & Vogenauer 2010
Beale, H., Fauvarque-Cosson, B., Rutgers, J., Tallon, D. & Vogenauer, S., *Cases, Materials and Text on Contract Law*, 2nd ed, Oxford, Hart Publishing, 2010.

Beale 2012
Beale, H., *Chitty on Contracts: General principles*, London: Sweet & Maxwell, 2012.

Beatson 2010
Beatson, J., et al, *Anson's Law of Contract*, 29th ed., Oxford Univ. Press 2010.

Bernstein 1992
Bernstein, L., "Opting out of the Legal System: Extra-legal Contractual Relations in the Diamond Industry", *The Journal of Legal Studies*, (21) 1992, p. 115–157.

Bernstein 1994
Bernstein, L., "Social Norms and Default Rules Analysis", *South California Interdisciplinary Law Journal*, (3) 1993–1994, p. 59–91.

Bernstein 1996
Bernstein, L., "Merchant Law in a Merchant Court: Rethinking the Code's Search for Immanent Business Norms", *University of Pennsylvania Law Review*, (144) 1996, p. 1765–1821.

Bernstein 2001
Bernstein, L., Private Commercial Law in the Cotton Industry: Creating Cooperation Through Rules, Norms, and Institutions, University Chicago Law & Economics, 2001, Olin Working Paper No. 133. Available at SSRN: <http://ssrn.com/abstract=281437 or http://dx.doi.org/10.2139/ssrn.281437>.

Birmingham 1970
Birmingham, R.L., 'Breach of Contract, Damage Measures, and Economic Efficiency', *Rutgers Law Review*, 1970, p. 273–284.

Bishop 1985
Bishop, W., 'The Choice of Remedy for Breach of Contract', *Journal of Legal Studies*, (14) 1985, p. 299–320.

Bridge 2009
Bridge, M., *The Sale of Goods*, 2nd ed., Oxford Univ. Press 2009.

Bridge et al 2010
Bridge, M. et.al., *Benjamin's Sale of Goods*, 8th ed., London: Thomson Reuters, 2010.

Brooks 2006
Brooks, R.R.W., The Efficient Performance Hypothesis, *Yale Law Journal*, 2006, p. 568–596.

Brown 2001
Brown, I., *Commercial Law*, 7th ed., Oxford Univ. Press, 2001.

Cahoy 2003
Cahoy, D.R., Oasis or Mirage? Efficient Breach as a Relief to the Burden of Contractual Recapture of Patent and Copyright Limitations, *Harvard Journal of Law and Technology*, (17) 2003, p. 135–178.

Calabresi & Melamed 1972
Calabresi, G. & Melamed, A.D., "Property Rules, Liability Rules, and. Inalienability: One View of the Cathedral", *Harvard Law Review*, (85) 1972, p. 1089–1128.

Cao (曹士兵) 2006
Cao, Shibing (曹士兵), "最高人民法院裁判、司法解释的法律地位",中国法学 ("The Status of Decisions and Judicial Interpretations of Supreme People's Court", *China Legal Science*), (3) 2006, p. 175–180.

Cao (曹守晔) 2009
Cao, Shouye (曹守晔), "最高人民法院 '关于适用　'中华人民共和国合同法若干问题的解释二'之情势变更问题的理解与适用"，法律适用 ("The Understanding and application of the Doctrine of Change of Circumstances, which is included in the 'Interpretation of the Supreme Court of Several Issues Concerning the Application of the Contract law of the People's Republic of China'", *Journal of Law Application*), 8 (2009), P. 44–49.

Chan 2011
Chan, Gordon Y. M., The Doctrine of Change of Circumstances in Chinese Contract Law, Sep 27th 2011, available at SSRN: http://ssrn.com/abstract=1934085.

Chen 2001
Feng Chen, The New Era of Chinese Contract Law: History, Development and a Comparative Analysis, Brooklyn Journal of International Law 1 (2001), p. 153–191.

Chen 2002
Chen, Yin-Ching, Civil Law Development, China and Taiwan, Stanford Journal of East Asian Affairs, (2) 2002, p. 8–14.

Chen (陈春隆) 2003
Chen, Chunlong (陈春隆),"中国司法解释的地位与功能",中国法学 ("The Status and the Function of Chinese Judicial Interpretation", *China Legal Science*), (1) 2003, p. 24–32 (China).

Chen 2008
Chen Jianfu, *Chinese Law: Context and Transformation*; Leiden: Martinus Nijhoff Publishers, 2008.

Chirico 2010
Chirico, F., "The Function of European Contract Law – An Economic Analysis" in: P. Larouche & F. Chirico, *Economic Analysis of the DCFR, The work of the Economic Impact Group within CoPECL*, München: Sellier European Law Publishers, 2010, p. 9–30.

Clarkson, Miller & Muris 1978

Clarkson, K.W., Miller, R. L. & Muris, T.J., Liquidated Damages v. Penalties: Sense or Nonsense?, *Wisconsin Law Review*, 1978, p. 351–390.

Craswell 1988
Craswell, R., 'Contract Remedies, Renegotiation, and the Theory of Efficient Breach', *Southern California Law Review*, 1988, p. 629–670.

Craswell 1989
Craswell, R., Contract Law, Default Rules and the Philosophy of Promising, *Michigan Law Review*, (88) 1989, p.489–529.

Craswell 2006
Craswell, R., Expectation Damages and Contract Theory Revisited", Stanford Law and Economics Working Paper No. 325, August 2006, available at SSRN: <http://papers.ssrn.com/sol3/papers.cfm?abstract_id=925980>.

Craswell 2009
Craswell, R., When is a Willful Breach 'Willful'? The Link between Definitions and Damages, *Michigan Law Review*, 2009, 1501–1515.

Coase 1960
Coase, R.H., The problem of social cost, *Journal of Law and Economics,* (3) 1960, p. 1–44.

Coleman 1984
Coleman, J.L., Economics and the Law: A Critical Review of the Foundations of the Economic Approach to Law, *Ethics*, (94) 1984, p. 649–679.

Collins 1999
Collins, H., *Regulating Contract*, Oxford: Oxford University Press, 1999.

Cotterrell 2004
Cotterrell, R., Using the Concept of Legal Culture, Australian Journal of Legal Philosophy (29) 2004, p. 1–28.

Cooter & Eisenberg 1985
Cooter, R. & Eisenberg, M. A., Damages for Breach of Contract, *California Law Review*, 73 (1985), p. 1432–1481.

Cooter & Ulen 2011
Cooter, R. & Ulen, T., *Law and Economics*, 6th ed, New York: Addison-Wesley Longman, 2011.

Cui (崔建远) 1992
Cui, Jianyuan (崔建远), 合同责任研究, 长春: 吉林大学出版社 (*Studies on Contract Liability*, Changchun: Jilin University Press), 1992 (China).

Cui 2010
Cui, Jianyuan (崔建远), 合同法, 北京: 法律出版社 (*Contract Law*, Law Press), 5th ed., 2010 (China).

Cunnington 2008
Cunnington, R.M., The Inadequacy of Damages as a Remedy for Breach of Contract, in: C. Rickett (eds.), *Justifying Private Law Remedies*, Oxford: Hart Publishing, 2008, p. 115–145.

De Geest & Wuyts 2000
De Geest, D. & Wuyts, F., Penalty Clauses and Liquidated Damages, in: B. Bouckaert & D.G. Geest (eds.), *Encyclopedia of Law and Economics, Volume III. The Regulation of Contracts*, Cheltenham, UK: Edward Elgar, 2000, p. 141–161.

De Geest 2010
De Geest, G., Specific performance, damages and unforeseen contingencies in the draft common frame of reference, in F. Chirico &P. Larouche (eds.), *Economic Analysis of the DCFR: the Work of the Economic Impact Group within CoPECL*, Munich: Sellier, 2010, p. 125–134.

De Geest 2012
De Geest, G., N Problems Require N Instruments, *Washington University in St. Louis Legal Studies Research Paper No. 12-05-20* (June 7, 2012), Available at SSRN: <http://ssrn.com/abstract=2079747 or http://dx.doi.org/10.2139/ssrn.2079747>.

Delfino 2013
Delfino, R., "European Community legislation and Actions", *European Review of Contract Law*, (9) 2013, p. 90–95.

De Long 1989
De Long, S.W., "The Efficiency of a Disgorgement as a Remedy for Breach of Contract", *Indiana Law Review*, (22) 1989, p. 737–775.

Demsetz 1968
Demsetz, H., "The Cost of Transacting", *The Quarterly Journal of Economics*, (82) 1968, p. 33–53.

Depoorter & Tontrup 2012
Depoorter, B. & Tontrup, S., "How Law Frames Moral Intuitions: The Expressive Effect of Specific Performance", *Arizona. Law Review*, (54) 2012, p. 673–717.

Diamond & Maskin 1979
Diamond, P. A. & Maskin, E., "An Equilibrium Analysis of Search and Breach of Contract, I: Steady States", *Bell Journal of Economics*, (10)1979, p. 282–316.

Di Matteo 2001
Di Matteo, L.A, "A Theory of Efficient Penalty: Eliminating the Law of Liquidated Damages", *American Business Law Journal*, (38)2001, p. 633–733.

Dong (董玉鹏) 2005
Dong, Yupeng (董玉鹏), "论商品房买卖中的惩罚性赔偿", 山东理工大学学报("Analysis of Punitive Damages in Contracts for Sales of Commodity Houses", *Journal of Shangdong University of Technology*), (21) 2005, p. 55–58. (China).

Edelman 2001
Edelman, J., *Exemplary Damages for Breach of Contract*, Law Quarterly Review (117) 2001, p. 539–545.

Edlin 1998
Edlin, S. A., "Breach Remedies", *The New Palgrave Dictionary of Economics and the Law*, London: Macmillan Press, 1998. Available at: http://works.bepress.com/aaron_edlin/25.

Eisenberg 2004
Eisenberg, M. A., *Remedial Theory in Contract Law: Compensation; the Theory of Efficient Breach; Cover: Actual and Virtual Specific Performance and Disgorgement*, Presentation in Law and Economics Workshop, Berkeley Program in Law and Economics, UC Berkeley (April 2004), at 55–62

Eisenberg 2005
Eisenberg, M.A., "The Limits of Cognition and the Limits of Contract", *Stanford Law Review*, (47) 1995, p. 211–259.

Eisenberg 2005
Eisenberg, M.A., 'Actual and Virtual Specific Performance, the Theory of Efficient Breach, and the Indifference Principle in Contract Law', *California Law Review* (93) 2005, p. 975–1050.

Eisenberg 2006
Eisenberg, M.A., "The Disgorgement Interest in Contract Law", Michigan Law Review, (105) 2006, p. 559–602.

Farber 1980
Farber, D. A., "Reassessing the Economic Efficiency of Compensatory Damages for Breach of Contract", *Virginia Law Review*, (66) 1980, p. 1443–1484.

Farnsworth 1970
Farnsworth, E.A., "Legal Remedies for Breach of Contract", *Columbia Law Review*, (70)1970, p. 1145–1216.

Fehr 1997
Fehr, E., Gächter, S & Kirchsteiger, G., 'Reciprocity as a Contract Enforcement Device: Experimental Evidence', *Econometrica*, 1997, p. 833–860.

Feltkamp & Vanbossele
Feltkamp, R. & Vanbossele, F., "The optional Common European Sales Law: Better Buyer's Remedies for Seller's Non-performance in Sales of Goods?", *European Review of Private Law*, (6)2011, p. 873–905.

Firoozmand 2007
Firoozmand M. R., Changed Circumstances and Immutability of Contract: a Comparative Analysis of *Force Majeure* and Related Doctrines, Business Law International (8) 2007, p. 161–185.

Fox 2001
Fox, D., "Restitutionary Damages to Deter Breach of Contract", *The Cambridge Law Journal*, (60) 2001, p. 33–35.

Fried 1981
Fried, B., *Contract as Promise: A Theory of Contractual Obligation*, Cambridge, MA: Harvard Uni. Press, 1981.

Friedman 1989
Friedman, D., "The Efficient Breach Fallacy", *The Journal of Legal Study*, (18)1989, p. 1–24

Fuller & Perdue 1936
Fuller, L.L. & Perdue, W.R., "The Reliance Interest in Contract Damages: 1", *the Yale Law Journal*, (46) 1936, p. 52–96.

Fuller & Perdue 1937
Fuller, F.F. & Perdue, W.R., 'The Reliance Interest in Contract Damages: 2', *The Yale Law Journal*, 1937, p. 373–420.

Furmston 2000
Furmston, M., Sale & Supply of Goods (3rded. Sydney, Cavendish Publishing 2000)

Gneezy & Rustichini 2000
Gneezy, U. & Rustichini, A., "A Fine Is a Price", *The Journal of Legal Studies*, (29) 2000, p. 1–17.

Goetz & Scott 1977
Goetz, C.J. & Scott, R. E., 'Liquidated Damages, Penalties and the Just Compensation Principle: Some Notes on an Enforcement Model and a Theory of Efficient Breach', *Columbia Law Review*, 1977, p. 554–594.

Goode 2004
Goode, R., Commercial Law (3rd ed. Lexis Nexis 2004).

Gotanda 2003
Gotanda, J.Y., "Renegotiation and Adaptation Clauses in International Investment Contracts, Revisited", *Vanderbilt Journal of Transnational Law*, (36) 2003, p. 1461–1473.

Guo (郭士辉) 2003
Guo, Shihui (郭士辉), "规范房产交易市场 依法审理商品房买卖合同纠纷, 最高法院民一庭庭长孙华璞就关于商品房买卖合同纠纷司法解释有关问题答记者问",人民法院报 ("Regulate Housing Market and Resolve Disputes over Contracts on Purchase and Sales of Commodity Houses According to Law, an Interview of the Chief Judge of the No.1 civil tribunal in the SPC over the Interpretation on Sales of Commodity Houses", *People's Ct. Daily*), July 8, 2003 (China).

Han (韩强) 2010
Han, Qiang (韩强), "情势变更原则类型化研究", 法学研究 ("Different Types of Substantial Changes of Circumstance", *Chinese Journal of Law*), 4 (2010), pp. 57–69.

Han (韩世远) 1999
Han, Shiyuan (韩世远), 违约损害赔偿研究, 北京:法律出版社 (*A Study of Damages for Breach*, Beijing: Law Press), 1999 (China).

Han (韩世远) A 2011
Han, Shiyuan (韩世远),合同法总论, 法律出版社 (*General Theory of Contract Law*, Beijing: Law Press), 3rd ed., 2011(China).

Han (韩世远) B 2011
Han, Shiyuan (韩世远), "中国合同法和CISG", 暨南学报 ("Chinese Contract Law and CISG", *Journal of Jinan University*), (2) 2011, p. 7–13.

Han (韩世远) 2014
Han, Shiyuan (韩世远), "情势变更若干问题研究", 中外法学 ("A Study of Several Issues Concerning Changes of Circumstance", *Peking University Law Journal*). 3 (2014), pp. 657–675.

Harris & Ogus & Phillips 1979
Harris, D. & Ogus, A. & Phillips, J., Contract Remedies and the Consumer Surplus, Law Quarterly Review, (95) 1979, p. 581.

Harris 2005
Harris, D., et al., Remedies in Contract & Tort (2nd ed. Cambridge Univ. Press 2005).

Hart & Moore 1988
Hart, O. & Moore J., Contracts and Renegotiation, *Econometrica* (56) 1988, p. 755–785.

Hatzis 2003
Hatzis, A. N., "Having the cake and eating it too: efficient penalty clauses in Common and Civil contract law", International Review of Law and Economics (22) 2003, p. 381–406.

Havighurst 1961
Havighurst, H.C., *The Nature of Private Law*, Evanston: Northwestern Uni. Pres., 1961.

He (贺卫方) 1992
He, Weifang (贺卫方), "契约与合同之辨析", 法学研究 ("Analytical Differentiation between 'Contract' and 'Agreement'", *Jurisprudence Research*), (2)1992, p. 93–104 (China).

Heirbaut & Storme 2010
Heirbaut, D. & Storme, M.E., "The Historical Evolution of European Private Law", in: C. Twigg-Flessner (ed.), *The Cambridge Companion to European Union Private Law*, Cambridge, UK: Cambridge Uni. Press, 2010, pp. 20–32.

Hesselink 2008
Hesselink, M.W., *The Politics of a European Civil Code*, Kluwer Law Intl., 2008.

Herbots 2012
Herbots, J., "Interpretation of Contracts", in J. M. Smits (ed.), *Elgar Encyclopedia of Comparative Law*, 2nd ed., Cheltenham, UK; Northampton, MA, USA: Edward Elgar, 2012, p. 421–448.

Hicks 1935
Hicks, J.R., "A Suggestion for Simplifying the Theory of Money", *Economica*, (2) 1935, p. 1–19.

Holmes 1897
Holmes, O.W., *The Path of the Law*, Harvard Law Review, (10) 1897, p. 457.

Holmes 1981
Holmes, O.W., *The Common Law*, Boston: Little, Brown & Co., 1981.

Hondius & Grigoleit
Hondius, E. & Grigoleit, H. C., *Unexpected Circumstances in European Contract Law*, Cambridge: Cambridge Uni. Pres., 2011.

Houser, Xiao, McCabe, & Smith 2008
Houser, D., Xiao, E., McCabe, K. & Smith, V., "When punishment fails: Research on sanctions, intentions and non-cooperation", *Games and Economic Behavior*, (62)2008, p. 509–532.

Hsee & Weber 1997
Hsee, C.K. & Weber, E.U., "A fundamental prediction error: Self–others discrepancies in risk preference", *Journal of Experimental Psychology: General*, (126) 1997, p. 45–53.

Hsu 2007
Hsu, C. S., Contract Law of the People's Republic of China, *Minnesota Journal of International Law*, (16) 2007, p. 115–162.

Huo (霍存福) 2005
Huo, Cunfu(霍存福), "论中国古代契约与国家法的关系,以唐代法律与借贷契约的关系为中心", 当代法学 ("The Relation between Contract and Law in Ancient China, An Inquiry into Loan Contracts in Tang Dynasty", *Contemporary Law Journal*), (1) 2005, p. 44–56.

Huo (霍存福) 2008
Huo, Cunfu(霍存福), 中国古代契约精神的内涵及其现代价值, 吉林大学社会科学学报 (The Connotation and Its Modern Value of the Contract Spirits of Ancient China, Jilin University Journal Social Science Edition), (9) 2008, p. 57–64.

Hviid 2000
Hviid, M., 'Long-Term Contracts & Relational Contracts' in: B. Bouckaert & D.G. Geest (eds.), *Encyclopedia of Law and Economics, Volume III. The Regulation of Contracts, Cheltenham*, UK: Edward Elgar, 2000, p. 46–72.

Jansen & Zimmermann 2008
Jansen, N., & Zimmermann, R., 'Restating the Acquis Communautaire? A Critical Examination of the "Principles of the Existing EC Contract Law"', Modern Law Review, (71) 2008, p. 505–534.

Jiang 1996
Jiang Ping, Drafting the Uniform Contract Law in China, *Columbia Journal of Asian Law* (10)1996, p. 245–258.

Jody 2009
Jody S.K., The Correspondence of Contract and Promise, *Columbia Law Review*, 2009, p. 1603–1649.

Jones & Goodhart 1996
Jones, G. & Goodhart, W., *Specific Performance* (2nd ed.), London: Butterworths, 1996.

Kaplow & Shavell 2002
Kaplow, L. & Shavell, S., 'Economic Analysis of Law', in: *Handbook of Public Economics* (vol. 3), Auerbach & Feldstein, eds.; Elsevier, 2002, pp. 1661–1784.

Katz 2012
Katz, A.W., 'Virtue Ethics and Efficient Breach', *Suffolk University Law Review*, (45) 2012, p. 777–798.

Keirse 2011
Keirse, A., "European Impact on Contract Law: A Perspective on the Interlinked Contributions of Legal Scholars, Legislators and Courts to the Europeanization of Contract Law", *Utrecht Law Review*, (7) 2011, p. 34–51.

Kessedjian 2005
Kessedjian, C., Competing Approaches to *Force Majeure* and Hardship, International Review of Law and Economics (25) 2005, pp. 415–433.

Kessler & Fine 1964
Kessler, F. & Fine, E., Culpa in Contrahendo, Bargaining in Good Faith, and Freedom of Contract: A Comparative Study, *Harvard Law Review* (77) 1964, p. 401–449.

Khouri 2000–2003
Khouri, N.C.Z., Efficient Breach Theory in the Law of Contract: An Analysis, Auckland University Law Review, (9) 2000–2003, p. 739–763.

Klass 2013
Klass, G., 'Efficient Breach Is Dead; Long Live Efficient Breach', Georgetown Law Faculty Publications and Other Works, Paper 1185, (2013). Available at:
http://scholarship.law.georgetown.edu/facpub/1185.

Klein & Leffler 1981
Klein, B. & Leffler, K.B., 'The Role of Market Forces in Assuring Contractual Performance', *Journal of Political Economy*, 1981, p. 615–641.

Kötz, 1998
Kötz, *European Contract Law*, Oxford, Oxford University Press, 1997.

Kornet 2010
N. Kornet, Contracting in China: Comparative Observations on Freedom of Contract, Contract Formation, Battle of Forms and Standard Form Contracts, Electronic Journal of Comparative Law, (14) 2010, p.1–31.

Kornhauser 1985–1986
Kornhauser, L.A., 'An Introduction to the Economic Analysis of Contract Remedies', *University of Colorado Law Review*, 1985–1986, p. 683–725.

Kronman 1978
Kronman, A.T., "Specific Performance", *University of Chicago Law Review*, (45) 1978, p. 351–382

Kronman 1980
Kronman, A. T., Wealth Maximization as a Normative Principle, The Journal of Legal Studies, (9) 1980, p. 227–242.

Kull 2006
Kull, A., "Rescission and Restitution", *The Business Lawyer*, (61) 2006, p. 569–588.

Lando & Rose 2004
Lando, H. & Rose, C., On the enforcement of specific performance in Civil Law countries, *International Review of Law and Economics*, 24 (2004) 473–487.

Laycock 1990
Laycock, D., The Death of the Irreparable Injury Rule, *Harvard Law Review*, (103) 1990, p. 687–771.

Li (李胜利) 2006
Li, Shengli (李胜利), "购房者利益保护与惩罚性赔偿责任, 最高院一则司法解释相关条款之评析", 法商研究 ("Protection of the buyer's benefit and Punitive Damages in Sales of Commodity House, Commentary on an Interpretation by the Supreme People's Court", *Studies on Law and Business*), (5) 2006, p. 57–59. (China).

Li (李显东) 2005
Li, Xiandong (李显东), "民有私约如律令考", 中国政法大学学报 ("A Study on 'Private Contracts as Laws and Decrees'", *Journal of China University of Political Science and Law*), (3) 2005, p. 79–100.

Li (李晓英) 2003
Li, Xiaoying (李晓英), "汉代契约研究", 史学月刊 ("A Study of Contracts in Han Dynasty", *Journal of Historical Science*), (12) 2003, p. 87–94.

Li 1997
Wei Li, Judicial Interpretation in China, *Willamette Journal of International Law* (5) 1997, p. 87–112.

Liang (梁慧星) 2010
Liang, Huixing (梁慧星),中国民事立法评说：民法典、物权法、侵权责任法, 北京:法律出版社 (*A Commentary on China's Civil Legislation: the Civil Code, the Property Law and the Tort Liability Law*, Beijing: Law Press), 2010 (China).

Liang (梁书文) 2006
Liang, Shuwen (梁书文), "商品房销售面积误差纠纷的处理", 法律适用 ("Solutions to the Dispute over the Size of Commodity Houses", *Journal of Law Application*, (1) 2006, p. 128–130. (China).

Ling 2002
Ling, B., *Contract Law in China*, Hong Kong, Singapore and Malaysia: Sweet & Maxwell Asia 2002.

Linzer 1981
Linzer, P., 'On the Amorality of Contract Remedies--Efficiency, Equity, and the Second "Restatement"', *Columbia Law Review*, 1981, p. 111–139.

Liu (刘云生) 2000
Liu, Yunsheng (刘云生), 中国古代契约法, 西南师范大学出版社 (*The History of Contracts in Ancient China*, South-western Normal Uni. Publisher), 2000 (China).

Liu (刘正红) 2008
Liu, Zhenghong (刘正红), "履约风险规则及减损规则的适用", 人民司法::案例研究 ("Risks in Performance and the Application of Mitigation Rule", Ren Min Si Fa: An Li Yan Jiu), (16) 2008, p. 81–83. (China).

Liu & Avraham 2012
Liu, Z. & Avraham, R., Ex ante Versus ex post Expectation Damages, *International Review of Law and Economics*, (32) 2012, p. 339–355.

Lyons & Mehta 1997
Lyons, B. & Mehta, J., 'Contracts, Opportunism and Trust: Self-interest and Social Orientation', *Cambridge Journal of Economics*, 1997, p. 239–257.

Macaulay 1963
Macaulay, S., 'Non-Contractual Relations in Business', *American Social Review*, 1963, p. 45.

Mac Cormack 1985
Mac Cormack, G., "The law of contracts in China under the T'ang and Sung dynasties", *Revue internationale des droits de l'antiquité*, (32) 1985, p. 17–68.

Mackay 2005
Mackay, J. P. H., Halsbury's Laws of England, 41 Sales of Goods and Supply of Services (4th ed. LexisNexis 2005)

Macneil 1980
Macneil, I. R., *The New Social Contract: An Inquiry into Modern Contractual Relations*, New Haven: Yale Uni. Press, 1980.

Macneil 1982
Macneil, I.R., Efficient Breach of Contract Circles in the Sky, *Virginia Law Review*, 1982, p. 947–969.

Mac Queen 2012
Mac Queen, H.L., "Change of circumstances: CISG, CESL and a case from Scotland", *Journal of International Trade Law and Policy,* (11) 2012, p. 300–305.

Magnus 2012
Magnus, U., CISG and CESL, in M. J. Bonell, M. Holle & P. A. Nielsen (eds.),*Liber Amicorum Ole Lando,* Djøf Forlag, 2012, p. 225–255; Max Planck Private Law Research Paper No. 12/27, Available at: SSRN < http://ssrn.com/abstract=2165758>.

Mahoney 1995
Mahoney, P.G, Contract Remedies and Options Pricing, *Journal of Legal Study,* (24) 1995, p. 139–163.

Mahoney 2000
Mahoney, P.G., Contract Remedies: General Mitigation, in: B. Bouckaert & D.G. Geest (eds.), *Encyclopedia of Law and Economics, Volume III. The Regulation of Contracts,* Cheltenham, UK: Edward Elgar, 2000, p. 117–140.

Mak 2009
Mak, V., Performance-oriented remedies in European sale of goods law, UK & US: Oxford & Portland, Hart Publishing 2009.

Mankiw 2008
Mankiw, G. N., *Principles of Microeconomics,* 5th ed, USA: South-Western College Publisher, 2008.

Margolis 1987
Margolis, S. E., Two definitions of efficiency in law and economics, *The Journal of Legal Studies,* (16) 1987, p. 471–482.

Markovits & Schwartz 2011
Markovits, D. & Schwartz, A., 'The Myth of Efficient Breach: New Defenses of the Expectation Interest ', *Virginia Law Review*, (97) 2011, p. 1939–2008.

Mattei 1995
Mattei, U., "The Comparative Law and Economics of Penalty Clauses in Contracts", *The American Journal of Comparative Law,* (43)1995, p. 427–444.

Mattei 2003
Mattei, U., *The European Codification Process: Cut and Paste,* The Hague: Kluwer Law International, 2003.

Mc Bride 1995
McBride, N. J., *Case for Awarding Punitive Damages in Response to Deliberate Breaches of Contract,* Anglo-American Law Review (24) 1995, p. 369–390.

McBride 1996
McBride, N. J., *Punitive Damages*, in WRONGS AND REMEDIES IN THE TWENTY-FIRST CENTURY 175, (Peter Birks ed., Oxford, Clarendon Press 1996).

McKendrick 2003
McKendrick, E., 'Breach of Contract, Restitution for Wrongs and Punishment' in: Burrows & Peel (eds), *Commercial Remedies: Current Issues and Problems*, UK: Oxford University Press, 2003, p. 91–124.

Mckendrick 2010
Mckendrick, E., Goode on Commercial Law (4th ed., London: Penguin 2010).

McKendrick 2012
McKendrick, E., Contract Law: Text, Cases, and Materials (5th edition), Uk: *Oxford University Press*, 2012.

McKendrick 2013
McKendrick, E., *Force Majeure* and Frustration of Contract, 2nd ed., Oxon & New York: Informa law Routledge, 2013.

Medina 2005
Medina, B., "Renegotiation, 'Efficient Breach' and Adjustment: The Choice of Remedy for Breach of Contract as a Choice of a Contract-Modification Theory" in: N. Cohen & E. McKendrick (eds.), Comparative Remedies For Breach Of Contract, Oxford: Hart Publishing, 2005, p. 51–72.

Menetrez 2000
Menetrez, F., 'Consequentialism, Promissory Obligation, and the Theory of Efficient Breach', *47 UCLA Law Review*, 2000, p. 859–885.

Merryman 1985
Merryman, J.H., The Civil Law Tradition: An Introduction to the Legal Systems of Western Europe and Latin America, (2d ed., Stanford U. Press), 1985.

Miceli 1997
Miceli, T.J., *Economics of the Law: Torts, Contracts, Property and Litigation*, Oxford University Press 1997.

Mo 1999
Mo, J.S., "The Code of Contract Law of the People's Republic of China and the Vienna Sales Convention." American University International Law Review (15)1999, p. 209–270.

Moreno 2009–2010
Moreno, J. P., 'The Efficient Breach Hypothesis: Its Impact and. Effect on the Penalty Clause as Defined under Colombian Law', *The Illinois Business Law Journal*, 2009, p. 4–14.

Morrison 1994–1995
Morrison, R., Efficient Breach of International Agreements, *Denver Journal of International Law and Policy*, (23) 1994–1995, p. 183–222.

Moss 2011
Moss, G.C., Commercial contracts and European private law, in: C. Twigg-Flessner (ed.), *The Cambridge Companion to European Union Private Law*, Cambridge, UK: Cambridge Uni. Press, 2010, pp. 147–159.

Nelken 2004
Nelken, D., Using the Concept of Legal Culture, *Australian Journal of Legal Philosophy*, (29) 2004, p. 1–26.

Ogus 2006
Ogus, A. *Costs and Cautionary Tales: Economic Insights for the Law.* Hart Publishing, 2006.

Omar 2007
Omar, P. J., Lessons from the French experience: the possibility of codification of commercial law in the United Kingdom, *International Company and Commercial Law Review*, (18) 2007, p. 235–243.

Pelc 2010
Pelc, K.J., Eluding Efficiency: Why do we not see more efficient breach at the WTO?, *World Trade Review*, (9) 2010, p. 629–642.

Pelc & Urpelainen 2010
Pelc, K.J. & Urpelainen, J., On The Use of Efficient Breach in International Agreements, December 2010, Available at: <http://147.142.190.246/joomla/peio/files2011/papers/Pelc,%20Urpeleinen%2007.12.2010.pdf> (last accessed, 24th Jan. 2011).

Perillo 2000
Perillo, J.M., 'Misleading Oliver Wendell Holmes on Efficient Breach and Tortious Inference', *Fordham Law Review*, (68) 2000, P. 1085–1106.

Perritt Jr 2000
Perritt Jr, H. H., Dispute Resolution in Cyberspace: Demand for New Forms of ADR, *Ohio State Journal of Dispute Resolution*, (15) 2000, p. 675–702.

Phang 1992
Phang, A., Frustration in English Law, a Reappraisal, *Anglo-American Law Review*, (21) 1992, p. 278–309.

Polinsky 1983
Polinsky, A.M., 'Risk Sharing Through Breach of Contract Remedies', *Journal of Legal Studies*, 1983, p. 427–444.

Poole 2014
Poole, J. *Casebook on Contract Law* (12th ed. Oxford Uni. Press 2014).

Posner (A) 2000
Posner, E.A., 'Contact Remedies: Foreseeability, Precaution, Causation and Mitigation' in: B. Bouckaert & D.G. Geest (eds.), *Encyclopedia of Law and Economics, Volume III. The Regulation of Contracts*, Cheltenham, UK: Edward Elgar, 2000, p. 162–178.

Posner (B) 2000
Posner, E.A., "A Theory of Contract Law under Conditions of Radical Judicial Error", *Northwestern University Law Review*, (94)2000, p. 749–774.

Posner 2003
Posner, E.A., 'Economic Analysis of Contract Law After Three Decades: Success or Failure?', *Yale Law Journal*, 2003, p. 829–880.

Posner & Sykes 2011–2012
Posner, E.A. & Sykes, A.O., Efficient Breach of International Law: Optimal Remedies, 'Legalized Noncompliance,' and Related Issues, *Michigan Law Review*, (110) 2011–2012, p. 243–294.

Posner 1973
Posner, R. A., Economic Analysis of Law, 1st ed., Boston: Little Brown, 1973.

Posner & Rosenfield 1977
Posner, R.A. & Rosenfield, A.M., "Impossibility and Related Doctrines in Contract Law: An Economic Analysis", *Journal of Legal Study*, (6) 1977, p. 83–118.

Posner 2004
Posner, R.A., Law and economics in common-law, civil-law, and developing nations, *Ratio Juris*, (17) 2004, p. 66–79.

Posner 2007
Posner, R.A., *Economic Analysis of Law*, 7th ed., Boston: Aspen Publisher, 2007.

Perloff 1981
Perloff, J.M., 'The Effects of Breaches of Forward Contracts due to Unanticipated Price Changes', *The Journal of Legal Studies*, 1981, p. 221–235.

Polinsky 1987
Polinsky, A.M., 'Fixed Price versus Spot Price Contracts: A Study in Risk Allocation', *Journal of Law, Economics, & Organization*, 1987, p. 27–46.

Pound 1923
Pound, R., 'Theory of Judicial Decision', *Harvard Law Review*, 1922–1923, p. 802–825.

Qiao (乔宇) 2011
Qiao, Yu (乔宇), "完成行为的替代履行问题", 人民司法 ("The Question about Substitutive Performance of An Act", *People's Judicaure Case*), (10) 2011, p. 36–39. (China).

Rea 1984
Rea, S.A., "Efficiency Implications of Penalties and Liquidated Damages", *The Journal of Legal Studies*, (13) 1984, p. 147–167

Richard 2006
Richard, R. W. Brooks, 'The Efficient Performance Hypothesis', *The Yale Law Journal*, 2006, p. 568–596.

Roberts 2008
Roberts, C.L., 'Restitutionary Disgorgement for Opportunistic Breach of Contract and Mitigation of Damages' ', *Loyola of Los Angeles Law Review*, (42) 2008, p. 131–176.

Rodger 1992
Rodger, A. F., *The Codification of Commercial Law in Victorian Britain*, Law Quarterly Review, (109) 1992, p. 570–590.

Rogers 1998–1999
Rogers, C.A., "Gulliver's Troubled Travels, or the Conundrum of Comparative Law", George Washington Law Review, (67) 1998–1999, p. 149–190.

Rowan 2012
Rowan, H., Remedies For Breach of Contract, A Comparative Analysis of the Protection of Performance (Oxford Univ. Press 2012).

Rubin 1977
Rubin, P. H., Why Is the Common Law Efficient? *The Journal of Legal Studies*, (6) 1977, p. 51–63.

Rubin 1982
Rubin, P. H., Common Law and Statute Law, *The Journal of Legal Studies*, (11) 1982, p. 205–223.

Russell 2007
Russell, I.S., The Broken Promise of Efficient Breach: Sacrificing Certainty for False Efficiency', 2007, available at: <http://works.bepress.com/irma_russell/2> (last accessed, 5 February 2012>.

Scalise 2007
Scalise Jr, R.J., Why No "Efficient Breach" in the Civil Law?: A Comparative Assessment of the Doctrine of Efficient Breach of Contract, *The American Journal of Comparative Law*, (55) 2007, p. 721–766.

Schäfer & Ott 2004
Schäfer, H. & Ott, C., *The Economic Analysis of Civil Law*, Uk, Cheltenham & MA, USA, Northampton: Edward Elgar, 2004.

Schwartz 1979
Schwartz, A., "The Case for Specific Performance", *The Yale Law Journal*, (89) 1979, p. 271–306.

Schwartz 1990
Schwartz, A., The Myth that Promisees Prefer Supracompensatory Remedies: An Analysis of Contracting for Damage Measures, *Yale Law Journal*, (100)1990, p. 369–407.

Schwartz & Scott 2003
Schwartz, A. & Scott, R.E., 'Contract Theory and the Limits of Contract Law', *the Yale Law Journal*, 2003, p. 541–619.

Schwartz 2008
Schwartz, A. & Scott, R. E., *Market Damages, Efficient Contracting, and the. Economic Waste Fallacy*, Columbia Law Review (108) 2008, p. 1610–1669.

Schwenzer 2012
Schwenzer, I., "The Proposed Common European Sales Law and the Convention on the International Sale of Goods", *Uniform Commercial Code Law Journal*, (44) 2012, p. 457–481.

Senden 2004
Senden, L., Soft Law in European Community Law, *Oxford: Hart Publishing*, 2004.

Shavell 2004
Shavell, S., *Foudations of Economic Analysis of Law*, USA, Belknap Press of Harvard University Press, 2004.

Shavell 2006
Shavell, S., 'Specific Performance versus Damages for Breach of Contract: An Economic Analysis', Tex. Law Review, 2006, p. 831–867.

Shiffrin 2007
Shiffrin, S.V., The Divergence of Contract and Promise, *Harvard Law Review*, p. 708–753.

Shuzo 1998
Shuzo, Shiga, "中国法文化的考察,以诉讼的形态为素材", 选自王亚新&梁治平编: 明清时期的民事审判与民间契约, 北京:法律出版社("Investigation on Chinese Legal Culture, Litigation Pattern as Material ", in Y., Wang & Z., Liang (eds.):*The Civil Trial and Social Contract During the Ming and Qing Period*, Beijing: Law Press), 1998 (China).

Siems 2003
Siems, M., Disgorgement of Profits for Breach of Contract: A Comparative Analysis, *Edinburgh Law Review*, (7) 2003, p. 27–59.

Siems 2014
Siems, M., *Comparative Law*, Cambridge: Cambridge Uni. Press, 2014

Sidhu 2006
Sidhu, D.S., The Immorality and Inefficiency of an Efficient Breach, *Transactions: The Tennessee Journal of Business Law*, (8) 2006, p. 61–100.

Sidhu 2011
Sidhu, D.S., A Crisis of Confidence and Legal Theory: The Economic Downturn and the End of the Doctrine of Efficient Breach, *Georgetown Journal of Legal Ethics*, (24) 2010, p. 357–397.

Slapper & Kelly 2010–2011
Slapper, G. & Kelly, D., *The English Legal System* (11th ed.), Oxon: Routledge 2010–2011.

Smith 1994
Smith, L.D., "Disgorgement of the Profits of a Breach of Contract: Property, Contract and Efficient Breach", *Canadian Business Law Review*, (24)1994, p. 121–140.

Smith 2004
Smith, S. A., *Contract Theory*, Oxford, UK: Oxford Univ. Press, 2004.

Smith, Houser, Xiao & McCabe 2008
Smith, V.L., Houser, D., Xiao, E. & McCabe, K., "When Punishment Fails: Research on Sanctions, Intentions and Non-Cooperation" Games and Economic Behavior, (62) 2008, p. 509–532.

Smith 2010
Smith, J.M., European Private Law and the Comparative Method, in: C. Twigg-Flessner (ed.), *The Cambridge Companion to European Union Private Law*, Cambridge, UK: Cambridge Uni. Press, 2010, pp. 33–43.

Smythe 2009
Smythe, D. J., Impossibility and Impracticability, *Encyclopedia of Law and Economics*, 2009, Forthcoming. Available at SSRN: http://ssrn.com/abstract=1439922.

Spier & Whinston 1995
Spier, K.E. & Whinston, M., "On the Efficiency of Privately Stipulated Damages for Breach of Contract: Entry Barriers, Reliance, and Renegotiation", *Rand Journal of Economics*, (26)1995, p. 180–202.

Stavins 1995
Stavins, R., Transaction Costs and Tradeable Permits, Journal of Environmental Economics and Management, (29)1995, p. 133–148.

Stolle & Slain 1997
Stolle, D. P. & Slain, A. J., Standard form contracts and contract schemas: a preliminary investigation of the effects of exculpatory clauses on consumers' propensity to sue, *Behaviour Science & Law*, (15)1997, p. 83–94.

Sun (孙良国) 2009,
Liangguo Sun (孙良国), "期望损害赔偿的实现, 替代交易的研究", 当代法学 ("Realizing the Expectation Damages: the Study on Substitutive Performance", *Contemporary Law Review*), (6) 2009, p. 86–94. (China).

Sunstein 1997
Sunstein, C.R., Behavioral Analysis of Law, *The University of Chicago Law Review*, (64) 1997, p. 1175–1195.

Thel & Siegelman 2009
Thel, S. & Siegelman, P., Willfulness versus Expectation: A Promisor
Based Defense of Willful Breach Doctrine, *Michigan Law Review*, (107) 2009, p. 1517–1531.

Tong (佟柔) 1990
Tong, Rou (佟柔), 中国民法, 北京: 法律出版社 (*Chinese Civil Law*, Beijing: Law Press), 1990 (China).

Treite 1988
Treite, G., *Remedies for Breach of Contract: A Comparative Account*, Oxford University Press, 1988.

Treitel 2002
Treitel, G., *Some Landmarks of Twentieth Century Contract Law*, Oxford Clarendon Press, 2002.

Treitel 2003
Treitel, G., *The Law of Contract* (17th ed., London: Sweet & Maxwell), 2003

Triantis 1992
Triantis, G.G., Contractual Allocations of Unknown Risks: A Critique of the Doctrine of Commercial Impracticability, *the University of Toronto Law Journal*, 1992, p. 450–483.

Twigg-Flesner 2008
Twigg-Flesner, C., *The Europeanisation of Contract Law: Current Controversies in Law* (1st edition), UK: Routledge-Cavendish, 2008.

Twigg-Flesner 2008
Twigg-Flesner, C., Introduction: key features of European Union Private Law, in: C. Twigg-Flessner (ed.), *The Cambridge Companion to European Union Private Law*, Cambridge, UK: Cambridge Uni. Press, 2010, p. 1–19.

Ulen 1984
Ulen, T.S., the Efficiency of Specific Performance: Toward a Unified Theory of Contract Remedies, *Michigan Law Review*, 1984, p. 341–403.

Uribe 2011
Uribe, R.M., "The Effect of a Change of Circumstances on the Binding Force of Contracts – Comparative Perspectives", NL: *the auspices of METRO, the Instiute for Transnational Legal Research of Maastricht University, Intersentia*, (94) 2011.

Van Kogelenberg 2013
Van Kogelenberg, M., *Motive Matter, An Exploration of the Notion "Deliberate Breach of Contract" and its Consequences for the Application of Remedies*, Cambridge: Intersentia, 2013.

Van Zelst 2008
Van Zelst, B., *The Politics of European Sales Law: A Legal-Political Inquiry into the Drafting of the Uniform Commercial Code, the Vienna Sales Convention, the Dutch Civil Code and the European Sales Directive in the Context of the Europeanization of Private Law*, the Netherlands: Kluwer Law International BV, 2008.

Von Bar 2009
Von Bar, C. et al., "Principles, Definitions and Model Rules of European Private Law, Draft Common Frame of Reference (DCFR)" (eds.), 2009.

Waddams 2000
Waddams, S.M., Breach of Contract and the Concept of Wrongdoing, *Supreme Court Law Review*, 2000, p. 1–29.

Walt 2011
Walt, S., Penalty Clauses and Liquidated Damages, in: D.G. Geest, (ed.), *Contract Law and Economics*, 2d ed., Cheltenham, UK: Edward Elgar, 2011, p. 178–206.

Wang 1997
Wang Chengguang, An Emerging Legal System, in: Xianchu Zhang (ed.), *Introduction to Chinese Law*. Hongkong &London: Sweet & Maxwell Asia, 1997, p. 4–8.

Wang 1992
Wang Liming, Specific Performance in Chinese Contract Law: An East-West Comparison, *Asian Pacific Law Review* (1) 1992, p. 18–38.

Wang (王利明) 1996
Wang, Liming (王利明), 违约责任论, 北京:中国政法大学出版社 (*Study on the Liability for Breach of Contract*, Beijing: Publishing House of China University of Politics and Law), 1996 (China).

Wang & Xu 1999
Liming Wang & Chuanxi Xu, Fundamental Principles of China's Contract Law, *Columbia Journal of Asian Law* (13) 1999, p. 1–33.

Wang (王利明) 2001,
Wang, Liming (王利明),合同法要义与案例析解,总则, 北京:中国人民大学出版社 (*Contract Law, Fundamentals and Case Analysis, General Theory*, Beijing: People's University Publishing House), 2001 (China).

Wang (王利明) 2003
Wang, Liming (王利明),合同法研究, 北京:中国人民大学出版社 (*Study on Contract Law*, (Vol. II), Beijing: People's University Publishing House), 2003 (China).

Wang (王洪亮) 2012
Wang, Hongliang(王洪亮), "强制履行请求权的性质及其行使", 法学 ("The Nature of Compelled Performance and the Enforcement of It", *Law Study*), (1) 2012, p. 104–114, (China).

Wathne & Heide 2000
Wathne, K. H & Heide, J.B., 'Opportunism in Interfirm Relationships: Forms, Outcomes, and Solutions', *Journal of Marketing*, 2000, p. 36–51.

Warkol 1999
Warkol, C.S., "Resolving the Paradox between Legal Theory and Legal Fact: The Judicial Rejection of the Theory of Efficient Breach", *Cardozo Law Review*, (20)1998–1999, p. 321–354.

Webb 2006
Webb, C., "Performance and Compensation: An Analysis of Contract Damages and Contractual Obligation", *Oxford Journal of Legal Studies*, (26) 2006, pp. 41–71.

Wehberg 1959
Wehberg, H., "Pacta Sunt Servanda", *American Journal of International Law* (53)1959, p. 775–786.

Whincup 1992
Whincup, M.H., *Contract Law and Practice: The English System and Continental Comparisons*, 2nd ed., Deventer & Boston: Kluwer Law & Taxation Pub., 1992.

Williamson 1981
Williamson, O.E., 'The Modern Corporation: Origins, Evolution', *Journal of Economic Literature*, 1981, p. 1537–1568.

Wilhelmsson 1993
Wilhelmsson, T., *Perspectives of Critical Contract Law*, UK: Ashgate, 1993.

Wilkinson-Ryan & Baron 2009
Wilkinson-Ryan, T. & Baron, J., 'Moral Judgment and Moral Heuristics in Breach of Contract', *Journal of Empirical Legal Studies*, 2009, p. 405–423

Wilkinson-Ryan 2010
Wilkinson-Ryan, T., 'Do Liquidated Damages Encourage Breach? A Psychological Experiment', *Michigan Law Review*, (108)2010, p. 633–671.

Wilkinson-Ryan 2014
Wilkinson-Ryan, T., 'Demand for Breach', *University of Pennsylvania Institute for Law & Economic Research Paper*, No. 14–19 (Apr. 20th 2014). Available at SSRN: http://ssrn.com/abstract=2428775.

Wladis 1987
Wladis, J. D., *Common Law and Uncommon Events: The Development of the Doctrine of Impossibility of Performance in English Contract Law*, Georgetown Law Journal (75) 1987, p. 1575–1631.

Woo 1999
Woo, M., Law and Discretion in the Contemporary Chinese Courts, *Pacific Rim Law & Policy Journal*, (8)1999, p. 581–614.

Xiao & Qi (肖丕国&祁圣友) 2006
Xiao, Pi'guo & Qi, Shengyou (肖丕国&祁圣友), "商品房买卖中的惩罚性赔偿研究", 人民司法 ("A study on the Punitive Damages in Sales of Commodity Houses", *People's Judicature*), (1) 2006, p. 42. (China),

Xin (信春鹰) 1999
Xin, Chuying (信春鹰), 中国的法律制度及其改革, 北京:法律出版社 (*Chinese Legal System and Current Legal Reform*, Beijing: Law Press), 1999 (China).

Xing (刑建东) 2006
Xing, Jiandong (刑建东), 合同法总则, 学说与判例注释, 北京:法律出版社 (*General Rules of Contract Law, Commentary and Case Study*, Beijing: Law Press), 2006 (China).

Xu (许慎) 2001
Xu, Shen (许慎), 说文解字, 北京:九州出版社 (*Words and Expressions*, Beijing: Jiuzhou Publisher), 1st ed., 2001 (China).

Yorio 1982
Yorio, E., In Defense of Money Damages for Breach of Contract, *Columbia Law Review* (82) 1982, pp. 1365–1424.

Yorio 2012
Yorio, E., Contract Enforcement: Specific Performance and Injunctions (2nd ed. New York, Wolters Kluwer Law & Business 2012).

Zeng (曾世雄) 2001
Zeng, Shixiong (曾世雄), 损害赔偿法原理, 北京:中国政法大学出版社 (*The Principle in the Law of Damage Compensation*, Beijing: Publishing House of China University of Politics and Law), 2001 (China).

Zeng (曾宪义) 2000
Zeng, Xianyi et (曾宪义等), 中国法制史, 北京大学出版社 (*Chinese Legal History*, Beijing University Press), 2000.

Zeng (曾宪义) 2009
Zeng, Xianyi (曾宪义), "关于中国传统调解制度的若干问题研究", 中国法学 ("Studies of Several Issues about the Institution of Mediation in Traditional China", *China Legal Science*), (4) 2009, p.34–46.

Zhang (张传玺) 1991
Zhang, Chuanxi (张传玺), "论中国历代契约资料的蕴藏及其史料价值", 北京大学学报 ("Sources of Deeds in Various Periods and Their Value as Historical Data", *Journal of Beijing University*), (3)1991, p. 112–128.

Zhang (张晋藩) 1999
Zhang, Jifan (张晋藩), 中华法制文明的演进, 北京:中国政法大学出版社 (*Evolution of the Chinese Legal Civilization*, Beijing: Publishing House of China University of Politics and Law), 1999 (China).

Zhang (张晋藩) 2009
Zhang, Jinfan(张晋藩), 中国法律的传统与近代转型, 北京:法律出版社 (*The Tradition and Modern Transformation of Chinese Law*, Beijing: Law Press), 1997 (China).

Zhang 2006
Zhang Mo, Chinese Contract Law: Theory and Practice, Leiden: Martinus Nijhoff Publishers, 2006.

Zhang & Huang 2000
Zhang Y. & Huang, D., New Contract Law in the People's Republic of China and the UNIDROIT Principles of International Commercial Contracts: A Brief Comparison, Uniform Law Review 5 (2000), p. 429–440.

Zhao (赵刚) 2010
Zhao, Gang (赵刚), "减损规则的适用与违约损害赔偿计算", 社会科学期刊 ("Application of the Mitigation Rule and Measure of Damages for Breach of Contract", *Social Science Journal*), (3) 2010, pp. 111–114 (China).

Zheng (郑显文) 2003
Zheng, Xianwen (郑显文), "中国古代关于商品买卖的法律文书研究", 中国经济史研究 ("A Study of Legal Documents for Sales Contracts in Chinese History", *Study on the History of Chinese Economy*),(2) 2003, p. 52–62.

Zhong & Yu 1999
Zhong Jianhua & Yu Guanghua, China's Uniform Contract Law: Progress and Problems, UCLA Pacific Basin Law Journal (17) 1999, p.1–31.

Zhou 2008
Zhou, Q., 'Is Seller's efficient breach possible under English sale law', 2008,
Available at: <http://works.bepress.com/qi_zhou/1> (last accessed, 16 December 16 2011).

Zhu 2005
Zhu, N., A Case Study of Legal Transplant: The Possibility of efficient breach in China, *Georgetown Journal of International Law*, (36) 2005, p. 1145–1171.

Zhu (朱佳木) 2007,
Zhu, Jiamu (朱佳木), "毛泽东对计划经济的探索及其对社会主义市场经济的意义", 中共党史研究("Mao Zedong's Theory of Planned Economics and Its Significance to the Socialist Market Economy", *Journal of Chinese Communist Party History Studies*), (2) 2007, p. 3–11 (China).

Zelst 2008
Zelst, B.V., "The Politics of European Sales Law: A Legal-Political Inquiry into the Drafting of the Uniform Commercial Code, the Vienna Sales Convention, the Dutch Civil Code and the European Sales Directive in the Context of the Europeanization of Private Law", the Netherlands: *Kluwer Law International BV*, 2008.

Zhu 2005
Zhu, Ni, A Case Study of Legal Transplant: The Possibility of Efficient Breach in China. Georgetown Journal of International Law, Vol. 36, p. 1145–1171, 2005.

Zimmermann 2009
Zimmermann, R, "Present State of European Private Law", *The American Journal of Comparative Law*, (57) 2009, p. 479–512.

Živković 2013
Živković, V., Hardship in French, English and German Law, Strani pravni život (Foreign Legal Life) – Časopis Instituta za uporedno pravo u Beogradu (Institute for Comparative Law in Belgrade review), Jan. 2013, available at SSRN: http://ssrn.com/abstract=2158583.

Zweigert & Kotz 1998
Zweigert, K. & Kotz, H., Introduction to Comparative Law, 3rd rev. ed. Oxford: Oxford University Press, 1998.

TABLE OF LEGISLATION AND EUROPEAN OR INTERNATIONAL INSTRUMENTS

International

- Convention on Contracts for the International Sales of Goods (CISG)
- Unidroit Principles of International Commercial Contracts (PICC)
- ICC *Force Majeure* Clause 2003.

European Union

- Treaty Establishing the European Community (TEC);
- Treaty on Functioning of the European Union (TFEU);
- A Green Paper on "policy options for progress towards a European Contract Law for consumers and businesses COM (2010) 348 final;
- *A More Coherent European Contract Law, An Action Plan* (the "Action Plan");
- Draft Common Frame of Reference of European Private Law (DCFR);
- Principles of European Contract Law (PECL) (Lando Principles);
- Directive to protect the consumer in respect of contracts negotiated away from business premises (85/577/EEC), 20 December 1985, (Doorstep Selling Directive);
- Directive on package travel, package holidays and package tours (90/314/EEC) 13 June 1990;
- Directive on unfair terms in consumer contracts (93/31/EEC), 5 April 1993;
- Directive on the protection of purchasers in respect of certain aspects of contracts relating to the purchase of the right to use immovable properties on a timeshare basis (94/47/EC) 26 October 1994;
- Directive on the protection of consumers in respect of distance contracts (97/7/EC), 20 May 1997;
- Directive on Consumer protection in the indication of the prices of products offered to consumers (98/6/EC), February 1998;
- Directive on certain aspects of the sale of consumer goods and associated guarantees (1999/44/EC), May 1999;
- Directive concerning the distance marketing of consumer financial services and amending Council Directive 90/619/EEC and Directives 97/7/EC and 98/27/EC (2002/65/EC), September 2002;

- Directive on injunctions for the protection of consumer' interests (98/27/EC), 23 April 2009;
- Directive on consumer rights (2011/83/EU), 25 October 2011;
- Directive on Common European Sales Law Directive COM (2011) 635 final (CESL);
- Proposal for a Directive of the European Parliament and of the Council on Consumer Rights, COM (2008) 614;
- Resolution of the European Parliament on action to bring into line the Private Law of the member state, [OJ 1989 C 158/400];
- Resolution of the European Parliament on the harmonization of certain sectors of the Private Law of the member states, [OJ 1994 C 205/518].

England

- The Law Reform (Frustrated Contract) Act 1943;
- Sales of Goods Act 1979 (SGA 1979);
- Supreme court act 1981;
- Sales of Goods Act 1893 (SGA 1893);
- The Sale and Supply of Goods to Consumers Regulation 2002;

China

Legislation

- 中华人民共和国民法通则 [The General Principles of Civil Law of the People's Republic of China]， promulgated by Order No. 37 of the President of the People's Rep. of China, 12 April 1986, effective as of 1 January 1987 (GPCL);
- 中华人民共和国海商法[the Maritime Law of the People's Republic of China], promulgated by Order No. 64 of the President of the People's Rep. of China, 7 November 1992, effective as of 1 July 1992;
- 中华人民共和国经济合同法 [The Economic Contract Law of the People's Republic of China], promulgated by Nat' People's Cong., 13 December 1981, effective as of 1 July 1982, expired in 1999 (ECL);
- 中华人民共和国涉外经济合同法 [Law of the People's Republic of China on Economic Contracts Involving Foreign Interest], promulgated by Order No. 22 of the President of the People's Rep. of China, 21 March 1985, effective as of 1 July 1985, expired in 1999 (FECL);
- 中华人民共和国技术合同法[The Law of the People's Republic of China on Technology Contracts], promulgated by Nat' People's Cong., 23 June 1987, effective as of 1 November 1987, expired in 1999. (TCL);
- 中华人民共和国合同法[Contract Law of the People's Republic of China], promulgated by Nat' People's Cong., 15 March 1999, effective as of 1 October 1999 (CCL);
- 中华人民共和国城市房地产管理法 [Urban Real Estate Administration Law of the People's Republic of China], promulgated by the Standing Comm. Nat' People's Cong., 5 July 1994, effective as of 1 January 1995, amended 30 August 2007.

- 中华人民共和国食品安全法 [Regulation on the Implementation of the Food Safety Law of the People's Republic of China], promulgated by Nat' People's Cong., 8 July 2009;
- 中华人民共和国侵权责任法 [The Tort Law of the People's Republic of China], promulgated by Standing Comm. Nat' People's Cong., 26 December 2009, effective as of 1 July 2010.
- 中华人民共和国民事诉讼法 [Civil Procedure Law of the People's Republic of China], promulgated by Nat' People's Cong., 9 April 1991, 1st revised by the Standing Comm. Nat' People's Cong., 28 October 2007, 2nd revised 31 August 2012, effective as of 1 January 2013 (民事诉讼法[CPL]);
- 中华人民共和国消费者权益保护法 [Law of the People's Republic of China on the Protection of Consumer Rights and Interests], promulgated by Standing Comm. Nat' People's Cong., 31 October 1993, effective as of 1 January 1994, revised 25 October 2013 (消费者保护法[consumer protection law]);

Supreme People Ct' Interpretations

- 最高人民法院关于适用《中华人民共和国合同法》若干问题的解释(一) [Interpretation I of the Supreme People's Court of Several Issues concerning the Application of the Contract Law of the People's Republic of China], promulgated by the Judicial Comm. of the Sup. People's Court, 1 December 1999 (合同法司法解释一 [Interpretation over the CCL I]);
- 最高人民法院关于审理商品房买卖合同纠纷案件适用法律若干问题的解释 [Several Issues Concerning the Application of Law in Trial of Dispute Cases Involving Commodity Premises Sales and Purchase Contracts Interpretation], promulgated by the Judicial Comm. of the Sup. People's Court, 24 March 2003, effective as of 1 June 2003 (商品房买卖司法解释 [Interpretation on Sales of Commodity Premises]);
- 最高人民法院关于司法解释工作的规定 [Provisions of the Supreme People's Court on the Judicial Interpretation Work], promulgated by No. 12 [2007] of the Sup. People's Court, 23 March 2007;
- 最高人民法院关于适用《中华人民共和国合同法》若干问题的解释(二) [Interpretation II of the Supreme People's Court of Several Issues concerning the Application of the Contract Law of the People's Republic of China], promulgated by the Judicial Comm. of the Sup. People's Court, 9 February 2009 (合同法司法解释二 [Interpretation over the CCL II]);
- 关于当前形势下审理民商事合同纠纷案件若干问题的指导意见[Guiding Opinions on Several Issues Concerning Trials of Civil and Commercial Contract Disputes Under Current Circumstances], promulgated by the Sup. People's Court, 7 July 2009. (合同指导意见 [Guiding Opinions]);
- 最高人民法院关于审理买卖合同纠纷案件适用法律问题的解释 [Interpretations of the Supreme People's Court on Certain Issues concerning the Application of Contract Law of the People's Rep. of China], promulgated by the Sup. People's Court, 10 May 2012. (买卖合同司法解释[Interpretation over Sales Disputes]).

Other Jurisdiction

- Basic Law (the German constitution);
- Civil Code (German) (BGB);
- Code Civil (France);
- Uniform Commercial Code (USA);
- Restatement (Second) of Contracts (USA);
- Massachusetts consumer protection law (USA);

Report and News

U.S. Department of Justice, Civil Jury Cases and Verdicts in Large Countries, available at www.bjs.gov/content/pub/pdf/cjcavilc.pdf (1992).

U.S. Department of Justice, Civil Jury Cases and Verdicts in Large Countries, available at www.bjs.gov/content/pub/pdf/ctcvlc01.pdf (2001).

U.S. Department of Justice, Punitive Damage Awards in State Courts, available at www.bjs.gov/content/pub/pdf/pdasc05.pdf (2005).
European Commission, A New Start: European Commission work plan to deliver jobs, growth and investment, 16 December 2014, available at: http://europa.eu/rapid/press-release_IP-14-2703_en.htm.

CASES

England

- *Alghussein Establishment v Eton College* [1988] 1 W.L.R. 587.
- *AV Pound & Co Ltd v M W Hardy & Co Inc* [1956] AC 588.
- *Azimut-Benetti Spa v Healey* [2011] 1 Lloyd's Rep 473 (QB.
- *Baily v. De Crespigny* [1869] 4 L.R. 180 (Q.B.).
- *Bank of England v. Vagliano Bros* [1981] A C 107.
- *Behnke v Beda Shipping Co Ltd* [1927] 1 KB 649.
- *British Westinghouse Electric & Manufacturing Co Ltd v Underground Electric Rlys Co Ltd* [1912] A.C. 673.
- *CCC Films v Impact Quadrant Films,* [1984] 3 All ER 298.
- *Chandelor v. Lopus,* 79 Eng. Rep. 3 (K.B. 1603).
- *Cheall v. Association of Professional Executive Clerical and Computer Staff* [1983] 2 A.C.
- *Cohen v Roche* [1927] 1 KB 169.
- *Co-operative v Argyll* [1998] AC 1 (HL).
- *Cory v Thames Ironworks and shipbuilding Co Ltd* [1868] LR 3 Q.B. 181.
- *Cullinane v British 'Rema' Manufacturing Co Ltd* [1954] 1 Q.B. 292.
- *Currie v. Misa* (1875) LR 10 Ex 153.
- *Duffen v FRA Bo Spa* (No 2) [2000] 1 L. R. 180.
- *Dunlop Pneumatic Tyre Co. Ltd. v. New Garage & Motor Co.* [1915] A.C. 79.
- *Dunkirk Colliery Co v. Lever* (1878) 9 ChD 20, CA.
- *Dunlop Pneumatic Tyre Co. Ltd v New Garage & Motor Co.* [1915] A.C. 79.
- *Erie County Natural Gas and Fuel Co Ltd v Samuel S. Carroll* [1911] A.C. 105.
- *Evans Marshall & Co v Bertola SA* [1973] 1 W.L.R. 349, M Co.
- *Experience Hendrix LLC v PPX Enterprises Inc* [2003] EWCA Civ 323.
- *Fibrosa Spolka Akcyjna v Fairbairn Lawson Combe Barbour Ltd* [1943] AC 32.
- *Ford v Cotesworth* [1870] 5 L.R. 544 (Q.B.).
- *Ford Motor Co v Armstrong* [1915] 31 TLR 267 (CA).
- *France v Gaudet* [1871] L.R. 6 Q.B. 199.
- *Francis v Cowcliffe* [1976] 33 P & CR 368 (CH).
- *Francis Milton Gibson v J T Allen Agency* [1965] W.Y. 51 407 P.2d 708.
- *George v Ascot Supreme Ltd* [2002] EWHC 1978 (Q.B.).

- *Hadley v Baxendale* [1854] 9 EX 341.
- *Hadley v Clarke* [1799] 101 E.R. 1377.
- *Hinde v. Liddell* [1975]L.R. 10 Q.B. 265.
- *Howell v. Coupland* [1876] 1 Q.B.D. 258 (C.A.)Re Badische Co Ltd [1921] 2 Ch 331.
- *Hyman and Wife v Nye & Sons* [1880–81]L.R. 6 Q.B.D. 685.
- James Finlay & Co Ltd v NV Kwik Hoo Tong Handel Maatschappij.
- *Jarvis v Swans Tours Ltd* [1972] EWCA Civ 8.
- *J Lauritzen AS v Wijsmuller BV (The Super Servant Two)* [1990] 1 Lloyd's Rep. 1.
- *Koufos v Czarnikow Ltd (The Heron II)* [1969] 1 A.C. 350.
- *Land Rover Group Ltd v UPF* (UK) *Ltd* [2002] EWHC 3183.
- *Logan v Le Mesurier.* [1847] 6 Moo PC 116.
- *Lord Elphinstone v. Monkland Iron and Coal Co.* [1886] 11 A. C. 332.
- *McMaster & Co Ltd v Mc Euen & Co Ltd* [1921] S.C. (HL) 24.
- *McRae v Commonwealth Disposals Commission* [1952], 84 C.L.R. 377.
- *Meng Leong Development Pte Ltd v Jip Hong Trading Co Pte Ltd* [1985] AC 511.
- *Murray v Leisureplay plc* [2005] EWCA Civ 963 (CA) (employment contract).
- *M&J Polymers Ltd v Imerys Minerals Ltd* [2008] EWHC 344 (QB) (sales contract).
- *Oscar Chess Ltd v Williams* 1 ALL ER 325 (1957).
- *Payzu Ltd v Saunders* [1919] 2 K.B.581, C.A.
- *Philips Hong Kong Ltd v The AG of Hong Kong* [1993]61 BLR 41 (PC).
- *Re R & H Hall and W H Pim (Junior) & Co Ltd* [1928] All ER Rep 763.
- *Royal Bank of Canada v W Got Associates Electrical Ltd* [1999] 3SCR 408.
- R Pagnan & Fratelli v. Corbisa Industrial Agropacuaria Limitada.
- *Sealace Shipping Co. Ltd v. Oceanvoice Ltd, The Alecos M* [1991] 1 Lloyd's Rep. 120.
- *Sky Petroleum Ltd v VIP Petroleum Ltd* [1974] 1 WLR 576.
- *Société des Industries Métallurgiques SA v Bronx Engineering Co Ltd* [1975] 1 Lloyd's Rep 465 (CA).
- *Splidt v Heath* [1809] 170 E.R.1080.
- *Steam Herring Fleet Ltd v VS Richards & Co Ltd* [1901] 17 T.L.R. 731.
- *Staffordshire Area Health Authority v South Staffordshire Waterworks Co, [1978] 3 All ER 769, Court of Appeal (1978), [1978] 1 W.L.R. 1387.*
- *Stuart v Wilkins*, 99 Eng. Rep. 15 (K.B. 1778).
- *Sudbrook Trading Estate Ltd v Eggleton* [1983] 1AC 444 (HL).
- *Tai Hing Cotton Mill Ltd v Kamsing Knitting Factory*[1979] AC 91.
- *Taylor v Caldwell* [1863] EWHC J1 (QB), 122 ER 309, 3 B & S 826.
- *Thames Guaranty Ltd v Campbell* [1985] Q.B. 210 (C.A.)
- *The Arpad* [1934] P189 at 212, per Greer LJ.
- *Thorn v Commissioners of Works and Public Buildings* [1863] 32 Beav. 490.
- *Tito v Waddell* (No 2) [1977] CH 106.
- *Tradax Export SA v Andre & Cie SA* [1976] 1 Lloyd's Rep. 416.Krell v Henry [1903] 2 K.B. at 749.
- *Tsakiroglou & Co Ltd v Noblee & Thorl GmbH* [1962] AC 93.
- *Tullett Prebon Group Ltd v El-Hajjali [2008] EWHC 1924* (QB) (employment contract).
- *Victoria Laundry (Windsor) Ltd v Newman Industries Ltd* [1949] 2 K.B. 528.
- Wedgwood v Adams [1843] 49 E.R. 958.

- *Wertheim v Chicoutimi* [1911] AC 301.
- *Willson v Love* [1896] 1 Q.B. 626.
- *Wilson v. United Counties Bank Ltd.* [1920] A.C. 102.

China

Changchun Foreign Economic and Trade Co. Ltd. Vs. Chaoyang Real Estate Development Co. Ltd.

Changchunshi Duiwai Jingji Maoyi Gongsi Su Changchunshi Chaoyang Fangdichan Kaifa Gongsi Gouxiao Fangwu Yin Qingshibiangeng er Yinqi de Jiakuan Jiufen An (长春市对外经济贸易公司诉长春市朝阳房地产开发公司购销房屋因情势变更而引起的价款纠纷案) [Changchun Foreign Economic and Trade Co. Ltd. Vs. Chaoyang Real Estate Development Co. Ltd.], Renming Fayuan Anli Xuan (人民法院案例选) [Selected Cases from the People's Courts] 4, p. 127.

Chengdu Bai Shun Shi Ye Co.Ltd. & China Building Technique Group Co., Ltd. (CBTGC)

Chengdushi Baishun Shiye You xian Gongsi Su Zhongguo Jianzhu Jituan Youxian Gongsi (成都市百顺实业有限公司诉中国建筑技术集团有限公司中国建筑技术集团有限公司) [Chengdu Bai Shun Shi Ye Co.Ltd. & China Building Technique Group Co., Ltd. (CBTGC)], (Sichuan High People's Ct. 13 August 2011) (PKUlaw).

Great Wall Company v. Ocean Plaza Company

Changcheng Gongsi Su Yuanyang Dasha Gongsi Shangpinfang Maimai Hetong Jiufen An (长城公司诉远洋大厦公司商品房买卖合同纠纷案) [Great Wall Company v. Ocean Plaza Company], 2004 Sup. People's Ct. Gaz. 10 (No. 1 Beijing Interm. People's Ct. 2004) (China).

Guangdong Changhong Highway Engineering Co. Ltd. Vs. Fujian Rongyuan Construction Co.Ltd.

Guangdong Changhong Gonglugongcheng Youxian Gongsi yu Fujiansheng Rongyuan Jianshe Gongcheng Youxian Gongsi Jianshe Gongcheng Shigong Hetong Jiufen Shangsu An (广东长宏公路工程有限公司与福建省榕源建设工程有限公司建设工程施工合同纠纷上诉案) [Guangdong Changhong Highway Engineering Co. Ltd. Vs. Fujian Rongyuan Construction Co.Ltd.] (Shangluo Interm. People's Ct, 12 May 2014) (PKUlaw).

Hainan Yuya saltworks vs. Taikun Real Estate Development Co. Ltd.

HainanSheng Yuya Yanchang Deng yu Sanya Taikun Fangdichan Kaifa Youxian Gongsi Tudi Shiyongquan Zhuanrang Hetong Jiufen Shangsu An (海南省榆亚盐场等与泰坤房地产开发有限公司土地使用权转让合同纠纷上诉案) [Hainan Yuya saltworks vs. Taikun Real Estate Development Co. Ltd.] (Hainan High People's Ct., 21 December 2007). (Chinalawinfo)

Li Mou v. Huang Xiaoling
Limou Su Huang Xiaoling Fangwu Maimai Hetong Jiufen An (李某诉黄晓玲房屋买卖合同纠纷案) [Li Mou v. Huang Xiaoling] (Zhejiang Ningbo Dist. People's Ct. 22 December 2011) (Chinalawinfo).

Wuhan Municipal Coal Gas Corp. v. Chongqing Measuring Instrument Factory
Wuhanshi Meiqi Gongsi Su Chongqing Jiance Yibiaochang An (武汉市煤气公司诉重庆检测仪表厂煤气装配线技术转让合同， 煤气表散件购销合同纠纷案) [Wuhan Municipal Coal Gas Corp. v. Chongqing Measuring Instrument Factory], 1996 Sup. People's Ct. Gaz2, (Wuhan Interm. People's Ct. 1996) (China).

Zhongji Tongyong Import and Export Co. Ltd. vs. Tianjin No.2 Port Co. Ltd
Zhongji Tongyong Jinchukou Gongsi Su Tianjin Gangbu Di er gangYouxian Gongsi Gangkou Zuoye Hetong Jiufen An, 中机通用进出口公司诉天津港埠第二港有限公司港口作业合同纠纷案, [Zhhongji Tongyong Import and Export Co. Ltd. vs. Tianjin No.2 Port Co. Ltd], 2000 Sup. People's Ct. Gaz. 5 (Tianjin High People's Ct. 2000) (China).

Zhong Jian Sanju JIanshenggongcheng Gufen Youxiang Gongsi Su Anhui Sheng Youbang Hunningtu Youxian Gongsi (中建三局建设工程股份有限公司诉安徽省友邦混凝土有限公司) [China Construction Third Engineering Bureau Co. Ltd. vs. Anhui concrete Co. Ltd.], (Hefei High People's Ct. 2007).

VALORIZATION ADDENDUM

1. Social Relevance of This Research

Firms care about economic profits. But should firms only pursue economic welfare? Many debates have been raised up about the trade off between economic value and other values impacting a firm's decision. One of these is related to the theory of efficient breach proposed by law and economic scholars. The traditional efficient breach theory depicts a situation where breach of a contract compared to its performance creates more wealth to the breaching party while leaving the non-breaching party indifferent between breach and performance. Thus, it is assumed that contract law should be shaped in such a way that efficient breaches will be encouraged and otherwise breach is prevented. The remedy of expectation damages is assumed to be able to realize this goal since it enables a potential breaching party to escape from the obligation of performance as long as he is willing to pay damages equal to the other party's expected loss. In this sense, the meaning of a contract commitment is consistent with the famous statement made by Judge Oliver Wendell Holmes that a contract only depicts a duty to pay damages when it is broken but nothing else. A firm is encouraged to breach a contract if this brings out higher economic profits than performance does. Sitting on the other side of the table, moralists argue that firms should not only be driven by economic efficiency but also by promissory morality, which requires a firm to comply with the promise it has made. Following this idea, moralists would suggest that contract law should always serve the purpose of enforcing promise, which points in the direction of the remedy of specific performance. The conflict between a firm's goal of making profits and its moralistic obligation of keeping promise provided the initial impetus for the development of this research, which in return contributes to the balance between moralism and economic efficiency.

Setting the above debate aside, a question to be met by contract parties is that they do meet several unexpected events which may have altered the utility of the contract and rendered the contract less profitable for one party after the conclusion of the contract. Contract law enforces a contract because the parties want it in order to increase the social welfare shared by the parties. However, a complete and perfect contract does not exist, given the fact that contracting parties have limited foresight and they cannot afford the high transaction costs for drafting a fully stipulated contract. For this reason, parties in some circumstances do not want a contract to be performed and they would have chosen non-performance at the time when the contract is concluded had they foreseen those circumstances. This is also the starting point for the proposition of the efficient breach theory, according to which the approach of breach and payment of expectation damages is considered to be the optimal solution in the above circumstances. However, there are other options to avoid non-performance when performance compared to non-performance incurs higher costs to the promisor. The result of this research is relevant since it essentially discusses a very practical problem that every contracting party might have to face if performance of a contract turns out to be burdensome.

2. Audience besides Academic Community

Policy makers might be intended in the results of this research. This research is concerned with a central question regarding how to improve the normative framework of contract law in order to facilitate welfare-maximization. The research addresses a number of important questions that policy makers need to answer in relation to the design of contract law. What is the optimal default contract remedy? Should parties be allowed to freely stipulate ex-ante contract damages? When should non-performance of a contract be considered to be efficient? What options do parties have when an unexpected contingency happens and alters the equilibrium of a contract? The answers to the above questions will be found in this research. In addition, inspiration can be drawn from this research regarding the possibility and needs of legal transplantation. This research compares different contract law systems regarding the choice of default contract remedy, the effect of damages stipulation and reactions of the law to unexpected events. More importantly, the historical development of a specific contract law system and the cultural environment where each legal system works have been equally studied so that the operation of a specific legal rule can be better understood. Last decades have witnessed an increase in the scale of legal transplantation. It is important for policy makers in one legal system to understand not only the differences between laws but also the cultural and historical elements that shape those differences.

Business will be another group who can benefit from the results of this research. On the one hand, this research has provided a comprehensive overview of breach, non-performance and remedies in Chinese contract law, European Union law and English sales law. This will be helpful for companies that are planning or have already chosen either Chinese law, English law or EU law as the applicable law to their contracts. Business will have a general picture in mind regarding the structure of a specific contract law system and base their contracting strategies (e.g. damages stipulation or risk allocation) on their prediction of legal consequences resulting from specific contract terms. For example, when negotiating over the remedies for breach of a contract, contracting parties will always have to know how to stipulate contract remedies by themselves, to what extent they are allowed to stipulate the amount of contract damages and what will happen if a damages clause is considered to be punitive. Business will find the above information in this research. On the other hand, developing the possible solutions to deal with unexpected risks is an important task undertaken by this research. When conditions and circumstances have changed, contract parties face the choices of either continuing performance, breaching the contract, renegotiating with each other or seeking for remedies from a third party. In this respect, this research also provides a lot of hints and ideas for business regarding the possible solutions offered by a specific contract law system to unexpected risks.

In addition to policy makers and businesses, judges, lawyers and other legal professions may also benefit from the results of this research. This has some particular meaning to legal professions who deal with Chinese law. In the past 30 years, there is a sharp increase in the scale of China-related transactions and investment against a global market and in return this creates more needs for legal professions with a knowledge of Chinese law. But for many lawyers or judges, Chinese law still seems to be an alienated legal system with a lot of uncertainties. Part II of this thesis provides an extensive discussion of Chinese contract law and legal culture in comparison to European Union law and English law. By referring to the result of this thesis, the western legal audience could find out to what degree the Chinese legal system differs from basic contract law theories that are well-known by European lawyers when it comes to breach, damages and unexpected contract risks.

3. Publication of the Research Results

First, the results of this research will be published into a book by intersentia in its *Ius Commune* Europaeum series. The book will be available to students and researchers who have special interests in the topics of either contract law, comparative law or law and economics. By referring to this book, they can develop their own arguments and ideas, for instance, regarding the justifications for breaches, the optimal solution to control contract risks or the justification for a default contract remedy.

Second, some chapters or sections in this thesis have already been or are in the pipeline for being published in law journals or book chapters. For instance, the Syracuse Journal of Internal Law and Commerce in 2014 has published the paper "Efficient Breach in the Common European Sales Law (CESL)", which has discussed the possibility of applying the efficient breach theory in the Common European Sales Law.

Third, since 2012 and 2015 some results in this research have been presented in conferences and workshops, such as the Joint Seminar "*The Future of Law and Economics*" in Paris or the "*European Master in Law and Economics Midterm Meeting*" in Bologna. Presentations of the papers in front of audiences with different backgrounds facilitate the exchange of ideas, suggestions and critiques over the topic of the efficient breach theory from various perspectives. More importantly, feedbacks from the audiences have made a great contribution to the improvement of this research.

4. Innovativeness of the Research

For a long time, contract law scholars have been making a lot of efforts to solve the contract law design problem by adopting different methodologies. The central question that they tried to answer was how to optimally design contract law rules in order to realize some specific goals. Law and economics scholars use efficiency as the standard for optimizing the design of contract law and proposed the efficient breach theory, which is concerned with the choice of contract remedy rule. This research studies the applicability of efficient breach in different legal systems and examines what extent such a theory is consistent with the contract laws in those legal systems. To summarize, this research is assumed to contribute to literature at least from three perspectives.

From a theoretical perspective, this research re-examines the theory of efficient breach and reconsiders the implications that the theory of efficient breach theory will provide to the normative framework of contract law. In the previous literature, the focus of the theory of efficient breach has been placed on the interactive relationship between expectation damages and a promisor's decision of breach. As a result, the theory of efficient breach presented in previous literature has been heavily criticized for its indeterminacy and inaccuracy since it has ignored many other efficiency-related factors and the multiple effects on people's behavior created by contract remedies. By taking those criticisms as well as the concept of economic efficiency into consideration, this research has analyzed two scenarios of efficient breach as well as the relationship between efficiency and different contract law rules instead of using a general efficient breach scenario. This research realizes that the initial question triggering the debates over the theory of efficient breach is that performance of a contract in certain circumstances might turn out to be inefficient since it is costly for parties to include all the possible contingencies in their contract. In terms of contingencies altering the utility of a contract, this research concludes that only unfortunate contingencies which increase the burden of performance or alter the equilibrium of a contract will lead to a result that performance of the contract should be refrained. In contrast, the scenario of efficient breach in relation to a fortunate contingency is only plausible in theory but not in reality when a number of factors are taken into consideration, such as the cost of enforcing remedies, the property law rules and the possibility of substitutive transactions, etc. Moreover, this research argues that breach of a contract is merely one solution that a promisor could choose; but there are also other solutions available to contract parties for avoiding inefficient performance of a contract, such as renegotiation of a contract in order to terminate or modify it. In this sense, there might be a new terminology – inefficient performance – better indicating the problem to be solved by the efficient breach theory and hereby our attention should also be paid on the entire framework of contract law rules instead of merely on the choice of the default remedy.

Except for re-framing the efficient breach theory, this thesis also tries to extend this theory to the study of specific contract law systems. As is realized by some law and economics scholars (e.g. Posner 2003), the early literature has the problem of failing to produce predictable and correct theories for understanding and reforming the existing contract law since it has largely ignored to analyze the current system of law. A few studies have discussed the efficient breach theory against the background of specific contract law systems. This research attempts to make a bridge between the theory of efficient breach and different legal systems and to test if this theory is consistent with those systems. In order to fulfill this goal, this research studies contract remedy systems in different jurisdictions by analyzing how exactly those laws react to breach and what solutions adopted by them to the question to be solved by the theory of efficient breach. This provides some inspiration to the future law and economics study regarding how economic theories can contribute to the reform and understanding of the current contract law system.

This research will also contribute to the comparative law and economics literature. After re-examining the theory of efficient breach and its relationship with different remedy models, this thesis studies the applicability of the efficient breach theory in the context of European contract law, English sales law and Chinese contract law. The comparison among these three systems is more than a mere description of the differences and similarities that existed in the content. More importantly, the comparative research also analyzes whether or not the differences among those systems will influence the level of efficiency produced by each legal system by taking account of the judicial traditions and the concepts of contracts involved in each legal system. The answer to this question is particularly important before people conclude that one legal system is definitely better than the other two.

5. How will this/these plan(s) for valorization be shaped?

First, social media, such as newspapers or blogs, can provide a platform for publicizing the results of this research into articles. The public can freely access those articles and get information regarding a large number of topics including the concept of efficient breach, contracting strategies, Chinese contract law tradition, Europeanization of contract law and even some classical contract cases, etc. The readers will also be able to participate in discussions by following those articles with comments and critiques and this in turn is going to promote more extensive debates. Second, business and legal service providers might be interested in receiving handbooks or brochures indicating the rules in a specific contract law system, some common types of contract risks and possible strategies for coping with those risks. Such types of handbooks have practical significance for those entities that prepare to refer the contracts to Chinese law or English law. In one way, the handbooks and booklet will help lawyers or legal counsels to frame their legal opinions in serve-providing process and in another way they will be reframed as guidance tools for business in their decision-making. Third, the results of this research can be made available to policy makers as recommendations for the improvement of law. This will be achieved via proposals sent to policy makers (e.g. European Commission or National People's Congress in China) or presentations and discussions in conference. To be mentioned, this research does not only explore the applicability of the efficient breach theory, but also shed some lights on new topics (e.g. opportunistic breaches; influence of law on renegotiation) and methodologies (comparative law and economics, behavioral analysis) to be developed in the future research. In this sense, this research also stimulates more research over topics closely related to the theory of efficient breach.

IUS COMMUNE EUROPAEUM

A peer-reviewed book series in which the common foundations of the legal systems of the Member States of the European Union are the central focus.

The *Ius Commune Europaeum* series includes horizontal comparative legal studies as well as studies on the effect of treaties within the national legal systems. All the classic fields of law are covered. The books are published in various European languages under the auspices of METRO, the Institute for Transnational Legal Research at Maastricht University.

Recently published:
Volume 128: *Tradition, Codification and Unification. Comparative – Historical Essays on Developments in Civil Law*, J.M. Milo, J.H.A. Lokin and J.M. Smits
Volume 129: *Nobody's Perfect. Comparative Essays on Appeals and Other Means of Recourse Against Judicial Decisions in Civil matters*, A. Uzelac and C.H. van Rhee (eds.)
Volume 130: *Legal Aid in the Low Countries*, B. Hubeau and A. Terlouw (eds.)
Volume 131: *State Aid and Public Procurement in the European Union*, S. Schoenmaekers, W. Devroe and N. Philipsen (eds.)
Volume 132: *Property Law Perspectives III*, A. Apers, S. Bouly et al. (eds.)
Volume 133: *Multi-Party Redress Mechanisms in Europe: Squeaking Mice?*, V. Harsági and C.H. van Rhee (eds.)
Volume 134: *Europe at the Edge of Pluralism*, D. Gozdecka and M. Kmak
Volume 135: *Cooperative Agreements between Public Authorities. The Influence of CJEU Case Law on National Legal Systems*, K. Wauters
Volume 136: *Common Core, PECL and DCFR: Could They Change Shipping and Transport Law?*, W. Verheyen, F.G.M. Smeele and M.A.I.H. Hoeks
Volume 137: *Who does What? On the Allocation of Competences in European Private Law*, B. Akkermans, J. Hage, N. Kornet and J.M. Smits
Volume 138: *The Nature of Mutual Recognition in European Law*. W. van Ballegooij
Volume 139: *Evidence in Contemporary Civil Procedure. Fundamental Issues in a Comparative Perspective*, C.H. van Rhee and A. Uzelac (eds.)
Volume 140: *The Effect of D&O Insurance on Managerial Risk Taking*, M. Gaber
Volume 141: *Information and notification duties*, M.B.M. Loos and I. Samoy (eds.)

www.ingramcontent.com/pod-product-compliance
Ingram Content Group UK Ltd.
Pitfield, Milton Keynes, MK11 3LW, UK
UKHW051926100926
8556IPUK00022B/1388

9 781780 683560